Java Network Programming

Java Network Programming

MERLIN AND CONRAD HUGHES
MICHAEL SHOFFNER
MARIA WINSLOW

MANNING

Greenwich
(74° w. long.)

For electronic browsing of this book, see http://www.browsebooks.com

The publisher offers discounts on this book when ordered in quantity. For more information, please contact:

> Special Sales Department
> Manning Publications Co.
> 3 Lewis Street
> Greenwich, CT 06830
>
> Fax: (203) 661-9018
> email: orders@manning.com

Library of Congress Cataloging-in-Publication Data
Hughes, Merlin.
    Java network programming / Merlin Hughes . . . [et al.].
       p.   cm.
    Includes index.
    ISBN 1-884777-34-1
    1. Java (Computer program language) 2. Computer networks.
  I. Hughes, Merlin, 1972 –
  QA76.73.J38J377   1996   96-44002
  005.2'762—dc21   CIP

Manning Publications Co.
3 Lewis Street
Greenwich, CT 06830

Copyeditor: Margaret Marynowski
Typesetter: Aaron & Heather Lyon
Cover designer: Leslie Haimes

Printed in the United States of America
  3 4 5 6 7 8 9 10 – CR – 00 99 98 97

contents

preface

We founded our company, Prominence Dot Com, with the commitment to provide clients with advanced Internet-based solutions for business needs. When we first set up shop, the hot new technology for the Internet was the World Wide Web. Applications-oriented Web sites became our first order of business.

We began evaluating Java for Web applications development during its alpha-2 phase, in the summer of 1995. At the time, CGI applications of various sorts represented the cutting edge of Web-based products. It was immediately apparent that Java presented unique and powerful features that enabled "real" distributed applications which could run over any TCP/IP network.

Of course, all of that is ancient history in Internet terms. Slightly more than a year later, Java is hotter than the coffee which inspired its name. In fact, at the time of this writing, the coffee market itself is in a bit of a lull, but Java's popularity continues to surge.

Java's appearance in the right place at the right time with the answers to hard problems is earning it a place in the toolkits of developers worldwide. From a developer's standpoint, Java's cross-platform, secure, object-oriented, and network-centric features make it useful. Its clean syntax makes it fun and relatively easy to use. Most importantly, its status as the only high-level cross-platform language with native Web browser support makes it a must for serious Web- and intranet-oriented development efforts—precisely the sort of efforts that require the use of the secure networking codebase and techniques developed in this book.

Java Network Programming arose out of a set of professional courseware that we developed in response to the widespread need for a comprehensive reference on advanced features of the Java language. This book therefore covers everything from the basics of Java networking to in-depth techniques for implementing high-level secure networked applications. It is simultaneously a complete tutorial on networking and cryptography, a Java networking API reference, and a collection of production codebase contained on a companion CD-ROM.

We sincerely hope and believe that the material in this book will be as useful to you as it has been to us. Please give *Java Network Programming* a good home and dogear it, so that it knows it is loved.

acknowledgments

Putting this book together brought us severe pain and torture. We would all be dead now were it not for the kind help of several people. Many thanks are owed to Marjan Bace, our publisher, for his advice along the way and his patience with missed deadlines. Grant Gainey and Dave Zimmerman of WidgetWorks, Inc. kindly donated their notes from a lecture on RMI to be used as a reference for the RMI chapter. Thanks are also due to David Barrett for permission to use some of his DES optimizations. Keith Brady and Kevin Jeffay reviewed the appendices on cryptography and networking, respectively. Thanks are owed to Len Dorfman for getting us started in the first place. Dinesh Manocha demonstrated infinite patience during this time; Kevin Jeffay, Don Smith, Bert Dempsey, and Donal O'Mahony gave valued lectures on networking over the years, and Lee Tien, Michael Froomkin, and Bruce Schneier offered advice on publishing cryptographic algorithms in the US.

We would all like to thank our friends and family for not abandoning us permanently even though we abandoned them temporarily, and Dr. Dumas for much-needed sanity and reality checks.

Merlin would particularly like to thank Simon Rooney, David Graham, and the TCD crowd for their support, and Michael wants to add special thanks to Trey Harris, Judd Knott, Chris Colomb, the folks at UNC Geology, and the old UNC Sunsite crew for all of their help. Without you all, it wouldn't have been possible.

Sa-lute!

guide to the reader

Intended audience

Java Network Programming offers something for every Java networker, from the beginner to the experienced developer. In addition to developing practical networking classes, advanced features such as custom cryptography and Remote Method Invocation are covered in detail. The library of code developed in the book is also included on a companion CD-ROM, along with a generic chat application ready to be extended for custom uses.

- *Beginners* can take advantage of the Preliminaries part of the book, which contains overviews of networking and cryptography as well as highlights of the Java security model. Comprehensive appendices provide additional detailed background on networking and cryptographic topics.

- *Experienced Java programmers* will be able to jump right in at the point most appropriate for their needs. For example, programmers already familiar with sockets and TCP/IP networking—but unfamiliar with Java's `SecurityMananger`—can start at the Java security model portion of Preliminaries. These programmers can then move on to the chapters covering the `java.io` and `java.net` packages, which develop practical classes to provide hands-on experience in developing applications using the API.

- *Experienced C and C++ programmers* will find that networking with Java is quite a bit cleaner and more rewarding than networking in C and C++. For example, Java's exception mechanism facilitates robust handling of common problems that occur during I/O and networking operations, and the threading facilities provide a way to easily implement powerful servers.

Networking with Java

The Java programming language is ideally suited to networked applications programming. The core API comes with a standard set of classes which provide uniform access to networking protocols across all of the platforms to which the Java Virtual Machine has been ported. The language abstracts away from issues such as hardware byte order so that programmers need not concern themselves with the traditional problems of cross-platform interoperability. Basic network access is provided through classes from the `java.net` package. These are complemented by classes from the `java.io` package that provide a uniform streams-based interface to communications channels. These classes can be extended to provide sophisticated high level functionality to serve custom communications needs.

Both applications and embedded applets can benefit from the networked facilities provided by the language. Applets can communicate with central information storage to access a central information store and to provide true real-time collaboration between users distributed across the World Wide Web. Applications can also benefit in a number of ways above and beyond the usual advantages that Java enjoys over traditional programming languages. The secure and dynamically linked nature of Java permits development of servers which can be extended with new code at run-time. Examples of this include a Web server that can dynamically and securely execute code that is supplied by a client, or a search engine which can accept searches in the form of "searchlet" code fragments.

Extensions to the language API are being developed which further abstract away from the underlying nuts and bolts of networking. These extensions include a Remote Method Invocation API which provides transparent access to the methods of an object executing in a remote virtual machine. Parameters and results of remote method calls are implicitly transmitted over a network connection between the virtual machines. Another API and set of tools will provide CORBA compatibility, providing universal access to CORBA objects. Additional extensions will provide a cryptographic framework, networked multimedia access and interfaces to telephony products, and a commerce framework. Further down the road, JavaSpace promises globally distributed tuple spaces for truly distributed applications.

Contents and layout

In this book, we cover the `java.io` and `java.net` packages extensively with examples covering all of the techniques that are necessary to develop networked applications in Java, including a treatment of threads and exceptions. Following this introduction we document and discuss some practical examples of networked applications programming, developing a high-level communications library along the way. We proceed to develop a set of cryptographic classes for secure Internet and intranet applications. We then discuss object serialization and remote method invocation (RMI). Overviews of both networking and cryptography are provided for those readers less familiar with these topics.

The book is organized into five parts: Part I provides preliminary information, including an introduction to TCP/IP, cryptography, and the Java security model. Part II covers the `java.io` and `java.net` packages in detail, providing both API details and example code and extensions. Part III significantly extends the Java API by developing extensive networking classes, and a cryptographic framework that includes implementations of common encryption and authentication techniques. Part IV covers the object serialization and RMI technologies. These are new features of the programming language that significantly ease the development of networked applications. Part V consists of appendices, including in-depth networking and cryptography overviews, as well as some useful tables.

PART I

Preliminaries

The Preliminaries part of this book provides the programmer with overviews of important concepts for Java networking, cryptography, and the Java security model. More in-depth appendices are provided at the end of the book, should further questions arise.

Chapter 1: Introduction to networking   This chapter presents the basics of networking with TCP/IP, including the concept of stacks and layers, IP, TCP, UDP, ports, and sockets, and the TCP family of services.

Chapter 2: Introduction to cryptography   This chapter introduces the field of cryptography, which we can use to provide privacy and authentication across public networks. Private and public key encryption, secure hashing, and digital signatures are discussed.

Chapter 3: The Java security model   This chapter outlines browser restrictions on client resource access. The `SecurityManager` class places certain limitations on the operations that applets may perform. An understanding of these limitations is useful if networked applications are to be embedded on the Web as applets. A brief discussion of considerations imposed by firewalls is also provided, along with an overview of Java's "sandbox" security model.

chapter 1

Introduction to networking

A network is simply a collection of interconnected information devices which speak the same data transmission protocol.

1.1 Stacks and layers

Networking involves moving data from one device on a network to other devices on the network. In order for devices to communicate, they must all speak the same data transmission language. Protocols provide that language.

When a given unit of data is being transferred across a network, an array of related networking protocols is involved in everything from pushing the relevant voltages (or pulses of light) over the physical links to delivering continuous data streams to applications that use the data. The relationship of these protocols to one another is most naturally visualized as a *stack* or *layer* system, with the bottom layer being hardware and the top being the networked applications actually producing and consuming the data. The middle layers handle intermediate functions such as bridging different physical networks into larger networks. Each networking layer performs a discrete function and talks only to the layers immediately above and below it in the stack (Figure 1.1).

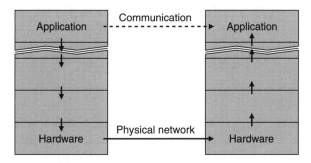

Figure 1.1   A network stack

The point of the stack abstraction is that each layer in the stack need handle only its specific function, and may in fact be implemented by several different interchangeable protocols. For example, the standard Ethernet LAN (a datalink protocol with associated hardware) found in many office complexes may simultaneously carry IP, IPX (Novell), and AppleTalk, all of which are distinct network-layer protocols. The two most important examples of network stacks are described below.

1.1.1 OSI seven-layer model

The open systems interconnect (OSI) model is a seven-layer stack specified and implemented by the International Standards Organization. The actual OSI protocols never caught on in the US, but the general model is a good one to use when designing network stacks. The OSI model is often used to illustrate principles of network layers (Figure 1.2).

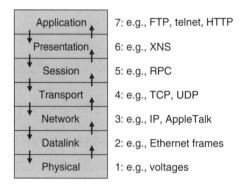

Figure 1.2   The OSI networking stack

1.1.2 TCP/IP suite

Since the Internet and intranet are TCP/IP networks, the TCP/IP suite is the stack of interest to the Inter/intranet applications programmer. The TCP/IP family of networking protocols subdivides networking functions into five conceptual layers instead of seven (Figure 1.3).

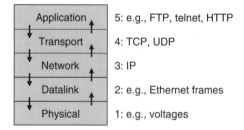

Figure 1.3   The TCP/IP networking stack

1.1.3 Encapsulation

Each layer talks only to the layers immediately below and above it in the stack. This arrangement is accomplished by means of encapsulation and decapsulation. Encapsulation is the process of embedding each layer's packets into the packets of the layer immediately below it. Decapsulation is the reverse process—stripping lower level packets as the data moves up the receiving machine's protocol stack (Figure 1.4).

The process works as follows: an application generates a stream of data. In the case of TCP/IP this stream is handed to the transport layer, which encapsulates the data packets in TCP segments and performs other transport layer functions, such as error correction. TCP then passes the segments to the IP layer, which puts them into IP datagrams and performs other network layer functions, such as routing. The datagrams next go to the datalink layer, which in many cases is an Ethernet.

The Ethernet encapsulates the datagrams into frames, which it then prepares to put on the physical cable. The frames move onto the wire as a voltage, to be picked up by

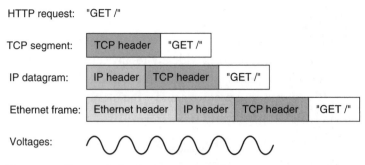

HTTP request: "GET /"

TCP segment: | TCP header | "GET /" |

IP datagram: | IP header | TCP header | "GET /" |

Ethernet frame: | Ethernet header | IP header | TCP header | "GET /" |

Voltages:

Figure 1.4   Encapsulation between protocol layers

another Ethernet card or interface somewhere else on the physical network. If the original data stream is bound for a local machine, the Ethernet card of the local destination machine will pick up the frames directly from the wire. Otherwise they will be picked up by the Ethernet interface of a gateway of some sort, possibly an IP router. The IP router will then decapsulate the frames into IP packets, make routing decisions about them, re-encapsulate them for the correct outbound interface, and ship them off toward the destination machine's network (Figure 1.5).

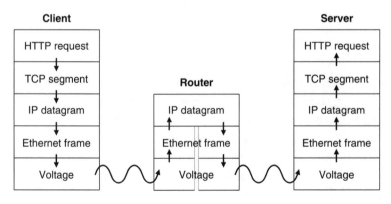

Figure 1.5   TCP/IP communication

When the remote host receives the frames addressed to it, the process of decapsulation begins. Each packet is stripped out of its containing packet as the incoming data are passed up the stack to the application layer. The receiving application ends up seeing the stream generated by the originating application. As far as the receiving application is concerned, the stream from the network is no different from a stream from the local filesystem, keyboard, or other device, despite the fact that it may have originated thousands of miles away.

1.2 The Internet

An *internet* is a collection of more than one network with any-to-any connectivity based on a network (layer 3) protocol. The *Internet* is specifically the worldwide network of TCP/IP networks which use IP addresses and protocols under the ultimate jurisdiction of the Internet Society (Figure 1.6).

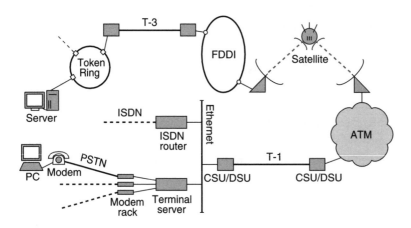

Figure 1.6   An internet

The networks which comprise the Internet are quite varied. They include every-thing from permanent enterprise-level corporate networks and university networks to SLIP/PPP accounts from Internet service providers (ISPs). All of these self-contained networks connect to larger regional providers via wide area networking (WAN), which in turn connect at peering points to exchange Internet traffic. Most of the networks that connect to the Internet are permanent local area networks (LANs), but many are also transient dialup accounts which originate from a pool of IP addresses provided by ISPs.

1.2.1 IP: the internet protocol

TCP/IP is the network stack implemented on the Internet. TCP/IP has as its founda-tion the internetworking protocol (IP). IP is a layer 3 (network) protocol for addressing hosts and routing data packets (datagrams) between them. IP overlays datalink layer networks of vastly different sorts to link machines on different types of physical networks as if they were on the same network. The current version of IP is formally known as IPv4.

1.2.2 IP addresses and networks

IP addresses take the form *x.x.x.x*, where each *x* is one byte, such as `152.2.254.81`. Every IP address falls into a *network*, which is a block of IP addresses grouped for administrative purposes.

Networks fall into different *classes*. The number of hosts in the network is determined by the class of which it is a member. There are 5 classes, and every network falls into only one of them, based on the first byte in its address.

- Class A: 1–126 (16M hosts each)
- Class B: 128–191 (65536 hosts each)
- Class C: 192–223 (256 hosts each)
- Class D: 224–239 (multicast mode)
- Class E: 240–255 (reserved for future use)

The class scheme was designed to provide a range of network sizes so that organizations could match the network size to the actual number of hosts required. The class scheme subsequently had to be modified to avoid technical problems with routing table overload. These problems are discussed in Appendix A in Section A.4.7.

1.2.3 IP subnets

IP makes use of subnets, which are logical divisions of a network into smaller networks, each of which consists of a range of addresses from the original IP net. Subnets are necessary in order to configure an IP network which is made up of more than one broadcast-based network such as Ethernet. Each subnet contains its own broadcast address.

IP networks and subnets have a broadcast address. Packets to this address are picked up by every host on the network or subnet. A non-subnetted IP address uses a default broadcast address based on the class of the IP address. For example, the Class C address `198.86.40.81` has a default broadcast address of `198.86.40.255`.

The netmask is a binary mask that covers the network number portion of the IP address. If the network is not subnetted, the netmask is the default netmask for whichever class of network contains the IP address. For example, a non-subnetted Class B address has a netmask of `255.255.0.0` and a non-subclassed Class C has the netmask

`255.255.255.0`. For a subnetted address, the netmask will extend into some portion of the address beyond the default. The portion of the address that is not the network and subnet addresses is the host address (Figure 1.7). All hosts which share a subnet are configured to have the same netmask and broadcast address.

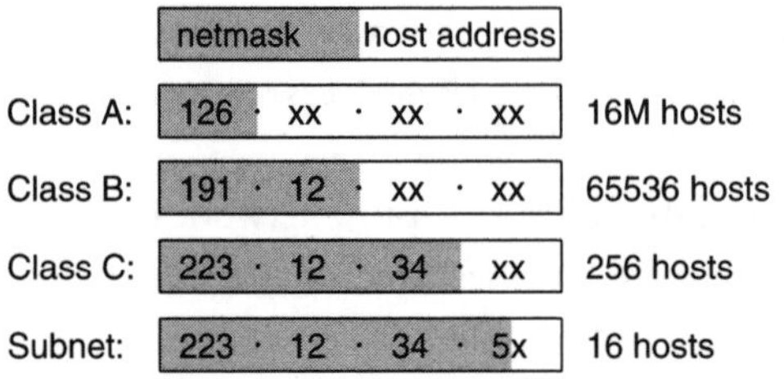

Figure 1.7 **IP classes and subnets**

1.2.4 ARP

The address resolution protocol (ARP) is used by IP to find the hardware address associated with a given IP address. When a host tries to send an IP packet, it first encapsulates the packet into the frames of the datalink layer protocol below it. It sends an ARP request, which is sent on the hardware broadcast address, to get the hardware address of the host in question. If the host is not on the local subnet, IP will use the broadcast to ask for the hardware address of the local IP gateway.

1.2.5 IP datagrams

An IP datagram consists of a header and a protocol data unit (PDU). The header contains information about fragmentation, length, time to live (TTL), and similar parameters. The PDU contains the data being encapsulated, which usually means a TCP segment or UDP packet.

IP uses Internet Control Message Protocol (ICMP) to correct routing problems on the fly. ICMP supports various messages for managing packet flow. The most important ICMP messages are:

- *Destination unreachable*   When a router destroys a packet because the destination is unreachable, it sends this message back to the originating host.

- *Redirect*   The redirect message is sent by a router to a host when it discovers that the host is using an inefficient route that is passing through it.

- *Echo* An echo message asks the destination to respond with an echo reply message, which proves that the remote end is up and functioning. Programs like ping and traceroute use echo to debug network connectivity.

- *Source quench* A source quench is sent to a packet source to get it to slow its transmission rate.

1.2.6 IP routing

Conceptually, IP networks are based on hosts and routers (Figure 1.8). The hosts implement IP stacks and do transmission flow control, error-checking (if any), and other data processing. The routers concern themselves only with discovery of the optimal path through the network.

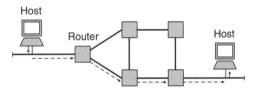

Figure 1.8 IP routing

The key to IP is its routing capability. An IP router has several network interfaces, and examines each packet that appears on them. It then calculates a least-cost route to the destination by means of its routing protocol, and forwards the packet down the appropriate interface toward the destination. A simple router does not need global knowledge of the network. It must simply know which of its local interfaces the packet should be forwarded to, based upon the destination address.

1.3 TCP: transmission control protocol

TCP is a connection-oriented transport protocol that sits on top of IP. TCP packets, called *segments*, are encapsulated into IP datagrams. TCP encoding and decoding occur at the hosts which form the endpoints of the communications channel. Along the way, the intermediate routers examine the IP packets only to make routing decisions.

TCP provides applications with data streams in which all transmitted data are guaranteed to appear at the destination host's applications layer in the order that they were transmitted. TCP is not isochronous, which means that it it makes no guarantee about the exact arrival time or rate at which the segments will appear on the remote end, only that they will appear uncorrupted and in the correct order.

1.3.1 TCP's features

TCP provides a number of mechanisms to implement quality of service (QOS) over the connectionless, nonguaranteed IP layer:

- *Multiplexing (ports)* A given host can support more than one TCP-based connection simultaneously because the TCP layer does multiplexing and demultiplexing based on port numbers (Figure 1.9). Well-known services such as telnet, HTTP, and SMTP have port numbers assigned by a central authority. Custom applications may make private use of other ports. Ports with numbers below 1024 are known as *privileged*, and are reserved for authorized services. Ports 255 and below should not be used by programmers, as they are typically allocated for system purposes.

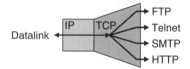

Figure 1.9 Multiplexing TCP virtual streams

- *Guaranteed, unique delivery* A sequence number is assigned to each segment that the sending TCP transmits. On the remote end, a checksum is performed, and if data are missing, the receiving end informs the sending end to retransmit. If the data are intact, the receiving end sends an acknowledgment, called an *ACK*. TCP automatically removes duplicate segments so that the receiving end sees each segment only once.

- *Streams* TCP supports virtual streams across a network. Each TCP session is a connection between two machines and designated ports on those machines. TCP makes use of the network to present remote applications with a point-to-point connection that resembles a direct byte-oriented stream.

- *Slow start* Congestion is the number one cause of packet loss in the Internet. This problem arises if packets are arriving at a router too quickly, and it must drop some to prevent buffer overflows. TCP uses a slow start algorithm that initially limits a new connection's bandwidth, so that it does not transmit excessive amounts of data if the network is congested. Slow start leads into TCP's flow control mechanism.

- *Flow control* Flow control enables TCP to adjust the sender's send rate and thereby avoid buffer overflows on the receiving machine. TCP accomplishes this with a variable-length sending window, which both ends adjust based on data acknowledgment.

- *Full-duplex transmission* TCP connections simultaneously transmit and receive, which saves the time required for a turnaround signal required by a half-duplex connection.

1.3.2 Ports and sockets

A socket represents a TCP connection between two applications across a TCP/IP network, and is specified by IP addresses and port numbers at both ends of the connection, although typically only the server's port number is encountered by the programmer. At the server, a process listens on a particular port. Every time a connection is made to the port, a TCP stream is created between the server and the client.

Sockets are the basis of most applications layer network communications. TCP is useful when network overhead is not a significant problem and reliable data transfer is required (Figure 1.10).

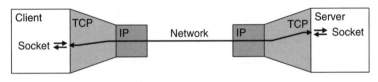

Figure 1.10   Ports and sockets

1.4 UDP: user datagram protocol

UDP is a connectionless transport layer protocol that sits on top of IP. Unlike TCP, UDP provides no state management and data integrity functions except for a checksum. UDP provides no congestion avoidance, and no packet delivery guarantees. If the receiving IP stack receives the packet and finds that the UDP datagram is corrupted, it simply throws it away.

1.4.1 UDP sockets

UDP provides sockets in much the same way that TCP does. A UDP socket is identified by the local IP address and the UDP port. Packets may be sent to anywhere or received from anywhere through a UDP socket.

1.4.2 Uses for UDP

UDP is appropriate when transport layer overhead must be minimized or data reliability is not crucial. This is the case when the application calls for small, independent packets. Examples of well-known services that use UDP are NFS, DNS, and SNMP. When using UDP, it is important to keep in mind that zero, one, or more than one copy of a datagram may get to the receiving end (Figure 1.11).

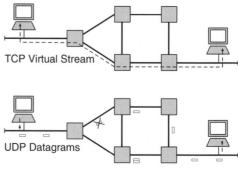

Figure 1.11   TCP versus UDP

UDP packet length is stored in sixteen bits, so when using UDP it is important to limit data size. It is also particularly important to limit packet size to avoid fragmentation. Fragmentation arises if a packet must be broken into several smaller packets for transmission purposes. This reduces the chances of data delivery because if any of the fragments is lost, the entire packet will be discarded.

1.5 The TCP/IP family of services

The TCP/IP family of services is largely applications layer services that are usually found bundled into TCP/IP stacks or in system applications. The specific port numbers that the services use are specified and published by a central authority. All TCP/IP services are client/server in nature.

1.5.1 FTP

File transfer protocol is one of the original TCP/IP protocols. FTP is used for transferring documents and binary files. FTP works by allowing a user to log on and request documents for downloading or uploading. FTP uses TCP port 21 for initiating and controlling connections, and TCP port 20 for data transfer.

1.5.2 Telnet

Telnet is an application that allows users to log in to (telnet to) a machine and use the equivalent of a direct console or terminal. Telnet uses TCP port 23.

1.5.3 Gopher

Gopher is a precursor to HTTP that organizes and presents information in a text-based menu format. Gopher has been largely obviated by HTTP. Gopher uses TCP port 70.

1.5.4 Finger

The finger protocol is used to find out information about users on a particular host. It can also provide information about currently logged-in users. Finger uses TCP port 79.

1.5.5 WAIS

Wide area information services is a system of indexing and searching a filesystem. WAIS consists of two components, an indexer and a search engine. The indexer indexes information in a filesystem and creates a lookup table. The search engine accepts search strings from the user and queries the lookup table.

WAIS is becoming obsolete, replaced by more advanced systems that operate on similar principles over the Web.

1.5.6 NNTP

Network news transport protocol is used to transfer articles among servers (and NNTP-enabled clients) in the USENET Internet news system. NNTP uses a flooding protocol to make sure that a given article gets transferred to every server in the system. NNTP uses TCP port 119.

1.5.7 SMTP

Simple mail transfer protocol is the protocol used to transfer email between mail transport agents (MTAs) over the Internet. Sendmail is the most widely-used MTA. ESTMP is a new extended version of SMTP that supports additional commands for MTA communication. SMTP uses TCP port 25.

1.5.8 SNMP

Simple network management protocol is used to remotely manage network devices. SNMP allows manipulation of a management information base (MIB) for a networked object. Network interface cards, ethernet hubs, and routers are possible examples of SNMP-enabled network devices. SNMP uses UDP ports 161 and 162.

1.5.9 HTTP

Hypertext transfer protocol is the World Wide Web protocol, and uses TCP port 80. HTTP supports transfer of multiple multipurpose internet mail extension (MIME) data types, including images and text. A document's MIME type is specified in an HTTP document's header by a major type, such as `text`, and a minor type, such as `html`, with the syntax `Content-type: text/html`. HTTP 1.0 is the currently implemented version of HTTP.

Standard HTTP is a stateless protocol. The client opens a connection to the server and makes a request. The server responds to the request by passing the requested information to the browser, and then closes the connection. HTTP documents consist of headers, which contain type and other information, and a data body. Normally, the browser masks the headers so that the user does not see them.

The uniform resource locator URLs are used to point to resources of all types on the World Wide Web, including HTTP documents. A URL is made up of a protocol part, a server designation, and a file (path) designation (Figure 1.12).

Figure 1.12 URL composition

Common gateway interface HTTP provides for server-side extensions that conform to the CGI standard. CGI programs typically reside in specified directories, usually called `cgi-bin`, on the server and are invoked by HTML browsers based on user action.

CGIs can be used in HTML documents as images, links, and as the action for forms. When the user activates the CGI, the browser opens a connection to the server and passes a set of information to it. The server then starts a copy of the CGI program and passes this information to it as environment variables and its standard input. Whatever the CGI writes to its standard output is sent back to the browser via the server (Figure 1.13).

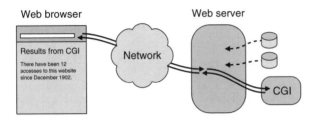

Figure 1.13   CGI

The browser can pass environment information to the server in three ways. The get method puts this information in an environment variable, usually called `QUERY_STRING`. The post method puts the information in the CGI's standard input. Information may also be encoded as the end part of the URL used to invoke the CGI, and appears in the `PATH_INFO` variable.

CGIs can indicate whether the server should process, or parse, the header information on the return trip or pass it through to the browser unparsed. In the default case the server parses the data. To indicate to the server that it is not to parse the data, the CGI filename typically must begin with the string `nph-`, although this designation may differ depending on the server.

1.6 DNS

The domain naming system (DNS) is a distributed mapping system between host names and IP numbers which allows for hosts to have one or more names that resolve to a varying number of IP addresses. In general, each host on the Internet with a registered name has one name associated with its IP number. The entire hostname, including the domain and subdomain component, is known as the host's fully qualified domain name (FQDN). Resolving the same FQDN to more than one IP address is known as round-robin DNS. Round-robin DNS is used to distribute load for one service, such as a Web host, across multiple machines.

DNS performs two functions. It provides lookup services, or name resolution, to hosts that are trying to find the IP number of a given hostname. It also provides the database that defines these mappings. Both of these functions are provided by nameservers, which are hosts that provide name resolution services.

DNS is implemented by a hierarchical system of nameservers that resolve different components of the FQDN. The root level is maintained by InterNIC. InterNIC is responsible for assigning domain names in all root level domains, including EDU, COM, MIL, NET, ORG, and others, and creating entries for each domain in the root nameservers. These entries list the authoritative nameservers for each domain (Figure 1.14).

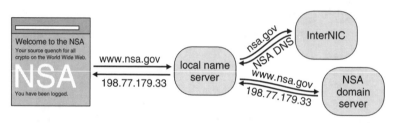

Figure 1.14   DNS in action

1.6.1 Authoritative and caching-only nameservers

Authoritative nameservers are specific machines on the Internet which provide listings for all of the machines and subdomains for a given organization's block of IP numbers. Authoritative nameservers have entries that either give the hostname-IP mappings directly or point to other nameservers which give these mappings.

1.6.2 Hostname lookup

Each host that needs to resolve hostnames is configured to use a DNS server to make name resolution queries. This server is provided by an ISP or the local network administration. When a new hostname needs to be looked up, the host queries its nameserver. A special type of nameserver used only for lookups is known as a caching-only nameserver. Caching-only nameservers diminish network traffic by performing a lookup only once and then retaining the results for a preset period, typically 14 days.

1.6.3 Reverse lookups

Standard DNS is a one-way mapping from hostname to IP number. Reverse mappings are sometimes useful, usually for verification purposes. Organizations may list their IP numbers and associated hostname in a special domain, `in-addr.arpa`, to facilitate reverse lookups on their IP numbers.

1.7 Firewalls and proxy servers

For security reasons, many organizations choose to partition their internal networks from the Internet by means of firewalls (Figure 1.15). Firewalls may be configured to restrict traffic in a variety of fashions, and, as a result, not all options will be open in certain situations. For example, a heavily firewalled site may permit traffic only to port 80 of the Webserver, in which case a stand-alone server running on a dedicated port will not be accessible from a client running outside the firewall.

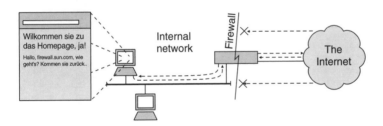

Figure 1.15   Firewalls

    Firewalls come in two primary flavors: packet filters and application-layer gateways. Packet filtering happens at the IP layer, usually at routers with external interfaces. Packet filtering employs an access control list to allow or deny packet delivery to inside hosts based on the source and destination address in the packet. Attempts to reach hosts behind the firewall are blocked and sometimes logged.

    Applications level gateways are also known as proxies. A proxy is a server that is interposed between an internal client and an outside service when the client attempts to make an outside connection. For example, an HTTP proxy server accepts connections from internal clients that are directed toward an outside host's port 80. It then makes the connection to the outside itself and relays the response to the client. This insulates the client and hides details about the internal network from the outside service. Proxies are typically able to do more logging and implement more sophisticated access control criteria than packet filters.

Proxies have the unfortunate effect of eliminating true streams between client and server. Since the HTTP proxy is in effect the server for the internal client, there is no way for the client and the actual remote server to communicate in any way except through the specific services the proxy supports. Supported service usually means only port 80 traffic. This effectively prevents many Web-based networked applications from operating through firewalls, except through HTTP requests.

1.8 Conclusion

TCP/IP networking fundamentals are the foundation of most Java networking, including the classes developed in this book. Java code based on these APIs and the core APIs may also utilize the TCP/IP family of applications layer services such as DNS, SMTP, and HTTP. Appendix A contains further information on these and other netowrking topics.

chapter 2

Introduction to cryptography

When you sign a contract or a check nobody will dispute that it was you who signed it. If you drop a sealed envelope into the mail nobody will look inside. If you regularly put a backup of your computer system in the bank nobody can get at it. If you buy a bunch of flowers with your credit card nobody but the assistant sees your card number and you can be confident that the number won't be used by someone else to defraud you. You lock your front door when you leave in the morning: nobody will get inside and take your possessions.

This is security. You take it for granted. It is part of your everyday life. On a computer—particularly on a network—an analogous concept should exist, so that you can sign something and people will know that you wrote it; send a message and know that only the intended recipient will read it; buy goods and be confident that fraudsters won't spend money using your credit card number; store your work or messages without the fear that crackers will break into your machine and steal or destroy the files.

That is the way it should be; unfortunately it is not the way things are. The Internet has been the source of many stories of security breaches over the years, from Robert Morris and his Internet Worm (which brought most of the Internet to a standstill and cost many thousands of dollars) through Clifford Stoll's hunt for Berferd (who, as documented in Stoll's *The Cuckoo's Egg*, broke into computer systems all over the world in an attempt to find valuable information), all the way to more recent front page news such as the short-lived security flaws in Netscape's Navigator software. As regards the particular issues described above, it is the work of an instant to create an identical copy of a computer file, or part thereof, so how can you "sign" a computer file if anyone else can copy your signature and add it to his or her own files? If you send a password (or a credit card number) over the Internet, many people are in a position to see that information as it travels to its destination, so how can credit card purchases, private letters, or network security on your computer work?

These problems can usually be solved with a *cryptographic protocol*—a series of steps using the digital technologies of *encryption* and *signatures*. See Figure 2.1. This chapter

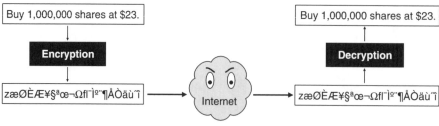

Figure 2.1 Encryption

introduces these three concepts, along with some supporting ideas and techniques for using them successfully: many "secure" computer systems turn out not to be so despite using all the right tools, because the tools have been used in the wrong way. Mistakes analogous to leaving the key under the doormat or signing a blank check crop up frequently, so care must be exercised.

2.1 Encryption

Encryption is the process of writing a message in such a way that only certain (desired) people can read it. Julius Caesar is reputed to have done this when sending messages to his officers over 2,000 years ago: he didn't trust the messengers, so he shifted the alphabet three places, writing *d* when he meant *a*, *e* when he meant *b*, all the way back around to *c* when he meant *z*. The receiving officer could reverse this process very easily.

The Caesar Cipher isn't very good for a number of reasons, the first one being that if anyone knew how the system worked, then he or she could always work out what the original message (called the *plaintext*) was if they could ever get hold of the encrypted message (the *ciphertext*). This means that Caesar couldn't have felt very secure when some of his officers defected to the enemy—it would have been very useful to be able to change the cipher in an easy way without having to think up a completely new one. The answer to this is to vary the number of places by which the alphabet is shifted: sometimes shift it by two places, sometimes by fifteen. If Caesar shifted the message by a different amount for each officer then one treacherous officer couldn't blow the whistle on his entire message network. This idea is called having a *shared secret key*: the *key* is the amount by which a particular message has been shifted, and both Caesar and the message recipient share this information, but keep it secret from everyone else. Incidentally, a Caesar Cipher with a key of thirteen is still used today on USENET—it's called rot13, and is used to encrypt messages whose content some people might not want to see (such as how a film ends, or the answer to a riddle). It's not really encryption since most people on USENET know how to decode it, but rot13 remains useful as something similar to writing the answer upside down at the bottom of the page.

The study of methods of performing encryption is called *cryptography* (hidden writing); the study of methods of working out what encrypted messages mean (as an outsider, not as one of the communicating parties) is called *cryptanalysis*. A cryptanalyst would have no difficulty working out what was going on in any Caesar Cipher message because there are only twenty-five different amounts that you can shift the alphabet by (shift it twenty-six times and you're back where you started). First pretend that only one shift was made and see if that produces a sensible message, then pretend that two were made, then three, and so on until one shift produces a message that makes sense—the chance of two different shifts producing messages which make sense is pretty small, particularly if the message is long. This trick, which amounts to guessing which key was used by trying every possible key and seeing which ones make sense, is called a brute force key search attach, and is often the most straightforward (but rarely the most efficient) way of trying to crack somebody else's codes. Having only 25 different keys means that the modified Caesar Cipher isn't a particularly good improvement on the original: modern computer encryption techniques have many more keys—ranging from 1,099,511,627,776 up to 340,282,366,920,938,463,463,374,607,431,768,211,456 and beyond!

2.2 Public key encryption

Encryption like the Caesar Cipher, where two people share some secret and then use that secret to transform the messages they send between each other in a way that prevents anyone else from understanding them, is called *symmetric* key encryption. The shared secret, the key, is the same for both of them: the recipient just has to use it a little differently than the sender (Figure 2.2). There's another kind of encryption, called *asymmetric* (or *public*) key encryption

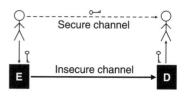

Figure 2.2   Symmetric encryption

(Figure 2.3), where the two parties don't have the same key; they have a special matched pair of keys. Anything encrypted using one key can only be decrypted using the other (and usually vice versa), but it's almost impossible to work out what the first key is if you know only the second (and possibly vice versa).

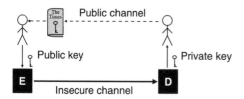

Figure 2.3   Public key encryption

Why would such a system be useful? Consider the problems of using a symmetric cryptosystem among a group of *N* people (Figure 2.4): every pair of people wishing to communicate privately must share a key, so the number of keys needed is $N(N-1)/2$, which increases in proportion to the square of the number of people present. Getting the keys to all of these people would be a nightmare. There's still a problem if even one key needs to be transported: the two people sharing the key have to communicate in a secure manner at some point. (They could meet face-to-face away from surveillance, for example.) Beyond even that, either of the two owners of each key may compromise the system (accidentally, unwillingly, or

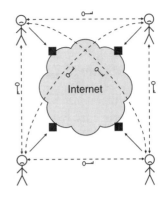

Figure 2.4 Symmetric encryption for a group

deliberately), and if they do, then every message that either of them ever sent using that key is compromised.

Compare this to a public key system (Figure 2.5). The classic implementation is RSA (Rivest, Shamir, Adleman, after its authors), where each person has a key pair: the literally named *private* and *public* keys. The private key always remains a personally held secret of the key pair's owner, while the public key is usually disseminated as far and wide as possible by the owner. This is safe because it is almost impossible to work out what the private key is using the public key. There are two important consequences:

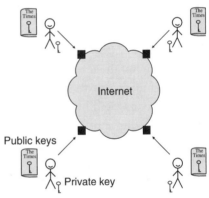

Figure 2.5 Asymmetric encryption among a group of people

- Anybody wishing to send a secret message to someone else obtains just the recipient's public key (which should be easy) and encrypts the message with that. Because of the nature of the public key system (any message encrypted with one key can only be decrypted using the other key of the pair), it is now safe to send the message to the recipient by any desired means, even the front page of the national newspaper, because the only person who can decrypt the message is the owner of the private key.

- If someone wishes to have his or her name associated with a document (as is the case when signing a check, for example), they encrypt the document using their *private* key. This isn't much good as encryption, since everybody who wants to can get hold of the author's public key and decrypt the document. What it is good for is the fact that everyone knows that the *only* person who could have encrypted the message is the owner of the private key—the author. Thus it is possible to sign a document in a unique and unforgeable manner using public key cryptography.

While public key cryptography has been in use and under mathematical scrutiny for over twenty years, the mathematical community has not been able to prove that trapdoor one-way functions (this is the mathematical name for a public key cryptosystem) or one-way functions (covered in Section 2.3) exist. In twenty years, nobody has been able to find a fast way of reversing RSA, but neither has anybody been able to prove that it's impossible to find such a thing.

2.3 Hash functions and digital signatures

While public key cryptography can be used directly to sign a digital document, having to encrypt an entire document just to sign it seems to be more work than one would hope to have to do (particularly considering that all currently known public

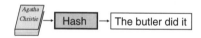

Figure 2.6   Hash functions

key cryptosystems are many orders of magnitude slower than their symmetric key cousins). In addition, it is a shame to render the entire document unreadable (at least in the sense that it is not obviously readable, and takes some computational effort to read) when a mere signature is required. These twin problems are solved (at a small security risk) in conventional digital signatures by using *hash* (or *digest*) functions (Figure 2.6)— functions which take the entire document being signed as input, and produce a (usually) much shorter output (20 bytes, for example)—the *digest*—irrespective of how long the original document was.

These functions are specially selected for a number of properties, particularly:

- *One way*   While it is easy to compute the digest of a document (i.e., to go from document to digest), it is almost impossible to create a document which hashes to a particular digest (i.e., to go from digest to document, the reverse process).

- *Collision resistance*   It should be very difficult to produce two messages with the same digest. Note that this doesn't necessarily follow from the one-way property.

A digital signature (Figure 2.7) is made by hashing a document and encrypting only the digest with the author's private key. It now becomes apparent why the above properties are necessary: if the hash function were not one way, then fraudsters could take someone's signature from an old document, and append it to a document which they had written specially to have the same digest as the original but to say something completely different (such as "victim owes fraudster a holiday in the Canaries"). If the hash function were not collision resistant, a fraudster could easily create two different documents, ask the victim to sign one and then safely substitute the other.

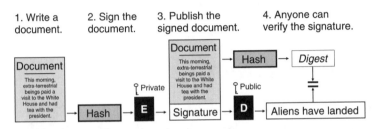

Figure 2.7   Digital signatures

The security risk inherent in using hash functions is that since digests are much smaller than the original documents, there must be very many different documents which hash to the same digest, so the frauds described in the last paragraph must be possible anyway. The special properties for which the hash functions are chosen or designed ensure that fraudulent activity requires huge computing resources and lots of time (preferably something on the order of the lifetime of the universe). Unfortunately, as with public key cryptosystems, mathematicians haven't proven that hash functions with these properties actually exist, but most hash functions currently in use have proven resistant to every attempt to invert them. Aside from this there are security risks inherent in encrypting large documents with private keys anyway.

2.4 Conclusion

Threat and risk evaluation is the first step along the path to securing a system. Some risks (such as someone else having exactly the same signature as you) are extremely unlikely, while some threats (such as military attack) are extremely difficult or costly to defend against; in such cases it may be preferable to buy insurance. The remaining threats—those against which it is economical to defend—can be thwarted effectively using the algorithms presented later in this book. While new technologies in computation and mathematics seem threatening, they are a long way off yet, assuming they even come to fruition, and they will almost certainly bring solutions to the new problems with them.

All of the fields touched on in this book develop at an astonishing rate, so the most important thing of all is to keep in touch with developments. If you are concerned about security, read some of the references supplied and keep in touch with the online world—and bear in mind that while you can secure your own software, your operating system vendor may not have secured his or hers, so paying attention to noncryptographic security announcements is also critically important.

2.5 Further information

Appendix B contains further information on some fundamentals of digital security, along with brief comments on a selection of algorithms (chosen for popularity, excellence, or political significance) and a taste of what may happen in the future.

Read these:

- Bruce Schneier, *Applied Cryptography*, John Wiley & Sons, 1996.
- `comp.risks` newsgroup.
- `sci.crypt` newsgroup.
- `cypherpunks` mailing list.

chapter 3

The Java security model

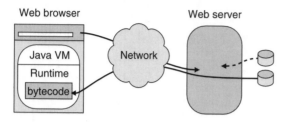

Figure 3.1   Java execution flow

A basic working knowledge of the Java security model is indispensable for any programmer who wishes to make use of Java for serious applications. Since Java is designed to run in a distributed manner and provide assurances of safety in the client environment, Java implementations necessarily impose restrictions on application access to system resources such as networks and file systems (Figure 3.1). This chapter provides an overview of the main points in the security model which affect the networked applications programmer.

Java provides two levels of security: low-level intrinsic security and resource-level security. Java's intrinsic security relates to the integrity of bytecodes that come across a network, and consists of a bytecode verifier and a `ClassLoader`. The verifier attempts to make sure that incoming bytecodes do not perform illegal type conversions, memory-accesses, or other similar forbidden activities. The `ClassLoader` partitions the namespaces of classes loaded from across the network and prevents collisions and related name resolution problems. The `ClassLoader` also ensures that local classes are loaded first to prevent spoofing of system classes. On top of this, Java provides resource access restriction through a `SecurityManager` class (Figure 3.2).

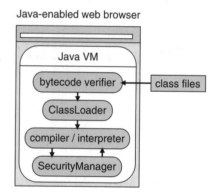

Figure 3.2   Java's security model

Java's intrinsic security measures are extremely important, but they are for the most part transparent to the programmer. Java's resource-level security restrictions are much more relevant for applications developers because they directly affect the higher level system resources available for networking purposes.

3.1 SecurityManager and resources

Java's security model is often described as a *sandbox*, where the sandbox is the area considered safe for untrusted code (Figure 3.3). Java-enabled browsers currently treat all code as untrusted and therefore restrict it all to the sandbox.

The sandbox policy is implemented with Java's `SecurityManager`, which determines the level of I/O access for runtime objects. Since an applet in a Web page is instantiated and runs within the runtime of the browser, the browser's built-in `SecurityManager` governs the applet's I/O capabilities. The applet programmer cannot override the browser's `Security-Manager` to gain additional access.

The `SecurityManager` imposes a variety of restrictions on resources, including file system access, access to native methods, thread modification, network resources, and access to system properties. Current browser `SecurityManager` classes allow applets no file system access, no ability to spawn processes on the client, and no native code execution.

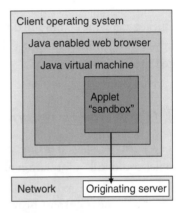

Figure 3.3   The Java sandbox model

3.1.1 System properties

Browsers provide read-only access to a limited set of system properties. These properties usually include those listed in Table 3.1, among others, and are accessible through the `getProperty()` and `getProperties()` methods of the `System` class.

Table 3.1   Standard Java system properties

Property name	Property meaning
os.name	Operating system name
os.arch	Operating system architecture
file.separator	Local OS' file separator (e.g., \ for Windows)
path.separator	Local OS' path separator (e.g., ; for Windows)
line.separator	Local OS' line separator

Table 3.1   Standard Java system properties (continued)

Property name	Property meaning
`java.version`	Java version
`java.vendor`	Java vendor's string
`java.vendor.url`	Java vendor URL
`java.class.version`	Java class library version

3.1.2 Threads

Threads may not be modified by an applet that does not own them. In fact, in certain browsers the priority of applet threads may not be modified even by the applet that created them!

3.1.3 Network resources

For security reasons, it is important to restrict access to network resources; otherwise an applet could leak information about a firewalled network, for example.

Sockets   Under current browsers, sockets can only be opened to the host that is the applet's source or the host specified in the applet's CODEBASE parameter. If the two are not the same, the CODEBASE takes precedence. Attempts to open sockets to any other host result in a `SecurityException`.

URLs   URLs have similar restrictions imposed on them by the current `Security-Manager`. URLs may be opened only to the host that is the applets' source or the host specified by the CODEBASE parameter. If the two are not the same, the CODEBASE takes precedence. Attempts to open URLs to any other host cause the Java runtime to throw a `SecurityException`.

Firewalls   Firewalls effectively turn off all socket-based networking for Java applets, since the applets are not allowed to open a connection through a firewall. Proxy servers allow applets to fetch images from the server they came from via proxy HTTP requests, but no other sort of access is allowed through firewalls.

DNS   Applets are very limited in the hostname lookups that they can perform. DNS requests actually form a covert channel that lets an applet leak information to a machine (the nameserver) that is not the host that served it. For this reason, an applet may only be able to perform name lookup for the host that served it. It is also important to note that applets that should operate behind firewalls must have a codebase specified as an IP number, because DNS lookups for applets may be turned off entirely.

3.2 Conclusion

Applet resource restrictions imposed by the `SecurityManager` are subject to change as new versions of browsers are released. Future Java APIs will provide authentication capabilities which will enable trusted code to execute outside of the sandbox, thereby enabling applets with the same class of resource access afforded to stand-alone Java applications.

PART II

Introducing the API

This part of the book introduces the classes and interfaces supplied in the `java.net` and `java.io` packages. These packages contain all the tools needed for building complex networked applications. An exhaustive description of the available stream classes begins this section. Streams are crucial in Java networking; they represent the programmer's connection to a communications channel. Client-side and server-side networking follow, with descriptions of simple clients and servers. We develop a multithreaded echo server and client in these chapters; this serves as a simple basis for other multithreaded server behavior. The UDP protocol and its uses are examined next, followed by the URL classes, where we step through an example demonstrating how to create custom browser function. Two refresher chapters are included in this section, covering exceptions and threads. Both are very important to Java networking, and it may be helpful to refer to these chapters at various times while reading this section.

Chapter 4: An introduction to streams A *stream* is a high level abstraction representing a connection to a communications channel, which is any entity that may *receive* or *send* data. A socket and a memory buffer could both be considered communications channels by this definition. Streams can either read from the endpoint or write to it, so they are divided into two classifications, input and output streams. In this chapter we take a look at these characteristics and put the abstract concepts into perspective with examples. If the reader is not proficient in Java exceptions and threads, we recommend that he or she refer to the relevant refresher chapters.

Chapter 5: File access through streams   File streams are available to use when it may be convenient to treat files as communications channels. Applications can then stream data to files as easily as they can stream data to other channels. An overview of file-related classes is given in this chapter before moving on to the file streams. We step through a simple example, then describe how to create custom file streams, using more complex examples.

Chapter 6: Extending streams with filters   Filter streams are wrappers for the lower level streams that allow for a higher level of abstraction in communications. They connect to simpler streams and generally provide added function. In this chapter, we give an introduction to the issues surrounding filter streams. The generic `FilterInputStream` and `FilterOutputStream` classes are introduced, a quick overview of the available filter streams is given, and we implement a few examples.

Chapter 7: Supplied filter streams   The filter streams that are discussed in detail here are `DataInput/OutputStream` and `BufferedInput/OutputStream`; however, `PrintStream` and `SequenceInputStream` are also described. These filter streams add additional function on top of the facilities provided by the various basic stream classes. An implementation of buffered streams is shown and described to further highlight the issues surrounding them. We conclude this chapter with a custom filter output stream that can seamlessly transmit data to several output streams simultaneously.

Chapter 8: Memory I/O streams   The Java API provides two streams that use memory as a communications channel: `ByteArrayInput/OutputStream` and `PipedInput/OutputStream`. The byte array streams allow data to be streamed into and out of a memory buffer, and the piped streams allow data to be streamed between threads of an application. This chapter begins with descriptions of these streams followed by a few examples, including a simple example of extending `ByteArrayOutputStream`.

Chapter 9: Client-side networking   This chapter begins the discussion of TCP/IP. IP is the low level network protocol that makes up the transport layer of the Internet. TCP is an internet protocol, running on top of IP, that establishes a virtual connection over an IP-based network. The `InetAddress` class represents a unique address on the network; every node on an internet has at least one IP address. Once a client has obtained a remote machine's IP address, a socket is used to establish a connection to that machine. The `Socket` class represents a TCP connection to a particular IP address. These classes are described with examples, and issues unique to network programming are covered. Client-side programming is introduced with further examples.

Chapter 10: Server-side networking   The `ServerSocket` class is used to implement servers; its purpose is to receive connections from remote clients. This class is first described, and an echo server is developed to demonstrate the principles involved. Issues that make server-side programming more complex than client-side programming are discussed, and an example of a nonblocking server is given. Finally, a more sophisticated server is developed which makes use of the multithreading features of the language to cleanly handle multiple simultaneous connections using threads.

Chapter 11: Datagram networking   Datagram networking uses the UDP protocol in place of TCP. UDP is a packet-based protocol with no guarantee of delivery or correct ordering of packets. Because it does not have the overhead of TCP, it should be used when network latency is a serious concern, but the guarantees of correct and complete delivery that TCP provides are not required. This chapter gives an overview of the classes relevant to UDP, and we develop an application to demonstrate datagram network programming. A discussion of when to use UDP rather than TCP concludes the chapter.

Chapter 12: Using the URL classes   The URL-related classes provide a framework for creating custom browser function. The URL class represents an object addressable by a URL on the World Wide Web, or indeed any protocol that can be addressed with the URL format. Several classes and interfaces form a framework that allows custom protocols and content types to be easily integrated. These classes are described, and an example is given that implements HTTP access to text files.

Chapter 13: An overview of multithreading   The Java language natively supports multithreading, which can be very important in writing powerful client and server applications. This chapter gives an overview of this capability, the relevant classes, and some of the issues that arise with multithreading.

Chapter 14: An overview of exceptions   The Java exception handling model is introduced in this chapter, along with the relevant classes, how to make use of exceptions, how to define your own exceptions, and why.

chapter 4

An introduction to streams

Streams are an extremely important part of network programming, and the Java API provides several stream classes with which to work. A stream is a high level abstraction representing a connection to a communications channel, such as a TCP/IP network connection or a memory buffer. Streams can either read from a communications channel or write to it, so they are divided into two classifications, input and output streams.

In this chapter, we first discuss the characteristics of streams, then move on to the two generic stream classes: `OutputStream` and `InputStream`. These are the superclasses of all other streams. The methods of these classes are detailed, then demonstrated with examples. A brief discussion of the basic stream types supplied by the API concludes the chapter. We will look at all of these streams in detail in later chapters.

4.1 Overview

Streams are the underlying abstraction behind communications in Java. A stream represents an endpoint of a one-way communications channel, as shown in Figure 4.1.

Figure 4.1 OutputStream and InputStream

The communications channel usually connects an output stream to a corresponding input stream. Everything that is written to the output stream can subsequently be read from the input stream. This connection can take the form of a link through a network, a memory buffer between threads, a file, or a terminal to the user. Streams provide a uniform data interface for applications, no matter what communications channel is actually used.

All of the I/O classes in Java are supplied by the package `java.io`. As a result, this package must be imported into all applications which make use of streams-based communication.

4.1.1 FIFO

Streams are FIFO (first-in first-out). This means that the first thing that is written to an output stream will be the first thing that is read from the corresponding input stream. If a sequence of numbers is written to an output stream, then it will be read in the same order from the corresponding input stream.

4.1.2 Sequential access

Streams provide sequential access to the communications channel; you can write a sequence of bytes one after the other, or read a sequence of bytes in the order that they were written. Most streams provide no random access; it is not possible to skip around and read or write bytes at just any position. Very little facility is provided for reading or writing data in anything other than a purely sequential manner, i.e., in order, one byte after another.

4.1.3 Read-only or write-only

The various stream classes provide either only reading functions or only writing functions. An output stream writes data into a communications channel, an input stream reads data out of a communications channel. There is no stream class which allows both reading and writing.

In cases where we wish to both write to and read from a single communications channel, we must use one stream to write (the output stream) and a different stream to read (the input stream). As we will see later when we look at networking applications, when you open a network connection you obtain two streams—an input stream to read from the network and an output stream to write to the network.

4.1.4 Blocking

An important issue that arises with streams is that of *blocking*. If a thread tries to read from a user's keyboard, it cannot read any data until the user actually types something. While the thread is waiting for some data to arrive (which in this case, requires the user to type something in), it is *blocking*. Similarly, if a thread tries to write data to a disk, it may take a while for the data to actually be written; while the thread is waiting for the I/O operation to complete, it is *blocking*.

Blocking refers to a thread going to sleep because it attempts to read data and there is none available, or it attempts to write data and the operation does not happen immediately. The Java environment will let other threads run while one is blocking; the blocking thread will wake up only when data arrive or the I/O operation completes.

There is little facility for nonblocking I/O in Java. Nonblocking I/O refers to being able to read some data and return immediately if there is none available, or to write some data and to return immediately if there will be a delay. We will look at the existing nonblocking facilities when we start building network servers.

4.2 Class OutputStream

The OutputStream class represents a gateway onto a communications channel: you can write data to an OutputStream and it will travel down the attached communications channel.

4.2.1 Constructors

There are no usable constructors for the base class OutputStream. Simply creating an OutputStream by itself is meaningless; it must be connected to a communications channel. As such, OutputStreams can only be instantiated by creating a subclass such as a FileOutputStream to a file or a PipedOutput-Stream to a pipe, or any subclass which actually connects to something. An OutputStream is like an

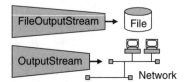

Figure 4.2   Various Output-Streams

entrance: you can't just create an entrance by itself; you must create an entrance to *something*, such as a cave or a room or a hallway. In the same way you must create an output stream to *something*, such as a file or network (Figure 4.2).

Obviously, with Java's inheritance model, if you create a FileOutputStream, then you can subsequently pass it as just a generic OutputStream.

4.2.2 Methods

The OutputStream class provides the superclass for all concrete output stream implementations. As such, it declares the standard methods that you can expect of all output streams, whether to a file or to a network. In the same way that you can enter any entrance, whether it is to a cave or room, you can write bytes to any output stream, whether it is to a terminal or a memory buffer.

The `OutputStream` class in fact provides only a few simple methods for communication: you can write a byte or a sequence of bytes. It also provides a few control methods to flush or close the communications channel. Any of the methods may block the calling thread.

abstract void write(int b) throws IOException   This method accepts a single byte and writes it to the attached communications channel. The argument is of type `int` but only the bottom eight bits are actually written.

This method is abstract because its implementation must be provided by a subclass which is attached to an actual communications channel such as a file.

void write(byte b[], int off, int len) throws IOException   This method accepts an array of bytes b, an initial index `off`, and a number of bytes `len`, and writes `len` bytes from b starting from index `off` to the attached communications channel.

The default implementation of this method is to repeatedly call the single-byte `write()` method. Subclasses will usually override this with a more efficient implementation.

void write(byte b[]) throws IOException   This method accepts an array of bytes b and writes the entire array to the attached communications channel.

The default implementation of this method is to call the previous `write()` method on the entire array.

void flush() throws IOException   This method flushes any buffers that the `Output-Stream` may have. Sometimes, for reasons of efficiency, the data which are being sent to a communications channel are kept temporarily in memory buffers. This method forces any buffered data to actually be written.

If the stream is attached to a network connection, any waiting data will be sent across the network. If the stream is attached to a file, the data will be written to disk.

void close() throws IOException   This method flushes and closes the underlying communications channel and then frees up any system resources which it is using. Any data that have been sent before this call is made will still be sent when the stream is flushed; this call may thus block until the data are written.

What actually happens when a stream is closed depends on the entity to which it is attached. If it is attached to a network connection, then the network connection is closed down; if it is attached to a memory buffer then nothing happens.

4.2.3 IOException

Every `OutputStream` method can throw an exception of type `IOException`. The exact type of `IOException` thrown depends on the problem and the entity to which the stream is actually connected.

Even closing a stream can throw an exception: if a stream is buffered, then the data must be sent before the stream can be closed, and an error may occur at this point. For example, a file system may become full while there is still buffered data in memory. Closing a file stream requires that the data be actually written, and this may not be possible.

4.3 A simple OutputStream example

As noted above, an `OutputStream` must always be attached to some underlying communications channel, whether it is a memory buffer or a network connection. The most easily accessible stream is `System.out`, which is connected to the system's standard output stream, as shown in Figure 4.3.

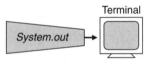

Figure 4.3 System.out

Every byte that is written to `System.out` is displayed on the user's terminal. For a standalone application, this will be the terminal where the application was run. For an applet, this will be the Java Console window or its equivalent.

The following piece of code prints out each of the command line parameters using a `println()` method that we will define next:

```
import java.io.*;

public class SimpleOut {
   public static void main (String args[]) throws IOException {
      for (int i = 0; i < args.length; ++ i) {
         println (args[i]);
      }
   }
   // public static void println (String msg) throws IOException ...
}
```

We declare that the `main()` method may throw exceptions of type `IOException`. We are not interested in actually handling exceptions which may be thrown by the `println()` method, and so we pass them on and let the main execution thread halt.

The comment describes the signature of the `println()` method; we will look at this method next.

```
public static void println (String msg) throws IOException {
   synchronized (System.out) {
      for (int i = 0; i < msg.length (); ++ i)
         System.out.write ((byte) msg.charAt (i));
      System.out.write ('\n'); // write one-byte LineFeed
   }
   System.out.flush ();
}
```

The `println()` method uses the `write()` methods of `System.out` to print out its argument.

All of the `write()` methods of class `OutputStream` are declared as throwing `IOException` and so we must prepare for such exceptions. We are not interested in handling exceptions at this point and so we simply pass them on by declaring that this method may throw any exceptions raised. In practice, `System.out` is unlikely to throw an exception, but because the declaration of the `OutputStream` class states that exceptions may be thrown, we must be prepared for their occurrence.

We synchronize on `System.out` to ensure that no other threads can write to the terminal in the middle of this message and then print the `String`. We print the `String`, composed of 16-bit Unicode characters, by converting it into a series of bytes; the `Output-Stream` class can only transmit bytes. We loop through the message, extracting each character, casting it to a byte and writing it. Note that casting a `char` to a `byte` will simply discard the high bits of the character. We finally write out a newline character and flush the stream to ensure that any buffered data are displayed immediately.

Looping through each character is quite slow. The `String` class actually declares a method `getBytes()` that efficiently converts the `String` into an array of bytes, discarding the high bits of each character. With this approach, we can use the multibyte `write()` method of `OutputStream` to efficiently write a `String`:

```
byte buffer[] = new byte[msg.length ()];
msg.getBytes (0, msg.length (), buffer, 0);
System.out.write (buffer);
```

This code fragment creates a byte buffer that is the size of the `String`, uses the `getBytes()` method to extract the `String` into the buffer, and writes the buffer to `System.out`.

4.3.1 ASCII characters

In this example, we are writing to an ASCII device (the user's terminal) and so we don't want to transmit full Unicode 16-bit characters. To convert Unicode to ASCII we can simply discard the high bits of each character. Unicode was designed as a superset of ASCII to make a Unicode transition easier; the crude translation of just discarding the high bits will be correct for most common messages.

If, however, the message should include unusual Unicode characters, then this translation will garble the message. In order to communicate with traditional ASCII programs and devices, we must restrict our messages to contain only ASCII characters.

4.3.2 Synchronization

Readers unfamiliar with the threading features and classes of Java should refer to Chapter 13 for an overview of this topic.

The `println()` method synchronizes on `System.out`. While this is not important in this particular example, it might be useful in a more complex program. Synchronization ensures that no other thread may write to the terminal while this thread is writing the message and newline (Figure 4.4).

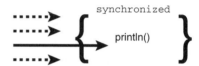

Figure 4.4 Synchronization between threads

`OutputStream` methods frequently block while writing, because communications channels are usually slow. Other threads can execute during this period and so it would be quite common for another thread to attempt to write to `System.out` in the middle of this thread's writing. Using synchronization prevents this problem.

Of course, synchronization helps only if other threads which try to access `System.out` are also synchronized on it. The various `print()` methods of class `PrintStream` are all synchronized, and so the user of these methods will be safe. Be aware, however, that the `write()` methods are not synchronized, and so it is still possible to interrupt a message.

In this particular case, the problems of synchronization simply pose an aesthetic challenge. In a networked application they pose real difficulties. It could be disastrous for two threads to simultaneously write messages to a single network connection without synchronization.

Bad Thread Interaction   Figure 4.5 demonstrates how threads could interact badly. In this example, two threads are both printing *Hello world!* to the same stream without synchronization. Because the message is written as a sequence of bytes, one thread may block at any point while its message is being written; during this time the other thread may proceed to write its own message.

Figure 4.5 I/O without synchronization

4.4 Class InputStream

The InputStream class represents a gateway that lets us read data *out* of a communications channel. Data that have been written into a communications channel by an OutputStream can be read by a corresponding InputStream.

4.4.1 Constructors

The InputStream class is abstract, like the Output-Stream class. A subclass must be constructed, such as a FileInputStream, that is actually attached to a communications channel. In the same way that the Output-Stream is like an entrance, the InputStream class is like an exit. You cannot just create an exit, you must create an exit from *something* such as a room. By reading from a stream, you read data through the exit. In the

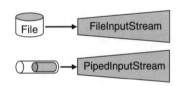

Figure 4.6 Various Input-Streams

case of an InputStream, you must create a concrete implementation such as a File-InputStream or a PipedInputStream. These streams let you read data from a file or a memory pipe (Figure 4.6).

4.4.2 Methods

The InputStream class is the superclass for all input streams, and so declares those methods that will be supplied by all input streams, whether they read from files, network connections, or memory buffers.

The InputStream class provides a few simple methods for reading a byte or a sequence of bytes, as well as methods to determine the amount of data available for reading without blocking, to skip and reread data, and to close the communications channel.

Attempting to read from an InputStream that has no data ready will cause the caller to block until data become available. If the data have already arrived from the communications channel (for example, delivered by a network transport protocol), then they will be waiting in a memory buffer and so will be available immediately without the need to block.

abstract int read() throws IOException   This method reads and returns a single byte, blocking if none is available. The method returns −1 if the end of the file (EOF) is reached. EOF will be caused by reaching the end of a file, by reaching the end of a closed network connection, or by whatever is appropriate for the communications channel.

This method is abstract because its implementation must be provided by a subclass that is attached to an actual communications channel.

int read(byte b[], int off, int len) throws IOException   This method attempts to read len bytes into array b, starting at index off. The array must already have been allocated. The method will block if no data are available, and will return the number of bytes successfully read or −1 if the end of the file is reached.

The method may not actually read len bytes for two possible reasons: if there are fewer bytes left in the stream before the end of the file, then only the remaining bytes will be read. Subsequent reads will return EOF. Alternatively, if some data are available to read immediately without blocking, but are fewer than the entire array, then only those bytes will be read. More data may subsequently become available and will be returned from later reads.

The default implementation of this method is to repeatedly call read() for a single byte. Subclasses will usually override this with a more efficient implementation.

int read(byte b[]) throws IOException   This method attempts to read as many bytes into b as possible, up to the length of the array. The method returns the number of bytes actually read, or −1 if the end of the file is reached. Again, fewer than b bytes may actually be read.

The default implementation of this method is to call the previous read() method for the entire array.

int available() throws IOException   This method returns the number of bytes that can be read from the stream without blocking. For example, an InputStream attached to a network connection will return the number of bytes that have actually been received down the network connection and are in memory but have not yet been read.

void close() throws IOException   This method closes the attached communication channel. Any data that has not yet been read will be discarded, and any system resources will be freed. In the case of an `InputStream` from a network connection, `close()` will close down the network connection.

long skip(long n) throws IOException   This method attempts to skip n bytes of input. This is useful if you know that you want to ignore a number of bytes, and is more efficient than just reading and ignoring them. It may not be possible for the method to actually skip as many bytes as were requested, so this method returns the number of bytes that were successfully skipped.

4.4.3 Mark and reset methods

The `mark()` and `reset()` methods allow a place in a stream to be marked, some data read, and then for the stream to be reset; subsequent reads will reread data from the marked point onwards (Figure 4.7).

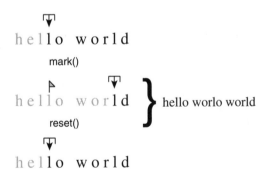

Figure 4.7   The mark() and reset() methods

This operation is frequently a very useful one, particularly in a situation such as decoding an image of an unknown format. If an `InputStream` is attached to an image file, then it may be necessary to pass the stream to several image decoders in order to determine which one actually understands the format.

A GIF decoder must read six bytes before it can determine whether or not it can understand the file. If it is not a GIF file, it must return the bytes to the stream. The stream can then be passed to a JPEG decoder which will read the first eleven bytes to determine whether it can understand the file, and so forth.

The GIF decoder should mark the beginning of the file before reading the header. If it cannot decode the file, then it can simply reset the stream so that the next decoder will start reading again from the beginning. Otherwise, there is no easy facility to return the six bytes to the stream, and so it would have to be closed and reopened for the next decoder.

As an example of this operation, consider an `InputStream` with three bytes, abc, available. If a program reads one byte, calls `mark()`, reads another byte, calls `reset()` and then reads two more bytes, it will have read abbc.

boolean markSupported()   None of the basic `InputStream` classes support `mark()` and `reset()`, but we will see later how to add mark/reset functions to any stream. The `markSupported()` method can be used to test whether a particular `InputStream` supports these methods.

void mark(int readlimit)   This instructs the stream to mark its current location. The parameter `readlimit` specifies the maximum number of bytes that may be unread by a subsequent call to `reset()`. If more than `readlimit` bytes are read, a call to reset may fail.

In the example given, a GIF decoder would specify 6 bytes, and a JPEG decoder would specify 11 bytes.

void reset() throws IOException   This instructs the stream to return to the previously marked location; i.e., subsequent reads will continue from the position in the stream where mark was last called. This may fail if more bytes have been read than were initially indicated.

4.4.4 IOException

All methods but `markSupported()` and `mark()` may throw an exception of type `IOException`. The nature of the `IOException` depends upon the problem and the underlying communications channel. Reaching the end of a file will not cause an `IOException` from a plain `InputStream`. Instead, the `read()` methods will return -1. We will later see how some variants of `InputStream` may throw an `IOException` if a premature EOF occurs.

4.5 A simple InputStream example

This is a simple example which demonstrates reading from System.in. Terminal input to a Java application, i.e., keyboard input to a command-line application, is available through System.in (Figure 4.8). This stream is not frequently used by Java applications, but it is useful as an example InputStream.

Figure 4.8   System.in

The following piece of code reads bytes from System.in and writes them back to System.out:

```
import java.io.*;

public class SimpleIn {
   static public void main (String args[]) throws IOException {
      int charRead;
      while ((charRead = System.in.read ()) >= 0)
         System.out.write (charRead);
   }
}
```

We declare that the main() method may throw an IOException; this may occur from either the read() or write() call. We then sit in a loop, reading bytes from System.in and writing them out to System.out. The loop terminates when read() returns −1; this corresponds to the end of the file. This particular example is reading from the keyboard; EOF is signalled under UNIX when the user types control-D, and under DOS when the user types control-Z.

It is fairly inefficient to transfer individual bytes in this manner; it would be better to use a small buffer for reading and writing multiple bytes, as in the following piece of code:

```
byte buffer[] = new byte[8];
int numberRead;
while ((numberRead = System.in.read (buffer)) >= 0)
   System.out.write (buffer, 0, numberRead);
```

Here, we create a small buffer and read as many bytes as possible into it using the read() method. This call returns the number of bytes read, or −1 at the end of the file. If some data have actually been read, we write out as many bytes as were read in and loop again.

Note that a newline is not printed after each buffer. The newlines that are printed are part of the input stream from the user, inserted whenever Return is typed, just like all other characters.

4.6 A tee class example

In this example, we implement a class which operates in a similar fashion to a plumbing tee joint. We will take input from one InputStream and allow it to be written out to multiple OutputStreams. What we will implement is not itself actually a stream; however, we will develop a proper tee stream class later on.

We define a class that reads data from an InputStream and stores it in an internal buffer. We will also provide a method that writes this buffer to an OutputStream. This method can be called repeatedly to write the buffer to multiple streams (Figure 4.9):

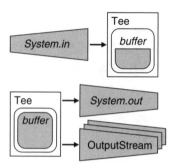

Figure 4.9   Class Tee

```
import java.io.*;
public class Tee {
  // public Tee (InputStream i, int n) throws IOException ...
  // public Tee (InputStream i) throws IOException ...
  // public void writeTo (OutputStream o) throws IOException ...
}
```

The Tee class provides two constructors; both require an InputStream i from which data will be read, the first also accepts an initial buffer size specification. The class provides one public method, writeTo(), that writes the buffered data to the specified OutputStream o:

```
  protected byte buffer[];
  protected int buffSize, numBytes;

  public Tee (InputStream i, int n) throws IOException {
    buffSize = n;
    buffer = new byte[buffSize];
    readFrom (i);
  }

  // protected void readFrom (InputStream i) throws IOException ...
```

To create a new `Tee` object you must supply an `InputStream` as a parameter to the constructor. It will read data from this stream until the end of the file, storing this data in the internal buffer.

We will store the data that we read in the `buffer` array. This array must be able to grow to accept as much data as is supplied, so we will also need to keep a record of the current size of the buffer, `buffSize`, and the amount of data which we have read into it, `numBytes`.

Because our buffer automatically grows, we can make the initial buffer as small or large as we like. Creating an initial buffer that is too small will be inefficient because we will need to increase the buffer size an unnecessary number of times. Creating one that is too large will simply waste some memory. In this case we let the user specify an initial size. We use the `readFrom()` method to actually fill the buffer from the supplied stream:

```
public Tee (InputStream i) throws IOException {
   this (i, i.available () + 1);
}
```

This constructor calls the previous constructor with a buffer size that is just larger than the number of bytes that are available for reading from `i`. If the value returned by `available()` happens to correspond to the entire amount of data that can be read, then we will not need to expand the buffer when reading:

```
public void readFrom (InputStream i) throws IOException {
   numBytes = 0;
   int justRead;
   while ((justRead = i.read (buffer, numBytes, buffSize - numBytes))
       > -1) {
     numBytes += justRead;

     if (numBytes == buffSize)
       increaseBufferSize ();
   }
}

// protected void increaseBufferSize () ...
```

The `readFrom()` method reads and buffers data from the specified `InputStream`, increasing the buffer size as necessary.

The `numBytes` variable corresponds to the number of bytes which we have actually read into the buffer; initially, we set this to zero. We then loop, reading from the `Input-Stream` into this buffer.

We use a multibyte `read()` method, specifying that it should read into our buffer, starting just beyond the data that we have already read. We attempt to read as many bytes as are left in the buffer; initially this will be the entire buffer size.

If the `read()` method returns –1 then we have reached EOF and so can exit the loop. Otherwise, we add the number of bytes that we just read to the total number of bytes we have read altogether. If the buffer is then full, we must increase its size, and so we call the `increaseBufferSize()` method:

```
protected void increaseBufferSize () {
   buffSize *= 2;
   byte newBuffer[] = new byte[buffSize];
   System.arraycopy (buffer, 0, newBuffer, 0, numBytes);
   buffer = newBuffer;
}
```

This method allocates a new, larger buffer for incoming data. It is not possible to reallocate an existing buffer, so to increase the buffer size we must first create a new, bigger buffer and then copy the contents of the old buffer into the new buffer.

To increase the buffer's size, we double it. By doubling its size, we allow our buffer to grow very rapidly. In only twenty calls to this method, we can grow a buffer from one byte up to one megabyte. We also make use of the `System.arraycopy()` method to efficiently copy the old buffer data to the new buffer. To start using the new buffer, we simply reassign our `buffer` reference. Garbage collection will take care of freeing memory allocated to the old buffer:

```
public void writeTo (OutputStream o) throws IOException {
   o.write (buffer, 0, numBytes);
}
```

The last method in this class is the `writeTo()` method. This writes the current buffer contents to the specified `OutputStream`. We write all of the valid contents of `buffer`, i.e., as many bytes as we have read.

4.7 Basic stream types

Streams can be connected to a variety of communications channels. Regardless of the underlying communications channel, the stream will provide the basic methods of `InputStream` or `OutputStream`. Depending upon what the stream is actually connected to, however, there may be some additional methods for manipulating the underlying channel.

Up to this point, we have referred to a *communications channel* as underlying streams. With some of the classes we shall look at, it may not be entirely obvious that there is a communications channel. We shall look at `ByteArrayOutputStream` which just writes data into an array of bytes. What makes this a communications channel, however, is that we can transport this array of bytes by any means we desire: UDP packet or carrier pigeon. Another thread somewhere else can then take this array of bytes and read out from it exactly what was written into it using a `ByteArrayInputStream`. So we have a communications channel, albeit an indirect one. A file is a similar indirect communications channel; you can read out of it what you formerly wrote into it.

In subsequent chapters, we will look at the various classes that provide streams access to different communications channels such as files, memory buffers, and network connections. The following is a quick listing of the main relevant classes (Figure 4.10). You may notice that there is no stream specifically devoted to network connections. The actual stream classes corresponding to a network connection, `SocketInputStream` and `SocketOutputStream`, are not made public, and so we will see the streams only as a generic `OutputStream` and `InputStream`.

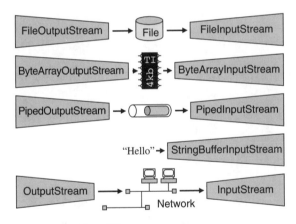

Figure 4.10   The different stream types

4.7.1 FileOutputStream and FileInputStream

These streams can be used to read and write files in a simple sequential manner. We will look at these classes in detail in the next chapter.

4.7.2 ByteArrayOutputStream and ByteArrayInputStream

These streams can be used to write data into an array of bytes and to read data out of an array of bytes. They are very useful classes for producing complex streams such as encrypted streams and message streams; we can write data into an array and manipulate it before transmission. They also provide a very easy mechanism to temporarily buffer stream data.

4.7.3 PipedOutputStream and PipedInputStream

These streams can be used for streams-based communications between threads in a single application. They are usually created in pairs; everything that is written to the output stream of a pipe can subsequently be read on the corresponding input stream. This is useful for simple streams-based interthread communications.

4.7.4 StringBufferInputStream

This stream provides a facility for reading bytes from a `StringBuffer`. This is very similar to a `ByteArrayInputStream`.

4.8 Wrapping up

This chapter has introduced the general concept of streams-based communications. Streams allow threads and applications to communicate over a variety of underlying communications channels in a uniform byte-I/O manner.

In the following chapters we will look at the various concrete stream classes that are provided by the `java.io` package. These classes will provide us with stream interfaces to files, networks, and other devices. We will also look at developing our own stream classes to provide us with function that is not provided by the supplied classes.

In later chapters we will begin developing networked applications. Streams provide the basis for most networked interapplication communications, and we will see how to develop significant networking libraries using the streams interface. We will implement a library of message-streams tools, as well as a set of streams that provide encryption and authentication capabilities that can help in the development of secure Internet applications.

chapter 5

File access through streams

Figure 5.1   FileInputStream and FileOutputStream

`FileOutputStream` and `FileInputStream` (Figure 5.1) are the two standard classes that supply streams access to files, providing the basic byte-oriented streams interface. This chapter is primarily concerned with a treatment of stream classes. Although files can also be accessed using the `RandomAccessFile` class, it is frequently useful to be able to access them through a streams interface; an application designed to read from an `InputStream` will accept input from the keyboard, from a file, or from a network connection without modification.

Other file-related classes include the `File` and `FileDescriptor` classes. For completeness, we will begin this chapter with an overview of these classes as well as an introduction to `RandomAccessFile`. Because they are not strictly related to networking, we go no further than discussing their respective APIs; we provide a more thorough treatment of the file stream classes.

5.1 Class File

This class represents a system-independent filename (Figure 5.2). It provides various methods to determine information about the actual file of the specified name, as well as methods to modify the file's attributes. With this class, a programmer can query whether a file of a particular name exists, whether it is readable, and so on.

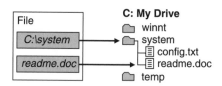

Figure 5.2   Class File

One possible use of the `File` class is to take a directory name and a filename and join them to obtain a complete path to the file. The directory separator is different in different operating systems, and so it is not reasonable to simply append, for example, a / character to the pathname and then append the filename to this. As an example, the AWT `FileDialog` class returns a pathname and a filename; it is up to the programmer to join them, preferably using this class. The class can also, however, be used to rename files, to create directories, to get a listing of the files in a directory, and so forth.

CHAPTER 5   FILE ACCESS THROUGH STREAMS

5.1.1 Constructors

An instance of `File` can be created from an entire system-dependent pathname, from a pathname and a filename, or from an existing `File` object and a filename. In the latter case, the `File` object must be a directory. The new `File` object will then refer to a particular file in the directory.

File(String path)   This constructor creates a `File` object for the specified system-dependent pathname `path`. The file can subsequently be manipulated with the methods supplied by this class.

File(String path, String name)   This constructor creates a `File` object for the specified file `name` on the specified path `path`. Usually this involves concatenating the pathname and the filename, separated by the directory separator character.

File(File dir, String name)   This creates a `File` object for the specified file `name` in the specified directory `dir`.

5.1.2 Methods

The `File` class provides various methods to test whether a file exists, whether it is a directory or a file, and so on. It also provides methods to create directories, and to remove and rename files. The `File` class is commonly used to provide a platform-independent naming mechanism, although it can also be used to provide these file management facilities.

   Note that none of these methods throw `IOExceptions`. Instead, they usually return a flag indicating whether they were successful.

boolean canRead()   This method returns `true` if the file exists and is readable.

boolean canWrite()   This method returns `true` if the file exists and is writable.

boolean delete()   This method attempts to delete the file, and returns `true` if successful.

boolean exists()   This method returns `true` if the file exists.

String getAbsolutePath()   This method returns the system-dependent absolute path-name of the corresponding file.

String getName()   This method returns the leaf name of the `File` object; this is just the filename, without the preceding path.

String getParent()   This method returns the parent directory name of the `File` object; for a file, this is the file's directory.

String getPath()   This method returns the pathname to the file represented by the `File` object; this may be a relative or absolute path.

boolean isAbsolute()   This method returns `true` if the pathname represented by the `File` object is an absolute pathname.

boolean isDirectory()   This method returns `true` if the `File` corresponds to a directory.

boolean isFile()   This method returns `true` if the `File` corresponds to a file.

long lastModified()   This method returns the date on which the corresponding file was last modified. See `java.util.Date`.

long length()   This method returns the length of the corresponding file.

String[] list()   This method returns an array of every filename in the corresponding directory.

String[] list(FilenameFilter filter)   This method returns an array of every file in the corresponding directory which matches the specified `FilenameFilter filter`. The `FilenameFilter` class provides a convenient way to select only those files in a directory with, for example, a particular suffix.

boolean mkdir()   This method creates a directory corresponding to the `File` object, returning `true` upon success.

boolean mkdirs()   This method creates a directory corresponding to the `File` object, and as many parent directories as are necessary, returning `true` upon success.

boolean renameTo(File dest)   This method attempts to rename the file to the specified destination file `dest`, and returns `true` upon success.

5.1.3 SecurityException

Access to files is restricted by the `SecurityManager`. Most of the methods listed above may fail with an exception of type `SecurityException` if the program is not permitted to perform the requested operation. Applications do not have a `SecurityManager` and so can access files arbitrarily. Applets under most browsers currently may not open any file for reading or writing, or may access only a certain restricted directory.

Note that a `SecurityException` may be thrown even though it is not listed in any `throws` clause. This is because it is a subclass of `RuntimeException`, which may be thrown at run-time without being declared.

5.2 Class FileDescriptor

A `FileDescriptor` object is a handle to a low-level system file-descriptor. A file-descriptor represents an open file, and includes information such as the current file position for reading and writing. This class is not commonly used.

Java has no facilities for creating or manipulating `FileDescriptors` other than by the `RandomAccessFile`, `FileOutputStream`, and `FileInputStream` classes.

5.3 Class RandomAccessFile

The `RandomAccessFile` class offers an easy way to handle files without using the streams interface of `FileOutputStream` and `FileInputStream` (Figure 5.3). The advantage of using this class is that it provides both reading and writing methods and allows, as the name suggests, random access to the file. The file stream classes are limited by their streams nature to provide only sequential access, and either only read access or only write access through any single stream.

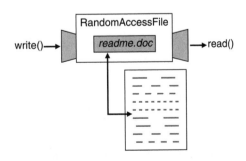

Figure 5.3   Class RandomAccessFile

5.3.1 Constructors

Random access files can be constructed from filenames or `File` objects. Whether access is read/write or read-only is specified in the constructor. Writing into an existing file *overwrites* the data at the current file-access position; it does not insert the data at the current position, and *does not truncate* the file.

public RandomAccessFile(String name, String mode) throws IOException
This constructor creates a `RandomAccessFile` with the specified system-dependent file name `name` and the specified mode `mode`. Mode `"r"` is for read-only and mode `"rw"` is for reading and writing.

 Remember that filenames are not portable across platforms. Under UNIX, a filename may have the form `/etc/rc.d/rc.sysinit`, while under DOS the filename may have the form `C:\WINDOWS\SYSTEM.INI`. Unless the user is supplying a filename, it is better to use the next constructor.

public RandomAccessFile(File file, String mode) throws IOException This constructor creates a `RandomAccessFile` from a specified `File` object `file` and mode `mode` (`"r"` or `"rw"`).

5.3.2 Methods

This class provides a lot of methods that have very similar signatures to those of `Output-Stream` and `InputStream`. It provides facilities to read and write bytes, as well as many higher level functions, such as reading a line of ASCII text or reading an `int` value. These methods have the same signatures as the `DataOutputStream` and `DataInput-Stream` classes, which we shall look at in Chapter 7. This class actually implements the `DataInput` and `DataOutput` interfaces that declare a standard set of these methods.

public final FileDescriptor getFD() throws IOException This method returns the system-level file descriptor object that is being used by the `RandomAccessFile`.

public int read() throws IOException This method reads a byte of data. It blocks if no input is available, and returns the value –1 if the end of the file is reached.

public int read(byte b[], int offset, int len) throws IOException This method reads a subarray as a sequence of bytes. It reads `len` bytes into array `b`, starting at index *offset.* As with the `InputStream` class, this method may not read the requested number of bytes. The number of bytes successfully read is returned.

public int read(byte b[]) throws IOException This method attempts to read a complete array of bytes using the previous `read()` method.

public final void readFully(byte b[], int off, int len) throws IOException This method fully reads the specified subarray of b. If EOF is reached before enough bytes have been read, then an exception of type `EOFException` is thrown.

public final void readFully(byte b[]) throws IOException This method fully reads the specified array b using the previous `readFully()` method.

public int skipBytes(int n) throws IOException This method skips the specified number of bytes n. It blocks until n bytes have been skipped, throwing an `EOFException` if EOF is detected prematurely. The returned value is meaningless because it is always n.

public void write(int b) throws IOException This method writes a byte of data. Although the parameter b is an `int`, only the low eight bits are written.

public void write(byte b[], int off, int len) throws IOException This method writes the specified subarray of `len` bytes from array b starting at index `off`.

public void write(byte b[]) throws IOException This method writes an array of bytes using the previous `write()` method.

public long getFilePointer() throws IOException This method returns the current location of the file pointer. This is the byte offset in the file at which the `RandomAccessFile` is currently reading or writing.

public void seek(long pos) throws IOException This method sets the file pointer to the specified absolute position.

public long length() throws IOException This method returns the length of the file.

public void close() throws IOException This method closes the file.

public final boolean readBoolean() throws IOException   This method reads a `boolean` value, as written by the `writeBoolean()` method. All of these methods throw an exception of type `EOFException` if a premature EOF is reached.

public final byte readByte() throws IOException   This method reads a `byte` value. Unlike the `read()` method, this method throws an `EOFException` if the EOF is reached.

public final short readShort() throws IOException   This method reads a `short` value, as written by the `writeShort()` method.

public final int readInt() throws IOException   This method reads an `int` value. Note that this is read as four binary bytes; the value is not decoded from a text file.

public final long readLong() throws IOException   This method reads a `long` value (eight bytes).

public final int readUnsignedByte() throws IOException   This method reads an unsigned `byte` value; thus, the `byte` 255 will be treated as the `int` 255.

public final int readUnsignedShort() throws IOException   This method reads an unsigned `short` value, returning the corresponding `int`.

public final float readFloat() throws IOException   This method reads a `float` value.

public final double readDouble() throws IOException   This method reads a `double` value.

public final char readChar() throws IOException   This method reads a 16-bit `char` value.

public final String readUTF() throws IOException   This method reads a UTF formatted `String`. UTF format is briefly described with the `DataInputStream` and `DataOutputStream` classes.

public final String readLine() throws IOException   This method reads a line of ASCII characters terminated by a newline or EOF.

public final void writeBoolean(boolean b) throws IOException   This method writes a `boolean` value.

public final void writeByte(int i) throws IOException   This method writes a single byte.

public final void writeShort(int i) throws IOException   This method writes a 16-bit `short`.

public final void writeInt(int i) throws IOException   This method writes a 32-bit `int`.

public final void writeLong(long l) throws IOException   This method writes a 64-bit `long`.

public final void writeFloat(float f) throws IOException   This method writes a 32-bit `float`.

public final void writeDouble(double d) throws IOException   This method writes a 64-bit `double`.

public final void writeChar(int c) throws IOException   This method writes a 16-bit `char`.

public final void writeChars(String s) throws IOException   This method writes a `String` as a sequence of 16-bit characters. Neither the string length nor a delimiting character are written.

public final void writeUTF(String str) throws IOException   This method writes a `String` in Unicode Text Format (UTF).

public final void writeBytes(String s) throws IOException   This method writes a `String` as a sequence of ASCII bytes. The top byte of every character in the `String` is ignored.

5.3.3 IOException

All of the methods listed above may throw an IOException if there is a problem with the read or write. All of the higher level read methods (for integers, etc.) will throw an EOFException (a subclass of IOException) if the EOF is reached prematurely.

5.3.4 SecurityException

All file access is restricted by the current SecurityManager. Creating a RandomAccess-File may cause a SecurityException if the specified file access is prohibited.

5.4 Class FileOutputStream

The FileOutputStream class allows sequential data to be written to a file (Figure 5.4). The usual constructors take a filename or File object and create a corresponding new file, destroying any existing file having the same name.

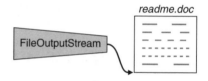

Figure 5.4   Class FileOutputStream

5.4.1 Constructors

Constructing a FileOutputStream will create the specified file and then provide the capability to write to it. The close() method should be called when writing to the file is finished. If this is not done, then the file is automatically closed when the File-OutputStream is garbage collected.

FileOutputStream(String name) throws IOException   This constructor creates a file with the specified filename name, destroying any existing file having the same name. The FileOutputStream provides sequential write access to the new file.

FileOutputStream(File file) throws IOException   This constructor creates a file corresponding to the specified File object file, destroying any existing file having the same name. To use this constructor, a File object with the desired name must be created first, followed by the associated FileOutputStream.

FileOutputStream(FileDescriptor fdObj)   The `FileDescriptor` object provides access to the system-specific data structure for open files. This constructor allows a `FileOutputStream` to be constructed from the `FileDescriptor` of a file which is already open, for example, one which is open for random access. This constructor does *not* create the file. It takes an existing, open file and writes to it.

This constructor will not throw an `IOException` because the `FileDescriptor` is assumed to be already attached to an open file.

5.4.2 Methods

The `FileOutputStream` class provides one method in addition to the usual methods of `OutputStream`.

FileDescriptor getFD() throws IOException   This method returns a `File-Descriptor` object for the file which is being written.

5.4.3 IOException

The methods and constructors described above may all throw exceptions of type `IOException` if an I/O error occurs. Possible causes include an invalid filename, the file being locked, or the disk becoming full.

5.4.4 SecurityException

Creating a `FileOutputStream` may throw an exception of type `SecurityException` if the current `SecurityManager` does not permit file writing.

5.5 Class FileInputStream

The `FileInputStream` class allows one to read sequential data from a file (Figure 5.5). The file must already exist. Creating a `FileInputStream` for a nonexistent file will throw an exception of type `IOException`.

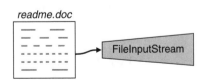

Figure 5.5   Class FileInputStream

5.5.1 Constructors

Constructing a `FileInputStream` opens a stream for reading from the specified file.

FileInputStream(String name) throws IOException   This constructor opens a file with the specified filename `name` for reading. The `FileInputStream` then provides sequential read access to this file. As before, be aware of the differences between filenames on different operating systems.

FileInputStream(File file) throws IOException   This constructor opens a file corresponding to the specified `File` object `file` for reading.

FileInputStream(FileDescriptor fdObj)   This constructor creates a `FileInputStream` attached to the existing `FileDescriptor fdObj`. The `FileDescriptor` must be a valid descriptor for a file which is open for reading.

5.5.2 Methods

The `FileInputStream` class provides an additional method to those of `InputStream`. The `markSupported()`, `mark()`, and `reset()` methods take their default implementations of unsupported.

FileDescriptor getFD() throws IOException   This method returns a reference to the system-level `FileDescriptor` object to which the `FileInputStream` is attached. Creating a new `FileInputStream` automatically creates such a `FileDescriptor` object.

5.5.3 IOException

Most of the methods and constructors described above may throw an exception of type `IOException`. The exact nature of the `IOException` depends upon the I/O error, but the most common cause is a file not existing. The `read()` methods do not throw an exception at EOF, but as with `InputStream` they return the value -1.

5.5.4 SecurityException

Creating a `FileInputStream` may throw an exception of type `SecurityException` if the operation is not permitted by the `SecurityManager`.

5.6 A simple file streams example

This example presents a trivial file copier (Figure 5.6). It takes two filename parameters and copies the first file to the second.

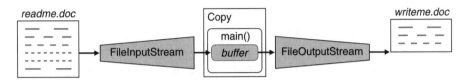

Figure 5.6   File copying

```
import java.io.*;

public class Copy {
   static public void main (String args[]) throws IOException {
      if (args.length != 2)
         throw (new RuntimeException ("Syntax: Copy <src> <dst>"));
      FileInputStream in = new FileInputStream (args[0]);
      FileOutputStream out = new FileOutputStream (args[1]);

      byte buffer[] = new byte[16];
      int n;
      while ((n = in.read (buffer)) > -1)
         out.write (buffer, 0, n);

      out.close ();
      in.close ();
   }
}
```

All of the code resides in the `main()` method. We declare that this method may throw any exceptions that may occur from attempting to copy the file. We verify that the correct number of parameters have been supplied, and throw an explanatory exception if not.

We open a `FileInputStream` from the first parameter and a `FileOutputStream` to the second parameter. These provide the basic `InputStream` and `OutputStream` interfaces for accessing the files. We then copy the first file to the second file using a small intermediate buffer for efficiency. We have seen this type of loop in the previous chapter: we read as many bytes into the buffer as possible and then write them to the `OutputStream`.

When the `read()` method returns the value −1 we have reached the EOF, and so we exit the loop and close the two files.

5.7 Creating an AppendFile-OutputStream

We will now look at creating a custom `OutputStream`. This class is very similar to a `FileOutputStream`, except that it will append written data to the end of an existing file rather than always creating a new file. The file will be created if it does not exist (Figure 5.7).

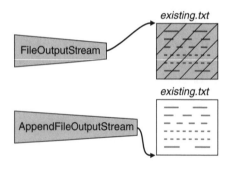

Figure 5.7 Class AppendFileOutputStream

```
import java.io.*;

public class AppendFileOutputStream extends OutputStream {
  // public AppendFileOutputStream (String fileName) throws IOException ...
  // public void write (int b) throws IOException ...
  // public void close () throws IOException ...
}
```

Our class extends `OutputStream` and provides the minimum number of methods necessary to actually implement an `OutputStream`.

```
protected RandomAccessFile file;

public AppendFileOutputStream (String fileName) throws IOException {
  file = new RandomAccessFile (fileName, "rw");
  file.seek (file.length ());
}
```

We make use of a `RandomAccessFile file` to perform all I/O; the constructor creates this `RandomAccessFile` with the specified filename `fileName`. The Random-

AccessFile class automatically creates the file if it does not exist, or opens it for random access if it already exists. The rest of the classes makes use of methods of this class to perform the actual I/O; we seek the end of the file so that new data will be appended to the file, rather than overwriting the original contents.

```
public void write (int b) throws IOException {
    file.write (b);
}
```

This method calls the `write()` method of the `RandomAccessFile`.

```
public void close () throws IOException {
    file.close ();
}
```

This method calls the `close()` method of the `RandomAccessFile`.

We could obviously implement the multibyte `write()` methods to call those of `RandomAccessFile`; however, for illustrative purposes, this is the minimum number of methods necessary to implement this class.

There are actually several alternative implementations for this class; we will now look at a few of these.

5.7.1 An alternative AppendFileOutput-Stream method

Another approach to this problem is to make use of the `FileOutputStream` constructor that attaches to an already open `FileDescriptor` object. We can open a file for random access, find its end, and create a `FileOutputStream` attached to the underlying `FileDescriptor`. The following method does just this:

```
FileOutputStream getAppendFileOutputStream (String fileName) throws IOException {
    RandomAccessFile file = new RandomAccessFile (fileName, "rw");
    file.seek (file.length ());
    return new FileOutputStream (file.getFD ());
}
```

This method creates a `RandomAccessFile`, finds its end, and then returns a `FileOutputStream` attached to the underlying `FileDescriptor`. The `FileDescriptor` has been positioned at the end of the file by the `seek()` call. We can use this method to create `OutputStreams` which append to the end of existing files.

It is necessary to understand the `FileDescriptor` class to understand this code. Java creates a `FileDescriptor` object for every open file. This `FileDescriptor` includes information such as a reference to the actual file and a read/write position in the file. If a file is opened twice for reading, then each `InputStream` will have a different `FileDescriptor`. Reading from one will not affect the read position of the other. Alternatively, you can open a file once and create several `FileOutputStreams` attached to the single `FileDescriptor`. Any operation which modifies the read/write position of this `FileDescriptor` will affect all of these streams.

In this piece of code we open the file once when we create the `RandomAccessFile`. We set the read/write position using the `seek()` method, and then we create a `FileOutputStream` attached to the existing `FileDescriptor`. Both the `RandomAccessFile` and the `FileOutputStream` share the same `FileDescriptor`, which is positioned at the end of the file.

5.7.2 A second alternative AppendFileOutputStream class

The previous `getAppendFileOutputStream()` method suggests a much simpler implementation of our `AppendFileOutputStream` class:

```
import java.io.*;

public class AltAppendFileOutputStream extends FileOutputStream {
   protected FileInputStream file;

   public AltAppendFileOutputStream (String fileName) throws IOException {
      super ((new RandomAccessFile (fileName, "rw")).getFD ());
      file = new FileInputStream (getFD ());
      int n = file.available ();
      do {
         n -= file.skip (n);
      } while (n > 0);
   }

}
```

This piece of code makes use of the existing `FileOutputStream` implementation. We inherit the superclass implementations of `OutputStream` methods that directly access a `FileDescriptor` object, and are thus very efficient.

The constructor is somewhat obscure. It creates a `RandomAccessFile`, much as before, and then calls the superclass constructor with the `FileDescriptor` of this `RandomAccessFile`. Creating a `RandomAccessFile` in this manner does not erase an existing file, so after the constructor call we will have a `FileOutputStream` attached to an existing file, but positioned at the beginning.

We then create a `FileInputStream` attached to the same `FileDescriptor`. The `FileInputStream` and `FileOutputStream` both share the same system-level `FileDescriptor`, so the `skip()` method sets the access position for both the `FileInputStream` and this `FileOutputStream`.

The reason we do not create the `RandomAccessFile`, call its `seek()` method, and then call the superclass constructor is that this is *prohibited* by the Java language. The superclass constructor call must be the *first* statement in a constructor.

It would seem that we could use a superclass constructor call of the form `super((rFile = new RandomAccessFile(fileName, "rw")).getFD())` to leave a reference to the `RandomAccessFile` in a variable `rFile`. Unfortunately, it is technically illegal to access an instance variable from a superconstructor call.

5.8 Building a mark/reset FileInputStream

In the previous chapter we discussed the `mark()` and `reset()` methods of `InputStream`. The default `FileInputStream` does not provide these methods, even though they are provided by the underlying filesystem. In this example, we will create a `FileInputStream` that supports the `mark()` and `reset()` methods (Figure 5.8).

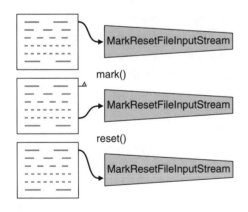

mark()

reset()

Figure 5.8   Class MarkResetFileInputStream

```
import java.io.*;

public class MarkResetFileInputStream extends FileInputStream {
   public static MarkResetFileInputStream create (String fileName)
       throws IOException {
     RandomAccessFile file = new RandomAccessFile (fileName, "r");
     return new MarkResetFileInputStream (file);
   }
```

```
// public MarkResetFileInputStream (RandomAccessFile file)
//     throws IOException ...
// public boolean markSupported () ...
// public void mark (int n) ...
// public void reset () throws IOException ...
}
```

This class is a `FileInputStream` that incorporates an alternative technique that we could have used in the previous implementation of the `AppendFileOutputStream` class. We supply a `static create()` method that returns a new `MarkResetFileInputStream`. We create a `RandomAccessFile` that opens the specified file for reading; we then create a new `MarkResetFileInputStream` that attaches to the same `FileDescriptor` as the `RandomAccessFile`, and uses methods of the `RandomAccessFile` to change the read position.

It would, of course, also be appropriate to implement a `create()` method that accepts a `File` parameter. The code would be very similar, so we have omitted this alternative.

```
protected long markedPos;
protected RandomAccessFile file;

public MarkResetFileInputStream (RandomAccessFile file) throws IOException {
    super (file.getFD ());
    this.file = file;
    markedPos = -1;
}
```

In our constructor, we accept a `RandomAccessFile file` attached to the chosen file, and then call the superclass constructor that attaches to the underlying `FileDescriptor` object of this file. We keep a reference to the `RandomAccessFile` in `file`.

To perform `mark()` and `reset()`, we store the marked position in the `markedPos` variable. We set the marked position to the value `-1`, indicating that no position has been marked.

Note that we cannot use the same implementation as before (with `AltAppendFileOutputStream`) for this class, because there is no facility to rewind a `FileDescriptor` without using a `RandomAccessFile`, and there is no way to attach a `RandomAccessFile` to an existing `FileDescriptor`.

```
public boolean markSupported () {
    return true;
}
```

We override the default implementation of `markSupported()` to indicate that this class does indeed support the `mark()` and `reset()` operations.

```
public void mark (int n) {
   try {
     markedPos = file.getFilePointer ();
   } catch (IOException ex) {
     markedPos = -1;
   }
}
```

To mark a position in the file we must take note of the current reading position in the file. To do this, we can call the `getFilePointer()` method of the `RandomAccess-File`. Note that the `getFilePointer()` method may throw an `IOException`, but the signature for `mark()` specifies that it may not, so we must catch any potential exception and set the marked position to -1.

```
public void reset () throws IOException {
   if (markedPos == -1)
     throw new IOException ("No mark set.");
   file.seek (markedPos);
}
```

The `reset()` method first checks to see that a mark has been set. If none has, then we throw an explanatory `IOException`. Otherwise we use the `seek()` method of `RandomAccessFile` to reset the reading position of the underlying `FileDescriptor`. Both this `FileInputStream` and the `RandomAccessFile` are attached to the same `FileDescriptor`, so calling the `RandomAccessFile seek()` method will also reposition the reading position of the `FileInputStream`.

Using this stream, we can make use of the mark/reset `InputStream` methods to efficiently implement file format discriminators and other such classes. To implement this without using a `RandomAccessFile`, we would have to buffer the data as we read it and then reread from the buffer in case of a reset.

5.9 Wrapping up

In this chapter we have looked at the file stream classes. More importantly, we have seen how we can extend these classes and provide additional function beyond what is provided by the basic API. The classes which we have developed are very small because we can leverage off the existing codebase. This ability is one of the tremendous advantages of object-oriented programming. In addition, we have provided all of these facilities on top of the uniform streams interface, so they are readily usable by any code that makes use of the stream classes.

The classes that we have implemented provide only additional functionality for file streams. They are not directly usable for byte array streams, networked streams, or indeed any other stream class. In the next chapters, we will look at filter streams that provide enhanced function on top of any underlying stream connection.

chapter 6

Extending streams with filters

Up to this point, we have just looked at simple streams that support writing bytes and byte arrays. Obviously, communication at such a level is more awkward than it need be. We have seen how to extend an existing stream and add function; however, this is limited because we can extend only a single stream, and so must implement the extension for all communication channels that we will use.

We would like to be able to develop streams that allow us to attach higher level functions to any type of stream in a generic manner. This chapter introduces the concept of a *filter stream*, a stream that provides additional function on top of an existing stream. We will be able to develop streams that allow us to communicate all of the primitive Java data types over any underlying stream connection, among other things.

6.1 Providing higher level communications

There are several obvious ways of providing higher level communications over a stream which can handle only bytes. We can use general-purpose methods that convert data into bytes and transmit the bytes over a separate stream; alternatively, we can subclass a stream and provide these methods directly. The last and most general option is to make a filter stream that provides enhanced stream function on top of another existing stream.

6.1.1 General purpose methods

In this example, we implement a pair of general-purpose methods that write an integer as four bytes into an `OutputStream` and read an integer as four bytes from an `Input-Stream` (Figure 6.1).

Figure 6.1 General-purpose methods

```
void writeInt (OutputStream o, int x) throws IOException {
   o.write (x >>> 24);
   o.write (x >>> 16);
   o.write (x >>> 8);
   o.write (x);
}
```

This method writes the integer x to the `OutputStream` o as a series of four bytes, high-byte first. Note that the `write()` method just writes the bottom eight bits of the integer parameter.

The operator `>>>` shifts the integer right by the specified number of bits, so the value x `>>>` 24 is just the top byte of x.

```
int readInt (InputStream i) throws IOException {
    int x0 = i.read ();
    int x1 = i.read ();
    int x2 = i.read ();
    int x3 = i.read ();
    if (x3 == -1)
        throw (new IOException ("EOF while reading int"));
    return x3 + (x2 << 8) + (x1 << 16) + (x0 << 24);
}
```

This method reads four bytes from the `InputStream` i and adds them together to produce the integer result. If we reach EOF before reading the entire integer we throw an `IOException`. The operator `<<` shifts the value left by the specified number of bits.

This manner of communication is quite adequate in a simple situation; methods can be provided for communicating all of the default types. The problem with this approach is that every application which needs to communicate these types must agree on a format, and provide the code in the form of these methods.

6.1.2 Enhanced OutputStreams

In the previous example, we read the integer from the stream, so it would be nice if the stream provided the method to read an integer directly; this is the nature of object-oriented programming. The following class extends the `FileOutputStream` class and provides a `writeInt()` method; we would obviously implement a corresponding `Data-FileInputStream` that mimics the `readInt()` method above (Figure 6.2).

Figure 6.2 Enhanced streams

```
import java.io.*;

public class DataFileOutputStream extends FileOutputStream {
    // public DataFileOutputStream (String fileName) throws IOException ...
    // public void writeInt (int x) throws IOException ...
}
```

This class extends `FileOutputStream` and adds a `writeInt()` method that writes an integer to the attached file as four bytes.

```
public DataFileOutputStream (String fileName) throws IOException {
    super (fileName);
}
```

In the constructor, we call the superclass constructor with the specified filename `fileName`. For reasons of simplicity, we don't implement any of the other constructors.

```
public void writeInt (int x) throws IOException {
    write (x >>> 24);
    write (x >>> 16);
    write (x >>> 8);
    write (x);
}
```

The `writeInt()` method writes the integer as four separate bytes, as before.

This approach is cleaner than the first approach; we can call the `writeInt()` method directly on the `OutputStream`. The drawback of this approach is that we must provide an implementation of `writeInt()` for every `OutputStream` available. We have demonstrated an implementation for a `FileOutputStream`; we also would have to provide an implementation for `PipedOutputStream` and so forth.

6.1.3 Filter streams

The mechanism for adding higher level function to streams in Java is filter streams. A `FilterInputStream` is a stream that attaches to an existing `InputStream` and provides additional function on top of that which is already provided. Similarly, a `FilterOutputStream` attaches to an existing `OutputStream` and enhances its function. In this rest of this chapter we will look at some of the supplied filter streams (Figure 6.3).

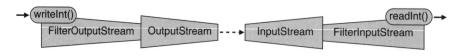

Figure 6.3   Filter streams

One important thing to note about filter streams is that they are subclasses of `OutputStream` and `InputStream`, and so provide all of the normal methods of these superclasses. Usually the superclass methods will be passed on directly to the attached stream, so writing to a `FilterOutputStream` will write directly to the attached `OutputStream`.

Because filter streams are themselves streams, we can attach several filter streams in series together and obtain their combined functions.

6.2 Class FilterOutput-Stream

This class is a template for filter output streams. It does not provide any additional function other than the ability to attach to an existing `OutputStream` and to make use of its methods.

In fact, a plain `FilterOutputStream` is functionally indistinguishable from the `OutputStream` to which it is attached; all of the methods perform the relevant action on the attached stream. The `FilterOutputStream` can thus be passed as an `Output-Stream` parameter with no visible difference. This class is used by subclasses which will add to the basic function provided here.

6.2.1 Constructors

`FilterOutputStreams` attach to existing `OutputStreams`, hence the single constructor:

FilterOutputStream(OutputStream out)   This constructor creates a new `Filter-OutputStream` attached to the `OutputStream` out. It is not possible to call this constructor directly; it may only be called by a subclass.

6.2.2 Methods

The default methods just call the corresponding action on the attached stream.

void close() throws IOException   This calls the corresponding method on the attached stream, i.e., closing a `FilterStream` closes the stream to which it is attached. It is thus not necessary to also close the attached stream.

void flush() throws IOException   This calls the corresponding method on the attached stream.

void write(int b) throws IOException This calls the corresponding method on the attached stream.

void write(byte b[]) throws IOException This calls the corresponding method on the attached stream.

void write(byte b[], int off, int len) This calls the corresponding method on the attached stream.

6.3 Class FilterInputStream

This class is a template for filter input streams. It does not provide any function other than the ability to attach to an existing `InputStream` and to pass requests on to methods of this attached stream.

6.3.1 Constructors

`FilterInputStream`s attach to existing `InputStream`s, hence the single constructor:

FilterInputStream(InputStream in) This constructor creates a new `Filter-InputStream` attached to the `InputStream in`. It is not possible to call this constructor directly; it may be called only by the constructor of a subclass.

6.3.2 Methods

The default methods just call the corresponding action on the attached stream.

int available() throws IOException This returns the number of bytes available on the attached stream.

void close() throws IOException This closes the attached stream.

void mark(int readlimit) This calls the corresponding method on the attached stream.

boolean markSupported()   This calls the corresponding method on the attached stream.

int read() throws IOException   This calls the corresponding method on the attached stream.

int read(byte b[]) throws IOException   This calls the corresponding method on the attached stream.

int read(byte b[], int off, int len) throws IOException   This calls the corresponding method on the attached stream.

void reset() throws IOException   This calls the corresponding method on the attached stream.

long skip(long n) throws IOException   This calls the corresponding method on the attached stream.

6.4 Supplied filter streams

There are many possible uses for filter streams, and the Java environment comes with several such streams already defined. These are streams which can attach to any existing stream, including other filter streams, and provide additional function. They include:

6.4.1 BufferedOutputStream and Buffered-InputStream

These streams provide input and output buffering on top of an existing stream. Buffering is a useful function because it makes I/O more efficient (Figure 6.4).

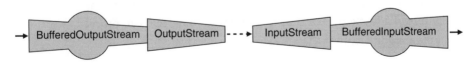

Figure 6.4   Buffered streams

Without buffering, every call to a stream will pass through to the local operating system, which can incur a lot of overhead. By buffering the communications, the majority of reads and writes can occur directly to a memory buffer, and the operating system must be only occasionally called. Output buffers can be flushed using the `flush()` method; this writes any buffered data to the attached `OutputStream`. These streams will also flush automatically if the buffer becomes full.

6.4.2 DataOutputStream and DataInput-Stream

These streams provide high-level communications capabilities on top of an existing stream which can only read and write bytes. Methods are provided to communicate all of the primitive language types, such as `Strings` and floating point numbers (Figure 6.5).

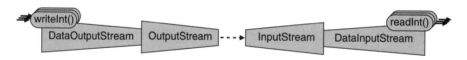

Figure 6.5   Data streams

6.4.3 PushbackInputStream

A pushback stream is an input stream that supports a very simple form of *unreading*: a single byte of data can be pushed back into the input stream, and this byte will subsequently be available for reading again (Figure 6.6). In an ear-

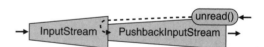

Figure 6.6   Class PushbackInputStream

lier example, we used the `mark()` and `reset()` methods to permit, for example, a GIF decoder to read some of a file and then to restore the stream if it does not understand the image. We can achieve the same effect with a `PushbackInputStream` if a decoder needs only to read a single byte of data to determine whether it can proceed. This is, in fact, a common requirement of a language scanner.

6.4.4 SequenceInputStream

This filter stream is interesting because it allows a series of Input-Streams to be sequenced one after another (Figure 6.7). All of the data are read from the first stream until the end of the file is reached, at

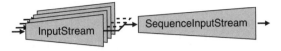

Figure 6.7   Class SequenceInputStream

which point reading switches to the next stream. End of file is signalled only when the end of the last InputStream is reached. Because this is a filter stream, it appears as just a single long InputStream, even though it reads sequentially from several underlying streams.

6.4.5 LineNumberInputStream

This stream provides rudimentary line numbering: it proceeds as a normal InputStream, but increments an internal counter with every line that it reads (Figure 6.8). The current line number can be queried using a special method; this

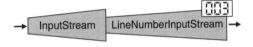

Figure 6.8   Class LineNumberInputStream

permits an application to easily identify the line number of a text file which it is reading without having any additional code. The mark() and reset() methods are modified to restore the line number.

6.4.6 PrintStream

This class provides the capability of ASCII textual data output. It provides methods for writing all of the standard data types to an OutputStream, formatting the values as plain text. The System.out stream is in fact a PrintStream attached to the user's terminal;

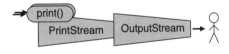

Figure 6.9   Class PrintStream

all data written to System.out using the print methods are thus formatted in ASCII for human use (Figure 6.9).

6.4.7 StreamTokenizer

The `StreamTokenizer` class is a fairly involved filter stream that provides the capability to parse an `InputStream` as a sequence of language tokens (Figure 6.10). The class is oriented around the Java language, and is of real use only to programmers who are interested in parsing Java source files.

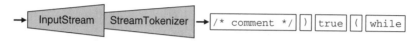

Figure 6.10   Class StreamTokenizer

6.5 Using filter streams

In this example we will look at using a few filter streams together (Figure 6.11). We will look at the various filter streams in detail in the next chapter.

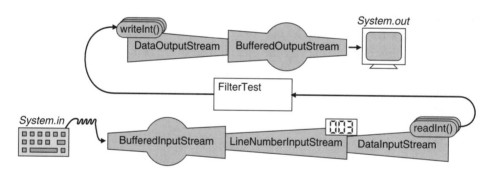

Figure 6.11   Using filter streams

This example reads lines of input and writes them out again, in uppercase, preceded by the line number. What makes this unusual, other than using methods of `DataInputStream` and `DataOutputStream` to read and write ASCII lines, is that we buffer the input and the output. Buffering the input has little obvious effect; however, buffering the output has the effect of delaying the actual writing out of data until we flush the stream or until the buffer becomes full. Hence, we do not see our input written out again until either we have written a lot (512 bytes by default), or until we terminate the input using control-D (UNIX) or control-Z (DOS) and the output is flushed.

```java
import java.io.*;

public class FilterTest {
  public static void main (String args[]) {
    BufferedInputStream buffIn = new BufferedInputStream (System.in);
    BufferedOutputStream buffOut = new BufferedOutputStream (System.out);

    LineNumberInputStream lineIn = new LineNumberInputStream (buffIn);

    DataInputStream dataIn = new DataInputStream (lineIn);
    DataOutputStream dataOut = new DataOutputStream (buffOut);
    try {
      String input;
      while ((input = dataIn.readLine ()) != null) {
        String msg = lineIn.getLineNumber () + " : " +
          input.toUpperCase () + "\n";
        dataOut.writeBytes (msg);
      }
      dataOut.flush ();
    } catch (IOException ex) {
      System.err.println (ex);
    }
  }
}
```

The first thing we do is to create a `BufferedInputStream` `buffIn` and a `BufferedOutputStream` `buffOut` attached to the user's terminal. Everything that we read from or write to these streams ultimately comes from or goes to the user's terminal; however, memory buffers make the I/O more efficient. We attach a `LineNumberInputStream` `lineIn` to the input to keep a count of the current line number.

We subsequently create a `DataInputStream` `dataIn` and a `DataOutputStream` `dataOut` attached to these streams. Again, what we read and write goes through the buffered streams which are attached to the user's terminal. These data streams provide us with a filter for higher level communications on top of the lower level streams, which can handle only bytes.

We subsequently read lines from the input, process them and write them to the output. Notice here that we do this processing until the `readLine()` method returns null. Some methods of `DataInputStream` indicate to us that we have reached the end of the file by throwing an `EOFException`. The `readLine()` method simply returns null. Our loop is thus terminated when the user types control-D (or control-Z). We subsequently flush the output.

The use of a `DataOutputStream` is actually unnecessary here. We could have simply used the `println()` methods of `System.out`; however, this serves as an example of attaching multiple streams together.

6.6 Building ASCII filter streams

There are many uses for filter streams in networking which we shall look at later. In this example we will create a pair of filter streams that permit us to read and write integers in ASCII format. We define an `ASCIIOutputStream` and an `ASCIIInputStream` that attach to an existing stream and provide methods to read and write strings and integers in ASCII format. The `ASCIIOutputStream` is analogous to the predefined `PrintStream` class which provides methods to write all of the standard data-types in ASCII. Streams such as these are very useful for communicating with human beings, as well as with servers that communicate in plain-text.

6.6.1 Class ASCIIOutputStream

This class is a `FilterOutputStream` that attaches to an existing stream and provides some capability for communicating in ASCII over the stream. Because the normal `write()` methods are passed directly to the attached stream, these ASCII communication methods are provided in addition to the usual methods of `OutputStream`.

```
import java.io.*;

public class ASCIIOutputStream extends FilterOutputStream {
   // public ASCIIOutputStream (OutputStream out) ...
   // public void writeInt (int x) throws IOException ...
   // public void writeString (String s) throws IOException ...
}
```

This class extends `FilterOutputStream` and provides methods `writeInt()`, which writes an integer value in ASCII, and `writeString()`, which writes a `String` in ASCII.

```
public ASCIIOutputStream (OutputStream out) {
   super (out);
}
```

The constructor calls the superclass constructor, attaching to the specified Output-Stream out.

```
public void writeInt (int x) throws IOException {
   Integer y = new Integer (x);
   writeString (y.toString ());
}
```

This method writes an integer x to the attached stream in ASCII. We make use of the toString() method of class Integer, which converts an integer value into a String, and then use the writeString() method.

```
public void writeString (String s) throws IOException {
   byte b[] = new byte[s.length ()];
   s.getBytes (0, s.length (), b, 0);
   write (b);
}
```

This method writes a String s to the attached stream in ASCII. In this process, we must strip the top byte from every character before transmission. The char primitive in Java is a Unicode 16-bit character, whereas an ASCII character is only 8 bits wide. The most convenient conversion from Unicode to ASCII is to simply ignore the high byte of each character.

We perform this conversion by creating a byte buffer just large enough to hold the String, and then using the getBytes() method of class String that copies the String into a supplied buffer, stripping the high byte from each character. We then write this buffer to the attached OutputStream using the write() method. Note that when we call write() here, we are making use of the write() method that is inherited from the superclass FilterOutputStream. This inherited write() method simply calls the write() method of the attached stream.

6.6.2 Class ASCIIInputStream

This stream is a FilterInputStream that attaches to an existing stream and provides rudimentary function for reading ASCII data from the stream. We provide a method ws() that skips whitespace in the stream, a method readInt() that reads an integer in ASCII from the stream, and a method readWord() that reads an ASCII word, where a word is considered to be any consecutive sequence of non-whitespace characters.

```
import java.io.*;

public class ASCIIInputStream extends FilterInputStream {
   // public ASCIIInputStream (InputStream in) ...
```

```
   // public int read () throws IOException ...
   // public int read (byte b[], int o, int l) throws IOException ...
   // public void ws () throws IOException ...
   // public int readInt () throws IOException ...
   // public String readWord () throws IOException ...
}
```

This class extends `FilterInputStream` and adds methods to read ASCII data. To do this, we must provide a very similar function to the `PushbackInputStream` class. For this reason, we provide new implementations of the `read()` methods that let us unread a single byte of data in addition to adding the `ws()`, `readInt()`, and `readWord()` methods.

```
public ASCIIInputStream (InputStream in) {
   super (in);
}
```

In the constructor we call the superclass constructor, attaching to the `InputStream` in.

```
protected int pushback = -2;

public int read() throws IOException {
   int c = pushback;
   if (pushback == -2)
      c = super.read();
   else
      pushback = -2;
   return c;
}
```

This `read()` method supports an unreading function that lets us insert a single byte back into the `InputStream`, so that a subsequent call to `read()` will reread this byte. The `pushback` variable holds this unread byte, or the value –2, if none has been unread. Our implementation of this method therefore checks to see whether a byte has been unread; if so, then we return this value and set `pushback` to –2. Otherwise we read a byte from the attached stream.

The reason that we use the value –2 to indicate that no data have been unread, is that we wish to also support unreading of the EOF. The native `PushbackInputStream` does not support this because it uses –1 (EOF) to indicate that no data have been unread.

This EOF pushback facility is important when reading from `System.in`, because when the user types control-D (or control-Z), EOF will be signalled only once; a subsequent call to `read()` will wait for another character to be entered on the keyboard. By unreading the EOF, we allow keyboard EOFs to be correctly processed by this stream.

```java
public int read(byte b[], int o, int l) throws IOException {
   if (l == 0)
      return 0;
   else if (pushback == -2)
      return super.read (b, o, l);
   else if (pushback == -1) {
      pushback = -2;
      return -1;
   } else { b[o] = (byte) pushback;
      pushback = -2;
      return 1;
   }
}
```

This method supports unreading using the multibyte `read()` method. We first check to see whether the read request was for zero bytes; if so, we return zero (no bytes were read). Next, we check to see whether a byte has been unread; if not, then we return a multibyte read from the attached stream.

Otherwise, a byte has been unread; we check to see if this was the EOF; if so, then we reset `pushback` and return EOF. Otherwise we insert `pushback` into the read array b, reset it, and return 1 (one byte was successfully read).

```java
protected void unread (int x) {
   pushback = x;
}
```

This method unreads a single byte by placing it in the `pushback` variable. Note that you can only unread a single byte at a time; unreading a second byte will overwrite the first.

```java
public void ws () throws IOException {
   int x;
   while (((x = read ()) != -1) && Character.isSpace ((char) x)) {
   }
   unread (x);
}
```

The `ws()` method skips over any immediate whitespace in the stream. To skip whitespace, we must read bytes until we reach a character that is not whitespace; we use an empty `while` loop for this. Our loop reads a character, tests to see whether it is the EOF or a whitespace character, and exits the loop as soon as a non-whitespace character is encountered.

Once we encounter a non-whitespace character, we discover our need for the unreading: this method is only supposed to skip whitespace, but we must loop until we actually read a non-whitespace character. We must therefore undo the last read that we performed with our `unread()` method. Note that we will even pushback the EOF.

When the user next calls `read()` after calling this method, it will, as expected, read the first non-whitespace character in the stream.

```
public int readInt () throws IOException {
    ws ();
    StringBuffer s = new StringBuffer ();
    int x = read ();
    if ((x == '-') || Character.isDigit ((char) x)) {
        s.append ((char) x);
        while (((x = read ()) != -1) && Character.isDigit ((char) x))
            s.append ((char) x);
    }
    unread (x);
    if ((s.length () == 0) || ((s.length () == 1) && (s.charAt (0) == '-'))) {
        if (x == -1)
            throw new EOFException ("EOF while reading ASCII integer");
        else
            throw new IOException ("Failed to read ASCII integer");
    }
    return Integer.parseInt (s.toString ());
}
```

This method reads an ASCII integer from the attached stream. An ASCII integer is considered to be any consecutive sequence of digits on the attached stream.

We first call the `ws()` method to skip any immediate whitespace. We then create a new `StringBuffer` s in which to build up the digits of the integer that we are reading. We use a similar loop to that of `ws()` to copy all of the following digits from the stream into s; we can then evaluate s as an integer. This loop is augmented with an `if` statement to read a preceding minus sign.

We use the `isDigit()` method of the `Character` class to determine whether a particular character is a digit; we exit the loop when we encounter a non-digit, and unread this last character. Again, we must unread a character because we must actually read a non-digit character to locate the end of an integer.

If s is empty, and we have therefore failed to read an integer, then we throw an appropriate exception. If we have reached the EOF, then we throw an `EOFException` that explains that the stream ended prematurely; we otherwise throw an `IOException` that explains that no digits could be read. Otherwise, we have successfully read an integer and so we parse the ASCII string using the `parseInt()` method of class `Integer` and return the result.

The `readInt()` method expects to encounter a non-digit character after the sequence of digits; however, the `writeInt()` method does not write any subsequent whitespace. It is up to the programmer to ensure that if two integers are to be written back-to-back, then a whitespace or other non-digit character separates them.

```
public String readWord () throws IOException {
    ws ();
```

```
StringBuffer s = new StringBuffer ();
int x;
while (((x = read ()) != -1) && !Character.isSpace ((char) x))
    s.append ((char) x);
unread (x);
if ((x == -1) && (s.length () == 0))
    throw new EOFException ("EOF while reading ASCII word");
return s.toString ();
}
```

This method reads an ASCII word from the attached stream. A word is considered to be any contiguous sequence of non-whitespace characters. This method is very similar to the `readInt()` method. We first skip any immediate whitespace characters using the `ws()` method. We then construct a `StringBuffer s` and read characters into this until we reach EOF or a whitespace character. As before, we must unread the last character that we read.

Finally, if we have reached the EOF without reading any characters, then we throw an explanatory `EOFException`. We otherwise return the `String` that we have just read.

These two classes provide us with basic functions to read and write ASCII values from or to any underlying streams-based communications channel. The `ASCIIInput-Stream` is obviously extensible to allow us to read other data-types in ASCII, and so can be very useful for reading data from the user or from a textfile. A generic method that could read a sequence of characters matching a specified search pattern would be an obvious aid to extending this class further.

6.7 Wrapping up

We have provided a broad introduction to filter streams in this chapter, and it should be obvious that they are very powerful. We can essentially implement arbitrarily complex filter streams that extend the functions provided by existing filter streams and that work over any streams-based communications channel.

Considerable effort is expended in later chapters on developing powerful filter stream libraries. Simply opening a communications channel between two remote applications is a trivial task. Where the complexity of networked applications arises is in the definition of application-level protocols that can operate in a robust fashion in the presence of problems such as concurrency issues and communications failures. We will see later that we can hide many of these protocol complexities behind a fairly clean and simple filter-streams based interface.

chapter 7

Supplied filter streams

We have already introduced the concept of filter streams and provided a terse overview of those provided by the language environment. In this chapter, we will take a detailed look at several of those filter streams, in addition to developing more of our own.

The important filter streams that we will examine are the data streams and the buffered streams. In addition, however, we will briefly look at the `SequenceInputStream` class prior to developing a similar output stream, and the `PrintStream` class.

7.1 Class DataOutput-Stream

This class provides function for high-level data communications by supplying methods to write all of the primitive language types over a byte-oriented `OutputStream` (Figure 7.1). A corresponding `DataInputStream` decodes the written data at the remote end.

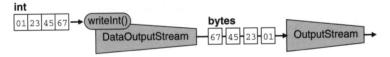

Figure 7.1   Class DataOutputStream

The methods here may be familiar because they are the same as those provided by `RandomAccessFile`. Both classes, in fact, implement a `DataOutput` interface that declares a standard set of methods for higher level data communications.

7.1.1 Network byte order

Values written by this class are written in *network byte order*, i.e., high byte first. This is particularly important for interfacing with clients and servers that are not written in Java.

Network byte order is a widely recognized byte-ordering standard for network communications on the Internet. It specifies the order in which the constituent bytes of an `int` or `short` should be written when such a value is being sent across a network connection. Specifically, the high byte should be written first, and the low byte written last. In the `writeInt()` method from the previous chapter, we wrote the bytes in network byte order.

Applications written in C and C++ make use of the `htons()` and `htonl()` functions (host to network `short`, host to network `long`) to convert 16-bit and 32-bit values from the byte order of the machine architecture into that of the Internet. There are corresponding functions `ntohs()` and `ntohl()` for decoding data from the network. These functions are directly interoperable with the methods of `DataOutputStream` that write `short` and `int` values.

The issues of communicating text are usually solved by communicating in ASCII using the `writeBytes()` method of `DataOutputStream`. The UTF format is also a public standard, however, so it is equally possible for non-Java applications to interpret UTF strings, as written by the `writeUTF()` method.

7.1.2 Constructors

Like most filter streams, there is only one constructor:

DataOutputStream(OutputStream out)   This constructs a `DataOutputStream` attached to the specified `OutputStream out`. All data are broken down into bytes and transmitted over the attached stream.

7.1.3 Methods

These methods allow us to transmit high-level data across a communications channel; the various types are broken up into a sequence of bytes. There are several methods provided in addition to those that transmit just the basic language types.

void writeBoolean(boolean v) throws IOException   This method writes a `boolean` value to the attached stream in a format that can be understood by a `DataInputStream`.

void writeByte(int v) throws IOException   This method writes a `byte` value to the attached stream.

void writeShort(int v) throws IOException   This method writes a `short` to the attached stream.

void writeInt(int v) throws IOException   This method writes an `int` to the attached stream.

void writeLong(long v) throws IOException   This method writes a `long` to the attached stream.

void writeFloat(float v) throws IOException   This method writes a `float` to the attached stream.

void writeDouble(double v) throws IOException   This method writes a `double` to the attached stream.

void writeChar(int v) throws IOException   This method writes a `char` to the attached stream.

void writeChars(String s) throws IOException   This method writes a `String` to the attached stream as a sequence of characters. Each character is written as a pair of bytes that can be read as a character by a `DataInputStream`. Neither the length of the `String` nor a terminator is written.

void writeUTF(String str) throws IOException   This method writes a `String` to the attached stream in modified Unicode UTF-8 format. This is the usual mechanism for communicating strings between Java applications. The UTF format specifies that the `String` be written in a special encoding such that each each character is written as one, two, or three bytes. ASCII characters are written in just a single byte, whereas very rarely used characters are written as three bytes. The majority of text-based communications between applications are usually in ASCII, so this encoding is very efficient for transmitting most common text. The length of the encoded `String` is also written to the stream, so the encoded `String` can be automatically decoded by a `DataInputStream`.

void writeBytes(String s) throws IOException   This method writes a `String` to the attached stream as a sequence of bytes. Only the low byte of each character in the `String` is written, so this is suitable for transmitting ASCII data to a device such as to a conventional terminal or a client written in the C programming language. The length of the `String` is not indicated; the programmer should usually terminate strings with a newline.

int size()   This method returns the number of bytes that have been written thus far to the attached stream.

7.1.4 IOException

All of the transmission methods make use of the `write()` methods of the attached stream and so can correspondingly throw exceptions of type `IOException`.

7.2 Class DataInputStream

This class provides methods to read all of the standard data types from a byte-oriented `InputStream` (Figure 7.2).

Figure 7.2   Class DataInputStream

As with the `DataOutputStream` class, the methods that read `short` and `int` values are compatible with network byte order, and so can read values that were written by a C program that uses the `htons()` and `htonl()` functions. ASCII text-based communications can be achieved with the `readLine()` method, which reads a line of ASCII text.

7.2.1 Constructors

As with most filter streams, there is only one constructor:

DataInputStream(InputStream in)   This constructs a `DataInputStream` attached to the specified `InputStream in`. When a method is called to read a value, the individual bytes are read from `in`.

7.2.2 Methods

All of the methods to read data make use of the read() methods of the attached stream. Note that unlike the read() methods of InputStream, these higher level methods cannot simply return the value -1 to indicate that the end of the file has been reached. If, for example, we are reading an integer and the attached stream reaches EOF, then we cannot return the value -1 because that is a perfectly valid integer to read. Instead, these methods throw an EOFException to indicate that the EOF of the attached stream has been reached.

The simple read() methods to read bytes and arrays of bytes still return -1; it is vital that filter streams provide exactly the same function for these methods as an InputStream; otherwise, we could not attach another filter stream to the data stream and get the desired result.

void readFully(byte b[]) throws IOException   This method fully reads an array of bytes. This is similar to the multibyte read() method, except that it blocks until all of the bytes have been read, and throws an EOFException if EOF is reached prematurely.

void readFully(byte b[], int off, int len) throws IOException   This method fully reads a subarray of len bytes into array b at offset off. This is similar to the multibyte read() call, except that it blocks until all of the bytes have been read, and throws an EOFException if EOF is reached prematurely.

boolean readBoolean() throws IOException   This method reads a boolean value from the attached stream, as written by a DataOutputStream.

byte readByte() throws IOException   This method reads a byte value from the attached stream, throwing an EOFException on premature EOF.

short readShort() throws IOException   This method reads a short value from the attached stream.

int readInt() throws IOException   This method reads an int value from the attached stream.

long readLong() throws IOException   This method reads a long value from the attached stream.

int readUnsignedByte() throws IOException This method reads a `byte` value from the attached stream and treats it as an unsigned value, thus returning a positive `int`.

int readUnsignedShort() throws IOException This method reads a `short` value from the attached stream and treats it as an unsigned value, thus returning a positive `int`.

float readFloat() throws IOException This method reads a `float` value from the attached stream.

double readDouble() throws IOException This method reads a `double` value from the attached stream.

char readChar() throws IOException This method reads a `char` value from the attached stream.

String readUTF() throws IOException This method reads a `String` in UTF encoding from the attached stream.

static String readUTF(DataInput in) throws IOException This `static` method reads a `String` in UTF encoding from the specified `DataInput in`.

String readLine() throws IOException This method reads a `String` in ASCII. An ASCII `string` is defined as a sequence of 8-bit characters terminated by LF, CR, CR/LF, or EOF. This method is frequently used to read input from the keyboard or from another application written in C which communicates using conventional ASCII data. This method returns `null` on EOF; it does not throw an `EOFException`.

7.2.3 IOException

All of the methods may throw an `IOException` if an error occurs in the underlying stream. The other exceptions thrown by this class (`EOFException` and `UTFDataFormat-Exception`) are subclasses of `IOException`, and so can be caught by a single `catch (IOException ex)` clause.

7.2.4 EOFException

This is a subclass of IOException, and indicates that the end of the file was reached while a method of DataInputStream was still expecting more data. The most common cause of an EOFException is that a network connection has been closed.

7.2.5 UTFDataFormatException

This is a subclass of IOException, and indicates that data were received by a readUTF() method that were not in UTF format. Typically this is a result of attempting to read a String when some other data have been written.

These data stream classes are used by almost all networked applications; it is otherwise very inconvenient to have to perform data communications at the byte level. Because this function is provided by filter streams, the basic OutputStream and Input-Stream classes can be very simple; yet we can still achieve higher level function when desired.

7.3 Class BufferedOutput-Stream

Buffering is used to make communications more efficient. This class buffers output until either flush() is called or the buffer becomes full. An output buffer is basically an area of memory in which data are stored between being written by an application and being written to the attached stream (Figure 7.3). We buffer data because it is considerably more efficient to call an operating system write() function once using a 512-byte block than 512 times using 1-byte blocks. We can store data in a buffer until there are a reasonable number of them and then write them all at once to the operating system in a single operation.

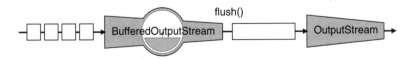

Figure 7.3   Class BufferedOutputStream

The DataOutputStream implementations of the high level communications methods are much the same as methods we developed; they consist of a series of single-byte writes. Writing data using a DataOutputStream is thus a lot more efficient if it goes through a buffer, rather than directly to a communications channel.

Buffering is particularly important in a networked application. The network usually carries data in packets; each packet consists of a header (40 bytes in the case of TCP/IP) and the body data. If we attach a DataOutputStream directly to a network connection and then call writeInt(), it is highly probable that the first byte written will be sent in a packet of its own; this is very inefficient because we are sending 41 bytes yet transporting only one useful byte. Efficiency may be even less if the packet travels over a datalink layer that has a minimum packet size. The minimum frame size over Ethernet is 64 bytes; higher values such as 576 are common for other media. If we use a BufferedOutputStream, then we can make sure to write a reasonable amount of data before calling flush() and so make more efficient use of the network.

7.3.1 Constructors

There are two constructors for the BufferedOutputStream class; the stream can be created using either the default buffer size or a user-specified buffer size.

BufferedOutputStream(OutputStream out)   This creates a BufferedOutput-Stream attached to the specified OutputStream out with the default buffer size (which is usually 512 bytes). Data are written to the attached stream only when the Buffered-OutputStream is flushed or becomes full. When the buffer is flushed, its contents can be written in just one call to the write() method of out.

BufferedOutputStream(OutputStream out, int size)   This creates a Buffered-OutputStream attached to the specified OutputStream out with the specified buffer size size.

7.3.2 Methods

The BufferedOutputStream class provides exactly those methods that are defined on an OutputStream and no more. The only difference is that the class performs internal buffering and implements the flush() method. It should be noted that the default implementation of close() for all FilterOutputStreams is to first flush the stream, and then to close the buffer. This means that closing a buffered stream or a filter stream attached to a buffered stream will first flush any buffered data and then close the stream, so buffered data will not be lost.

7.3.3 IOException

As with the `FilterOutputStream` class, many methods of `BufferedOutputStream` can throw exceptions of type `IOException`.

7.4 Class BufferedInput-Stream

This class adds buffering to an `InputStream` (Figure 7.4). It may not be so obvious why this is useful, but it basically removes the need for every `read()` to call the operating system. When a `read()` method of this class is first called, the class attempts to read a full buffer from the attached stream. Subsequent `read()` calls just return bytes from this memory buffer, making the calls much more efficient. This `FilterInputStream` also implements the `mark()` and `reset()` methods; this permits us to add mark/reset functions to any `InputStream` .

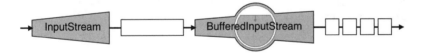

Figure 7.4   Class BufferedInputStream

7.4.1 Constructors

As with `BufferedOutputStream`, there are two constructors:

BufferedInputStream(InputStream in)   This creates a `BufferedInputStream` attached to the specified `InputStream` in, with the default buffer size. Subsequent `read()` calls to this class will buffer the data read from in and thus be more efficient.

BufferedInputStream(InputStream in, int size)   This creates a `BufferedInput-Stream` attached to the specified `InputStream in`, with a buffer of the specified size `size`.

7.4.2 Methods

This class provides all of the standard methods of `InputStream`, providing buffering on the `read()` methods and implementing the `mark()` and `reset()` methods.

7.5 Writing a buffered input stream

In this example, we will look at implementing our own `BufferedInputStream`. We won't support `mark()` and `reset()`, as they add a fair amount of complexity to the code. This example should demonstrate the ease with which we can extend basic stream functions in a transparent manner.

The basic idea behind this implementation is very simple: when we create the stream, we create a buffer to hold data. When a `read()` method is called, we check to see whether our buffer currently contains any data. If the buffer is empty we must refill it from the attached stream; otherwise we can efficiently return data straight from our buffer without making any operating system calls.

```
import java.io.*;

public class MyBufferedInputStream extends FilterInputStream {
    // public MyBufferedInputStream (InputStream i) ...
    // public MyBufferedInputStream (InputStream i, int size) ...
    // public int available() throws IOException ...
    // public int read() throws IOException ...
    // public int read (byte buf[], int off, int num) throws IOException ...
}
```

The class is a buffered `FilterInputStream`; we provide modified implementations of the `read()` methods and the `available()` method.

```
    public MyBufferedInputStream (InputStream i) {
        this (i, 512);
    }
```

This constructor calls the next constructor, with the default buffer size of 512 bytes.

```
protected byte buffer[];
protected int buffSize, buffIndex;

public MyBufferedInputStream (InputStream i, int size) {
   super (i);
   buffSize = buffIndex = 0;
   buffer = new byte[size];
}
```

This constructor accepts an `InputStream` and a specified buffer size. It initially calls the superclass constructor with the attached stream, and then initializes the buffer.

Buffered data are stored in the byte array `buffer`; the `buffSize` variable indicates the quantity of valid data in the buffer. This is the amount of data that have been successfully read into the buffer, and may be less than the actual size of the buffer. The `buffIndex` variable is the current read index in the buffer. Buffer initialization consists of creating the buffer and initializing these variables. The initialization of both variables to zero indicates to the `read()` methods that the buffer must be refilled.

```
public int available() throws IOException {
   return (buffSize - buffIndex) + in.available ();
}
```

This method returns the number of bytes available to read without blocking. This is equal to the number of remaining bytes in our buffer plus the number of bytes that can be read from the attached stream without blocking. The stream `in` is inherited from the `FilterInputStream` superclass, and corresponds to the attached stream.

```
public int read() throws IOException {
   if (buffIndex >= buffSize)
      fillBuffer();
   if (buffSize < 0)
      return -1;
   return buffer[buffIndex++];
}

// protected void fillBuffer () throws IOException ...
```

This method reads a single byte. If the buffer is empty (the read index is beyond the valid data) we call the `fillBuffer()` method, which attempts to fill the buffer from the attached stream. If, after this, the buffer capacity is –1, then EOF has been reached and we return the value –1. Otherwise, we return a byte of buffered data at the current read index and increment the index.

```
protected void fillBuffer () throws IOException {
   buffIndex = 0;
   buffSize = in.read (buffer);
}
```

This is an internal method called by the `read()` methods when the internal buffer is empty and must be refilled. All we do is to use the `read()` method of the attached stream to read data into the buffer, attempting to read a full buffer. We set the buffer reading index to zero and the amount of data in the buffer to be the value returned by the `read()` call. If the end of the attached stream is reached, then our buffer size will be set to -1.

```
public int read (byte buf[], int off, int num) throws IOException {
   if (buffIndex >= buffSize)
      fillBuffer ();
   if (buffSize < 0)
      return -1;
   if (num <= buffSize - buffIndex) {
      System.arraycopy (buffer, buffIndex, buf, off, num);
      buffIndex += num;
      return num;
   } else {
      int rem = buffSize - buffIndex;
      System.arraycopy (buffer, buffIndex, buf, off, rem);
      buffIndex += rem;
      int got = (in.available () > 0) ? in.read (buf, off + rem, num - rem) : 0;
      return rem + ((got > 0) ? got : 0);
   }
}
```

This method reads a subarray of bytes. If the buffer is empty we call the `fill-Buffer()` method. If the buffer capacity is -1, then EOF has been reached and we return immediately.

Otherwise, we determine whether we have a sufficient number of bytes in our buffer to service the request. If we have enough buffered data, then we can just copy a block of data from our internal buffer to the destination buffer using the `System.arrayCopy()` method, increment our read index, and return the number of bytes read.

If we have fewer data in our buffer than the request, we may still be able to read the requested number of bytes. We must first copy all the remaining data from our internal buffer into the destination buffer, updating the read index accordingly. We can then attempt to read the remainder of the request directly from the attached stream using a single large multibyte read. We then return the amount of data that we read from the attached stream, plus the amount of data that we copied from our internal buffer. We must first check, however, that the `read()` method did not return EOF; if we ignored this check, then we would lose a byte of buffered data on EOF.

It is arguable whether we should go to this complexity to allow large reads to occur. If a read request comes in that is one byte larger than the amount of data in our buffer, then we will make a single-byte read request to the attached stream, which is slightly inefficient. If we did not take this effort, however, it would be very inefficient to read a very large amount of data through this stream because it would be transferred in many buffer-sized amounts. In fact, we can overcome the small-read problem by checking to see whether the final read request is for less than a buffer size, and if so, to go through the internal buffer as usual.

7.6 Class PrintStream

We've looked at the most commonly used filter streams provided by the runtime. Of the other filter streams, `PrintStream` is commonly used with `System.out`; `Sequence-InputStream` can be used to string together multiple streams; and the others, `PushbackInputStream` and `StreamTokenizer`, are most commonly used by language parsers.

The `PrintStream` class attaches to an existing stream and provides a series of `print()` and `println()` methods that write out all of the primitive language types in ASCII (Figure 7.5). The `println()` methods print a newline after every value, whereas the `print()` methods print the values with no newline.

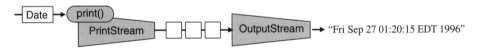

Figure 7.5 Class PrintStream

`PrintStream` has a few peculiarities. None of the methods will throw an `IOException`; this makes it considerably easier to write applications that print out information to the terminal because it is not necessary to handle exceptions whenever information is printed. Instead, a `checkError()` method is provided to query whether an exception has ever been encountered on the underlying stream. Exceptions can thus essentially be ignored. Additionally, by default this stream flushes the attached stream whenever it encounters a newline, whether this is a result of `println()` or just a newline in a string. An additional constructor is provided to override this behavior when it is inappropriate.

```
// Object o ...
System.out.print ("The object is ");
System.out.print (o);
System.out.println (".");
```

The `PrintStream` class provides `print()` and `println()` methods that take an `Object` parameter. With these methods, we can print any `Object` in ASCII. These methods actually call the `toString()` method of the `Object` parameter and then convert this `String` to ASCII.

The default `PrintStream` class is not very successful in terms of efficiency. In fact, it is extremely inefficient. If this is an issue, then an enhanced version of the `ASCII-OutputStream` that we developed in the previous chapter should probably be used.

7.7 Class SequenceInput-Stream

`SequenceInputStream` is a filter stream that allows us to sequence together several `InputStreams` to appear as a single long `InputStream` (Figure 7.6). The observant reader will notice that it is not in fact a subclass of `FilterInputStream`. The default implementations of all the `FilterInputStream` methods are not particularly useful for this class, and so it is more appropriate to subclass `InputStream` and provide the implementations directly. The `FilterInputStream` class is simply a useful superclass to use if the implementation that it provides is appropriate for a particular filter stream. When `FilterInputStream` is not a useful superclass, it is better to subclass `InputStream` directly.

Figure 7.6   Class SequenceInputStream

The following is a simple example using `SequenceInputStream`:

```
FileInputStream f1 = new FileInputStream ("file1.txt");
FileInputStream f2 = new FileInputStream ("file2.txt");
InputStream i = new SequenceInputStream (f1, f2);
```

This example creates three streams. The first two are normal `FileInputStreams` that read from files. The third is a `SequenceInputStream` constructed from the two file streams.

Reading from the `InputStream` i reads from `f1` until the EOF is reached and then reads from `f2`, only reporting EOF when the end of this second stream is reached. We can thus transparently read from the concatenation of several `InputStreams`.

We could sequence together many streams by using i as an input to yet another `SequenceInputStream`. The following is another way of sequencing many streams:

```
Vector v = new Vector ();
v.addElement (new FileInputStream ("file1.txt"));
v.addElement (new FileInputStream ("file2.txt"));
v.addElement (new FileInputStream ("file3.txt"));
InputStream i = new SequenceInputStream (v.elements ());
```

This uses an alternative constructor for `SequenceInputStream` that accepts an `Enumeration` of `InputStreams` and sequences through all of the elements of this `Enumeration`. `Enumeration` is an interface defined in the `java.util` package; the `Vector` class provides a simple means by which to create an `Enumeration` of objects. This piece of code will sequence in order through all the elements of the `Vector`.

7.8 Building a tee filter stream

At the beginning of the discussion of streams, we developed a primitive tee joint for streams. It operated by buffering up data from an `InputStream`, and then subsequently writing this buffer to several `OutputStreams`. In this example, we reimplement the tee joint as a filter stream. See Figure 7.7. We provide constructors to attach the tee stream to several `OutputStreams`, and everything that is written to the tee stream is written to all of the attached streams.

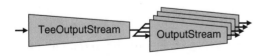

Figure 7.7   Class TeeOutputStream

To implement this stream, we keep a list of all of the OutputStreams to which we are attached and override our write() methods to write to each. We also override the other methods of OutputStream to call the appropriate method of all attached Output-Streams. In this manner, we can transparently take a single stream of data and redirect it to as many targets as we desire.

```java
import java.io.*;
import java.util.*;

public class TeeOutputStream extends OutputStream {
    // public TeeOutputStream (OutputStream o1, OutputStream o2) ...
    // public TeeOutputStream (Enumeration os) ...
    // public void flush () throws IOException ...
    // public void close () throws IOException ...
    // public void write (int b) throws IOException ...
    // public void write (byte b[], int off, int len) throws IOException ...
}
```

Our class extends OutputStream instead of FilterOutputStream because none of the methods provided by FilterOutputStream are appropriate for this class. It is more appropriate in this case to subclass OutputStream directly. We provide implementations of all of the necessary methods of class OutputStream. Note that we don't provide an implementation of the full array write() method; we thus inherit the superclass implementation which just calls our subarray write() method.

```java
protected Vector out;

public TeeOutputStream (OutputStream o1, OutputStream o2) {
    out = new Vector ();
    out.addElement (o1);
    out.addElement (o2);
}
```

This constructor allows us to attach our TeeOutputStream to two OutputStreams o1 and o2. We maintain a list of the target streams in the Vector out. We create a new Vector for this purpose and add to it the two specified OutputStreams.

```java
public TeeOutputStream (Enumeration os) {
    out = new Vector ();
    while (os.hasMoreElements ())
        out.addElement (os.nextElement ());
}
```

This constructor allows us to attach our TeeOutputStream to an arbitrary number of OutputStreams specified by the Enumeration os. We create a new Vector out as before, and transfer every element of the Enumeration into out. The caller can create an Enumeration of OutputStreams in many ways. One way to do this is to create a

Vector of the OutputStreams and use its elements() method, much as we did in the SequenceInputStream example. We cannot repeatedly use the supplied Enumeration for the purposes of this class, because it is possible to iterate through the elements of an Enumeration only once; in this class, we must do it repeatedly, for every call.

```
public void flush () throws IOException {
   IOException problem = null;
   for (int i = 0; i < out.size (); ++ i) {
      OutputStream o = (OutputStream) out.elementAt (i);
      try {
         o.flush ();
      } catch (IOException ex) {
         problem = ex;
      }
   }
   if (problem != null)
      throw problem;
}
```

When our flush() method is called, we wish to sequence through all of the attached OutputStreams and call the flush() method on each. This is complicated somewhat by the fact that any call to flush() may throw an IOException.

There are two ways we could handle this situation. One option would be to just call flush() and if an OutputStream throws an exception, exit the loop and not flush the rest of the OutputStreams. Instead, however, we call flush() on each Output-Stream and if one throws an exception, we catch it, store it, and rethrow it only after we have flushed all of the OutputStreams. To achieve this, we store any exception that occurs in the variable problem, and after we have flushed all the streams, we rethrow this exception.

The stack trace that is stored in an exception is formed when the exception is created, and so by rethrowing the exception, we keep the original stack trace and exception detail message.

```
public void close () throws IOException {
   IOException problem = null;
   for (int i = 0; i < out.size (); ++ i) {
      OutputStream o = (OutputStream) out.elementAt (i);
      try {
         o.close ();
      } catch (IOException ex) {
         problem = ex;
      }
   } if (problem != null)
      throw problem;
}
```

This method is very similar to the `flush()` method; we sequence through all of the `OutputStream`s, calling their respective `close()` methods. If an exception occurs, we store it in the `problem` variable and rethrow it after closing all the streams.

```
public void write (int b) throws
  IOException { IOException problem = null;
  for (int i = 0; i < out.size (); ++ i) {
    OutputStream o = (OutputStream) out.elementAt (i);
    try {
      o.write (b);
    } catch (IOException ex) {
      problem = ex;
    }
  }
  if (problem != null)
    throw problem;
}
```

This method writes a single byte to each of the attached streams. This class thus presents all of the usual methods of `OutputStream` to the caller, but every byte that is written to this stream is transparently written to all of the attached streams. Again, we store and rethrow any exception that occurs, so if one `OutputStream` fails, then the data will still be sent to all the other attached streams.

```
public void write (byte b[], int off, int len) throws IOException {
  IOException problem = null;
  for (int i = 0; i < out.size (); ++ i) {
    OutputStream o = (OutputStream) out.elementAt (i);
    try {
      o.write (b, off, len);
    } catch (IOException ex) {
      problem = ex;
    }
  }
  if (problem != null)
    throw problem;
}
```

This method writes the specified subarray to all of the attached streams in much the same manner as the previous methods.

This stream allows us to direct a single stream of data to multiple recipients through a completely transparent streams interface. There are several potential uses, from a server communicating with multiple clients at once, through a client engaged in group collaboration.

7.9 Wrapping up

The streams interface is a very powerful mechanism for building a high-level communications library. The Java environment comes with a set of filter streams that adds the necessary fundamental features to communicate meaningful data over a communications channel. As we see, it is comparatively easy to enhance these with significant extensions that operate through the same streams interface and so can build on top of each other.

In the next chapter we will revisit the `OutputStream` and `InputStream` classes and look at two pairs of stream classes that provide new communications channels. The byte array stream classes let us read and write data into and out of memory buffers, and the piped stream classes let us communicate between different threads of an application using a memory pipe.

chapter 8

Memory I/O streams

We have introduced the basic stream types and the concept of filter streams. In this chapter we will look at two more types of basic streams: `ByteArrayInputStream` and `ByteArrayOutputStream`, and `PipedInputStream` and `PipedOutputStream`. The former pair permits communication into and out of a memory buffer; the latter pair permits streams-based communications between the threads of an application.

The byte array stream classes turn out to be very useful because they provide a very convenient mechanism to buffer data prior to manipulation by a class such as a block encryption function. The piped stream classes are less frequently used; however, they complete our coverage of Java's stream APIs.

8.1 Class ByteArrayOutput-Stream

This class is an `OutputStream`, and as such, provides the basic writing methods. What is unusual about this class is that it is not attached to any real underlying communications channel; all of the data written to a `ByteArrayOutputStream` are written into an expanding memory buffer (Figure 8.1). This buffer can then be extracted from the stream and used, for example, with a packet-based networking protocol.

Figure 8.1   Class ByteArrayOutputStream

We will make use of this class in later chapters to build UDP packets, to build a messaging library and to provide encrypted stream classes, so it is an important class to understand. In the first `Tee` class example that we developed, we copied data from an `InputStream` into an expanding buffer. This class uses much the same mechanism, but with an `OutputStream` interface to the buffer.

8.1.1 Constructors

There are two `ByteArrayOutputStream` constructors; an initial size for the buffer may be specified, or the default size can be used.

ByteArrayOutputStream()   This creates a `ByteArrayOutputStream` with the default initial buffer size (32). The buffer grows arbitrarily as it is filled, so the small initial size is of no matter, except where efficiency is important.

ByteArrayOutputStream(int size)   This creates a `ByteArrayOutputStream` with the specified initial buffer size `size`. If the buffer becomes full, then a new buffer of twice the capacity is allocated and the old buffer is copied into it. Unless message sizes are known in advance and efficiency is important, specifying an initial size is unnecessary.

8.1.2 Methods

As an `OutputStream`, this class supports all of the usual methods. In addition however, the following methods are provided to access the internal buffer:

void reset()   This method empties the internal buffer. The existing contents are abandoned, so subsequent writes will start anew.

int size()   This method returns the number of valid bytes in the internal buffer. This is equal to the number of bytes that have been written since the stream was created or last reset.

byte[] toByteArray()   This method returns an array of bytes which is a copy of the valid data in the internal buffer. The internal buffer is *not* reset, so subsequent writes will continue to expand the buffer. The returned buffer is exactly as large as the quantity of valid data in the buffer.

String toString()   This method returns a `String` which is a copy of the internal buffer; each character of the `String` corresponds to a byte of the array with the top byte cleared. The internal buffer is not reset.

String toString(int hibyte)   This method returns a `String` which is a copy of the internal buffer; each character of the `String` corresponds to a byte of the array with the top byte set to the specified value `hibyte`. The internal buffer is not reset.

void writeTo(OutputStream out) throws IOException   This method writes the contents of the internal buffer to the specified `OutputStream out`. This is more efficient than calling the `toByteArray()` method and manually writing the returned copy to the `OutputStream`. The internal buffer is not reset.

8.1.3 IOException

The `writeTo()` method may throw an `IOException` if an error occurs while writing to the specified `OutputStream`.

8.2 A simple ByteArray-OutputStream example

We will look at using these streams more usefully in our later dealings with networking. For the moment we will look at a simple example which writes data into a `ByteArray-OutputStream` and then extracts it again.

This example copies all user input into a `ByteArrayOutputStream`. At EOF, it writes this back to the terminal and into every file specified on the command line. Before writing each file, it appends a message into the buffer (Figure 8.2).

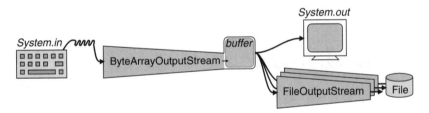

Figure 8.2 Using a ByteArrayOutputStream

```
import java.io.*;

public class ByteArrayOutputTest {
    static public void main (String args[]) throws IOException {
        ByteArrayOutputStream byteO = new ByteArrayOutputStream ();

        byte buffer[] = new byte[16];
        int n;
        while ((n = System.in.read (buffer)) > -1)
            byteO.write (buffer, 0, n);

        System.out.println ("Read " + byteO.size () + " bytes.");
        System.out.write (byteO.toByteArray ());

        PrintStream ascii = new PrintStream (byteO);
        for (int i = 0; i < args.length; ++ i) {
            ascii.println ("Written to " + args[i] + ".");
```

```
        FileOutputStream file = new FileOutputStream (args[i])
        byteO.writeTo (file);
        file.close ();
    }
  }
}
```

We first create a `ByteArrayOutputStream` byteO into which we will write all of our data. We then create a small buffer and copy `System.in` into byteO through this buffer. At EOF, we print the size of byteO and dump its contents to the terminal.

Note that we use the `toByteArray()` method, which returns a copy of the buffer contents, and then use the multibyte `write()` method of `System.out` to write this to the terminal. We then create a `PrintStream` attached to byteO which we will use to append text to the buffer.

For every command-line parameter, we append a message to the `ByteArray-OutputStream` and dump its contents to a new `FileOutputStream`. This time around we use the `writeTo()` method; this is functionally identical to using the `toByteArray()` method as before, but is more efficient. The only reason we use both alternatives is to demonstrate their application. Each file will thus contain the data typed in by the user and a list of all the files that the buffer has been written to thus far.

8.3 Class ByteArrayInput-Stream

This class is an `InputStream` that is constructed from an array of bytes. The `read()` methods read data from this array (Figure 8.3).

Figure 8.3   Class ByteArrayInputStream

8.3.1 Constructors

There are two constructors:

ByteArrayInputStream(byte buf[])　This creates a `ByteArrayInputStream` from the entire specified array of bytes `buf`. Calls to `read()` will read sequentially from this buffer until the end of the buffer is reached.

ByteArrayInputStream(byte buf[], int offset, int length)　This creates a `Byte-ArrayInputStream` from the specified subarray of `buf` starting at `offset`, of length `length`. Calls to `read()` will read sequentially from this subarray until `length` bytes have been read, and then return EOF.

8.3.2 Methods

This class provides only those methods defined by the `InputStream` class. Calls to `read()` will read from the array of bytes specified in the constructor, and EOF is indicated when the end of the array or subarray is reached. There is one change in semantics of interest:

void reset()　This method resets the stream so that it proceeds to read bytes again from the beginning of the array or subarray. This is different from the semantics of the mark/reset specification because it always resets to the initial position. The stream does not actually indicate that it supports mark/reset, so this should not cause any problems. Generally, we would call this method if we had modified the contents of the buffer and wanted to read from the beginning again.

8.4 A simple ByteArray-InputStream example

This example demonstrates the use of a `ByteArrayInputStream`; it echoes the user's input back to the terminal after the EOF is reached, preceding each line by its line number. Byte arrays are used intermediately (Figure 8.4).

```
import java.io.*;

public class ByteArrayInputTest {
    static public void main (String args[]) throws IOException {
        ByteArrayOutputStream out = new ByteArrayOutputStream ();
        byte buffer[] = new byte[16];
        int n;
```

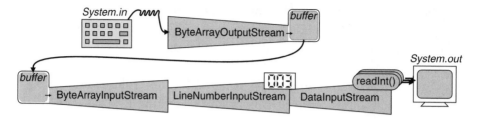

Figure 8.4   Using a ByteArrayInputStream

```
    while ((n = System.in.read (buffer)) > -1)
      out.write (buffer, 0, n);

    ByteArrayInputStream in = new ByteArrayInputStream (out.toByteArray ());
    LineNumberInputStream lIn = new LineNumberInputStream (in);
    DataInputStream dIn = new DataInputStream (lIn);
    String line;
    while ((line = dIn.readLine ()) != null)
      System.out.println (lIn.getLineNumber () + " : " + line);
  }
}
```

We first copy the user's input into a `ByteArrayOutputStream` until EOF is reached, as in the previous example. We then create a `ByteArrayInputStream` in from the contents of the `ByteArrayOutputStream`. From this we create a `LineNumber-InputStream lIn` to count lines and a `DataInputStream dIn` to read lines. We read one line at a time, and write out each line preceded by its line number.

In effect, a byte array is the communications channel connecting the user input to the code which reads one line at a time. This is all streams-based, and so is functionally indistinguishable from just connecting the `LineNumberInputStream` to `System.in` initially, except that the response is written only after all input has been received.

This example really makes sense only if you consider that we could transmit the buffer over a packet-based network such as UDP, and still use the streams interface for communications.

8.5 Class PipedOutput-Stream

The `PipedOutputStream` and `PipedInputStream` classes provide a streams-based interthread communications mechanism. The idea is that we can create a connected pair of piped streams; a thread can read from one end of the pipe and it will receive anything that is written into the other end by other threads (Figure 8.5).

Piped streams are created in pairs; one end is created unconnected, and then the other is created and connected to the first. It is only necessary to attach one stream to the other, not both to each other. Usually, one thread will block reading from the `PipedInputStream` end of the pipe; other threads will occasionally write data into the pipe, thus waking the listening thread.

Figure 8.5   Class Piped-OutputStream

8.5.1 Constructors

A `PipedOutputStream` can either be created and then manually connected to a `PipedInputStream`, or created and automatically connected to an existing `Piped-InputStream`.

PipedOutputStream()   This creates an unconnected `PipedOutputStream`. Writes will fail unless the stream is connected to a `PipedInputStream`.

PipedOutputStream(PipedInputStream snk) throws IOException   This creates a `PipedOutputStream` and connects it to the specified `PipedInputStream snk`.

8.5.2 Methods

This class provides all of the standard methods of `OutputStream` and one in addition, `connect()`, to attach to a `PipedInputStream`.

Writing to a `PipedOutputStream` throws an `IOException` with the message *Pipe broken* if the thread which was reading from the attached `PipedInputStream` has terminated. This behavior is necessary because piped streams are implemented using a memory buffer. If this buffer becomes full then a subsequent `write()` call will block until some data are read from the buffer. If there is no thread reading from the buffer, then the writer will block indefinitely.

void connect(PipedInputStream snk) throws IOException   This method attaches to the specified `PipedInputStream snk`. All data written to this stream will be subsequently available for reading from `snk`.

8.6 Class PipedInput-Stream

This is the corresponding read end for piped inter-thread communications (Figure 8.6).

Figure 8.6   Class Piped InputStream

8.6.1 Constructors

A `PipedInputStream` can either be created and then connected to a `PipedOutput-Stream`, or automatically connected to an existing `PipedOutputStream` upon creation.

PipedInputStream()   This creates an unconnected `PipedInputStream`.

PipedInputStream(PipedOutputStream src) throws IOException   This creates a `PipedInputStream` and connects it to the specified `PipedOutputStream src`.

8.6.2 Methods

This class provides all of the standard methods of `InputStream` and one in addition, to attach to a `PipedOutputStream`.

Unlike a typical `InputStream`, reading from an empty or closed `PipedInput-Stream` will not always block. If the thread which was writing to the attached `PipedOutputStream` has terminated, then after the second attempt to read from the empty stream, an `IOException` with the message *Pipe broken* will be thrown. This behavior is necessary, because if there were no longer a thread writing to the stream, then the reader would block indefinitely.

void connect(PipedOutputStream src) throws IOException   This method attaches to the specified `PipedOutputStrean src`. Subsequently all data written to `src` will be available for reading from this stream.

8.7 A piped stream example

This example demonstrates piping data between two threads in an application (Figure 8.7). The main thread reads from System.in and writes to a pipe; another thread reads from this pipe and writes to System.out in uppercase.

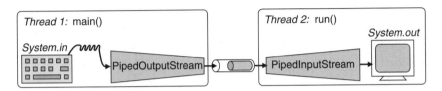

Figure 8.7   Using piped streams

This begins to bring together several important concepts: a connected Piped-OutputStream and PipedInputStream pair are created; a thread is then created, reading lines from the read end of the pipe and writing them to the terminal in upper case. The main thread sits in a loop reading user input and writing it to the write end of the pipe. We will use threads extensively in the networking sections.

```
import java.io.*;

public class PipeTest extends Thread {
    // public PipeTest (InputStream i) ...
    // public void run () ...
    // public static void main (String args[])
        throws IOException, InterruptedException ...
}
```

The PipeTest class inherits from Thread; this is one of the simplest ways to use threads. To start a thread, all we need to do is to create an instance of the class and call the start() method. The start() method creates a new thread which enters in the run() method.

```
    protected DataInputStream in;

    public PipeTest (InputStream i) {
        in = new DataInputStream (i);
    }
```

This is the constructor for our PipeTest class. The parameter i is the Input-Stream from which the thread will read. We create a DataInputStream in attached to i.

```
public void run () {
   try {
      String line;
      while ((line = in.readLine ()) != null)
         System.out.println (line.toUpperCase ());
      in.close ();
   } catch (IOException ex) {
      ex.printStackTrace ();
   }
}
```

This method is called when the thread is started. The method reads lines from the piped input stream and writes them in upper case to System.out until EOF is reached. We surround the code with a try ... catch statement to catch any exception that should arise.

```
public static void main (String args[])
      throws IOException, InterruptedException {
   PipedOutputStream o = new PipedOutputStream ();
   PipedInputStream i = new PipedInputStream (o);
   PipeTest p = new PipeTest (i);
   p.start ();

   byte buffer[] = new byte[16];
   int n;

   while ((n = System.in.read (buffer)) > -1) {
      o.write (buffer, 0, n);
      Thread.sleep (1000);
   }
   o.close ();
}
```

This is the main() method of the class. We initially create a pair of connected piped streams and an instance of our PipeTest class that is attached to the read end of the pipe. We then sit in a loop, reading data from System.in and writing it to the pipe.

Something of note, although not particularly of interest, is that we sleep for a second after writing to the PipedOutputStream. The reason we do this is that under some operating systems, if one thread is blocking on reading from System.in, then another thread cannot write to System.out. By sleeping for a second, we give our other thread a chance to write to System.out. This particular behavior is unusual and not typical of streams; it is unique to System.in and System.out. If we were not writing to System.out or were not interested in seeing the response immediately, we could omit the sleep() call. The sleep() method can throw an InterruptedException; we ignore this and let the main() method throw the exception.

If the main() method were to exit and the other thread were to continue attempting to read from the PipedInputStream, then it would receive an IOException to indicate that the pipe was broken. Because we first close the pipe, the other thread should, however, exit naturally.

8.8 An autoresetting Byte-ArrayOutputStream

The `ByteArrayOutputStream` class does not automatically reset its internal buffer after it is extracted using the `toByteArray()` method. This is actually a very common requirement; a lot of code ends up calling `reset()` immediately after every call to `toByteArray()`. This class is a very simple variant of the `ByteArrayOutputStream` class that automatically resets the buffer after a call to `toByteArray()` or any of the other similar methods.

```
import java.io.*;

public class ResetByteArrayOutputStream extends ByteArrayOutputStream {
    // public ResetByteArrayOutputStream () ...
    // public ResetByteArrayOutputStream (int size) ...
    // public byte[] toByteArray () ...
    // public void writeTo (OutputStream out) throws IOException ...
}
```

This class extends `ByteArrayOutputStream` and overrides the default methods to call `reset()` automatically after calling the corresponding superclass method.

```
public ResetByteArrayOutputStream () {
}
```

This constructor calls the default superclass constructor. A class does not inherit its parent's constructors, and so it is necessary to declare all the constructors that we wish to make available.

```
public ResetByteArrayOutputStream (int size) {
    super (size);
}
```

This constructor calls the corresponding superclass constructor.

```
public byte[] toByteArray () {
    byte result[] = super.toByteArray ();
    reset ();
    return result;
}
```

We wish to automatically reset the stream after a call to this method. We first call the superclass `toByteArray()` method, keeping the result in a temporary variable. We reset the buffer using the `reset()` method, and then return the superclass result. The `toString()` methods both call this method and so we need not alter them.

```
public void writeTo (OutputStream out) throws IOException {
    super.writeTo (out);
    reset ();
}
```

This method calls the superclass `writeTo()` method and then resets the stream. If an exception occurs while writing to the `OutputStream`, then the stream is not reset. If we wished to reset the stream regardless of whether an exception was thrown, we could surround the superclass `writeTo()` call with a `try ... finally` clause that calls the `reset()` method regardless of whether the call exits naturally or because of an exception.

It is debatable whether a class that is as simple as this is actually useful; after all, is it such a burden to call `reset()` manually? If it turns out that a significant amount of code calls the `reset()` method manually, then it probably is worth using this class. However, in the situation of a small applet, or where efficiency is at a premium, it is probably more appropriate to use a normal `ByteArrayOutputStream` and manually call `reset()`.

8.9 *Wrapping up*

This chapter should have served to illustrate that streams-based communications need not be carried over a file or network connection, but can also be carried through memory buffers. Later chapters will make extensive use of buffers because they allow us to manipulate the data very easily before and after transportation by a networking protocol.

The next few chapters introduce TCP and UDP. These are networking transport protocols that allow us to transport data between applications across a network. TCP naturally provides a virtual stream connection between two applications and so fits very cleanly into the Java streams-based communications model. UDP, on the other hand, provides packet-based communications for which we will need to make use of the byte array streams.

chapter 9

Client-side networking

123

Networking in Java is accomplished with the streams-related classes that we have already covered, and classes from the package `java.net` which provide access to IP addresses, TCP, UDP, and various URL-related mechanisms.

In this chapter, we will begin to look at the client side of networking with TCP. TCP provides a virtual-stream connection across a network that supports IP. This virtual stream provides streams-based facility to transport data from either end of the connection to the other.

IP addresses, which are used to address the target of TCP connections, are provided by the `InetAddress` class. TCP connections are created using the `Socket` class. Once a connection has been created we can obtain streams to and from the remote application, and then communicate through the streams interface. We can make use of the filter stream classes that we have looked at to add higher-level functions to this byte-oriented communications channel.

9.1 Class InetAddress

An IP address is the address of a computer on the Internet; it is currently a four-byte value. Data can be sent out onto a network, addressed to a specific IP address, and will be delivered to the target machine.

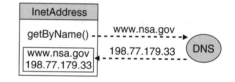

Figure 9.1 Class InetAddress

The `InetAddress` class provides abstracted access to IP addresses (Figure 9.1). The advantage of using this class to represent an IP address over, for example, a 32-bit `int`, is that applications will be transparently portable to IPv6, which will provide 128-bit addresses.

9.1.1 Constructors

There are no constructors for this class; instances must instead be created by using the `static` methods `getByName()`, `getLocalHost()` and `getAllByName()`.

9.1.2 Static methods

The following `static` methods are provided to create `InetAddress` objects:

static InetAddress getLocalHost() throws UnknownHostException   This method returns an `InetAddress` object corresponding to the local machine. In some cases, such as from behind a firewall, this may simply be the loopback address `127.0.0.1`.

static InetAddress getByName(String host) throws UnknownHostException This method returns an `InetAddress` object for the specified host `host`. The host can be specified either by name (`proxy0.att.com`) or by IP address (`127.0.0.1`). In either case, the host is specified as a `String`. There is no other client-side mechanism to construct an `InetAddress` for a remote host.

static InetAddress[] getAllByName(String host) throws UnknownHost-Exception   This method returns an array of `InetAddress` objects corresponding to every known IP address for the specified host. Typically, high-traffic web sites will register several IP addresses for a single hostname to distribute the load across several machines.

9.1.3 Instance methods

The following methods are provided to get information from an existing `InetAddress` object:

byte[] getAddress()   This method returns an array of bytes corresponding to the IP address represented by the `InetAddress`. The array is in network byte order, i.e., high byte first. Currently, under IPv4 this array will only be four bytes long. Future versions of IP will support longer addresses.

String getHostName()   This method returns the name of the host represented by the `InetAddress` object. If the hostname is not already known, an attempt is made to look it up using DNS, based upon the IP address. If this lookup fails, the numeric IP address is returned in `String` form.

For reasons of security, name lookups may be denied if an application is running behind a firewall.

9.1.4 UnknownHostException

This exception is a subclass of `IOException` and indicates that the named host could not be successfully identified.

9.1.5 SecurityException

A `SecurityException` may be thrown if the `SecurityManager` does not permit a specific operation. Currently an applet may construct an `InetAddress` object only for the host that is the web server from which it originated.

9.2 An InetAddress example

This example introduces the basics of creating and using `InetAddress` objects. It first prints out the local machine's address and then sits in a loop accepting hostnames and looking them up. The loop terminates on EOF.

```
import java.net.*;
import java.io.*;

public class InetEg {
  // public static void main (String args[]) ...
}
```

This example is just a demonstration of the application of `InetAddress` objects. The `main()` method makes use of a few `static` methods to print out `InetAddress` objects.

```
  public static void main (String args[]) {
    printLocalAddress ();

    DataInputStream in = new DataInputStream (System.in);
    try {
      String name;
      do {
        System.out.print ("Enter a hostname or IP address: ");
        System.out.flush ();
        name = in.readLine ();
        if (name != null)
          printRemoteAddress (name);
      } while (name != null);
      System.out.println ("exit");
    } catch (IOException ex) {
      System.out.println ("Input error:");
      ex.printStackTrace ();
    }
  }

  // static void printLocalAddress () ...
  // static void printRemoteAddress (String name) ...
```

The `main()` method first calls the `printLocalAddress()` method to print out the local machine name and address. It then sits in a loop that reads hostnames from `System.in` and uses the `printRemoteAddress()` method to print `InetAddress` information about every hostname that is entered. We flush `System.out` because we use the `print()` method, which does not automatically flush output.

If an exception occurs while we are reading from `System.in`, then we display the exception and exit; otherwise, we execute until EOF is reached.

```
static void printLocalAddress () {
  try {
    InetAddress myself = InetAddress.getLocalHost ();
    System.out.println ("My name : " + myself.getHostName ());
    System.out.println ("My IP : " + toText (myself.getAddress ()));
  } catch (UnknownHostException ex) {
    System.out.println ("Failed to find myself:");
    ex.printStackTrace ();
  }
}

// static String toText (byte ip[]) ...
```

This method uses the `getLocalHost()` method of `InetAddress` to get the IP address of the local machine. We print out the name of the local machine using the `getHostName()` method, and its address using the `getAddress()` method.

```
static String toText (byte ip[]) {
  StringBuffer result = new StringBuffer ();
  for (int i = 0; i < ip.length; ++ i) {
    if (i > 0)
      result.append (".");
    result.append (0xff & ip[i]);
  }
  return result.toString ();
}
```

This method takes an array of bytes and returns a `String` which is a textual representation of the byte array (e.g., `12.34.56.78` for the array `{12, 34, 56, 78}`). We use the `append()` method of a `StringBuffer` to accumulate the result; we append periods before every byte other than the first. When we are appending the value of a byte, we must first mask it with `0xff` to turn it into an unsigned integer; otherwise, bytes with the high bit set will be considered negative.

We could alternatively use the `toString()` method of `InetAddress`. This converts the `InetAddress` object to textual form, but we have no control over the formatting.

```
static void printRemoteAddress (String name) {
  try {
    System.out.println ("Looking up " + name + "...");
    InetAddress machine = InetAddress.getByName (name);
    System.out.println ("Host name : " + machine.getHostName ());
    System.out.println ("Host IP : " + toText (machine.getAddress ()));
  } catch (UnknownHostException ex) {
    System.out.println ("Failed to lookup " + name);
  }
}
```

This method takes a hostname `name` and uses the `getByName()` method of `Inet-Address` to determine its IP address. We then use the `getHostName()` and `get-Address()` methods of the returned `InetAddress` object to display its name and IP number. If the name that the user entered was a numeric IP address, then we will find the corresponding hostname only if the hostname is registered for reverse DNS lookup. If the name that the user entered was a hostname, we will now know one of its IP addresses.

9.3 Class Socket

A `Socket` is the Java representation of a TCP network connection (Figure 9.2). Using this class, a client can establish a streams-based communications channel with a remote host.

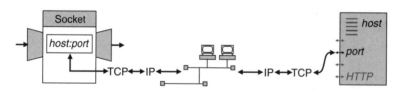

Figure 9.2 Class Socket

In order to communicate with a remote host using TCP/IP, the client must first create a `Socket` to the remote host. This automatically establishes a TCP connection, throwing an exception if it fails. In addition to specifying a host name, it is necessary to specify a port; this is an integer between 1 and 65535. Effectively, there are 65535 different addresses on every host. To connect to a host, you must specify the address on the host that you wish to connect to. There must be a server actively listening on the specified port, or the connection attempt will fail.

We have omitted some constructors and methods from the following description.

9.3.1 Constructors

Creating a `Socket` automatically connects to the specified host and port. There must be a server listening on the host port; otherwise an exception of type `IOException` will be thrown (*Connection refused*). Other possible errors result from network failures and unknown hostnames.

Socket(String host, int port) throws IOException   This creates a `Socket` and connects to the specified port `port` of the specified host `host`. The host is specified by name or by textual IP address; the port must be in the range 1–65535.

Socket(InetAddress address, int port) throws IOException   This creates a `Socket` and connects to the specified port `port` of the specified host `address`. The port must be in the range 1–65535.

9.3.2 Methods

The methods of class `Socket` permit identification of the remote host, and the local and remote port numbers, as well as extraction of streams for the purposes of communication.

To perform communications across a TCP connection, you must first create a `Socket`, and then use the `getInputStream()` and `getOutputStream()` methods to obtain streams with which to communicate with the remote server. The client and server will thus each have both an `InputStream` and an `OutputStream` for the purposes of communication.

InputStream getInputStream() throws IOException   This method returns an `InputStream` that permits streams-based communications across the TCP connection. All data written by the server at the far end of the connection may be read from this `InputStream`.

This method returns a stream of type `InputStream`; as we discussed earlier, the `InputStream` class is itself abstract. This method actually returns a `SocketInputStream`; however, this class is nonpublic, and so the user can treat it only as a generic `InputStream`.

Ultimately, data written to a `Socket` are segmented into packets for communication across IP. For all intents and purposes, however, the connection provides a continuous stream of data. For reasons of efficiency, `Socket` streams should usually be buffered.

OutputStream getOutputStream() throws IOException   This method returns an `OutputStream` that permits streams-based communications across the TCP connection. All data written to this stream may be read by the server at the far end of the connection. For reasons of efficiency, this `OutputStream` should be buffered; otherwise the first byte of a message will frequently be sent in an independent packet, wasting bandwidth.

```
// OutputStream out;

void writeInt (int x) throws IOException {
   out.write (x >>> 24);
   out.write (x >>> 16);
   out.write (x >>> 8);
   out.write (x);
}
```

This method is typical of many of the methods of `DataOutputStream` and demonstrates the reason why `Socket` streams should be buffered. If the TCP connection is idle and then this method is called, it is highly probable that the first `write()` call will result in a packet with just a single byte being sent. The subsequent three bytes will then be sent in a later packet. By buffering the stream, we can ensure that small packets like this are not inadvertently sent.

void close() throws IOException   This method closes the `Socket`, releasing any network and system resources being used. Any data which have been actually sent before this call *will* be successfully delivered to the remote end unless there is a network failure.

Note that if the `Socket`'s `OutputStream` has been buffered with a `Buffered-OutputStream`, then the `BufferedOutputStream` should be closed in preference to the `Socket`. Otherwise any data remaining in the buffer will be lost. Closing either the `Socket`'s `InputStream` or `OutputStream` will close down the network connection, so it is necessary to close only the `Socket`, its `InputStream`, or its `OutputStream`.

InetAddress getInetAddress()   This method returns the IP address of the remote host.

int getPort()   This method returns the port number of the remote host to which the `Socket` is connected.

int getLocalPort()   This method returns the local port number, i.e., the port number of the `Socket`. Every TCP connection in fact consists of the local and remote IP address, and a local and remote port number, which will usually be different. When a `Socket` is created and connected to a remote host, it is assigned a random unused local port number. This method is rarely used; it is most commonly used at a server that automatically assigns unused port numbers to its connections.

9.3.3 IOException

Many of the methods and constructors of the `Socket` class may throw `IOException` if an error is encountered.

9.3.4 SecurityException

The `SecurityManager` restricts the creation of `Sockets`. Applets, for example, may not open `Sockets` to anywhere other than the host from which they were served. Another significant restriction is that an applet behind a firewall may not be permitted to perform a DNS lookup, so it may be necessary to use a numeric IP address to target the connection instead of a hostname.

9.4 Getting Web pages with a socket

In this example, we will look at using a `Socket` to download pages from the Web. The program sits in a loop waiting for the user to type in URLs; for each URL entered, it creates a new `GrabPage` object. This object attempts to connect to the Web server and download the specified page; if successful, it displays the page contents to the screen (Figure 9.3).

We can achieve this same result automatically using just the `URL` class; however, it is instructive to perform the process manually to see what is involved in the World Wide Web protocols.

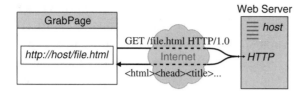

Figure 9.3   Downloading a Web page

```
import java.net.*;
import java.io.*;

public class GrabPage {
  // public GrabPage (String textURL) throws IOException ...
  // public static void main (String args[]) throws IOException ...
}
```

This class downloads and displays the Web-page specified in its constructor. We first parse the URL, then connect to the server, issue a HTTP request and display the response. This is all done upon creation of a GrabPage object.

The main() method demonstrates the application of this class by requesting URLs from the user and displaying the corresponding web pages.

```
  public GrabPage (String textURL) throws IOException {
    Socket socket = null;
    dissect (textURL);
    socket = connect ();
    try {
      grab ();
    } finally {
      socket.close ();
    }
  }

  // protected void dissect (String textURL) throws MalformedURLException ...
  // protected Socket connect () throws IOException ...
  // protected void grab () throws IOException ...
```

Creating an instance of GrabPage automatically fetches and displays the specified page. The constructor uses the dissect() method to dissect the URL; it next connects to the Web server using the connect() method. Finally, the grab() method requests the page and displays the result.

All of these helper methods may throw an IOException; we pass any that occur on to the caller. We should close the connection to the server when we exit, regardless of whether we are exiting successfully or as a result of an exception. To ensure that the

Socket is always closed, we surround the `grab()` call with a `try ... finally` clause that closes the Socket no matter how the body completes.

```
protected String host, file;
protected int port;

protected void dissect (String textURL) throws MalformedURLException {
   URL url = new URL (textURL);
   host = url.getHost ();
   port = url.getPort ();
   if (port == -1)
      port = 80;
   file = url.getFile ();
}
```

The URL classes supplied are very useful for dealing with URLs and other Web-related mechanisms. In this method we just use the URL class to dissect what the user types in; if the user types in the URL `http://www.att.com:8080/index.html`, we dissect it into the hostname host (`www.att.com`), the port port (8080) and the file file (`/index.html`). If the port number is omitted from the URL, then -1 is returned, so we need to use the default, which for HTTP is 80.

```
protected DataInputStream in;
protected DataOutputStream out;

protected Socket connect () throws IOException {
   System.out.println ("Connecting to " + host + ":" + port + "..");
   Socket socket = new Socket (host, port);
   System.out.println ("Connected.");

   OutputStream rawOut = socket.getOutputStream ();
   InputStream rawIn = socket.getInputStream ();
   BufferedOutputStream buffOut = new BufferedOutputStream (rawOut);
   out = new DataOutputStream (buffOut);
   in = new DataInputStream (rawIn);

   return socket;
}
```

This method connects us to the server. We open a Socket to the host and port determined by the `dissect()` method. If this succeeds (no exception is thrown), we create a `DataInputStream` in and a buffered `DataOutputStream` out, which allow us to communicate with the remote HTTP server.

```
protected void grab () throws IOException {
   System.out.println ("Sending request..");
   out.writeBytes ("GET " + file + " HTTP/1.0\r\n\r\n");
   out.flush ();
```

```
System.out.println ("Waiting for response..");
String input;
while ((input = in.readLine ()) != null)
   System.out.println (input);
}
```

This method sends a request to the remove server in HTTP/1.0 format. A typical request has the form:

```
GET /index.html HTTP/1.0
```

This tells the remote server that we want to get the file /index.html and that we understand HTTP version 1.0. By specifying HTTP/1.0, we tell the server that we want it to send us any informational headers that it can. It is possible to send more complex requests that specify the types of file that we can understand, etc. For the purposes of this example, we will keep things simple.

Note that we must follow the request with two newline characters; Web servers will usually wait for a blank line before processing a request. We must also flush the Output-Stream because we have attached a buffer to it; our request would otherwise just sit in the buffer.

After sending the request, we display the server's response. Typically, this will consist of a few lines of headers, a blank line, and then the contents of the file that we requested.

```
public static void main (String args[]) throws IOException {
   DataInputStream kbd = new DataInputStream (System.in);
   while (true) {
      String textURL;
      System.out.print ("Enter an URL: ");
      System.out.flush ();
      if ((textURL = kbd.readLine ()) == null)
         break;

      try {
         new GrabPage (textURL);
      } catch (IOException ex) {
         ex.printStackTrace ();
         continue;
      }

      System.out.println ("- OK -");
   }
   System.out.println ("exit");
}
```

In the main() method, we sit in a loop prompting the user to type in a URL. We create a new GrabPage object for each such URL; this attempts to display the specified page. On EOF, we exit the loop using the break statement.

We surround the call to `GrabPage` by a `try ... catch` statement to catch any exceptions that should occur. If an exception occurs, we print it and restart the loop using the `continue` statement. If the `GrabPage` constructor succeeds, then we have successfully displayed a page and so we display the message - `OK` -.

We declare that the `main()` method can throw `IOException` because the `read-Line()` call that reads from the keyboard declares that it may throw such an exception, and we wish to exit if this occurs.

Note that the code is a lot cleaner, because instead of handling exceptions at every possible occurrence, we pass them up and handle them at the highest level, which in this case is the `main()` method.

Also note that we are talking to a conventional application, probably written in C, and so we make use of the data stream methods that communicate ASCII strings.

9.5 Building a PostOutput-Stream class

In this example, we will develop an `OutputStream` class that performs a HTTP post operation.

To perform a post, you must open a connection to the Web server as before, and send the following header in ASCII:

```
POST <filename> HTTP/1.0
Content-type: <type>
Content-length: <length>
```

You must fill in the filename, content-type and content-length yourself. The content-type specifies the format of the following data; we use the mime-type `application/x-www-form-urlencoded`. The content-length specifies the length of the remaining data. Following this header you must transmit the body of the request; as before, it must be separated from the header by a blank line.

The body for this content-type (the content type that is submitted by standard HTML forms) has the following form:

```
<key>=<value>&<key>=<value>
```

You must fill in the keys and values for all of the variables which you want to send. The key and value text must be encoded in a special URL-encoding; this involves replacing any non-ASCII characters and certain ASCII characters with an escape sequence that consists of a percent character followed by the two-byte hexadecimal encoding of the character.

9.5.1 Class PostOutputStream

This is an `OutputStream` class that performs a HTTP post operation. It buffers up all of the data that are written to it, and when the `post()` method is called, it connects to the specified URL and posts the data, returning an `InputStream` from which the server response can be read (Figure 9.4).

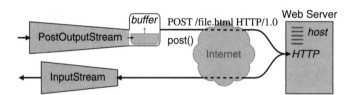

Figure 9.4   Performing a CGI post operation

Again, we can perform the same process using just the URL class; however, it is useful to understand how to do this manually. We will look at actually using the URL classes in a later chapter.

In addition to `post()` and the usual methods of `OutputStream`, this class provides a `writeBytes()` method that writes a `String` in ASCII, ignoring the high byte of every character, a `writeTag()` method that writes a variable-value pair in URL-encoding, and a `writeTags()` method that writes a `Hashtable` of variable-values pairs in URL-encoding.

```
import java.io.*;
import java.net.*;
import java.util.*;

public class PostOutputStream extends FilterOutputStream {
    // public PostOutputStream (URL url) ...
    // public PostOutputStream (URL url, String type) ...
    // public void writeBytes (String s) throws IOException ...
    // public void writeTag (String tag, String value) throws IOException ...
    // public void writeTags (Hashtable h) throws IOException ...
    // public InputStream post () throws IOException ...
}
```

This class extends `FilterOutputStream`; we will use the `FilterOutputStream` methods to buffer up data in a `ByteArrayOutputStream` prior to posting.

```
public PostOutputStream (URL url) {
   this (url, "application/x-www-form-urlencoded");
}
```

This constructor takes a single parameter `url` that specifies the URL which will be the target of the `post` request, and uses the default content-type for form-encoded data.

```
protected ByteArrayOutputStream byteO;
protected URL url;
protected String type;

public PostOutputStream (URL url, String type) {
   super (new ByteArrayOutputStream ());
   byteO = (ByteArrayOutputStream) out;
   this.url = url;
   this.type = type;
}
```

This constructor accepts both a target URL `url` and a content encoding `type`. It calls the superclass constructor, passing a new `ByteArrayOutputStream` to which to attach. We make a local reference to this in `byteO` for convenience. The `out` variable corresponds to the attached stream (what we supplied to the superclass constructor), and is inherited from the superclass. All data that are written to this `PostOutputStream` will thus be written to `byteO`, and so buffered up pending the actual post request.

```
public void writeBytes (String s) throws IOException {
   byte b[] = new byte[s.length ()];
   s.getBytes (0, s.length (), b, 0);
   write (b);
}
```

This method writes a `String` in ASCII by simply discarding the top byte of every character. This process is performed efficiently with the `getBytes()` method that copies a `String` into a byte array, discarding the top bytes; we then write out the resulting byte array.

```
public void writeTag (String tag, String value) throws IOException {
   if (byteO.size () > 0)
      write ('&');
   writeBytes (encode (tag));
   write ('=');
   writeBytes (encode (value));
}

// protected String encode (String s) ...
```

This method writes a variable-value pair in URL-encoding. We first check whether the `ByteArrayOutputStream` is empty; if not, then we assume that this is not the first variable-value pair and so we write an ampersand separator. We then URL-encode the variable name `tag` and write this out, followed by the equals separator, and the URL-encoded value `value`.

```
protected String encode (String s) {
    StringBuffer r = new StringBuffer ();
    for (int i = 0; i < s.length (); ++ i)
        r.append (encode ((char) (s.charAt (i) & 0xff)));
    return r.toString ();
}

// protected String encode (char c) ...
```

This method URL-encodes the specified `String s`. We create a new `String-Buffer r` in which to accumulate the result. We then loop through every character of `s`, appending the encoded character to `r`. We mask every character by 255 because the character encoding method only works for eight-bit values.

```
protected String encode (char c) {
    if (c < 16) {
        return "%0" + Integer.toString (c, 16);
    } else if ((c < 32) || (c > 127) || (" +&=%/~".indexOf (c) >= 0)) {
        return "%" + Integer.toString (c, 16);
    } else {
        return String.valueOf (c);
    }
}
```

This method URL-encodes a single character `c`. We return the escaped version of `c` if it is nonprintable (less than 32 or greater than 127) or one of space, plus, ampersand, equals, percent, slash, or tilde. Otherwise, we just return the character unmodified.

The escaped version of a character consists of a percent sign followed by the two-digit hexadecimal encoding of the character; plus becomes %2B, and so on. We special-case those characters that encode in a single hexadecimal digit (those less than 16) to insert a leading 0.

```
public void writeTags (Hashtable h) throws IOException {
    Enumeration e = h.keys ();
    while (e.hasMoreElements ()) {
        String key = (String) e.nextElement ();
        writeTag (key, (String) h.get (key));
    }
}
```

This method writes an entire `Hashtable` of attribute-value pairs. Every key in the Hashtable must be a `String` that maps to another `String`. We loop through every key, extracting the key and its corresponding value. We then use the `writeTag()` method to write out this variable-value pair.

```java
public InputStream post () throws IOException {
    int port = url.getPort ();
    if (port == -1)
        port = 80;
    Socket socket = new Socket (url.getHost (), port);
    try {
        OutputStream o = new BufferedOutputStream (socket.getOutputStream ());
        DataOutputStream dO = new DataOutputStream (o);
        dO.writeBytes ("POST " + url.getFile () + " HTTP/1.0\r\n");
        if (type != null)
            dO.writeBytes ("Content-type: " + type + "\r\n");
        dO.writeBytes ("Content-length: " + byteO.size () + "\r\n\r\n");
        byteO.writeTo (o);
        byteO.reset ();
        o.flush ();
        return socket.getInputStream ();
    } catch (IOException ex) {
        try {
            socket.close ();
        } catch (IOException ex2) {
        }
        throw ex;
    }
}
```

This method performs the CGI post operation and returns an `InputStream` from which to read the server response. We first open a `Socket` connection to the server, extracting the host name and port using the `getHost()` and `getPort()` methods of URL.

We then transmit a post header as described at the start of this section. The post target comes from the URL's `getFile()` method; the content-type is as specified in the constructor, or unspecified if null was passed, and the content length can be determined from the amount of data present in `byteO`.

After sending this header and a blank line, we transmit the contents of `byteO` using its `writeTo()` method. We finally flush our request and return an `InputStream` from which to read a response. The caller should close the `InputStream` when finished.

We surround the entire post operation with a `try ... catch` expression to catch any `IOException` that is encountered. If an `IOException` is encountered, then we can close the `Socket` connection before rethrowing the exception.

We could have extended the `ByteArrayOutputStream` class directly and added our new methods to this. We would then be able to buffer the data ourselves and use our own `writeTo()` method to send the request. The problem with doing this is that we would then have to make the standard `ByteArrayOutputStream` methods public, which while not particularly problematic, does not provide the cleanest public interface that extending `FilterOutputStream` does.

9.6 Wrapping up

Client-side networking with TCP is fairly simple; once you have established a connection to a server it is simply a case of communicating using the standard streams interface with which we have been working. Interfacing with many existing programs requires us to engage in ASCII communications, which basically involves the use of the `write-Bytes()` method of `DataOutputStream` and the `readLine()` method of `DataInput-Stream`. Interfacing with other existing applications may require transmitting data in network byte order; again, this is provided by the data streams.

An easy way to experiment with client-side networking is to write programs that interface with existing applications, of which HTTP is just one example. Most UNIX workstations support a number of standard TCP services. For example, if you open a TCP connection to port 79 of a public Unix host and transmit a username, it will respond with finger information about that user. If you open one to port 7, it will echo back to you everything that you send; port 13 responds to every connection with the current time. The beauty of networking is that you don't need to own a UNIX workstation to communicate with one.

In the next chapter we will introduce the server side of networking with TCP. Again, this will follow much the same model; once you have accepted a TCP connection you communicate using the streams interface. Server-side networking is complicated, however, by the fact that servers written in Java are commonly multithreaded which introduces all of the standard synchronization issues. Servers must also be robust and capable of operating in the midst of severe client failures. The advantages of writing your own server are manifold, particularly because you can extend the stream classes significantly and automate much of the networking process, as we shall see in the applications part of this book.

chapter 10

Server-side networking

We have just seen some examples of network client programming. What is primarily involved in building a client is opening a connection to a server and communicating over streams, using the server's application-layer protocol. The HTTP protocol is a fairly simple, text-based application-layer protocol, although we admittedly looked at only a small part of it. There are many other protocols in use, such as FTP and IRC, and we can develop similar clients for these.

In this chapter, we introduce the server-side of networking with TCP. At first glance, it is even simpler than client-side programming. A server picks a port number and listens for connections; whenever a client connects, the server receives a `Socket` through which to communicate with the client.

The complexities of developing servers arise with multithreading issues and the definition of an application-layer protocol that governs how clients will communicate with the server. This is complicated further if clients should be able to communicate with each other through the server. In the applications section of this book, we will develop some stream classes that provide a higher level transport layer that runs on top of TCP and provides many of these functions.

10.1 Class ServerSocket

The `ServerSocket` class is the mechanism by which a server can accept connections from clients across a network. The basic procedure for implementing a server is to open a `ServerSocket` on a particular local port number, and then to wait for connections. Clients will connect to this port, and a connection will be established.

The `ServerSocket` class creates a `Socket` for each client connection (Figure 10.1); the server can then handle these connections in the usual manner, typically by extracting an `InputStream` and an `OutputStream` and communicating with the client through the streams interface.

We have omitted some methods from the following description.

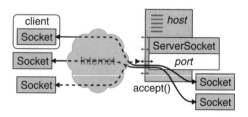

Figure 10.1 Class ServerSocket

10.1.1 Constructors

`ServerSockets` are constructed by choosing a port on the local machine. This port number must be in the range 1–65535; however, ports 1–1023 are reserved for system services and so can be used only by the machine administrator.

There is no easily accessible mechanism in the Internet for allocating port numbers to user applications; if you are serious, you must write to the IANA. Usually, an application just selects a port and sticks to it; ideally this port number will be user-configurable. Alternatively, if a port number of 0 is specified, then the operating system will select an arbitrary valid and free port every time that the application is run. The chosen port number can then be communicated to prospective clients by some other mechanism.

A server must explicitly accept a connection from a `ServerSocket` to obtain a `Socket` connection to a client; however, the operating system will actually start accepting connections from clients as soon as the `ServerSocket` is created. These connections will be placed in a queue and removed one-by-one as the server calls the `accept()` method. The `ServerSocket` constructor allows a server to specify how many connections it wishes the operating system to queue; the operating system will refuse any further connection requests that occur if the queue is full.

ServerSocket(int port) throws IOException   This constructs a `ServerSocket` that listens on the specified port `port` of the local machine; the default limit on outstanding connection requests (50) will be used. This means that the operating system should accept at most 50 clients in its queue of pending clients. Any additional connection attempts above this limit will be refused.

This is not a limit on the number of connections that the server can handle at once; it is a limit on the number that will be queued if the server is being slow about accepting new connections.

ServerSocket(int port, int count) throws IOException   This constructs a `Server-Socket` that listens on the specified port `port` of the local machine. The `count` parameter specifies the number of outstanding connection requests that should be queued by the operating system.

10.1.2 Methods

These methods permit connections to be accepted and information about the `Server-Socket` to be queried.

Socket accept() throws IOException   This method blocks (waits) until a client makes a connection to the port on which this `ServerSocket` is listening. A `Socket` is returned, corresponding to a TCP connection to the client. This `Socket` can be handled in the usual manner; frequently it is passed off to a separate handler and the main server loop returns to waiting in an `accept()` call.

void close() throws IOException   This method closes the `ServerSocket`. It does *not* close any of the connections which have been accepted and not yet closed, so a server may close its `ServerSocket` and maintain connections to its existing clients. Instead, this call instructs the operating system to stop accepting new client connections.

int getLocalPort()   This method returns the port on which this `ServerSocket` is listening. This is useful if you have specified a port number of 0 and so been assigned an available, unused port.

10.1.3 IOException

Creating a server socket can fail for various reasons, such as the requested port being a system port or if another application is already running on it. Other methods may also throw exceptions of this type.

10.1.4 SecurityException

Applets may not act as servers, so the `SecurityManager` will throw a `Security-Exception` if an applet creates a `ServerSocket`.

10.2 Building an echo server

This simple server accepts one connection and then echoes everything received on that connection back to the sender.

The server takes a single command-line parameter which is the port which it will listen on. It then waits for a connection, and subsequently echoes everything on that connection back to the sender (Figure 10.2).

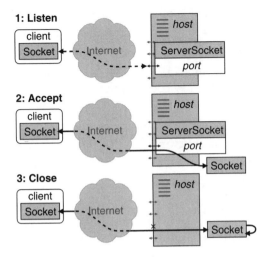

1: Listen

2: Accept

3: Close

Figure 10.2   A single-threaded echo server

```
import java.net.*;
import java.io.*;

public class STServer {
    // public static void main (String args[]) throws IOException ...
}
```

The echo server is a simple single-threaded application that executes in the `main()` method.

```
public static void main (String args[]) throws IOException {
    if (args.length != 1)
        throw new RuntimeException ("Syntax: STServer <port>");

    Socket client = accept (Integer.parseInt (args[0]));

    try {
    InputStream i = client.getInputStream ();
    OutputStream o = client.getOutputStream ();
    new PrintStream (o).println
        ("You are now connected to the Echo Server.");

        int x;
        while ((x = i.read ()) > -1)
            o.write (x);
    } finally {
        System.out.println ("Closing");
        client.close ();
    }
}

// static Socket accept (int port) throws IOException ...
```

When this application is run, the `main()` method is called. We first ensure that a port number argument has been provided and then call our own `accept()` method to accept a client connection on the specified port. Parsing the port number will throw a `NumberFormatException` if the number cannot be parsed. This is a `Runtime-Exception` that will halt the thread; it is assumed that any code can throw a `Runtime-Exception` so we don't need to declare it.

We extract the input and output streams from the resulting `Socket`, print a welcome message, and commence echoing back to the client everything that is received. We use a `finally` clause to close the `Socket` regardless of whether we terminate gracefully from an EOF, or due to an `IOException` from some problem.

```
static Socket accept (int port) throws IOException {
    System.out.println ("Starting on port " + port);
    ServerSocket server = new ServerSocket (port);

    System.out.println ("Waiting");
    Socket client = server.accept ();
    System.out.println ("Accepted from " + client.getInetAddress ());

    server.close ();
    return client;
}
```

This method accepts a single connection from a client on the specified port `port`. We first create a `ServerSocket` connected to the port; opening this may throw an `IOException` which we pass on. We then accept a single connection from a single client; we immediately close the server socket so that no more connection attempts can be made.

10.2.1 Testing the server

This server can be tested by using a telnet application to connect to the server; you can specify the host address `127.0.0.1` if you are connecting from the same machine that is running the server, and you must specify the port number that you have chosen.

The IP address `127.0.0.1` is a special address called the *loopback* address that directs IP packets back to the sending machine. You can usually also refer to this with the name `localhost`. You can easily test client-server applications on a single machine that is not connected to the Internet by running the server and then connecting to the loopback IP address.

10.3 Building a nonblocking server

A simple server, as described, is adequate for handling one connection at a time; however, it is unsuited to handling multiple connections. The `read()` method blocks if there are no data, and so if the server attempts to read from a client that has not transmitted any data, then the server will block.

There are two ways to get around this problem. One solution is to write a nonblocking server, the other is to write a multithreaded server. The multithreaded alternative is almost always considered a better solution.

This example demonstrates the operation of a nonblocking server. Earlier in the book, we said that there is no real capability for nonblocking I/O in Java. The `available()` method does, however, provide us with a crude workaround. The amount of nonblocking I/O that we can achieve is the ability to call a `read()` method that returns immediately if there are no data. We can simulate this by preceding every call to `read()` with a call to `available()` to ensure that there are data available.

The following server accepts two client connections and loops, echoing data between the clients. It uses the `available()` methods to simulate non-blocking I/O. (Figure 10.3). This is effectively a very simple two-person chat server.

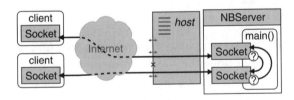

Figure 10.3   A nonblocking server

```
import java.net.*;
import java.io.*;

public class NBServer {
    // public static void main (String args[]) throws IOException ...
}
```

The server is a single thread that executes in the `main()` method.

```
static InputStream i0, i1;
static OutputStream o0, o1;
```

```
public static void main (String args[]) throws IOException {
  if (args.length != 1)
    throw new RuntimeException ("Syntax: NBServer <port>");

  try {
    accept (Integer.parseInt (args[0]));
    while (true) {
      int c0 = readNB (i0);
      if (c0 >= 0)
        o1.write (c0);
      int c1 = readNB (i1);
      if (c1 >= 0)
        o0.write (c1);
    }
  } finally {
    System.out.println ("Closing");
    try {
      if (o0 != null)
        o0.close ();
    } catch (IOException ex) {
        ex.printStackTrace ();
    } try {
      if (o1 != null)
        o1.close ();
    } catch (IOException ex) {
      ex.printStackTrace ();
    }
  }
}

// static void accept (int port) throws IOException ...
// static int readNB (InputStream i) ...
```

When the server is run, we first ensure that a port number has been specified on the command line. We then accept two connections using the `accept()` method, and commence echoing data between the two connections. We make use of the `readNB()` method that uses `available()` to test if there are any data to be read. If there are no data to be read, it returns the value -2; otherwise, it returns a byte of data.

Communication to the clients occurs through the streams $i0$ and $o0$ for the first client, and $i1$ and $o1$ for the second client; these are initialized by the `accept()` method.

We surround the entire body of this method with a `try ... finally` clause that serves to close both client connections when we exit. Note that even the `close()` call may throw an exception, so we must catch any exceptions that may occur, and thus ensure both `Socket`s close.

Going to such lengths to close `Socket`s is not particularly important for this particular server; when it exits, all `Socket`s will be closed anyway. It is usually, however, important that we clean up correctly when a client exits; most servers will stay operational for a long time, and so we could otherwise tie up system resources.

```
static void accept (int port) throws IOException {
    System.out.println ("Starting on port " + port);
    ServerSocket server = new ServerSocket (port);
    try {
        System.out.println ("Waiting..");
        Socket client0 = server.accept ();
        System.out.println ("Accepted from " + client0.getInetAddress ());
        i0 = client0.getInputStream ();
        o0 = client0.getOutputStream ();
        new PrintStream (o0).println ("Welcome. Please wait.");
        System.out.println ("Waiting..");
        Socket client1 = server.accept ();
        System.out.println ("Accepted from " + client1.getInetAddress ());
        i1 = client1.getInputStream ();
        o1 = client1.getOutputStream ();
        new PrintStream (o1).println ("Welcome.");
        new PrintStream (o0).println ("Proceed.");
    } finally {
        server.close ();
    }
}
```

This method accepts two client connections. We open a `ServerSocket server` on the specified port `port`, and then accept two connections, attaching the streams `i0`, `o0`, `i1`, and `o1` to the two `Sockets`.

Again, we surround the body of this method with a `try ... finally` clause that ensures that `server` is closed, regardless of how the method exits. Note that if an exception is thrown when accepting the second connection, then the first connection will be closed by the `finally` clause of the `main()` method.

```
static int readNB (InputStream i) throws IOException {
    if (i.available () > 0)
        return i.read ();
    else
        return -2;
}
```

This method performs a nonblocking read from the specified `InputStream i`, by first querying the `available()` method, and returning the value `-2` if there are no data available to be read.

Note that this method may not become aware when the client attached to `i` exits; the `available()` method will still return 0, even if the network connection has terminated. This is a major problem with nonblocking servers of this form: the only way to determine that a client has quit is to periodically write data to the client; if they are no longer listening, then an `IOException` will be thrown.

10.4 Building a multi-threaded echo server

Multithreaded servers overcome the blocking I/O problems by launching one or more threads per client connection. The main server thread will concern itself with accepting client connections, while the handler threads will serve existing connections. A handler thread can block on reading data from a client while all other threads keep processing.

This type of server has many advantages over the nonblocking alternative. Exceptions and other problems with a single connection are localized to the thread that is processing the connection; this generally leads to a more robust server. Under normal loads, all of the threads will spend most of their time blocking on I/O, unlike the nonblocking server, which must constantly monitor all client connections. The handler class also leads to a clean server implementation; all the code dedicated to accepting connections can be located in one class, and all of the code dedicated to handling a connection will be located in another.

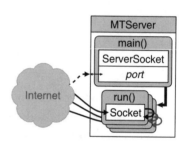

Figure 10.4 A multithreaded echo server

This server is a multithreaded version of the first echo server that we looked at. The main thread accepts connections, launching a new handler for each one. Each handler echoes all received data back to the sender (Figure 10.4).

```
import java.net.*;
import java.io.*;

public class MTEchoServer extends Thread {
    // MTEchoServer (Socket s) ...
    // public void run () ...
    // public static void main (String args[]) throws IOException ...
}
```

The `MTEchoServer` class extends `Thread`; we use the same class for both the mainline and the handlers. The main thread runs in the `main()` method, accepting new connections and creating new `MTEchoServer` threads to process these connections. When we start a client's handler thread, the `run()` method takes care of echoing data back to the client.

```
protected Socket s;

MTEchoServer (Socket s) {
   System.out.println ("New client.");
   this.s = s;
}
```

In the constructor, we accept a reference to the `Socket` that this handler will process. The caller must manually call our `start()` method to actually start a thread processing this connection.

```
public void run () {
   try {
      InputStream i = s.getInputStream ();
      OutputStream o = s.getOutputStream ();
      new PrintStream (o).println
         ("Welcome to the multithreaded echo server.");
      byte buffer[] = new byte[16];
      int read;
      while ((read = i.read (buffer)) >= 0)
         o.write (buffer, 0, read);
      System.out.println ("Client exit.");
   } catch (IOException ex) {
      ex.printStackTrace ();
   } finally {
      try {
         s.close ();
      } catch (IOException ex) {
         ex.printStackTrace ();
      }
   }
}
```

The thread that will process this connection enters the `run()` method. We open streams to and from the client, and send an introductory message using a temporary `PrintStream` object. We then loop, echoing any received data back to the client; we use a small buffer `buffer` to make this transfer more efficient. The copy loop reads data into this buffer; the `read` variable indicates how many data were just read. If this is a positive amount, then we echo the data back to the client; otherwise, EOF has been reached and we exit the loop.

As usual, when dealing with I/O, we must deal with exceptions. If an exception occurs in the body of the `run()` method then we print the exception and close down; the thread will halt when we leave the `run()` method. We use a `finally` clause to ensure that we close the `Socket`, regardless of whether we exit because of an exception, or naturally from an EOF.

```
public static void main (String args[]) throws IOException {
   if (args.length != 1)
      throw new RuntimeException ("Syntax: MTEchoServer <port>");
   System.out.println ("Starting on port " + args[0]);
   ServerSocket server = new ServerSocket (Integer.parseInt (args[0]));
   while (true) {
      System.out.println ("Waiting");
      Socket client = server.accept ();
      System.out.println ("Accepted from " + client.getInetAddress ());
      MTEchoServer c = new MTEchoServer (client); c.start ();
   }
}
```

The main() method is responsible for accepting new connections. We ensure that a port number has been specified on the command-line, and then open a new Server-Socket that listens on this port. We can then have a very simple main loop that just accepts new Sockets and starts a new handler thread for each such connection. These handler threads will process the connections in independent threads from this mainline.

Building a multithreaded server allows us to separate accepting connections from actually processing these connections. This leads to a cleaner implementation, and also protects the server from problems with individual connections. An example of the type of problem that we are protected from is that of the write() method blocking. TCP guarantees that any data that are successfully written to a Socket *will* be delivered to the client (or an error will be raised). In the case of client or network problems, this may mean that a write() method will take time to complete. If we only have a single thread handling multiple clients, then this blocking will delay all other clients.

10.5 Wrapping up

This part of the book is primarily concerned with introducing the Java API, and so the servers that we have looked at in this chapter are comparatively simple. There has been no application-level protocol to deal with; we have just echoed data back to the clients. In the applications part of this book we will look at developing servers that have application-level protocols with which we must interface.

The remainder of this part introduces UDP, and the URL classes, and provides a recap of threads and exceptions. Up to now, we have been primarily concerned with streams-based connections. Networking with TCP builds on this because the TCP networking protocol provides a virtual stream across the network. In the next chapter, we will look at the UDP networking protocol which is a datagram networking protocol; instead of a virtual stream, we must divide our transmissions into packets and send these as distinct units across the network.

chapter 11

Datagram networking

UDP is a *connectionless* transport layer protocol that operates on top of IP. It is packet-based, and revolves around constructing packets of information and dispatching them. Receipt is not guaranteed, but received packets are guaranteed not to be corrupt. Packets should be generated as byte arrays and then can be dispatched to a specified server.

The difference between TCP and UDP connections is best described with the following analogy. TCP is like a phone call: the number is dialed once, a connection is established, and the connection is available to both parties until someone closes the connection (hangs up the phone). UDP, on the other hand, is equivalent to having that same phone conversation through bionic couriers. Each message would be sent as a distinct package, and would arrive separately, requiring addressing each time. UDP packets can be lost and can overtake each other, and can even be duplicated. If a packet arrives, however, you can be very sure that it is intact. Both TCP and UDP operate over IP, and so both ultimately result in individual IP packets; UDP, however, brings the programmer much closer to the raw IP layer.

11.1 Class DatagramPacket

Sending a UDP packet involves creating a `DatagramPacket` object that consists of the message body and the target address (Figure 11.1); this `DatagramPacket` can then be placed into the network for delivery.

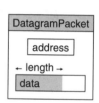

**Figure 11.1
Class Datagram-
Packet**

Receiving a UDP packet involves creating a `DatagramPacket` object and then accepting a UDP packet into it from the network; the source address and contents can subsequently be extracted from the `DatagramPacket`. You cannot specify who you wish to receive from; you will simply receive the next UDP packet that arrives with your address.

11.1.1 Constructors

There are two constructors for UDP datagrams. One is used for sending packets and requires the address to be specified; the other is used for receiving packets and just requires a memory buffer to be provided.

DatagramPacket(byte ibuf[], int ilength)   This constructor is used for receiving datagrams. The `ibuf` parameter is the byte array that will hold the packet contents when it arrives; you must provide a preallocated array to hold the packet. The `ilength` parameter is the maximum number of bytes that should be read from the UDP packet.

DatagramPacket(byte ibuf[], int ilength, InetAddress iaddr, int iport)   This constructor is used to create a datagram packet for transmission. The packet body consists of the first `ilength` bytes of array `ibuf`. The packet will be delivered to the specified port `iport` on the specified host `iaddr`; there must be a UDP server listening on the target port to receive the packet. Note that UDP and TCP port numbers are completely independent, so you can have both a UDP server and a TCP server listening on the same port number.

11.1.2 Methods

The contents and remote address of the `DatagramPacket` can be queried with the following methods. If the packet was received, then the addresses correspond to the source host; if the packet was created for transmission, then the addresses correspond to the destination host.

InetAddress getAddress()   This method returns the IP address of the packet source (or destination).

int getPort()   This method returns the port number of the packet source (or destination). This information allows you to respond to a UDP packet easily, because you can determine the source server's port number directly.

byte[] getData()   The `getData()` method is used to extract the packet data into a byte array. This will be the same buffer that was specified in the constructor; it will therefore have the initial buffer size, and not the exact packet size.

int getLength()   This method is used to find the length of the actual UDP packet; which will usually be less than the actual buffer size.

11.2 Class DatagramSocket

This class is used to both send and receive `DatagramPackets`; after creating a `DatagramSocket`, you can send and receive packets (Figure 11.2). As with TCP, a

`DatagramSocket` must listen on a particular port number between 1 and 65535; ports 1–1023 are reserved for system applications.

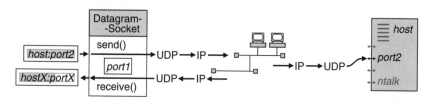

Figure 11.2   Class DatagramSocket

Remember that UDP is connectionless, so you use a single `DatagramSocket` to send packets to different destinations and receive packets from different sources.

11.2.1 Constructors

You can either specify a port for the `DatagramSocket` or let the operating system assign one to you. Usually a server will pick a particular port on which to operate, and clients will allow a random port to be assigned. The client's port number will be automatically inserted into every packet that it sends.

DatagramSocket() throws SocketException   This constructor creates a `Datagram-Socket` with a randomly chosen port number.

DatagramSocket(int port) throws SocketException   This constructor creates a `DatagramSocket` that listens on the specified port `port`.

11.2.2 Methods

The `DatagramSocket` class provides methods to send and receive `DatagramPackets` as well as methods to close the socket and determine the local port number.

void send(DatagramPacket p) throws IOException   This method sends the packet `p` to its destination address.

synchronized void receive(DatagramPacket p) throws IOException   This method receives a single UDP packet into the specified `DatagramPacket p`. The packet can then be inspected to determine the source IP number and port, and the length of the data. This method blocks until it has successfully received a packet.

int getLocalPort()   This method returns the port number on which the `Datagram-Socket` is operating.

synchronized void close()   This method closes the `DatagramSocket`.

11.2.3 IOException

Creating a `DatagramSocket`, and sending and receiving packets may all throw `IOExceptions` if a problem arises. The `SocketException` class is also a subclass of `IOException`.

11.2.4 SecurityException

The `SecurityManager` restricts access to UDP transmission and reception. Applets may neither send packets to nor receive packets from a server other than the one that originally served them. The receipt restrictions are performed by verifying the source address of every packet that is received.

11.3 Receiving UDP packets

In this example, we step through the process of receiving a UDP packet (Figure 11.3).

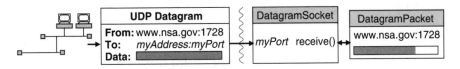

Figure 11.3   Receiving a UDP packet

```
DatagramSocket socket = new DatagramSocket (port);
```

We first create a `DatagramSocket` on a specified port. Specifying the port is optional; however, we want to pick our own port when we are planning on receiving packets so that we can give other applications an address to which to send their packets.

```
byte buffer[] = new byte[65536];
DatagramPacket packet = new DatagramPacket (buffer, buffer.length);
```

We next construct a reception packet. Remember that there are two constructors for the `DatagramPacket` class—one for transmission and one for reception; when receiving, we don't specify a destination address. The byte array, `data`, is the buffer into which we will receive the packet.

Note that the byte array is declared with a length of 65536 bytes. If we know that we will receive packets of a particular size, then we could choose a more appropriate value; however, this is the maximum size of any UDP packet (actually, it is slightly larger), because the UDP packet size is specified in just two bytes of the UDP header. If we provide a buffer that is too small, then part of the packet will be discarded.

```
socket.receive (packet);
```

The `receive()` method is called to wait for a packet to arrive. It takes a `DatagramPacket` as its parameter, and copies the received UDP packet into it.

```
InetAddress fromAddr = packet.getAddress ();
int fromPort = packet.getPort ();
int length = packet.getLength ();
byte data[] = packet.getData ();
// ...
```

Here we use methods of the `DatagramPacket` to determine its source address, port number, and data length. We then call `getData()` to get the packet contents; note that this is in fact the same buffer that we initially provided.

We can now dissect the data, and if necessary, respond to the `DatagramSocket` that originated the packet.

```
socket.close ();
```

When finished, we close the socket. This stops further reception and buffering of UDP packets.

11.4 Transmitting UDP packets

In this example, we step through the process of sending a UDP packet (Figure 11.4).

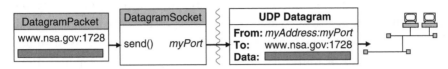

Figure 11.4 Transmitting a UDP packet

```
DatagramSocket socket = new DatagramSocket ();
```

We first construct a `DatagramSocket` for UDP transmission. UDP transfer is connectionless, but we still use a socket for transmission. In this case, we don't care about our local port number, so we accept a random one chosen by the operating system.

```
DatagramPacket packet = new DatagramPacket
  (data, data.length, InetAddress.getByName ("www.nsa.gov"), 1728);
```

We next create a `DatagramPacket` for transmission. We assume in this example that the `data` variable is an array of bytes. We construct a new `DatagramPacket` with this byte array, the length of the array, an `InetAddress` destination, and a port. These specify the destination to which the packet will be delivered; in this case, we are delivering to a server on port `1728` of the host `www.nsa.gov`. Remember that each packet must have its own addressing information, so we must use the constructor intended for transmission for each packet.

```
socket.send (packet);
```

Calling the `send()` method places the packet into the network for delivery to the target. On its way, it may be delivered out of order with earlier or later packets, it may be duplicated, or it may be lost. The local address and port number are automatically transmitted as part of the UDP header.

```
socket.close ();
```

We close the `DatagramSocket` when we are done.

11.5 A UDP example

It is often desirable to use UDP when latency is an issue; the overhead is considerably less than when TCP is used. Packet loss is, however, an obvious concern. This example uses an alarm to trigger a resend if no response is received to a transmission: we assume that the packet has been lost if we don't receive a prompt reply.

The server is a simple echo server; however, we have added code to simulate packet loss so that the behavior is more easy to observe. UDP packets usually will be lost only if a network is congested; across the Internet this may be quite common, but within a small LAN it is rare. The client sends a request to the server and awaits a response, using an alarm to trigger resends.

It is not advisable to use a much more complex mechanism than this to ensure reliable delivery with UDP. The more function you add, the closer you get to reimplementing TCP. TCP, however, has many special mechanisms that prevent network congestion and other problems. It is unlikely that any implementation of reliable delivery on top of UDP will address these issues successfully. If your data must get through intact, then use TCP.

11.5.1 Class Alarm

We will use this class in our UDP client to provide an alarm call mechanism (Figure 11.5). This allows us to schedule a callback to occur after a specified delay. In this example, we will send a packet and then wait for a response from the server; we schedule an alarm call to resend the request if we get no response within a reasonable time.

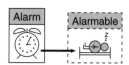

Figure 11.5 Class Alarm

This class implements the alarm mechanism, and is an extension of Thread. When the thread is started, it sleeps for a while and then issues an alarm call on its target object. An Alarm can be stopped by simply calling its stop() method.

```
public class Alarm extends Thread {
   // public Alarm (int time, Alarmable target) ...
   // public Alarm (int time, Alarmable target, Object arg) ...
   // public void run() ...
}
```

This class is a Thread that calls the alarmCall() method of the target object after a specified timeout. There are two constructors for the class; the timeout and target for the alarm call must be specified, and an additional parameter can optionally be specified to help identify the cause of an alarm callback.

```
public Alarm (int time, Alarmable target) {
    this (time, target, null);
}
```

This constructor calls the following constructor with a `null arg` value.

```
protected Alarmable target;
protected Object arg;
protected int time;

public Alarm (int time, Alarmable target, Object arg) {
    this.time = time;
    this.target = target;
    this.arg = arg;
}
```

This constructor takes three parameters: the `time` is the number of milliseconds to sleep before issuing an alarm call, the `target` is the alarmable object whose `alarmCall()` method should be called, and the `arg` is an arbitrary value that can be used to indicate the cause of the alarm call. One possible use of `arg` is as a `String` description of the cause for alarm.

```
public void run () {
    try {
        Thread.sleep (time);
        target.alarmCall (arg);
    } catch (InterruptedException ex) {
        ex.printStackTrace ();
    }
}
```

This method is called when the `Alarm` is started; we sleep for the specified time, then call the `alarmCall()` method of the target object. An alarm can be stopped by simply calling its `stop()` method; this method is inherited from the `Thread` superclass.

11.5.2 Interface Alarmable

This is the interface that must be implemented by any object that wishes to receive alarm calls. An `Alarmable` object is thus any object that might receive an alarm call to signal an event. In this example, we will use this mechanism to resend lost packets.

```
public interface Alarmable {
    public void alarmCall (Object arg);
}
```

The `alarmCall()` method is called when an `Alarm` reaches its timeout; the `arg` value is that which was passed to the `Alarm` object when the callback was initiated. This can be used to help determine the cause of the alarm call.

11.5.3 Class UDPEchoServer

This class implements a UDP echo server. It creates a UDP socket, then waits for transmissions, echoing back what was sent (Figure 11.6).

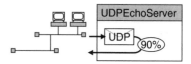

Figure 11.6   Class UDPEchoServer

```
import java.net.*;
import java.io.*;

public class UDPEchoServer {
  // public UDPEchoServer (int port) throws IOException ...
  // public void execute () throws IOException ...
  // static public void main () throws IOException ...
}
```

This is a simple class that listens on a specified UDP port and echoes back every packet that it receives to the sender.

```
protected DatagramSocket socket;

public UDPEchoServer (int port) throws IOException {
  socket = new DatagramSocket (port);
}
```

The constructor accepts a port number `port`; we open a `DatagramSocket socket` that listens on this port for incoming UDP packets.

```
public void execute () throws IOException {
  while (true) {
    DatagramPacket packet = receive ();
    if (Math.random () < .9)
      sendEcho (packet.getAddress (), packet.getPort (),
        packet.getData (), packet.getLength ());
    else
      System.out.println ("discarded");
  }
}

// protected DatagramPacket receive () throws IOException ...
// protected void sendEcho (InetAddress address, int port, byte data[],
//    int length) throws IOException ...
```

The execute() method loops, receiving UDP packets and echoing them back to the sender. We can easily return a packet to its sender because the source address and port are automatically provided by the networking protocol.

We simulate 10% packet loss to more clearly demonstrate the function of the subsequent client. Although UDP may drop packets naturally due to network congestion, this is not commonly observable on a small LAN.

```
protected DatagramPacket receive () throws IOException {
    byte buffer[] = new byte[65535];
    DatagramPacket packet = new DatagramPacket (buffer, buffer.length);
    socket.receive (packet);
    System.out.println ("Received " + packet.getLength () + " bytes.");
    return packet;
}
```

This method is essentially the same as the UDP reception code fragment shown earlier in the chapter. We create a new DatagramPacket, and a buffer into which to read the packet. We then receive a packet into the buffer using the receive() method of socket.

```
protected void sendEcho
        (InetAddress address, int port, byte data[], int length)
            throws IOException {
    DatagramPacket packet = new DatagramPacket (data, length, address, port);
    socket.send (packet);
    System.out.println ("Sent response.");
}
```

This method creates a new DatagramPacket from the specified packet contents, and transmits it to the specified address. We use this method to send a packet's contents back to its sender.

```
public static void main (String args[]) throws IOException {
    if (args.length != 1)
        throw new RuntimeException ("Syntax: UDPEchoServer <port>");
    UDPEchoServer echo = new UDPEchoServer (Integer.parseInt (args[0]));
    echo.execute ();
}
```

This method creates a new UDPEchoServer and calls the execute() method, which listens on the port specified as a command-line parameter, and echoes back every packet that is received.

11.5.4 Class SureDelivery

The SureDelivery class is a client to demonstrate the UDPEchoServer. This class attempts to protect against packet loss by resending a request if no response is received within a certain timeout. We use the Alarm class to perform this callback (Figure 11.7).

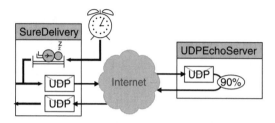

Figure 11.7   Class SureDelivery

```
import java.net.*;
import java.io.*;

public class SureDelivery implements Alarmable {
   // public SureDelivery (String message, String host, int port) ...
   // public void alarmCall (Object arg) ...
   // public static void main (String args[]) throws IOException ...
}
```

The SureDelivery class sends a message specified in the constructor to the specified UDP server and awaits a response. An Alarm is used to resend the message if no response is received within a 10-second timeout.

```
   protected DatagramSocket socket;
   protected DatagramPacket packet;
   protected Alarm alarm;

   public SureDelivery (String message, String host, int port)
       throws IOException {
     socket = new DatagramSocket ();
     packet = buildPacket (message, host, port);
     try {
       sendPacket ();
       receivePacket ();
     } finally {
       alarm.stop ();
       socket.close ();
     }
   }

   // protected DatagramPacket buildPacket (String message, String host,
   //     int port) throws IOException ...
```

```
// protected void sendPacket () throws IOException ...
// protected void receivePacket () throws IOException ...
```

In the constructor, we create a new `DatagramSocket socket` to be used for sending and receiving packets. We call the `buildPacket()` method to create a `Datagram-Packet packet`, which consists of the specified message, and which is addressed to the specified server.

We next send the packet and wait to receive a response. The `sendPacket()` method automatically starts an `Alarm alarm` that will alert us if no response is received within 10 seconds. When a response is received, we stop the alarm and terminate. Note the use of `finally` here—we wish to stop the alarm and close the socket, regardless of how we exit the constructor.

```
protected DatagramPacket buildPacket (String message, String host, int
    port) throws IOException {
    ByteArrayOutputStream byteO = new ByteArrayOutputStream ();
    DataOutputStream dataO = new DataOutputStream (byteO);
    dataO.writeUTF (message);
    byte[] data = byteO.toByteArray ();
    return new DatagramPacket (data, data.length, InetAddress.getByName
        (host), port);
}
```

The `buildPacket()` method takes a `String message` as a parameter, and a target host `host` and port `port`. We use a `ByteArrayOutputStream byteO` to create a byte array `data` that contains the specified message. We then construct a `DatagramPacket` with `data` as the contents, addressed to the specified host and port. We use the `get-ByName()` method of class `InetAddress` to obtain the IP address of the host.

Note that we are using the `ByteArrayOutputStream` class to create a UDP packet; we can thus use the streams interface to communicate over UDP. We attach a filter stream `dataO` to `byteO` and then write high-level data into the buffer. The `toByte-Array()` method of `byteO` lets us subsequently extract the data as an array of bytes.

```
protected void sendPacket () throws IOException {
    socket.send (packet);
    System.out.println ("Sent packet.");
    alarm = new Alarm (10000, this);
    alarm.start ();
}
```

This method sends the previously constructed packet `packet` over the `Datagram-Socket socket`, and starts a new `Alarm alarm` to warn us if no response is received within 10 seconds. Note that we don't need to explicitly provide an address or port for the server to respond to; this is taken care of by the UDP protocol.

```
protected void receivePacket () throws IOException {
   byte buffer[] = new byte[65535];
   DatagramPacket packet = new DatagramPacket (buffer, buffer.length);
   socket.receive (packet);
   ByteArrayInputStream byteI = new ByteArrayInputStream (packet.getData (),
      0, packet.getLength ());
   DataInputStream dataI = new DataInputStream (byteI);
   String result = dataI.readUTF (); System.out.println ("Received " +
      result);
}
```

The receivePacket() method creates a buffer buffer and a new Datagram-
Packet packet, then awaits a UDP response from the server. When we receive a
response we create a ByteArrayInputStream byteI that reads from the contents of the
packet. We attach a DataInputStream dataI to this, and display the contents of the
packet.

Note that the ByteArrayInputStream class lets us use the familiar streams interface to read the contents of a UDP packet, even though the UDP communications
channel is itself not streams-based.

```
public synchronized void alarmCall (Object object) {
   System.out.println ("alarm...");
   try {
      sendPacket ();
   } catch (IOException ex) {
      ex.printStackTrace ();
   }
}
```

This method is specified by the Alarmable interface and will be called by alarm
after a certain period of time if we don't first stop it.

We use this method in this class to resend the request if an echo response is not
received within a certain timeout. We presume that this means that a packet must have
been lost—either our request or the response—and so we must resend our request.

In this method, we resend the original packet using the sendPacket() method,
displaying any exception that should occur. The sendPacket() method automatically
schedules another alarm call should this request also be lost. We can thus simply return
after calling sendPacket().

```
public static void main (String args[]) throws IOException {
   if (args.length != 3)
      throw new RuntimeException ("Syntax: SureDelivery <host> <port>
         <message>");
   while (true) {
      new SureDelivery (args[2], args[0], Integer.parseInt (args[1]));
      System.out.println ("pause..");
      try {
```

```
        Thread.sleep (2000);
      } catch (InterruptedException ex) {
        ex.printStackTrace ();
      }
    }
  }
}
```

The main() method tests the classes we have discussed in these examples by repeatedly creating instances of the SureDelivery class that ping the server and await a response, resending requests if no response is received.

To run the example, first start the UDPEchoServer, then start the SureDelivery to ping the server machine. The output clearly shows what happens when a packet is dropped and the alarm call issues a resend.

11.6 Wrapping up

It is important to understand what UDP is useful for, before planning applications based on it. Because UDP is a connectionless protocol, the overhead is quite a bit lower than TCP, which must perform connection setup and ensure reliable delivery with automatic retransmission and flow control. TCP uses a transmission window to make this process more efficient; however, UDP is still a more efficient protocol, with lower overhead.

On the other hand, UDP does not guarantee delivery, it does not guarantee that the order of receiving is the same as the order of sending, and it does not guarantee that packets will not be duplicated; if you send a packet once, it may be received several times. UDP also has a limited packet size, and no network congestion control; if a large UDP packet is sent, it is likely to be broken into smaller IP packets which *significantly* increases the likelihood that a complete packet will be lost.

An example of when *not* to use UDP is in long data communications; if packets are reordered or lost, then the information becomes unusable. TCP is best in this case, when data requires correct and complete delivery. For data that does not have this requirement, UDP may be a good choice. Video and audio communications are good examples, since a few lost or reordered packets will not be very noticeable, and the lower overhead makes a real difference in delivery feasibility. Pinging a time server is another appropriate use of UDP; a server can listen for incoming UDP packets and respond to each one with the current time.

chapter 12

Using the URL classes

In this chapter, we take a look at a section of the networking API that is used to handle URL content types and to create browser functions. The URL handling classes and interfaces provide a framework for parsing URLs, opening streams based on the protocol type, and handling URL objects based on their content type.

At the time of this writing, the standard Java environment provides facilities for collecting and processing URLs with content types of GIF and JPEG images, and AU audio files. The getImage() and getAudioClip() methods of the Applet class use the URL classes for handling these content types.

The java.net package provides a framework for creating custom URL handling through several interfaces and abstract classes. These classes and interfaces allow new protocol and content types to be easily processed. Using this framework, it is possible to create Web browser function that can be embedded in any application.

By subclassing and implementing the classes and interfaces of this framework, it is possible to define custom ways of handling different types of data that are accessible through the URL addressing mechanism (Figure 12.1). Later in this chapter we will develop a simple application to collect and handle

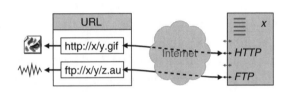

Figure 12.1   Using the URL class

URLs of MIME-type text/plain, i.e., plain-text files. This could easily be extended to handle more unusual content types. We begin with descriptions of the relevant classes; the classes are actually very comprehensive, and we provide only an overview of some of the methods supplied.

The purpose of these classes is to provide an extensible framework, which once in place, provides the programmer with a very simple interface for retrieving objects from the network. URL objects are automatically downloaded and converted from their native formats to one that is usable from Java, so images are automatically converted to Image objects that can be drawn to the screen, and so forth.

12.1 Overview

We will encounter six different classes and interfaces related to the URL classes, all of which are involved in downloading URL-addressable content. We will therefore begin with a brief overview of these classes.

The ultimate goal of these classes is that an application can create an URL object using the standard URL addressing scheme, such as `http://x.y.z/images/logo.gif` or `ftp://sunsite.unc.edu/pub/sound/screams.au`, and then simply call the `get-Content()` method to download and decode the addressed object. For the first example, the `URL` classes must connect to the web server, issue a request, parse the HTTP response headers, and decode the GIF image data, resulting in an `Image` object. For the second example, they must connect to the specified FTP site, log in, change directories, and download and decode the sound file, resulting in an appropriate `AudioClip` object.

To achieve this result, there are two chains of control. The first chain is based on the protocol (`http` or `ftp`) and allows us to obtain an `InputStream` from any URL-addressable object, based on the URL's protocol and address. The framework is extensible, so we can add new protocols such as `nntp`, and address objects across many different information systems.

The second chain of control is based on the type of the object; whether it is an image, formatted text, a soundclip, etc. The protocol chain identifies the type of the object, and then this chain picks an appropriate decoder. The decoder is responsible for reading from the protocol `InputStream` and constructing a useful Java representation of the object.

The first chain is achieved with the `URL–URLStream-HandlerFactory–URLStreamHandler–URLConnection` chain of classes (Figure 12.2). The `URL` object addresses the object; its `getContent()` method calls on an `URLStreamHandlerFactory` to return an `URLStreamHandler` appropriate for the URL's protocol. This `URLStreamHandler` is responsible for creating an `URL-Connection` object that can open an `InputStream` for reading from the addressed object.

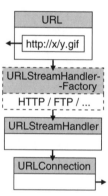

Figure 12.2 The URL protocol chain

The second chain of control, `URLConnection–Content-HandlerFactory–ContentHandler`, is then called upon to decode the object (Figure 12.3). The `URLConnection` class must be able to identify the content-type of the addressed object; it then calls on a `ContentHandlerFactory` to return a `ContentHandler` appropriate for the content-type. This `ContentHandler` must finally be able to decode a useful Java representation of the object.

What follows is a description of the API of these classes, followed by an actual implementation of a simple HTTP protocol chain and a `text/plain` content chain.

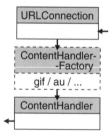

Figure 12.3 The URL content-type chain

12.2 Class URL

The URL class represents an object referred to by a Uniform Resource Locator, as used on the World Wide Web. An URL consists of four fields: the protocol, hostname, port number, and filename.

12.2.1 Constructors

There are several constructors for the URL class:

URL(String protocol, String host, int port, String file) throws Malformed-URLException   This constructor creates an absolute URL from scratch. The protocol `protocol` is the first field of the URL, typically `http` or `ftp`. The host `host` and port `port` specify the server where the URL object resides, and `file` specifies the object filename on the server.

URL(String protocol, String host, String file) throws MalformedURLException   This constructor assumes a default port number for the URL; the actual port used depends on the protocol, and must be handled by a protocol handler. Internally, the port is set to `-1`.

URL(String s) throws MalformedURLException   This constructor creates an URL from a complete textual specification, typically of the form `http://www.nsa.gov:80/index.html`.

URL(URL context, String s)   This constructor creates a new URL from an existing URL and a relative textual URL s. If the `String` s specifies an absolute URL, then the result is just an URL corresponding to s; otherwise the result is an URL that consists of s relative to the context `context`. For example, if `context` refers to `http://server/` and s is `index.html`, then the result will be an URL for `http://server/index.html`.

12.2.2 Methods

The following are some of the methods that allow an URL to be dissected and its contents to be obtained:

String getProtocol()   This method returns the protocol part of the URL as a String. This will be http, ftp, mailto, etc.

String getHost()   This method returns the String representing the hostname part of the URL.

int getPort()   This method returns the integer representing the port number part of the URL. If none was specified, then -1 is returned and the protocol default should be used.

String getFile()   This method returns the String representing the file part of the URL.

URLConnection openConnection() throws IOException   The openConnection() method returns an URLConnection object, which represents a protocol connection to the URL object. We can then use this class to access the contents of the URL. This class is described in detail later in this chapter.

InputStream openStream() throws IOException   This method opens a connection to the URL and returns an input stream for reading its contents.

In the case of the HTTP protocol, calling openStream() automatically sends a HTTP request and parses the resulting headers, so the stream returned will just read from the contents of the object.

This call is equivalent to first calling the openConnection() method, and then calling the getInputStream() method of the resulting URLConnection object.

Object getContent() throws IOException   The getContent() method collects the contents of the URL and returns it as an Object type. The actual type returned depends on the contents of the URL; if the URL refers to an image and an appropriate handler is installed, then an object of type Image should be returned. Similarly, if we have installed an appropriate handler for text files, then a text object should be returned as a String.

This method performs a series of operations to get the result: a connection must be made to a server, a request must be made, and the response must be processed. The response may indicate that the object actually resides elsewhere, in which case an appropriate protocol handler will automatically connect to the new address without any intervention from the user.

In practice, this method uses the openConnection() method to call on the protocol chain to make a connection, and then passes the result to the content-chain for automatic parsing.

12.2.3 Static methods

A `static` method is provided to install a protocol handler chain.

setURLStreamHandlerFactory(URLStreamHandlerFactory fac) This method sets the global `URLStreamHandlerFactory` for the current application. We will use this method when we look at developing a custom protocol handler. The `URLStream-HandlerFactory fac` must be able to return an appropriate handler for the supported `URL` protocol types. This method can be called only once; however, the environment comes with a default that services HTTP.

12.2.4 IOException

Many of the methods of this class may throw `IOExceptions` if an I/O problem arises.

12.2.5 MalformedURLException

A `MalformedURLException` can be thrown by any of the `URL` constructors, and indicates an attempt to create an `URL` object from incorrectly formed fields. This is a subclass of `IOException`.

12.3 Using the URL class

The default JDK comes with a protocol handler for HTTP, so we can use the `URL` class to easily access content on the Web without having to manually install a suite of protocol and content handlers (Figure 12.4).

The following code fragment downloads a configuration file using the `URL` class.

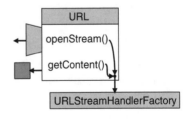

Figure 12.4   Class URL

```
URL url = new URL (getDocumentBase (), "config.txt");
InputStream in = url.openStream ();
DataInputStream dataIn = new DataInputStream (in);
Vector contents = new Vector ();
String line;
while ((line = dataIn.readLine ()) != null)
   contents.addElement (line);
dataIn.close ();
```

In this example we create an URL corresponding to the file config.txt, relative to the URL returned by getDocumentBase(). The getDocumentBase() method of class Applet returns an URL corresponding to the HTML document that contains the applet. We then call the openStream() method to get an InputStream in to read from this file, and attach the DataInputStream dataIn to this.

Behind the scenes, when we call openStream(), the default HTTP protocol handler sends an HTTP get request to the Web server that served this applet, parses the resulting headers, and returns an InputStream that lets us read from the contents of this object.

We can then read the contents of the textfile into the Vector contents using the usual streams interface, closing the stream when we're done.

Obviously, if an error is encountered (such as the server being down), then an IOException will be thrown by this piece of code.

12.4 Class URLConnection

The URLConnection class represents a protocol-specific connection to an URL object. This class is actually abstract; the protocol chain is responsible for providing suitable protocol-specific implementations.

12.4.1 Constructors

The URL object to which an URLConnection should connect is specified by the protocol chain in the constructor.

URLConnection(URL url)   This constructor creates a new URLConnection for the URL url. This constructor can only be called by a subclass of the URLConnection class; subclasses will actually provide implementations of the various URLConnection methods for a particular protocol.

12.4.2 Methods

This class represents a connection to an URL object and has many methods, several of which are optional in an implementation. We have omitted most of the methods for brevity.

abstract void connect() throws IOException This method connects to the URL that was specified in the constructor. The URLConnection class does not connect to the URL object until a method is called that requires a connection to be established.

Object getContent() throws IOException This method retrieves the contents of the URL. Since the contents could be anything, the return value has type Object. The actual type returned will depend on the content type. This processing is performed by the content handler chain.

InputStream getInputStream() throws IOException This method returns an InputStream that can be used to read from the URL object. If we have an URLConnection object, then we can call this method to obtain a raw stream to read from the URL object; this bypasses the content-handler chain used by the getContent() method.

OutputStream getOutputStream() throws IOException This method returns an OutputStream that allows an application to write to the URL; this would be used, for example, by an HTTP post operation.

12.4.3 Static methods

This class provides some internal methods that can be used to help in the implementation of a content handler and to install the content-handler chain.

void setContentHandlerFactory(ContentHandlerFactory fac) This method sets the static ContentHandlerFactory for the URLConnection class. This ContentHandlerFactory fac will be called upon to determine an appropriate content handler based on the content type of an URL. This method can be called only once.

protected String guessContentTypeFromName(String fname) This method can be used to try to determine a content type based on just the URL filename. We use this method in our example to guess the content type of an URL before we have opened a connection. The method operates by looking up the filename extension in an internal table, and is provided as an aid to the programmer.

protected String guessContentTypeFromStream(InputStream is) This method attempts to determine the contents of an URL by reading a few bytes from the InputStream is. It uses the mark() and reset() methods as we discussed in an earlier chapter, so that some data can be read and subsequently unread. This method is provided as an aid to the programmer.

12.4.4 IOException

As usual, problems with accessing an URL through an URLConnection are signaled by IOExceptions.

12.5 Using the URLConnection class

The URLConnection class gives us more control over the connection to an URL object (Figure 12.5). Most implementations of the JDK provide HTTP support for both get and post requests. In the following code fragment, we use methods of URLConnection to perform a CGI post operation. This can be used, for example, to submit information from an applet to a CGI program residing on a Web server.

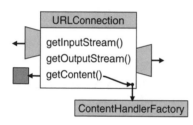

Figure 12.5 Class URLConnection

```
URL url = new URL (getCodeBase (), "/cgi-bin/update.cgi");
URLConnection c = url.openConnection ();
c.setDoOutput (true);
OutputStream out = c.getOutputStream ();
DataOutputStream dataOut = new DataOutputStream (out);
dataOut.writeBytes ("user=" + name + "&password=" + password + "\r\n");
dataOut.close (); InputStream in = c.getInputStream ();
DataInputStream dataIn = new DataInputStream (in);
String line;
while ((line = dataIn.readLine ()) != null)
   System.out.println (line);
dataIn.close ();
```

We first create an URL url that points to the CGI program /cgi-bin/update.cgi on the Web server that served this applet. This time, we use the getCodeBase() method of class Applet; this corresponds to the location of the class files from where this applet was served.

We then call `openConnection()` to create the `URLConnection` object c that corresponds to a protocol-specific connection to this URL object. We call the `setDoOutput()` method to indicate that we wish to send data through this connection; for HTTP, this corresponds to using a `post` operation as opposed to the usual read-only `get` operation. We then call `getOutputStream()` to get an `OutputStream` out to which we can send our data. Some protocols do not support sending and will throw an appropriate `IOException` at this point. We now send our data to this output stream using the usual streams interface, after which we close the stream. We finally call `getInputStream()` to get an `InputStream` in that lets us read a response from the server.

When we call `getInputStream()`, the protocol handler automatically makes a connection to the Web server, sends a `post` command and transmits the data which we wrote. We can then read the response of the CGI program from the returned stream.

12.6 Interface URLStream-HandlerFactory

The `URLStreamHandlerFactory` interface represents the first part of a custom protocol-handler chain. A class that implements this interface is responsible for creating new `URLStreamHandler` instances based on the protocol that is specified by an URL (Figure 12.6).

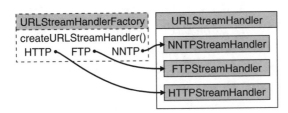

Figure 12.6   Interface URLStreamHandlerFactory

URLStreamHandler createURLStreamHandler(String protocol)   This method should create a new `URLStreamHandler` that can handle the specified protocol `protocol`.

When the URL class attempts to open a connection to an URL object, then it calls upon its `URLStreamHandlerFactory` to return an appropriate `URLStreamHandler` object for the protocol in question. For example, if the protocol type is `ftp`, then an FTP stream handler would be created.

To implement the protocol chain, a class must implement this interface, and then actually be installed using the `setURLStreamHandlerFactory()` method of class `URL`.

12.7 Class URLStream-Handler

Another abstract class to be implemented for the `URL` suite to be complete, the `URLStreamHandler` is responsible for creating connections for a specific protocol (Figure 12.7). An instance of this class will be created by the `URLStreamHandlerFactory` when the need arises.

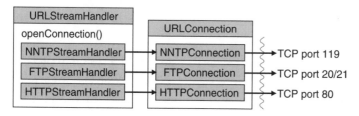

Figure 12.7   Class URLStreamHandler

URLConnection openConnection(URL u) throws IOException   This method should create an appropriate `URLConnection` object for the specified `URL u`.

Each `URLStreamHandler` is responsible for creating `URLConnection` objects that can process `URLs` using the relevant protocol. Usually for example, the HTTP `URLStreamHandler` will return subclasses of the `URLConnection` class that can communicate using the HTTP protocol. For this reason, it is necessary not only to implement `URLStreamHandlerFactory` and `URLStreamHandler`, but also to subclass the `URLConnection` class and provide implementations for the various protocols that are supported.

12.8 Interface Content-HandlerFactory

The `ContentHandlerFactory` interface represents the first part of the content handler chain. A class that implements this interface will be responsible for returning instances of the `Content-Handler` class appropriate for different MIME-types (Figure 12.8). Typical MIME-types include `text/plain`, `image/jpeg`, and so forth.

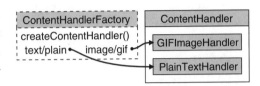

Figure 12.8   Interface ContentHandlerFactory

ContentHandler createContentHandler(String mimetype)   This method should create a new `ContentHandler` that can read an object of the specified content type `mimetype`.

The `URLConnection` class provides methods that can determine the content type of a particular `URL`; it uses the object name, as well as the first few bytes of the object itself, to determine this information. It then calls on its `ContentHandlerFactory` to return an appropriate handler for the object type. For example, if the type of an object is `text/html`, then an HTML content handler should be returned.

To implement a content-handler chain, a class must implement this interface and then be registered with the `URLConnection` class through its `setContentHandler-Factory()` method. This factory will then be called upon to return appropriate `ContentHandler` classes.

12.9 Class ContentHandler

This class is responsible for actually decoding the contents of an `URL` and producing a result that is usable by the Java runtime (Figure 12.9). When the `getContent()` method of class `URL` is called, then the protocol chain will make a connection to the object, and the content chain will call upon an instance of this class to actually decode the object.

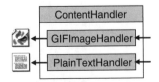

Figure 12.9   Class ContentHandler

abstract Object getContent(URLConnection urlc) throws IOException This method should use the methods of the supplied `URLConnection urlc` to read the contents of the `URL` object and to parse them as appropriate for the content type.

The actual type of the returned object will depend upon the application in question; however, for some types the result should be obvious. If this `ContentHandler` parses image files of some unusual format, then it should return an `Image` object; similarly, if it parses HTML files it should return an appropriate HTML object.

Only one `ContentHandler` will be created by the `ContentHandlerFactory` for a given MIME type; this `ContentHandler` will then be responsible for decoding all subsequent `URL`s of this type.

12.10 A plain-text HTTP framework

As we have seen, Web browsers send a `get pagename /HTTP/1.0` request to a Web server when a document is requested. The Web server responds with a series of headers, followed by the file. These headers can be examined to determine the type of the file, and the appropriate handler can then be invoked to deal with it.

In the following classes, we will implement the `URL` framework necessary to retrieve text files using the HTTP protocol (Figure 12.10). We will be able to extend this framework easily to obtain objects of different types. This lets an application simply call the `getContent()` method of an `URL` and receive an appropriate `Object` in return.

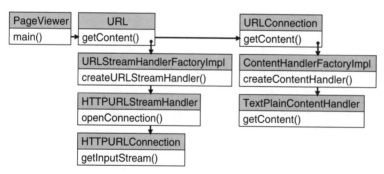

Figure 12.10   An URL-based plain-text HTTP framework

12.10.1 The PageViewer class

The `PageViewer` class is a simple application that takes an URL as a command line argument, and downloads and displays the page. If the content of the page is not plain-text (HTML files are not considered to be plain-text) then an exception will be thrown.

```
import java.io.*;
import java.net.*;

public class PageViewer {
   public static void main (String args[]) throws IOException {
      if (args.length != 1)
         throw new RuntimeException ("Usage: PageViewer <url>");
      URL.setURLStreamHandlerFactory (new URLStreamHandlerFactoryImpl ());
      URLConnection.setContentHandlerFactory (new ContentHandlerFactoryImpl ());
      URL page = new URL (args[0]);
      System.out.println (page.getContent ());
   }
}
```

This class sets two custom factories to put the URL framework in place. For the URL class, we set an `URLStreamHandlerFactoryImpl`; this is an implementation of the `URLStreamHandlerFactory` interface. For the `URLConnection` class, we set a `ContentHandlerFactoryImpl`, this is an implementation of the `ContentHandlerFactory` interface.

These factories will make use of the remainder of the framework that we must implement to allow us to call the `getContent()` method of an URL and receive in return a `String` corresponding to its contents.

We create an URL referring to the URL specified as a parameter, call its `getContent()` method to retrieve the contents and print this to `System.out`. Contrast this with the efforts we went to in earlier chapters, parsing the URL, sending requests and receiving responses. Of course, we still have to implement all of the networking, but this is hidden from the application within the URL framework.

12.10.2 Class URLStreamHandler-FactoryImpl

This class must return an `URLStreamHandler` appropriate for the protocol, in this case, HTTP.

```
import java.io.*;
import java.net.*;

public class URLStreamHandlerFactoryImpl implements URLStreamHandlerFactory {
   public URLStreamHandler createURLStreamHandler (String protocol) {
```

```
    if (protocol.equalsIgnoreCase ("http"))
       return new HTTPURLStreamHandler ();
    else
       return null;
  }
}
```

This implementation of URLStreamHandlerFactory is very simple; it checks for a protocol type of http, and returns an HTTPURLStreamHandler.

More complex implementations would check for several protocols, and return the stream handler for the appropriate protocol. If we wished to also implement the FTP protocol, then we could return an FTPURLStreamHandler for the protocol ftp. We can thus easily extend the URL framework to handle new protocols.

12.10.3 Class HTTPURLStreamHandler

This class must return an URLConnection appropriate to the protocol that it supports. In this case, this is the HTTP protocol.

```
import java.io.*;
import java.net.*;

public class HTTPURLStreamHandler extends URLStreamHandler {
   protected URLConnection openConnection (URL u) throws IOException {
      return new HTTPURLConnection (u);
   }
}
```

The openConnection() method of URLStreamHandler must return an appropriate URLConnection for the protocol. This example can handle only the HTTP protocol and so simply returns a new HTTPURLConnection for the supplied URL u.

12.10.4 Class HTTPURLConnection

This is the class that does most of the work of retrieving an URL. It must open a connection to the server, send appropriate requests, and determine the content type.

Note that a production implementation of an URLConnection class for HTTP must perform much more processing than we do here. An HTTP response includes a status field that indicates the success of the request. Among the various responses possible is a response that indicates that the client should try retrieving an alternative URL. A more complete URLConnection would parse these headers and automatically perform this redirection if necessary.

```
import java.net.*;
import java.io.*;
import java.util.*;

public class HTTPURLConnection extends URLConnection {
   // public HTTPURLConnection (URL url) ...
   // public void connect () throws IOException ...
   // public InputStream getInputStream() throws IOException ...
   // public String getContentType () ...
   // public String getHeaderFieldKey (int n) ...
   // public String getHeaderField (int n) ...
   // public String getHeaderField (String k) ...
}
```

Our `HTTPURLConnection` extends the `URLConnection` class and implements some of the methods that are provided by the `URLConnection` class. These include the `connect()` method to connect to the server, the `getContentType()` method that must determine the content type of the `URL`, and various methods to read the headers that were returned by the server.

```
protected Vector keys;
protected Hashtable headers;

public HTTPURLConnection (URL url) {
   super (url);
   keys = new Vector ();
   headers = new Hashtable ();
}
```

In our constructor, we call the superclass constructor with the specified `URL url`. We initialize the `Vector keys` and the `Hashtable headers`; these are used to hold the headers that are returned by the server.

```
protected InputStream in;

public void connect () throws IOException {
   if (!connected) {
      int port = (url.getPort () == -1) ? 80 : url.getPort ();
      Socket s = new Socket(url.getHost (), port);
      in = new BufferedInputStream (s.getInputStream ());
      sendRequest (s.getOutputStream ());
      readHeaders (in);
      connected = true;
   }
}

// protected void sendRequest (OutputStream o) throws IOException ...
// protected void readHeaders (InputStream i) throws IOException ...
```

The connect() method connects to the Web server. We first check the connected superclass variable to see if we are already connected. If not, then we create a Socket s connected the URL's hostname and port number fields. These are obtained from the variable url, which is inherited from the superclass and corresponds to the URL passed to the constructor.

We obtain a buffered input stream in to read from the socket, and then send an HTTP request to the server using the sendRequest() method. We read the headers that are returned by the server using the readHeaders() method, and set the connected variable to indicate that we are now connected.

```
protected void sendRequest (OutputStream o) throws IOException {
    new PrintStream (o).print ("GET " + url.getFile () + " HTTP/1.0\r\n\n");
}
```

The sendRequest() method creates a new PrintStream on the output stream, and sends a standard HTTP request.

```
protected void readHeaders (InputStream i) throws IOException {
    String line;
    DataInputStream in = new DataInputStream (i);
    while (((line = in.readLine ()) != null) && (!line.trim ().equals (""))) {
        int colon = line.indexOf (":");
        if (colon >= 0) {
            String key = line.substring (0, colon).trim ();
            String header = line.substring (colon + 1).trim ();
            keys.addElement (key);
            headers.put (key.toLowerCase (), header);
        }
    }
}
```

The readHeaders() method is called to read the HTTP headers from the server's response. These headers consist of a status response followed by a series of lines of the form key: value, followed by a blank line.

We read a line at a time, placing each header key into the Vector keys and each key-value pair into the Hashtable headers. The various methods that query the headers will read from these two data structures.

We keep reading lines until we encounter the end of the stream or a blank line. The data that follow these headers are the body of the URL object; we leave this data untouched, to be processed by a content handler.

```
public InputStream getInputStream () throws IOException {
    connect ();
    return in;
}
```

This method calls the `connect()` method and then returns the `InputStream` that is connected to the server. The contents of the URL can subsequently be read from this stream; the headers will already have been stripped by the `connect()` method.

```
public String getContentType () {
   if (connected) {
      if (getHeaderField ("content-type") != null)
         return getHeaderField ("content-type");
      else {
         try {
            return guessContentTypeFromStream (in);
         } catch (IOException ex) {
            return null;
         }
      }
   } else {
      String guess = guessContentTypeFromName (url.getFile ());
      if ((guess != null) && (!guess.equals ("content/unknown")))
         return guess;
      else {
         try {
            connect ();
            if (getHeaderField ("content-type") != null)
               return getHeaderField ("content-type");
            else
               return guessContentTypeFromStream (in);
         } catch (IOException ex) {
            return null;
         }
      }
   }
}
```

The `getContentType()` method is responsible for determining what kind of content the URL object represents. This implementation is fairly long and involved; it is so complex because there are a variety of ways that we can determine the content type.

If we are already connected, then we see if the server has supplied a content-type header. If so, then we can simply return the value that was given. Otherwise we use the `guessContentTypeFromStream()` that is supplied by the base `URLConnection` class. This method attempts to determine the content type based on the first few bytes of data.

If we are not connected, then we can use the `guessContentTypeFromName()` method to try and guess the content-type based on the URL filename. If this fails, then we must connect to the server and use the same methods as before to query the headers and the first few bytes of data.

```
public String getHeaderFieldKey (int n) {
   if (n < keys.size ())
```

```
      return (String) keys.elementAt (n);
    else
      return null;
  }
```

This method allows for lookup of header keys (not values) by number. Key n is the nth header that was returned by the server, starting from zero. If the server provided a header alpha: beta, then the key would be alpha.

```
public String getHeaderField (int n) {
  if (n < keys.size ())
    return getHeaderField ((String) keys.elementAt (n));
  else
    return null;
}
```

This method allows for lookup of header values by number. Again, indexing starts from zero; if the server provided a header alpha: beta then the value will be beta.

```
public String getHeaderField (String k) {
  return (String) headers.get (k.toLowerCase ());
}
```

This method allows for lookup of header values by key name. Using this we can, for example, look up the value corresponding to the key content-type. If the server provided a header content-type: text/html, then this would return text/html.

12.10.5 Class ContentHandlerFactoryImpl

This class is responsible for returning the appropriate content handler for any MIME content-types that we will support.

```
import java.io.*;
import java.net.*;

public class ContentHandlerFactoryImpl implements ContentHandlerFactory {
  public ContentHandler createContentHandler (String mimetype) {
    if (mimetype.equalsIgnoreCase ("text/plain"))
      return new TextPlainContentHandler ();
    else return null;
  }
}
```

The createContentHandler() method is the only method of the Content-HandlerFactory interface. In this case we are only supporting simple text, so we return a TextPlainContextHandler for the MIME-type text/plain and null for any other content types.

As with the `URLStreamHandlerFactory` implementation, we can easily add facilities to support new MIME types by simply returning an appropriate content handler.

12.10.6 Class TextPlainContentHandler

This class collects the contents of a plain-text URL. We return a `String` object consisting of the URL contents surrounded by descriptive comments.

```
import java.net.*;
import java.io.*;

public class TextPlainContentHandler extends ContentHandler {
   public Object getContent (URLConnection urlc) throws IOException {
     String line, content = "";
     DataInputStream in = new DataInputStream (urlc.getInputStream ());
     while ((line = in.readLine ()) != null)
       content = content + line + "\n";
     return "--Text/Plain--\n" + content + "--\n";
   }
}
```

The only method we need to implement is `getContent()`. This method takes an `URLConnection` object as a parameter and opens an input stream for reading from the URL object. We read the contents of the URL a line at a time, appending the contents to the `String` content. When we reach the end of the stream we return the contents, surrounded by descriptive comments.

If we were handling a more complex content-type, then we would probably need to do more processing here. An `image/gif` content-handler would have to decode the URL contents and then create a new `Image` based on the image data.

12.11 Wrapping up

The URL-related classes provide a framework for creating custom browser functions, but the process is not trivial. An application should first create and set a custom `URLStreamHandlerFactory` implementation that creates `URLStreamHandlers` corresponding to the URL protocols. The `URLStreamHandler` class returns instances of the `URLConnection` class particular to the protocol. These `URLConnection` classes are responsible for opening a connection to the URL object and returning communications streams to it. A `ContentHanderFactory` must be installed that returns a `ContentHandler` appropriate for the content of the `URLConnection`; these `ContentHandlers` must then actually download and decode the object.

We can actually install just a protocol chain if we wish to provide new protocols, but make use of the existing content-handlers; similarly, we can install just a content chain if we wish to handle new content types, but make use of the supported protocols.

The amount of work involved in this process is, as demonstrated, nontrivial. The advantage of going to this effort is that an application can then use a very simple interface to access URL-addressable objects. The `getContent()` method performs all of the protocol- and content-specific actions necessary to download and decode the referenced object. The framework is also easily extensible, and can be implemented to dynamically accept new content types.

For most purposes, luckily, it is unnecessary to implement this entire framework. If no `URLStreamHandlerFactory` is set, then some classes that are part of the standard Java distribution will be used (`sun.net.www.protocol.*`, `sun.net.www.content.*`). We can use these classes and the `getInputStream()` method to open a stream to any object using the HTTP or file protocols. We don't need to implement any content handlers to use the `getInputStream()` method; however, content handlers are currently also provided for plain text files, and GIF and JPEG images, among others. For these content types we can use the `getContent()` method to actually download and decode the object data.

The protocol handler that we provided for HTTP is lacking in many respects. Anyone who is seriously considering implementing a protocol handler should first obtain complete documentation for the desired protocol, so that a complete implementation can be provided.

This chapter completes our treatment of the `java.io` and `java.net` APIs. Although there remains in this part an overview of Java exception and thread handling, the significant remainder of this book discusses the actual implementation of some practical networking libraries and applications.

chapter 13

An overview of multithreading

Threading is a very important aspect of network programming in Java. It lets us write efficient and robust servers that process separate client connections in separate threads. We can use this to insulate different client handlers from each other, and to insulate applications from communication failures. We make extensive use of threads for both clients and servers in this book, so an appropriate understanding of the wherewithalls of thread usage is appropriate.

Traditionally, one considers only a single flow of execution through a program: execution begins at the start and flows along a single path until the program terminates (Figure 13.1).

The concept of multithreading is that there can be multiple flows, or threads, of execution in the same program at the same time (Figure 13.2). This is unlike multitasking, because the threads execute in the same data space; if a global variable is changed in one thread, all the other threads will observe the change.

On a multiprocessor machine, different threads may truly run concurrently on different processors. This provides an easy route to upgrading the processing power of a server, because even a single application will see the benefit.

Java supports threads natively at the language level. This makes programming with threads significantly more easy than if a helper library must be used, as was traditionally the case.

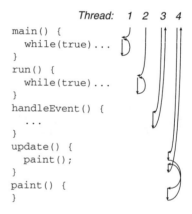

```
main() {
    execute();
}
execute() {
    logon();
    communicate();
    logoff();
}
logoff() {
}
communicate() {
}
logon() {
}
```

Figure 13.1 A single-threaded application

```
                    Thread:  1  2  3  4
main() {
    while(true)...
}
run() {
    while(true)...
}
handleEvent() {
    ...
}
update() {
    paint();
}
paint() {
}
```

Figure 13.2 A multithreaded application

The Java environment provides a `Thread` class for handling threads. There is a one-to-one correspondence between `Thread` objects and actual language threads. The language thread may be controlled by calling methods on its corresponding `Thread` object.

13.1 Variable scope in threads

Variables which are declared within the execution of a thread are local to that thread. That is to say, modifications made to the local variables of one thread, are not made to the local variables of another thread. *Local* in this context does not refer to instance variables, but to variables that are declared within a method; these are variables that are allocated memory in the thread's local stack.

Static class member variables will thus be common to all threads; other instance variables will be common to all threads accessing a particular instance of the class. All method parameters and local variables will be local to a single thread.

```
class Test {
  static int staticW;
  Vector instanceX;

  void aMethod(int paramY) {
    float localZ = staticW;
    instanceX.addElement (new Float (localZ));
  }
}
```

In this example, every thread that calls the aMethod() method will be allocated its own variables paramY and localZ. The instanceX instance variable will shared by all threads calling aMethod() on the same instance of the Test class, and the staticW will be shared among all threads in the runtime.

Obviously, a locally declared reference variable may refer to a nonlocal object, in which case any changes to the object will be nonlocal in scope.

13.2 Synchronization

Threads introduce a need for synchronization. Synchronization is a mechanism to allow the relative execution of different threads to be controlled, to prevent certain undesirable paths of execution. Consider the following code:

```
int balance;

boolean withdraw (int amount) {
  if (balance - amount >= 0) {
    balance -= amount;
    return true;
  }
  return false;
}
```

Ordinarily, this code would be perfectly correct; the withdrawal is performed only if the new balance would be positive. Consider, however, two threads executing this method simultaneously. See Figure 13.3 and Figure 13.4.

Figure 13.3   Two threads execute a method at the same time

If thread 2 happens to interrupt thread 1 at a critical point, then the balance could become negative (Table 13.1). To overcome this, we need *synchronization*.

Figure 13.4   Execution of a method rapidly switches between two threads

Table 13.1   Thread synchronization

Thread 1	Thread 2	balance
if (15 - 10 >= 0)		15
	if (15 - 10 >= 0)	15
balance -= 10		5
	balance -= 10	-5

A synchronized block is a region of code which can only be entered by a *single* thread at a time. In this thread example, two threads were executing in the `withdraw()` method at the same time. Note that it is not actually the block of code to which we wish to restrict access, but access to the `balance` variable of this object.

In Java, the `synchronized` statement allows us to mark regions of code as being accessible to just a single thread at a time.

```
synchronized (anObject) {
   // critical statements
}
```

The Java runtime will ensure that only one thread can execute the enclosed critical statements on `anObject` at a time.

13.2.1 Semaphores

Every class and object in Java has an associated semaphore. A semaphore is a special system object (not a Java object) that has two methods available to it: `get()` and `release()`. Only one thread can `get()` a semaphore at a time; all other threads which attempt to `get()` a semaphore which is already owned by another thread will be put to sleep. When the semaphore owner calls `release()`, one of the waiting threads will succeed in its `get()` request, and all the others will go back to sleep (Figure 13.5). With this mechanism, access to facilities can be restricted to just a single thread at a time; that which owns the semaphore. The nature of semaphores is entirely hidden from the Java programmer with the synchronized abstraction.

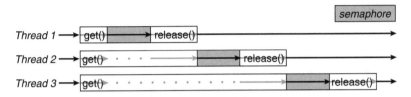

Figure 13.5 Using semaphores

Regions of code can be marked as being synchronized on a particular object or class. Before entering a synchronized block of code, a thread must obtain the semaphore on the specified object or class. If the semaphore is already taken, then the thread will block (go to sleep) until the semaphore is released.

In this manner, if a particular piece of code is a critical section for a certain object `obj`, it can be placed within a `synchronized (obj)` statement. In the previous example, the `withdraw()` method is a critical section for whichever instance of the object it is being called on.

Another use of the `synchronized` keyword is to declare that a method is synchronized. In this case, execution of that method must first obtain a semaphore on the object (or class, in the case of `static` methods). This is equivalent to surrounding the method body with a `synchronized(this)` statement.

13.2.2 Synchronizing

This code is a multithread-correct version of the previous example:

```
synchronized boolean withdraw (int amount) {
   if (balance - amount >= 0) {
      balance -= amount;
      return true;
   }
   return false;
}
```

Only one thread can execute this method on any particular object at any one time (Figure 13.6). This has the same effect as the following:

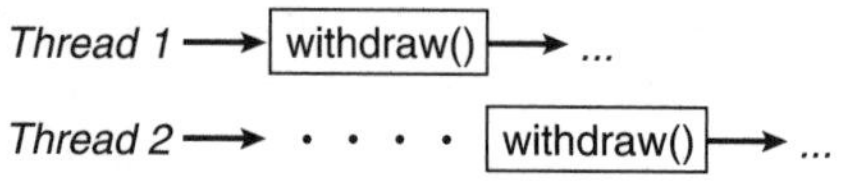

Figure 13.6   Only one thread can execute the method at one time

```
boolean withdraw (int amount) {
   synchronized (this) {
      if (balance - amount >= 0) {
         balance -= amount;
         return true;
      }
      return false;
   }
}
```

These examples state that the enclosed block of code cannot be executed until the semaphore of the corresponding object, this, has been obtained (this is a reference to the object on which the method was called).

If a thread already has the semaphore on a particular object and attempts to take that semaphore again, it automatically succeeds:

```
synchronized void a() {
   b(); // this method calls b while holding the current semaphore
}

// if called by a, the synchronized automatically succeeds
synchronized void b() {
}
```

If this were not the case, then method a() calling method b() would automatically block forever because the semaphore would be already taken.

It is frequently useful for an application that has multiple threads to be able to assign unique identifiers to each thread. The following code fragment allocates a unique identifier to every thread.

```
int id = 0;

public void run() {
   int myId;
   synchronized (this) {
      myId = id ++;
   }
}
```

By synchronizing around the assignment of the myId variable, we ensure that no other thread can interrupt the operation. Note, of course, that this is only of use if there are multiple threads in a single instance of an object. Extending this for all threads in an entire class, we need the following code:

```
static int classId = 0;

static synchronized int getId () {
   return classId ++;
}
```

By declaring that a `static` method is synchronized we require synchronization on the semaphore associated with the entire class, in order to execute. This permits only a single thread in the entire runtime to execute the `getId()` method at any time. We can thus use the `getId()` method to allocate unique identifiers to any thread in the runtime.

13.2.3 Life without semaphores

Without semaphores or a similar atomic mechanism, there is no way to write multi-thread-correct code. It is impossible to manually recreate the function of a semaphore. In particular, remember that different threads may be running concurrently on different processors. (This task is still impossible in the presence of preemption, even if there is just one processor.)

13.3 Class Thread

This class is the runtime representation of a thread (Figure 13.7). Given a `Thread` object, you can pause, resume and stop the corresponding system thread. There are many constructors and methods, of which we will list only a few.

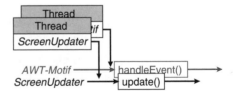

Figure 13.7 Class Thread

13.3.1 Constructors

These are the common constructors of `Thread`:

Thread(String name)   This creates a `Thread` having the name `name`. We can use thread names to identify the various threads of an application; this can make debugging easier because we can determine the purpose of the various threads that are active at any particular time.

Thread(Runnable target)   This creates a new `Thread` object; the corresponding thread will be asleep until the `start()` method is called. Calling the `start()` method on this new `Thread` object will result in the thread starting and calling the `run()` method of the `target` object.

Thread(ThreadGroup group, Runnable target)   This creates a new `Thread` object in the specified `ThreadGroup`, which will call the `run()` method of `target` when it is started. `ThreadGroups` allow us to group multiple threads and provide easy facilities to control the group of threads.

13.3.2 Static methods

There are several `static` methods that are useful for controlling the current thread (yourself) and finding out information about threads in the runtime.

static int activeCount()   This returns the number of currently active threads.

static Thread currentThread()   This returns the `Thread` object corresponding to the currently executing thread (yourself).

```
Thread myself = Thread.currentThread ();
```

static void sleep(long millis) throws InterruptedException   This causes the current thread (yourself) to sleep for the specified number of milliseconds. Other threads will run during this time. If another thread has a reference to your `Thread` object and calls your `interrupt()` method, then you will be awakened with an `Interrupted-Exception`.

```
try {
  Thread.sleep (1000); // sleep for a second
} catch (InterruptedException ex) {
  System.out.println ("I was interrupted.");
}
```

static void yield()   This causes the current thread (yourself) to yield the processor to any other waiting threads. The language does not guarantee preemption, so you should call this method if you are performing long computations without any pauses.

```
for (int i = 0; i < 1000; ++ i) {
   // some large computation
   Thread.yield (); // permit other threads to run
}
```

13.3.3 Instance methods

These instance methods control the thread represented by a `Thread` object.

int getPriority() This returns the thread's priority, a value between `Thread.`
`MIN_PRIORITY` and `Thread.MAX_PRIORITY`.

void setPriority(int newPriority) This sets the thread's priority. Higher priority
threads will preempt lower priority threads when they become ready to run. Thread priorities can be any integer value between `Thread.MIN_PRIORITY` and `Thread.`
`MAX_PRIORITY`, which are, respectively, 1 and 10.

```
Thread myself = Thread.currentThread();
myself.setPriority (Thread.MAX_PRIORITY); // raise my priority
```

A `ThreadGroup` can restrict the maximum priority of all of its member threads. As
a result, this `setPriority()` method may not succeed.

ThreadGroup getThreadGroup() This method returns the thread's `ThreadGroup`.

void start() This actually starts a thread. It is an error to call the `start()` method of
a `Thread` that is currently alive. When you call this method, the corresponding language
thread starts and enters the `run()` method. If the thread was created with a `Runnable`
`target` then this method will call the `run()` method of `target`.

```
Thread execution = new Thread (anObj);
// anObj must implement Runnable
execution.start ();
// a new thread starts and calls anObj.run()
```

void stop() This stops a thread; it can subsequently be started again. If restarted, it
will enter the `run()` method again.

void run() This method is called when a thread is started. If you create a subclass of
the `Thread` class, then this is the method that you should override and that will be executed by the language thread.

boolean isAlive() This returns a value indicating whether the thread is currently alive; a thread is alive if it has been started more recently than it has been stopped.

void suspend() This suspends a thread; its execution is paused.

void resume() This resumes a previously suspended thread.

void join() throws InterruptedException The caller blocks until the thread upon whose method this was called has stopped. Thus, if you have created and started a `Thread` object and want to wait for the thread to finish executing, you call its `join()` method.

```
Thread execution = new Thread (anObj);
execution.start (); // start the thread
try {
   execution.join (); // wait for the thread to finish
} catch (InterruptedException ex) {
   // I was interrupted.
}
```

13.3.4 SecurityException

The `SecurityManager` restricts the thread methods so that threads cannot take liberties with each other. This would be a problem if, for example, an applet were to stop all the threads of other applets running in the same browser. Calling any of the `Thread` class' methods may raise a `SecurityException` if the caller does not have permission to modify the target thread.

13.4 Interface Runnable

This interface is used to allow threads to easily be created in objects that do not extend the `Thread` class directly (Figure 13.8). If a class implements this interface, then a new `Thread` can be created to automatically call a `Runnable` object's `run()` method.

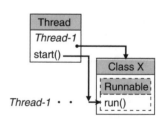

Figure 13.8   Interface Runnable

13.4.1 Methods

There is just one method defined:

void run()   The `Thread` class provides a constructor that takes a `Runnable` object as a parameter. When such a `Thread`'s `start()` method is called, a new thread will call this method. The thread stops automatically when this method completes.

13.5 Class ThreadGroup

The `ThreadGroup` class is used to group threads, to ease the maintenance of multiple threads (Figure 13.9). A limit can be placed on the maximum priority of any thread in a `Thread-Group`, and all the threads can be paused, resumed, and stopped with just a call to the `ThreadGroup`.

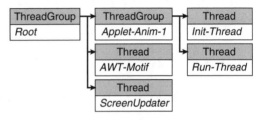

Figure 13.9   Class ThreadGroup

`ThreadGroups` can be used by Java-enabled browsers to keep different applets in separate execution spaces so that they can be more easily controlled.

13.5.1 Constructors

The are two constructors:

ThreadGroup(String name)   This creates a `ThreadGroup` with the specified name that is within the `ThreadGroup` of the currently executing thread (the caller).

ThreadGroup(ThreadGroup parent, String name)   This creates a `ThreadGroup` of the specified name that is within the specified `ThreadGroup`. You can have a hierarchy of `ThreadGroups` to ease thread management.

13.5.2 Methods

The methods of `ThreadGroup` can be used to control all of the threads in a `Thread-Group` simultaneously.

int activeCount()   This returns the number of active threads within the group.

int enumerate(Thread list[])   This fills in the array `list` with references to all active `Thread`s in the group, and returns the number inserted.

int activeGroupCount()   This returns the number of active `ThreadGroups` within the group.

int enumerate(ThreadGroup list[])   This fills in the array `list` with references to all active `ThreadGroups` in this group, and returns the number inserted.

void setMaxPriority(int pri)   This sets the maximum priority that any `Thread` in the group can have.

```
ThreadGroup appletGroup = new ThreadGroup ("Applet Group");
appletGroup.setMaxPriority (Thread.MIN_PRIORITY);
```

int getMaxPriority()   This returns the current maximum `Thread` priority for the group.

void stop()   This stops all of the `Thread`s and groups within this group.

```
Thread.currentThread().getThreadGroup().stop();
```

void suspend()   This suspends all of the `Thread`s and groups within the group.

void resume()   This resumes all of the `Thread`s and groups within the group.

void destroy()   This destroys a `ThreadGroup`; it must first have been stopped. This method releases all system resources held.

13.6 A Runnable example

One way to start a thread in an object is for the object to implement the `Runnable` interface. A `Thread` can be constructed with the object as an argument and then started. When the thread begins executing, it will call the target object's `run()` method. Many threads can be started in an object that implements `Runnable`, although we only use one in this example.

This is an example of using a thread in a `Runnable` application. We provide methods to start and stop the thread (Figure 13.10).

```
public class ThreadDemo implements Runnable {
    // public void begin () ...
    // public void end () ...
    // public void run () ...
}
```

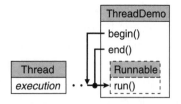

Figure 13.10   Class ThreadDemo

In this example, we implement the `Runnable` interface. This interface says that we must implement a `run()` method which will be called when we start a thread in this object. The `begin()` method starts a new thread if there is none currently running, and the `end()` method stops it.

```
protected Thread execution;

public void begin () {
    if (execution == null) {
        execution = new Thread (this);
        execution.setPriority (Thread.MIN_PRIORITY);
        execution.start ();
    }
}
```

This method is called to start executing a thread in this object. If this is the first call, we create a new `Thread` object passing, `this` as a parameter. This creates a thread which will call our `run()` method when it is started. We limit the thread's priority and then start it. We keep a reference to the new thread in the `execution` variable.

```
public void end () {
    if (execution != null) {
        execution.stop ();
        execution = null;
    }
}
```

This method is called to stop our thread. We use the `stop()` method of `execution`.

```
public void run () {
    try {
        // body
    } finally {
        execution = null;
    }
}
```

The new thread calls this method. We perform our long-running task here; a server connection handler is a typical task. If this method completes for any reason; natural or exceptional, we set our thread reference to `null`. This will prevent us from trying to `stop()` a completed thread, and will also allow garbage collection to free any system resources held by the `Thread`. This is not always necessary, but is just an example of a possible implementation.

13.7 A Thread subclass example

An alternative way to start a thread in an object is for the object to subclass `Thread` (Figure 13.11). The `start()` method, when called on this object, will automatically create a new thread which will enter through the `run()` method. Only one thread can be started in an object in this manner; there is a one-to-one mapping between `Thread` objects and language threads, so the `start()` method will affect only the one thread.

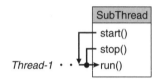

Figure 13.11   Class SubThread

```
public class SubThread extends Thread {
   public void run () {
      // ...
   }

   static public void main (String args[]) {
      SubThread t = new SubThread ();
      t.start ();
   }
}
```

In this example, we subclass `Thread` and override the `run()` method. When we create an instance of our `SubThread` class, a corresponding language thread is created. When we call the `start()` method on our `SubThread` object, the language thread starts and calls the `run()` method on our `SubThread` object.

13.8 Thread notification methods

The Object class defines some methods that are relevant to threads (Figure 13.12). Because these methods are declared by the Object class, they are defined on every Java object. The methods permit very efficient producer/consumer thread synchronization.

13.8.1 Notification methods of class object

The following methods provide a mechanism for threads to await notification of an occurrence, and to notify other waiting threads of the occurrence.

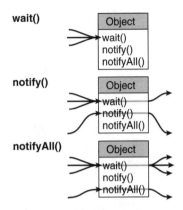

Figure 13.12   Thread notification methods

void wait() throws InterruptedException   Any thread can call this method on any object. The thread will then block until another thread calls the notify() method of the same object.

For example, if a thread finds that a Vector has no elements, it can then call the wait() method to wait for another thread to insert an object. If another threads inserts an object into the Vector, then it can call the Vector's notify() method to wake a sleeping thread.

void wait(long timeout) throws InterruptedException   This method waits for someone to call notify() on the object, or for the specified timeout to elapse. The granularity of the timeout is in milliseconds.

void wait(long timeout, int nanos) throws InterruptedException   This method waits for someone to call notify() on the object, or for the specified timeout to expire. This method allows the timeout to be specified in nanoseconds.

void notify()   This method wakes one Thread that is waiting on the target object.

void notifyAll()   This method wakes all threads that are waiting on the target object; most will immediately go back to sleep, but one will succeed.

A very important thing to note about the use of these methods is that a thread must be `synchronized` on the target object to call any of these methods. The `wait()` methods temporarily release the synchronization to let other threads access the target. After the `notify()` method has been called, and the caller of `notify()` releases the synchronization, the thread will regain synchronization on the object upon waking.

13.9 A producer-consumer example

This example demonstrates usage of the `wait()` and `notify()` methods to implement a simple producer/consumer (Figure 13.13).

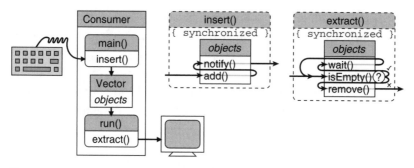

Figure 13.13   Class Consumer

```
import java.util.*;
import java.io.*;

public class Consumer extends Thread {
   protected Vector objects;

   // public Consumer () ...
   // public void run () ...
   // public void insert (Object o) ...
   // public static void main (String args[]) throws IOException,
        InterruptedException ...
}
```

This class represents a consumer. The class extends `Thread`; when the `start()` method is called, it proceeds to consume objects from the `objects` Vector. The `insert()` method allows producers to add objects to this `Vector` for consumption.

```
public Consumer () {
   objects = new Vector();
}
```

The constructor creates a new `Vector` which will hold the objects to be consumed.

```
public void run () {
   while (true) {
      Object object = extract ();
      System.out.println (object);
   }
}

// protected Object extract () ...
```

When the `start()` method is called on this consumer, a new thread enters the `run()` method. This thread repeatedly uses the `extract()` method to extract an object from `objects` and then prints this object.

```
protected Object extract () {
   synchronized (objects) {
      while (objects.isEmpty ()) {
         try {
            objects.wait ();
         } catch (InterruptedException ex) {
            ex.printStackTrace ();
         }
      }
      Object o = objects.firstElement ();
      objects.removeElement (o);
      return o;
   }
}
```

This method extracts an object from `objects`, using the `wait()` method to provide an efficient implementation. We synchronize on `objects`, and then sit in a loop that waits until the `Vector` is nonempty. Every time around the loop, we call the `wait()` method; this will sleep until another thread calls `notify()` on the object. If the `Vector` becomes nonempty, then we return the first element after removing it from the `Vector`.

Synchronizing on `objects` is necessary for two reasons. It allows us to call the `wait()` method; however, more importantly, it makes this code multithread-safe. To extract an object from the `Vector`, we must first call `firstElement()`, and then call removeElement (). If we were not synchronized on the Vector, then another thread could interrupt us between these two operations and remove the same object.

```
public void insert (Object o) {
   synchronized (objects) {
      objects.addElement (o);
      objects.notify ();
   }
}
```

This method adds an object to the Vector and then calls the notify() method. This will wake a thread that is waiting for the Vector to become nonempty. Note that we must be synchronized on the object to call its notify() method.

```
public static void main (String args[]) throws IOException,
   InterruptedException {
   Consumer c = new Consumer ();
   c.start ();
   DataInputStream i = new DataInputStream (System.in);
   String s;
   while ((s = i.readLine ()) != null) {
      c.insert (s);
      Thread.sleep (1000);
   }
}
```

This method shows the Consumer class in action. We first create a new consumer and start it; we then sit in a loop accepting input from the user. Every line that is entered is inserted into the consumer object. The insert() method will wake the consumer thread to consume the line and display it.

The wait() and notify() methods allow us to efficiently implement producer/ consumer classes. We will, in fact, make use of a very similar class in the applications part of this book.

13.10 Wrapping up

To make use of threads you must either implement the Runnable interface or extend the Thread class. Creating threads is fairly easy; however, managing synchronization issues can be more complex. Synchronization errors can be very hard to detect because they are not guaranteed to occur; they may happen only when some threads happen to be scheduled in a particular order. If you write a piece of code that is not multithread-correct, but does operate correctly under Java on one particular system, remember that multiprocessor machines are becoming widespread.

chapter 14

An overview of exceptions

An *exception* is an occurrence, usually some form of error, that disrupts the normal execution flow of a Java program. When an exception occurs, the normal flow of program execution is stopped, and control is transferred to a block of code that has been designated to handle the exceptional condition. If no such code is specified, then the exception propagates up to stop the affected thread and display the exception.

Java's exception mechanism is a lot cleaner than having to check for a possible error value after every method call, such as is required in C. The Java compiler requires the programmer to catch all predictable exceptions; this is useful because it ensures that the programmer is aware of potential problems.

14.1 Exception catching

At the language level, all exceptions are themselves classes that subclass from the `java.lang.Throwable` class and are handled using the `try ... catch` mechanism. The `try` clause surrounds a block of code that may throw certain exceptions. The `catch` clause handles a particular class of exception that may be thrown by this block.

The process of handling different classes of exception obeys the Java inheritance chain (Figure 14.1). A block of code that may throw an exception is surrounded with a `try` statement that has some associated `catch` clauses. Each `catch` clause indicates a particular class of exceptions to catch and has an associated handler. The `catch` clause will catch exceptions of the specified class, and any of its subclasses.

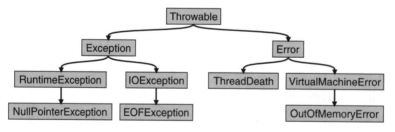

Figure 14.1 The exception inheritance chain

For example, catching exceptions of type `IOException` also catches any subclass of `IOException`, such as `EOFException`. This simplifies network programming because one does not have to name explicitly every possible exception that can occur. However, if a subclass must be dealt with in a different manner than the superclass, then either a catch clause for that class must be specified before the superclass catch clause, or the exception must be dealt with appropriately within the superclass' catch clause.

```
URL url;
try {
    url = new URL ("xyz");
    // ...
} catch (MalformedURLException ex) {
    // url is null.
} catch (IOException ex) {
    // any other IOExceptions
}
```

If an exception occurs as part of an assignment statement, then the assignment will not complete.

14.2 The major types of exceptions

In the Java environment, there are two major superclasses for exceptions, both of which themselves are subclasses of Throwable. The RuntimeException class also holds an important distinction worth noting.

14.2.1 Error

Exceptions that are a subclass of the class Error are serious errors in the Java runtime system, and in a correct system they should not occur. The major departure from this rule is the ThreadDeath exception that is used by the runtime to stop a thread. ThreadDeath will be thrown when a thread's stop() method is called.

No normal code should attempt to catch a subclass of Error.

14.2.2 Exception

Exceptions that are a subclass of the Exception class are normal errors that can occur during program execution, corresponding to problems such as communications failures and so forth. Common subclasses of Exception include IOException and InterruptedException. These exceptions must be explicitly handled by user code. The Java compiler will complain if these exceptions are not either caught or explicitly passed on.

14.2.3 RuntimeException

`RuntimeException` is a subclass of the class `Exception` that encompasses all exceptions that can happen at runtime but that cannot be predicted at compiletime. This includes problems such as array bounds exceptions and null pointer exceptions. If one of these errors is encountered, then a `RuntimeException` will be thrown. It is not *necessary* to declare that a `RuntimeException` may be thrown or to provide a `try ... catch` clause; however, if you know that one may occur and wish to handle it, then the normal exception handling mechanisms can be used.

14.3 Generating exceptions

Exceptions may be generated in several ways:

14.3.1 Method calls

If a method or constructor is declared to throw an exception, then calling that method or constructor may result in an exception of the declared class or a subclass. By declaring that it throws particular exceptions, the method is permitted to throw those exceptions and does not have to catch them in the method body. It is a compiletime error for a method body to throw an exception that is not declared in the `throws` clause, unless it is a subclass of `RuntimeException`.

```
int method () throws IOException ...
// ...
method (); // this call may throw an IOException
```

14.3.2 RuntimeException

A `RuntimeException` may occur even though the offending piece of code does not declare that it throws such an exception. Examples of `RuntimeException` include `NullPointerException` and `ArrayIndexOutOfBoundsException`. These exceptions can be thrown by a language statement or a method call. A `RuntimeException` is thrown by a method if the method executes a statement that throws the exception, and the method does not itself handle it.

```
int a[];
// ...
int i = a[100]; // this can throw an ArrayIndexOutOfBoundsException
```

14.3.3 User-generated exceptions

Exceptions can be manually thrown with the throw statement. This statement takes a single argument that must be a subclass of Throwable. The programmer can either throw an existing subclass of Throwable or declare a new one.

```
throw new Exception ("Problem");
```

14.4 Handling exceptions

If a piece of code can generate an exception by any of the mechanisms above, then unless the exception is a RuntimeException, it must be either caught or passed on. If a RuntimeException is not caught, then it will be passed on by default.

14.4.1 Passing on exceptions

Passing on an exception refers to a method declaring that it can throw that class of exception (Figure 14.2). The method body may then perform actions that can cause the specified types of exception to be thrown. Should such an exception be thrown, then it will be passed on

```
                                          Flow of Execution

void method () throws IOException {
  // ...
  out.close ();_ _ _ IOException _ _ _
  // ...
}
```

Figure 14.2 Passing on an exception

to the method's caller. Because the method has declared that it can throw a particular exception, the caller knows that it can occur, and must itself be able to catch the exception or pass it on. If an exception is not handled by any of the callers in the stack trace, then the current thread is stopped and the exception is printed to the terminal.

```
java.lang.NullPointerException
   at Consumer.extract(Consumer.java:47)
   at Consumer.run(Consumer.java:19) at
   java.lang.Thread.run(Thread.java)
```

14.4.2 Catching exceptions

Catching an exception refers to declaring that a block of code handles exceptions of a particular class. If an exception occurs then execution transfers to the corresponding piece of handler code (Figure 14.3).

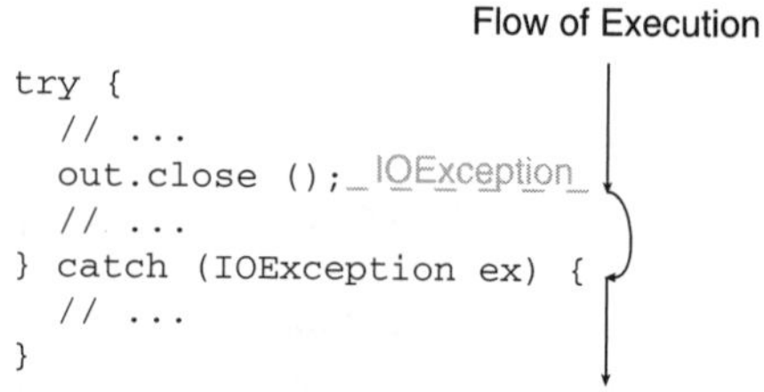

```
try {
  // block of code
} catch (ExceptionClass ex) {
  // handle exceptions of class ExceptionClass
} catch (ExceptionClass2 ex) {
  // handle exceptions of class ExceptionClass2
}
```

Flow of Execution

```
try {
  // ...
  out.close ();_ IOException_
  // ...
} catch (IOException ex) {
  // ...
}
```

Figure 14.3   Handling an exception

If the block of code here throws an exception that is of class `ExceptionClass` or any subclass, then execution will transfer to the first handler. Otherwise, if it throws an exception that is of class `Exception Class2` or any subclass, execution will transfer to the second handler.

More details   In a block of code surrounded with a `try ... catch` statement, the `try` clause is the piece of code that is to be attempted. The `catch` clauses are the handlers for the various possible exceptions. There may be one or more `catch` clauses for a single `try` clause. If an exception of a caught type occurs, then the corresponding handler code is executed and the exception that was thrown is placed in the variable declared in the `catch` statement. Note that if exceptions of several types are to be caught, and one is a subclass of the other, then the `catch` clause for the subclass must appear *before* that for the superclass. Only the first handler that can handle the exception will be called.

```
try {
  // any code can throw a RuntimeException
} catch (NullPointerException ex) {
  // a NullPointerException occurred
  System.err.println (ex); // calls ex.toString()
} catch (RuntimeException ex) {
  // some other exception occurred
  System.err.println (ex);
}
```

In this example, we want to distinguish between a `NullPointerException` and any other `RuntimeException`. If the `RuntimeException` clause came first, then it would always catch the `NullPointerException` and the other handler would never be executed.

14.4.3 The finally clause

A `finally` clause can be appended to a `try ... catch` statement as follows:

```
try {
  // ...
} catch (Exception ex) {
  // ...
} finally {
  // this clause is always executed
}
```

The `finally` clause is always executed after code leaves the `try` clause, regardless of the manner (Figure 14.4). If the `try` clause completes naturally, then the `finally` clause is executed. If an exception occurs and is caught, then the `finally` clause is executed after the exception handler. If there is a `return` statement or other exit from the `try` clause, the `finally` clause will be executed before the exit occurs. Even if the thread is stopped, the `finally` clause is executed. `Finally` is therefore very useful for performing cleanup after a particular piece of code, regardless of how the code exits.

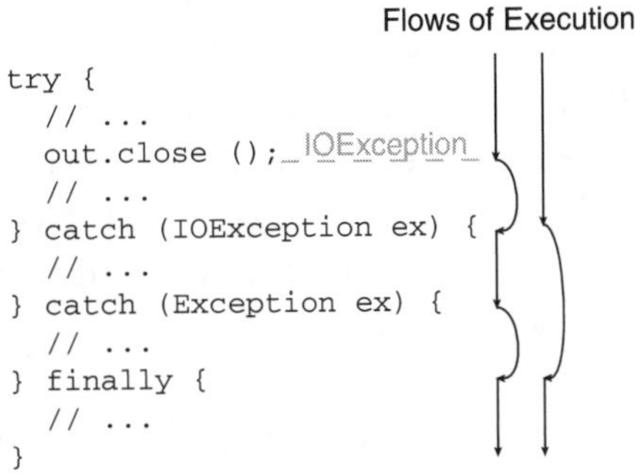

Flows of Execution

```
try {
  // ...
  out.close (); __IOException__
  // ...
} catch (IOException ex) {
  // ...
} catch (Exception ex) {
  // ...
} finally {
  // ...
}
```

Figure 14.4   The finally clause

14.5 Class Throwable

The `Throwable` class is the template for all exceptions, and most follow this model.

14.5.1 Constructors

`Throwable` has two constructors:

Throwable() This creates a `Throwable` object with no detail message. A detail message is a short description of the cause of the exception.

Throwable(String message) This creates a `Throwable` object with the specified detail message. A detail message is useful to help identify the cause when the exception stack trace is printed.

14.5.2 Useful methods

Throwable has several useful methods.

Throwable fillInStackTrace() This method inserts the current execution stack trace into the exception. The current stack trace is the list of method calls that has led up to the current point in execution; this is what is displayed when an exception is printed. Usually the exception constructor inserts the current stack trace, so when an exception is created, the list of method calls that led up to the exception being created will be automatically inserted. The `fillInStackTrace()` method can be used to alter an exception, so that it appears as if it originated at the rethrowing point, rather than at the original occurrence.

void printStrackTrace() This method prints the exception's stack trace, which displays the sequence of method calls that led to the exception being thrown. This method is very useful for tracking down errors.

void printStrackTrace(PrintStream out) This version of `printStackTrace()` prints the exception's stack trace to the specified `PrintStream out`.

String getMessage() The `getMessage()` method returns the exception's detail message.

String toString() The `toString()` method is overridden to include the exception class and the detail message.

14.6 User exceptions

Declaring your own exception is simply a case of declaring a class that subclasses the appropriate exception, and providing the appropriate constructors. You can then throw exceptions of the new class in the usual manner.

```
import java.io.IOException;

public class AuthException extends IOException {
  public AuthException () {
  }
  public AuthException (String detail) {
    super (detail);
  }
}
```

This code declares a new exception type that is a subclass of IOException. Networking code can throw exceptions of this type if an authentication error occurs.

It is important to subclass an appropriate exception type; for most networking code, this will be IOException or a subclass. Remember that the InputStream methods and OutputStream methods are declared as throwing IOExceptions; it does not matter that the AuthException class did not exist when these streams were defined. Because our new exception is a subclass of IOException, all existing code will be able to handle the new exceptions appropriately.

14.7 Wrapping up

Exceptions provide a very clean error-handling mechanism for the language. Code can be written without explicit error checks, and the appropriate exception handling code will automatically be called if a problem arises.

We can define our own exceptions that will fit within the standard exception model, and we can use finally clauses to perform cleanup operations where necessary, regardless of how the corresponding block of code exits.

14.8 Conclusion

This completes the API overview part of the book. The next part of the book is concerned with developing real applications, and classes to support such applications. We will look at a complete TCP client/server application, and then develop a set of message-stream classes that will permit us to develop generic server-based collaborative systems. We will also look at developing some encrypted communications channels that can be used to develop secure Internet applications. All of this new code fits within and builds upon the standard API framework that we have looked at thus far.

The purpose of the remainder of this book is severalfold. We first document and describe an extended communications library that is available for use on the supplied CD. We hope alsoto demonstrate how a generic, extensible and useful library can be built to augment the existing API and make the development of future applications easier.

PART III

Real networking applications

In this part of the book, we create real networked applications using the available classes in the API and a higher level communications library that we develop along the way. The Java API provides several options for streaming data, but we can add much more functionality if we extend the available classes to perform higher level operations common to client-server communications. We develop extended filter streams to handle message headers, to stream messages into queues for later processing, to add multiplexing and demultiplexing capability, and to add the ability to route messages to named recipients. We then look at a generic multithreaded server and client that uses this new library. The section concludes with a treatment of cryptographic streams, and a library for use in creating secure networked applications.

Chapter 15: Building a simple chat system In this chapter, we build a simple chat client and a multithreaded broadcast server. This is the first example of a full client-server system, and we implement it using the streams classes available in the API. The multithreading model of this server is useful for similar servers.

Chapter 16: Message streams Most networked applications make use of conceptual packets, or message units, instead of continuous byte streams as supplied by TCP. In this chapter, we develop a set of streams that encapsulates messages into discrete units that can be sent over TCP. By distinguishing separate messages, we will subsequently be able to add header information to messages, including information such as a list of intended recipients. We develop a `MessageOutputStream` and a `MessageInputStream` to accomplish this goal.

Chapter 17: Queuing message streams   There are times when the processing of a message may actually take a while, and it would be helpful to store the messages in a queue so that the communications layer of an application does not have to wait for the actual processing to complete. In this chapter, we develop a `Queue` data structure class, a `QueueInputStream` to place messages into the `Queue,` and a `QueueOutputStream` to read messages from the `Queue.`

Chapter 18: Multiplexing message streams   A feature that may be useful in many applications is the ability to multiplex independent data streams from different client-side applications down a single network connection. In this chapter we develop a set of streams that use the message stream classes to provide this multiplexing facility. We create a `MultiplexOutputStream` that adds a multiplexing header to each message and a `MultiplexInputStream` that reads these headers. An example of the use of these streams is given in a simple two-person collaborative tool.

Chapter 19: Routing message streams   In this chapter, we develop streams that can route messages to a list of recipients. This additional function greatly simplifies collaborative applications that need the ability to send messages between named clients of a central server. We develop the `RoutingInputStream` and `RoutingOutputStream` classes to serve this purpose.

Chapter 20: A generic message server   In this chapter, we develop a generic server class that uses the library of classes that we have developed so far. Servers written using this class can take advantage of the high level of abstraction it provides, and omit most of the network-related code. This `GenericServer` class can service arbitrary applications; it is not necessary to modify the server if the client changes.

Chapter 21: A generic message client   In this chapter, we develop the corresponding generic client that communicates with the generic server. Network client software written using this class can essentially ignore any networking issues. A simple interface is provided that allows clients to be written with a minimal of effort; these clients register with the `GenericClient` class, and all the network and message stream setup is performed automatically.

Chapter 22: A cryptographic framework   This chapter introduces a simple cryptographic framework that we will use to provide secure, authenticated communications channels. Readers are encouraged to read the corresponding security appendix if they are unfamiliar with cryptographic techniques. We develop a generic `Cipher` template for encryption algorithms and a generic `Hash` template for hashing algorithms.

Chapter 23: Cryptographic streams   The Java streams interface is a very powerful interface for communication. In this chapter, we develop a set of streams classes that transparently apply encryption and hashing algorithms to a byte-stream so we can supply security and authentication beneath any existing streams-based application. The `CipherOutputStream` and `CipherInputStream` classes provide encrypted communications, while the `HashOutputStream` and `HashInputStream` classes provide an authentication and integrity-checking mechanism.

Chapter 24: Encryption algorithms   In this chapter we actually implement some encryption algorithms using the Cipher template. We implement the basic DES algorithm, and then provide the triple-DES and DES-CBC variants that improve the basic security provided by DES. We do this in a generic manner, providing `EDECipher` and `CBCCipher` classes that can apply these strengthening techniques to almost any algorithm.

Chapter 25: Hash algorithms   Hash algorithms allow us to verify the integrity of a communications channel by computing digests of messages; the recipient can verify these digests to ensure that the message is intact. There are several subtle attacks that can be mounted on a secure communications channel; by adding a message authentication code, we can detect these attacks. We provide an implementation of SHS and SHS-MAC to provide these integrity checks.

Chapter 26: Using encryption   This final chapter completes the previous chapters by describing various key-generation techniques. We will use these techniques to produce encryption keys from textual passwords, and will also discuss session keys. A session key is an encryption key that is used only for the duration of a single conversation. If a session key is compromised, then only a single conversation is compromised, restricting the potential damage. We provide an implementation of the ANSI X9.17 standard for session key generation and demonstrate some code to perform user authentication.

chapter 15

Building a simple chat system

Now that we have given an in-depth description of the API, we will begin developing classes and applications that demonstrate its usage. In this chapter, we develop and discuss a multithreaded client-server chat system. This simple example of a client-server system is intended to demonstrate how to build applications using just the streams available in the standard API. In the following chapters, we will develop a set of classes that provide higher level facilities for building clients and servers.

15.1 Building a chat client

We will start with a simple graphical chat client. It takes two command-line parameters—the server name and the port number to connect to. It makes a socket connection and then opens a window with a large output region and a small input region (Figure 15.1).

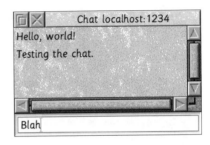

Figure 15.1   The ChatClient interface

After the user types text into the input region and hits Return, the text is transmitted to the server. The server echoes back everything that is sent by the client. The client displays everything received from the server in the output region. When multiple clients connect to one server, we have a simple chat system.

15.1.1 Class ChatClient

This class implements the chat client, as described. This involves setting up a basic user interface, handling user interaction, and receiving messages from the server.

```
import java.net.*;
import java.io.*;
import java.awt.*;

public class ChatClient extends Frame implements Runnable {
    // public ChatClient (String title, InputStream i, OutputStream o) ...
    // public void run () ...
    // public boolean handleEvent (Event e) ...
    // public static void main (String args[]) throws IOException ...
}
```

The ChatClient class extends Frame; this is typical for a graphical application. We implement the Runnable interface so that we can start a thread that receives messages from the server. The constructor performs the basic setup of the GUI, the `run()` method receives messages from the server, the `handleEvent()` method handles user interface events, and the `main()` method performs the initial network connection.

```
protected DataInputStream i;
protected DataOutputStream o;

protected TextArea output;
protected TextField input;

protected Thread listener;

public ChatClient (String title, InputStream i, OutputStream o) {
    super (title);
    this.i = new DataInputStream (new BufferedInputStream (i));
    this.o = new DataOutputStream (new BufferedOutputStream (o));
    setLayout (new BorderLayout ());
    add ("Center", output = new TextArea ());
    output.setEditable (false);
    add ("South", input = new TextField ());
    pack ();
    show ();
    input.requestFocus ();
    listener = new Thread (this);
    listener.start ();
}
```

The constructor takes three parameters: a title for the window, an input stream, and an output stream. The `ChatClient` communicates over the specified streams; we create buffered data streams i and o to provide efficient higher level communication facilities over these streams. We then set up our simple user interface, consisting of the `TextArea` output and the `TextField` input. We lay out and show the window, and start a `Thread` listener that accepts messages from the server.

```
public void run () {
    try {
        while (true) {
            String line = i.readUTF ();
            output.appendText (line + "\n");
        }
    } catch (IOException ex) {
        ex.printStackTrace ();
    } finally {
        listener = null;
        input.hide ();
        validate ();
        try {
            o.close ();
        } catch (IOException ex) {
```

```
      ex.printStackTrace ();
    }
  }
}
```

When the `listener` thread enters the `run()` method, we sit in an infinite loop reading `String`s from the input stream. When a `String` arrives, we append it to the output region and repeat the loop. An `IOException` could occur if the connection to the server has been lost. In that event, we print out the exception and perform cleanup. Note that this will be signalled by an `EOFException` from the `readUTF()` method.

To clean up, we first assign our `listener` reference to this `Thread` to null; this indicates to the rest of the code that the thread has terminated. We then hide the input field and call `validate()` so that the interface is laid out again, and close the `Output-Stream o` to ensure that the connection is closed.

Note that we perform all of the cleanup in a `finally` clause, so this will occur whether an `IOException` occurs here or the thread is forcibly stopped. We don't close the window immediately; the assumption is that the user may want to read the session even after the connection has been lost.

```
public boolean handleEvent (Event e) {
  if ((e.target == input) && (e.id == Event.ACTION_EVENT)) {
    try {
      o.writeUTF ((String) e.arg);
      o.flush ();
    } catch (IOException ex) {
      ex.printStackTrace();
      listener.stop ();
    }
    input.setText ("");
    return true;
  } else if ((e.target == this) && (e.id == Event.WINDOW_DESTROY)) {
    if (listener != null)
      listener.stop ();
    hide ();
    return true;
  } return super.handleEvent (e);
}
```

In the `handleEvent()` method, we need to check for two significant UI events. The first is an action event in the `TextField`, which means that the user has hit the Return key. When we catch this event, we write the message to the output stream, then call `flush()` to ensure that it is sent immediately. The output stream is a `DataOutput-Stream`, so we can use `writeUTF()` to send a `String`. If an `IOException` occurs the connection must have failed, so we stop the `listener` thread; this will automatically perform all necessary cleanup.

The second event is the user attempting to close the window. It is up to the programmer to take care of this task; we stop the `listener` thread and hide the `Frame`.

```
public static void main (String args[]) throws IOException {
    if (args.length != 2)
        throw new RuntimeException ("Syntax: ChatClient <host> <port>");

    Socket s = new Socket (args[0], Integer.parseInt (args[1]));
    new ChatClient ("Chat " + args[0] + ":" + args[1], s.getInputStream (),
        s.getOutputStream ());
}
```

The `main()` method starts the client; we ensure that the correct number of arguments has been supplied, we open a socket to the specified host and port and we create a `ChatClient` connected to the socket's streams. Creating the socket may throw an exception which will exit this method and be displayed.

15.2 Building a multithreaded server

We will now develop a chat server that can accept multiple connections and that will broadcast everything it reads from any client. It is hardwired to read and write `Strings` in UTF format.

There are two classes in this program: The main class, `ChatServer`, is a server that accepts connections from clients and assigns them to new connection handler objects. The `ChatHandler` class actually does the work of listening for messages and broadcasting them to all connected cli-

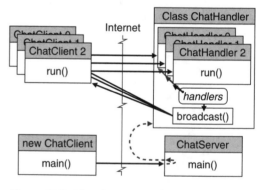

Figure 15.2   The chat system framework

ents. One thread (the main thread) handles new connections, and there is a thread (the `ChatHandler` class) for each client.

Every new `ChatClient` will connect to the `ChatServer`; this `ChatServer` will hand the connection to a new instance of the `ChatHandler` class which will receive messages from the new client (Figure 15.2). Within the `ChatHandler` class, a list of the current handlers is maintained; the `broadcast()` method uses this list to transmit a message to all connected `ChatClients`.

15.2.1 Class ChatServer

This class is concerned with accepting connections from clients and launching handler threads to process them.

```
import java.net.*;
import java.io.*;
import java.util.*;

public class ChatServer {
  // public ChatServer (int port) throws IOException ...
  // public static void main (String args[]) throws IOException ...
}
```

This class is a simple standalone application. We supply a constructor that performs all of the actual work for the class, and a `main()` method that actually starts it.

```
public ChatServer (int port) throws IOException {
  ServerSocket server = new ServerSocket (port);
  while (true) {
    Socket client = server.accept ();
    System.out.println ("Accepted from " + client.getInetAddress ());
    ChatHandler c = new ChatHandler (client);
    c.start ();
  }
}
```

This constructor, which performs all of the work of the server, is fairly simple. We create a `ServerSocket` and then sit in a loop accepting clients with the `accept()` method of `ServerSocket`. For each connection, we create a new instance of the `ChatHandler` class, passing the new `Socket` as a parameter. After we have created this handler, we start it with its `start()` method. This starts a new thread to handle the connection and so our main server loop can continue to wait on new connections.

```
public static void main (String args[]) throws IOException {
  if (args.length != 1)
    throw new RuntimeException ("Syntax: ChatServer <port>");
  new ChatServer (Integer.parseInt (args[0]));
}
```

The `main()` method creates an instance of the `ChatServer`, passing the command-line port as a parameter. This is the port to which clients will connect.

15.2.2 Class ChatHandler

This class is concerned with handling individual connections. We must receive messages from the client and resend these to all other connections. We maintain a list of the connections in a `static Vector`.

```
import java.net.*;
import java.io.*;
import java.util.*;

public class ChatHandler extends Thread {
  // public ChatHandler (Socket s) throws IOException ...
  // public void run () ...
}
```

We extend the `Thread` class to allow a separate thread to process the associated client. The constructor accepts a `Socket` to which we attach; the `run()` method, called by the new thread, performs the actual client processing.

```
  protected Socket s;
  protected DataInputStream i;
  protected DataOutputStream o;

  public ChatHandler (Socket s) throws IOException {
    this.s = s;
    i = new DataInputStream (new BufferedInputStream (s.getInputStream ()));
    o = new DataOutputStream (new BufferedOutputStream (s.getOutputStream ()));
  }
```

The constructor keeps a reference to the client's socket and opens an input and an output stream. Again, we use buffered data streams; these provide us with efficient I/O and methods to communicate high-level data types—in this case, `Strings`.

```
  protected static Vector handlers = new Vector ();

  public void run () {
    try {
      handlers.addElement (this);
      while (true) {
        String msg = i.readUTF ();
        broadcast (msg);
      }
    } catch (IOException ex) {
      ex.printStackTrace ();
    } finally {
      handlers.removeElement (this);
      try {
        s.close ();
      } catch (IOException ex) {
```

```
        ex.printStackTrace ();
      }
    }
  }

// protected static void broadcast (String message) ...
```

The `run()` method is where our thread enters. The first thing we do is to add our thread to the `Vector` of `ChatHandlers` `handlers`. The `handlers` `Vector` keeps a list of all of the current handlers. It is a `static` variable and so there is one instance of the `Vector` for the whole `ChatHandler` class and all of its instances. Thus, all `Chat-Handlers` can access the list of current connections.

Note that it is very important for us to remove ourselves from this list afterwards if our connection fails; otherwise, all other handlers will try and write to us when they broadcast information. This type of situation, where it is imperative that an action be done upon completion of a section of code, is a prime use of the `try ... finally` construct; we therefore perform all of our work within a `try ... catch ... finally` construct.

The body of this method receives messages from a client and rebroadcasts them to all other clients using the `broadcast()` method. When the loop exits, whether because of an exception reading from the client or because this thread is stopped, the `finally` clause is guaranteed to be executed. In this clause, we remove our thread from the list of handlers and close the socket.

```
protected static void broadcast (String message) {
  synchronized (handlers) {
    Enumeration e = handlers.elements ();
    while (e.hasMoreElements ()) {
      ChatHandler c = (ChatHandler) e.nextElement ();
      try {
        synchronized (c.o) {
          c.o.writeUTF (message);
        }
        c.o.flush ();
      } catch (IOException ex) {
        c.stop ();
      }
    }
  }
}
```

This method broadcasts a message to all clients. We first synchronize on the list of handlers. We don't want people joining or leaving while we are looping, in case we try to broadcast to someone who no longer exists; this forces them to wait until we are done.

Within this `synchronized` block we get an `Enumeration` of the current handlers. The `Enumeration` class provides a very convenient way to evaluate every element of a `Vector`. Our loop simply writes the message to every element of the `Enumeration`. Note that if an exception occurs while writing to a `ChatClient`, then we call the client's `stop()` method; this stops the client's thread and therefore performs the appropriate cleanup, including removing the client from `handlers`.

Note that the `writeUTF()` method is not synchronized, so we must explicitly perform synchronization to prevent other threads from writing to the stream at the same time.

15.3 Wrapping up

Multithreading is essential for servers with any sophistication. In this chapter, we have developed a multithreaded broadcast chat server and a simple graphical client. We used data streams to read and write messages in UTF format. Although this certainly makes more sense than breaking everything down into bytes, there is one drawback to this implementation: we can communicate only single `String` messages between clients. If we wish to communicate different information, then we must change both the client *and* the server. This can be a serious limitation when we want the server to perform a more generalized purpose, or when we want to extend the system to handle more than just text. We will look at a solution to this problem in the following chapters.

chapter 16

Message streams

TCP and sockets provide a streams-based communications channel; data arrive in a continuous stream of bytes. UDP, on the other hand, provides a packet-based communications channel; messages are packed into distinct packets for delivery.

In this and the following chapters, we will develop some message streams. Many applications communicate with conceptual packets: a command is sent to a server and a response is received, or an event is sent to a peer. All of these communications are characterized by the fact that the information being communicated is a self-contained unit. A byte-stream communication channel such as that provided by TCP is not necessary for these communications; all that is required is that a self-contained message be delivered.

UDP provides just such a packet-based transport mechanism. However, it is not a suitable transport protocol for most applications because it does not provide the reception guarantees of TCP; packets may be lost, reordered, and duplicated.

In the previous example, we saw how the server could only relay distinct one-String messages between clients. We need this concept of a message *packet* because the client cannot decode an arbitrary mix of data from different messages. If two Strings are written to the client at the same time, then the client will receive garbage. Instead, we must decide on a unit of information to send, or a packet, and use synchronization to ensure that we send individual packets separately.

Limiting the server to just relaying single-String messages is not very practical. The message streams that we develop here will allow us to write complex multiuser networked applications that communicate in units of a *message*, each of which can be an arbitrary volume and format of data.

16.1 Benefits of messages

There are many benefits of encapsulating messages into discrete packets, rather than transmitting a continuous stream of data (Figure 16.1).

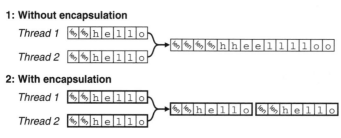

Figure 16.1 Encapsulation simplifies multiplexing

The first benefit is that we can transmit several distinct messages down a single connection, and they can each be extracted independently. Without encapsulation, the server must understand the format of every message so that it can ensure synchronization to successfully transmit distinct messages. This is a particular problem if the client is undergoing continuous development, because the server must keep pace.

Another benefit of encapsulation is that errors in a single message are not extended to affect all subsequent messages (Figure 16.2). Without encapsulation, we are assuming that every message has a particular format, so we cannot recover in the case of one being incorrectly formatted. Encapsulation allows us to extract messages separately, and even if a message is incorrectly formatted, subsequent messages will not be affected.

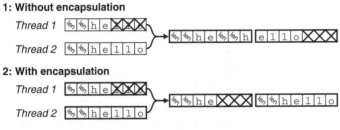

Figure 16.2   Encapsulation protects against errors

Another benefit of encapsulation is that we will always receive complete messages. If a network failure occurs during transmission of a message, then the message will not be partially delivered; instead, the part that was received will be discarded (Figure 16.3). If we trust that our messages will always be correctly formatted by the sender, then we need not worry about errors in messages. If a network failure occurs, then we will simply stop receiving messages; we will not receive erroneous messages. This simplifies applications development because error management can be confined to the application's networking layer; the higher layers can assume a reliable message transport layer.

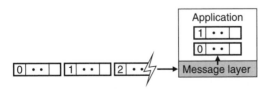

Figure 16.3   Encapsulation hides network failures

16.2 Class MessageOutput

This is the superclass for all message output streams. It is a `FilterOutputStream`; in fact, it extends `DataOutputStream` because the methods of `DataOutputStream` are so commonly required. The `MessageOutput` class therefore provides all the standard methods of `DataOutputStream`, and in addition adds three `send()` methods.

This is an abstract class; actual implementations are provided by concrete implementations that attach to different communications channels.

A message stream operates by encapsulating messages into packets that include a header in addition to the actual message body; it is, in effect, an encapsulation wrapper for a `DataOutputStream`. A message is transmitted only when the `send()` method is called; the data will therefore remain buffered until this time. The `send()` method attaches a header, sends the message, and resets the buffer. The header provides sufficient information for the packet to be extracted from a communications stream and presented at the receiving end as a complete message.

To write a message, you simply use the usual methods of `DataOutputStream`; all of the data that are written to the `MessageOutput` are stored away in a buffer. When you call `send()`, the message will be dispatched with appropriate headers (Figure 16.4). The exact headers that are attached depend on the nature of the message stream and the communications channel.

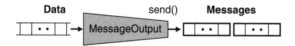

Figure 16.4   Class MessageOutput

In effect, the `MessageOutput` class provides a facility to box data; the `MessageOutput` is itself the box; as you write data into the stream, it is placed in the box. When you call `send()`, the box is closed and shipped, and a new box is opened to accept more data.

```
import java.io.*;

public abstract class MessageOutput extends DataOutputStream {
   public MessageOutput (OutputStream out) {
      super (out);
   }

   public abstract void send () throws IOException;
```

```
public void send (String[] dst) throws IOException {
  throw new IOException ("send[] not supported");
}

public void send (String dst) throws IOException {
  String[] dsts = { dst };
  send (dsts);
}
}
```

This is the definition of the MessageOutput superclass. We extend DataOutput-Stream and so inherit all its methods. The constructor accepts an OutputStream to which we will be attached; this is passed on to the DataOutputStream superclass, so the various methods of DataOutputStream will write directly to the specified stream. Usually this stream will be a ByteArrayOutputStream that buffers the data pending transmission.

The send() methods should transmit the message, along with whatever headers are necessary, to the communications channel for this message stream. No implementation of the normal send() method is mandated and so this class is declared abstract.

The send() methods that take a parameter will be used in a later chapter where we develop message streams that allow us to direct messages to specific recipients. Most message streams do not directly support these alternative methods, and so the default implementation throws an explanatory exception. The send() method that takes a single String parameter simply wraps it up as an array having one element.

16.3 Class MessageInput

This class is the superclass for all message input streams. As per the MessageOutput class, it extends DataInputStream to leverage off the function provided by that class. In addition to the usual methods of DataInputStream, a receive() method is defined.

A message input stream decapsulates messages from a stream and presents them to an application. The receive() method blocks until a complete message has been received, unwraps the body of the message from the header, and then makes the message body available for reading. The message body can be read directly from the Message-Input, using its DataInputStream methods. In the same way that the methods of MessageOutput do not write directly to the communications channel but into a message body, the methods of MessageInput do not read directly from the communications channel but out of a message body.

To read a message we thus call the `receive()` method; this waits until a new message is received. We can then read directly from the `MessageInput` class using the usual methods of `DataInputStream` and these will automatically read from the body of the message that has just been received (Figure 16.5).

Figure 16.5   Class MessageInput

In effect, the `receive()` method receives a message-box from the communications channel, opens the box and makes the contents available for reading. Calling `receive()` again will discard the current box and unpack a new one for reading.

```
import java.io.*;

public abstract class MessageInput extends DataInputStream {
   public MessageInput (InputStream in) {
      super (in);
   }

   public abstract void receive () throws IOException;
}
```

This is the definition of the `MessageInput` superclass. We extend `DataInput-Stream` and declare a `receive()` method. The `DataInputStream` superclass is attached to the stream that is specified in our constructor.

The `receive()` method will block until a message has been received and then allow reading to proceed from the body of the message. No implementation of this method is mandated and so this class is declared `abstract`.

16.4 Class MessageOutput-Stream

This class is an implementation of a `MessageOutput` that transmits messages over an attached `OutputStream`. It is essentially very similar to a `BufferedOutputStream` in that it buffers up all of the data that are written to it and only writes them to the attached stream when the `send()` method is called; this is equivalent to flushing a `BufferedOutputStream` (Figure 16.6).

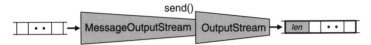

Figure 16.6   Class MessageOutputStream

Before writing the data to the stream, however, the `MessageOutputStream` class attaches a header that indicates the length of the message body data. This allows the receiver to determine in advance how large a message will be, without having to actually parse any of it.

Internally, buffering is accomplished with a `ByteArrayOutputStream`; this class provides an `OutputStream` interface to a dynamically expandable memory buffer (Figure 16.7).

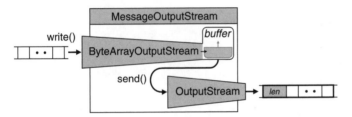

Figure 16.7   Internals of the MessageOutputStream class

This is the simplest concrete implementation of a `MessageOutput` and can be used to provide message transport over any streams-based communications channel, the obvious being, of course, a TCP network connection.

```
import java.io.*;

public class MessageOutputStream extends MessageOutput {
    // public MessageOutputStream (OutputStream o) ...
    // public void send () throws IOException ...
}
```

We extend the `MessageOutput` class and provide an implementation of the `send()` method. We will use a `ByteArrayOutputStream` to buffer messages; this buffer will be written to the stream specified in the constructor when `send()` is called.

```
protected OutputStream o;
protected DataOutputStream dataO;
protected ByteArrayOutputStream byteO;

public MessageOutputStream (OutputStream o) {
   super (new ByteArrayOutputStream ());
   byteO = (ByteArrayOutputStream) out;
   this.o = o;
   dataO = new DataOutputStream (o);
}
```

In this constructor we call the superclass constructor, specifying a new ByteArray-OutputStream to which to attach. All data written to this MessageOutputStream using the DataOutputStream methods will thus be stored in the ByteArrayOutputStream. For convenience, we keep a reference to this in byteO; we take this reference from out, which is inherited from the FilterOutputStream superclass. We attach a DataOutput-Stream dataO to the actual attached stream o; we will use this in the send() method.

Note that we do not attach the superclass to o, so closing this stream will not close the attached stream; it will instead call the close() method of byteO, which will have no effect.

```
public void send () throws IOException {
   synchronized (o) {
      dataO.writeInt (byteO.size ());
      byteO.writeTo (o);
   }
   byteO.reset ();
   o.flush ();
}
```

The send() method transmits the contents of the byte array to the attached stream. We synchronize on o to prevent another message being sent at the same time. We then transmit the length of the buffer, write the buffer to the stream, and finally reset the buffer so that it will begin refilling again. We also flush the OutputStream to ensure that the message is sent as soon as possible.

Note that we synchronize on o and not dataO. The latter is an object local to just this instance and so synchronizing on it would not prevent other classes from writing to o. Most write() methods do not actually synchronize on the stream being written to, so this synchronization really protects us only from other MessageOutputStreams; however, this is all that we require.

This class does not support the targeted send() method, so we inherit its default implementation.

16.5 Class MessageInput-Stream

This class is an implementation of a `MessageInput` that reads messages from an attached `InputStream`. The attached stream should provide a connection from a remote `MessageOutputStream`. When the `receive()` method is called, this class reads a message, as written by a `MessageOutputStream`, and then allows the contents of the message to be read using the usual `read()` methods of the superclass `DataInputStream` (Figure 16.8).

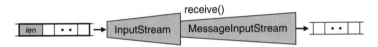

Figure 16.8   Class MessageInputStream

After reception and stripping of headers, received messages are internally stored in a `ByteArrayInputStream`; this provides a convenient `InputStream` interface for reading from an array of bytes (Figure 16.9).

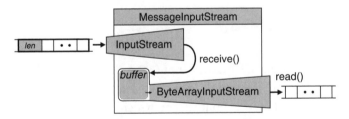

Figure 16.9   Internals of the MessageInputStream class

This is the simplest concrete implementation of a `MessageInput`, and is usually used at the receiving end of a network connection.

```java
import java.io.*;

public class MessageInputStream extends MessageInput {
    // public MessageInputStream (InputStream i) ...
    // public void receive () throws IOException ...
}
```

The `MessageInputStream` class extends `MessageInput` and provides an implementation of the `receive()` method. The constructor takes an `InputStream` parameter from which messages will be read. After a message has been read, the contents will be made available to read using the inherited `DataInputStream` methods of this class.

```
protected InputStream i;
protected DataInputStream dataI;

public MessageInputStream (InputStream i) {
  super (null);
  this.i = i;
  dataI = new DataInputStream (i);
}
```

This constructor is somewhat unusual in that we call the superclass constructor with a `null` parameter. This is because we initially have received no messages, and so have no data to provide from the superclass `read()` methods. If you call a `read()` method on this class without first calling `receive()`, a `NullPointerException` will be thrown.

```
byte[] buffer;

public void receive () throws IOException {
  synchronized (i) {
    int n = dataI.readInt ();
    buffer = new byte[n];
    dataI.readFully (buffer);
  }
  in = new ByteArrayInputStream (buffer);
}
```

This method receives a message from the attached input stream. We first read the length of the message, create a buffer `buffer` to hold it, and then read the whole message. This is all done while synchronized on the input stream, which prevents any other thread from reading from the input stream before the entire message has been read. Finally, we replace `in` with a new `ByteArrayInputStream` constructed from this buffer.

The `InputStream` in is inherited by the `FilterInputStream` class and is accessed by all of the methods of `FilterInputStream`. By reassigning `in` here, we therefore reassign the stream from which the `DataInputStream` methods will read. Any code which reads from this `MessageInputStream` class will thus read from the message that has just been received. Calling the `receive()` method again will discard the old message and start reading from a new message.

16.6 Using message streams

At the very simplest, we can use these streams as buffers. Instead of calling `flush()` we must call `send()` on a `MessageOutputStream`, and to read a buffer we must call `receive()` on a `MessageInputStream`.

```
void sender (OutputStream o) throws IOException {
  MessageOutputStream messageO = new MessageOutputStream (o);
  while (true) {
    messageO.writeUTF ("message");
    messageO.send ();
  }
}
```

The `sender()` method attaches a `MessageOutputStream` `messageO` to the `OutputStream` `o` and sits in a loop, sending messages.

```
void receiver (InputStream i) throws IOException {
  MessageInputStream messageI = new MessageInputStream (i);
  while (true) {
    messageI.receive ();
    System.out.println (messageI.readUTF ());
  }
}
```

The `receiver()` method similarly attaches a `MessageInputStream` `messageI` to the `InputStream` `i` and sits in a loop, receiving messages.

16.7 Class MessageCopier

The `MessageCopier` class is a very simple example of using message streams. The sole purpose of this class is to read messages from a `MessageInput` and write them straight to a `MessageOutput` (Figure 16.10). While this may seem a pointless exercise, we will use it later.

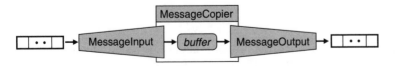

Figure 16.10   Class MessageCopier

Note that because we are relaying between a `MessageInput` and a `MessageOutput`, we could be relaying messages between arbitrary communications channels, with arbitrary headers. The particular classes in use—such as a `MessageOutputStream` and `MessageInputStream`—will take care of the specific encapsulation and decapsulation processes.

```
import java.io.*;

public class MessageCopier extends Thread {
    // public MessageCopier (MessageInput i, MessageOutput o) ...
    // public void run () ...
}
```

This class extends `Thread`; you can create an instance of it, start it, and messages will be copied by a new thread. The input and output streams are specified in the constructor; when the thread is started, the relaying process will begin.

```
    protected MessageInput i;
    protected MessageOutput o;

    static private int copierNumber;
    static private synchronized int nextCopierNum () { return copierNumber ++; }

    public MessageCopier (MessageInput i, MessageOutput o) {
        super ("MessageCopier-" + nextCopierNum ());
        this.i = i;
        this.o = o;
    }
```

Messages are transferred from the `MessageInput` i to the `MessageOutput` o. To maintain useful thread names, we make use of the static variable `copierNumber` and the static method `nextCopierNum()` which returns a unique identifier for each `Message-Copier` instance.

```
    public void run () {
        try {
            copy ();
        } catch (IOException ex) {
            ex.printStackTrace ();
        }
    }

    // protected void copy () throws IOException ...
```

The `run()` method is called when the `MessageCopier` is started (by calling the superclass `start()` method). We call the `copy()` method to actually copy messages from the `MessageInput` to the `MessageOutput`. If the `copy()` method throws an `IOException`, then we display the exception and the thread will terminate.

```
protected void copy () throws IOException {
   while (true) {
      i.receive ();
      byte[] buffer = new byte[i.available ()];
      i.readFully (buffer);
      o.write (buffer);
      o.send ();
   }
}
```

The `copy()` method simply loops, receiving messages on the `MessageInput` `i` and resending them unmodified to the `MessageOutput` `o`. We create a byte buffer `buffer` which is the size of the message body (as returned by the `available()` method). We read the body into the buffer and then write this to `o`.

To use this class, create an instance attached to the requisite streams and then call the `start()` method. A new thread will begin copying messages automatically. The copier can be stopped using the usual thread `stop()` method; however, care should be taken not to interrupt a message in mid transmission.

16.8 A transaction processing example

One of the things that makes these streams unusual is that multiple `MessageOutput-Streams` can be attached to a single `OutputStream`, and multiple `MessageInput-Streams` can be attached to a single `InputStream`. All of the `MessageStreams` will operate correctly together with multiple threads executing concurrently.

This is useful, for example, in a transaction-processing application. Requests may take a long time to process; they may require calling an external database which could take a while to respond. We can start multiple threads to receive messages concurrently; if one thread takes a long time to process the transaction, then the other threads will continue processing requests. Because we encapsulate each message, we do not have to parse the request to determine the start of the next message.

In this example, we develop a simple transaction-processing application. The server contains a `Hashtable` which maps attributes to values (both are `String` values). Clients can query the value of an attribute (`get`) at the server or assign a value to an attribute (put). The `get` and `put` operations are the transactions, and the server utilizes multiple threads to handle them.

16.8.1 Class TransactionClient

This is a very simple graphical client that connects to a corresponding server which we will develop next. It makes use of `MessageOutputStreams` and `MessageInputStreams` to communicate. The user interface presents two `TextFields` and two buttons.

The get button allows us to query the value of an attribute at the server, and the `put` button allows us to change the state of an attribute at the server (Figure 16.11).

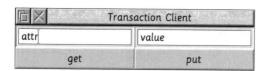

Figure 16.11   The TransactionClient interface

```
import java.awt.*;
import java.io.*;
import java.net.*;

public class TransactionClient extends Frame {
    // public TransactionClient (InputStream i, OutputStream o) ...
    // public boolean handleEvent (Event e) ...
    // public void listen () throws IOException ...
    // static public void main (String args[]) throws IOException ...
}
```

This is a simple graphical client and so we extend the `Frame` class. The constructor accepts an `InputStream` and an `OutputStream` over which to perform the message communications. The `main()` method opens a network connection, creates a new `TransactionClient`, and then calls the `listen()` method to receive messages from the server. The `handleEvent()` method processes user interactions.

```
    protected MessageInputStream mI;
    protected MessageOutputStream mO;
    protected Button get, put;
    protected TextField attr, value;

    public TransactionClient (InputStream i, OutputStream o) {
        super ("Transaction Client");
        mI = new MessageInputStream (i);
        mO = new MessageOutputStream (o);
```

```
        attr = new TextField (24);
        value = new TextField (24);
        get = new Button ("get");
        put = new Button ("put");
        setLayout (new GridLayout (2, 2));
        add (attr);
        add (value);
        add (get);
        add (put);
        pack ();
        show ();
    }
```

The constructor takes an `InputStream` i and an `OutputStream` o as parameters, and performs all communications over message streams that are attached to these. We create a `MessageInputStream` mI, a `MessageOutputStream` mO, and the GUI components, which consist of two `Buttons`, get and put, and two `TextFields`, attr and value. We lay these components out, and pack and show the frame.

```
public void listen () throws IOException {
    while (true) {
        mI.receive ();
        System.out.print ("attr: " + mI.readUTF ());
        System.out.println (" value: " + mI.readUTF ());
    }
}
```

This method loops and accepts messages on the `MessageInputStream` mI. We will be receiving responses from the `TransactionServer` class; every message consists of two strings: an attribute and its value. We print the attributes and values out to the console as they are received. Either receiving a message or reading a `String` may throw an `IOException`, and in this case we just pass it on to the caller.

```
public boolean handleEvent (Event e) {
    if ((e.id == e.ACTION_EVENT) && (e.target instanceof Button)) {
        try {
            if (e.target == get) {
                mO.writeUTF ("get");
                mO.writeUTF (attr.getText ());
            } else if (e.target == put) {
                mO.writeUTF ("put");
                mO.writeUTF (attr.getText ());
                mO.writeUTF (value.getText ());
            }
            mO.send ();
        } catch (IOException ex) {
            ex.printStackTrace ();
        }
    }
    return super.handleEvent (e);
}
```

This method handles user interactions. When the get button is pressed a message is sent to the `TransactionServer`, consisting of the command `"get"` and the name of the attribute; this is the label in the first `TextField`. When the put button is pressed, a message is sent consisting of the command `"put"`, the name of the attribute and a value to associate with this attribute (this is the label in the second `TextField`).

Every time a button is clicked, we write the message and send it. If an exception occurs, we print a stack trace to the console.

```
static public void main (String args[]) throws IOException {
    if (args.length != 2)
        throw new RuntimeException
            ("Syntax: TransactionClient <server> <port>");
    Socket s = new Socket (args[0], Integer.parseInt (args[1]));
    InputStream i = s.getInputStream ();
    OutputStream o = s.getOutputStream ();
    TransactionClient c = new TransactionClient (i, o);
    c.listen ();
}
```

The `main()` method starts a `TransactionClient`. We open a `Socket` to the server specified in the command-line parameters, and extract the input and output streams. We then create a `TransactionClient` attached to these streams and start it listening for server responses.

16.8.2 Class TransactionServer

This class is the transaction server. It makes use of the `MessageInputStream` and `MessageOutputStream` classes to allow multiple threads to concurrently process transactions. A simulated delay is introduced to denote a transaction taking time to complete (Figure 16.12).

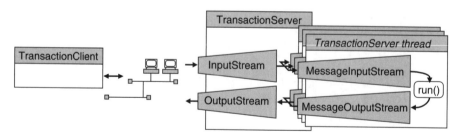

Figure 16.12   The transaction system framework

```
import java.io.*;
import java.util.*;
import java.net.*;

public class TransactionServer implements Runnable {
    // public TransactionServer (InputStream i, OutputStream o) ...
    // public void run () ...
    // static public void main (String args[]) throws IOException ...
}
```

This class implements `Runnable` instead of extending the `Thread` class; we wish to start multiple threads listening for requests to allow multiple transactions to be processed simultaneously, and so must use the `Runnable` interface.

The constructor accepts the streams over which to communicate. The `main()` method accepts a client connection and starts threads that process transactions; each thread enters the `run()` method after it is created.

```
protected Hashtable h;
protected InputStream i;
protected OutputStream o;

public TransactionServer (InputStream i, OutputStream o) {
    this.i = i;
    this.o = o;
    h = new Hashtable ();
}
```

This class communicates over the `InputStream i` and `OutputStream o`, and contains a `Hashtable h` which maps attributes to keys. The constructor performs the necessary initialization.

```
public void run () {
    MessageInputStream mI = new MessageInputStream (i);
    MessageOutputStream mO = new MessageOutputStream (o);
    try {
        while (true) {
            mI.receive ();
            try {
                Thread.sleep (1000);
            } catch (InterruptedException ex) {
            }
            String cmd = mI.readUTF ();
            System.out.println (Thread.currentThread () + ": command " + cmd);
            if (cmd.equals ("get")) {
                get (mI, mO);
            } else if (cmd.equals ("put")) {
                put (mI);
            }
        }
```

```
    } catch (IOException ex) {
      ex.printStackTrace ();
    }
  }


// void get (DataInputStream dI, MessageOutput mO) throws IOException {
// void put (DataInputStream dI) throws IOException {
```

Each thread that is started in a `TransactionServer` enters the `run()` method. Local message streams are created for communication by the thread. Each thread then sits in a loop, receiving messages. After receiving a message, the thread sleeps for a while to simulate processing time. The message is then processed; the command name is read from the message and the message is dispatched accordingly. Exceptions are caught and displayed.

```
void get (DataInputStream dI, MessageOutput mO) throws IOException {
  String attr = dI.readUTF ();
  mO.writeUTF (attr);
  if (h.containsKey (attr))
    mO.writeUTF ((String) h.get (attr));
  else
    mO.writeUTF ("null");
  mO.send ();
}
```

If the command is a get command, then the client is requesting the current value of an attribute. The server responds with a message which consists of the attribute name and value, or `null` if it has no value.

```
void put (DataInputStream dI) throws IOException {
  String attr = dI.readUTF ();
  String value = dI.readUTF ();
  h.put (attr, value);
}
```

If the command is a put command, the client is supplying a new attribute/value pair, which are put in the `Hashtable`.

```
static public void main (String args[]) throws IOException {
  if (args.length != 2)
    throw new RuntimeException
      ("Syntax: TransactionServer <port> <threads>");
  ServerSocket server = new ServerSocket (Integer.parseInt (args[0]));
  Socket s = server.accept ();
  server.close ();
  InputStream i = s.getInputStream ();
  OutputStream o = s.getOutputStream ();
  TransactionServer t = new TransactionServer (i, o);
  int n = Integer.parseInt (args[1]);
```

```
    for (int j = 0; j < n; ++ j)
        new Thread (t).start ();
}
```

The `main()` method opens a server socket on the specified port, accepts a single connection and then closes the server socket. A `TransactionServer` is created, attached to the socket streams. Finally, a user-specified number of threads is started in the `TransactionServer` to handle incoming transactions.

In essence, this is a very trivial database that allows us to insert and look up entries, although in practice it lacks a certain amount of database function. The purpose of the example, however, is to demonstrate how message streams can be applied to a problem that would traditionally be addressed with a basic stream connection.

Making use of the message streams provides us with the benefit that multiple threads can independently utilize a single communications channel. In this case, many threads may be concurrently reading from and writing to the connection; however, the message encapsulation protects us against the problems that we would otherwise encounter with interleaved messages.

16.9 Wrapping up

These message streams are very simple in concept, but also very useful; several variants will be developed later in this book. Many tasks require data to be encapsulated—not usually to allow multiple threads in this manner, but to allow the data to be manipulated and to allow more useful headers to be attached.

The message input and output streams that we have developed here attach directly to existing `InputStreams` and `OutputStreams`, so all message reading and writing involves direct access to the underlying streams. The headers that are attached to messages consist simply of the message length, as that is all the information required to decapsulate a message. In the next chapter we will look at providing an intermediate buffer in the form of a queue. This can provide a layer of insulation from the underlying communications channel, which will provide us with a few benefits, most notably insulation from problems with the communications channel.

chapter 17

Queuing message streams

A queue is a data structure that can store objects using a very simple interface: you can either add an object to the queue or remove an object from it. Queues have the FIFO property (first-in first-out); that is to say, the first object that is added to a queue will be the first object that is removed from it. Objects will thus come out of the queue in the same order in which they are added, much as boxes come off a conveyor belt in the same order in which they were added.

This chapter is concerned with developing a simple queue class and some associated streams that communicate through queues. Messages that are written into a queuing message stream will be placed in a queue for storage; messages that are read from a queuing message stream will be removed from a queue of messages. We will discuss the various advantages of using these queues as we encounter them.

17.1 Class Queue

This class provides the basic queue data structure (Figure 17.1). This queue implementation has one particularly interesting property: if you attempt to remove an object from an empty queue, you will be blocked (suspended) until an object becomes available to remove. A blocked thread will thus wake up when an object is next added to the queue.

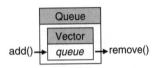

Figure 17.1   Class Queue

There are two significant methods, add() and remove(), which perform the corresponding operations on the queue structure. The elements of the queue are internally stored in a Vector.

```
import java.util.Vector;

public class Queue {
    // public Queue () ...
    // public Object remove () ...
    // public void add (Object item) ...
    // public boolean isEmpty () ...
}
```

The Queue class does not inherit from any other class; it defines the method add() to add an element to the queue, remove() to remove an element from the queue, and isEmpty() to determine whether the queue is empty.

```
    protected Vector queue;
```

```
public Queue () {
   queue = new Vector ();
}
```

Internally, we keep all of the objects in the `Vector` `queue`. The constructor allocates a new `Vector` to store the queue elements.

```
public Object remove () {
   synchronized (queue) {
      while (queue.isEmpty ()) {
         try {
            queue.wait ();
         } catch (InterruptedException ex) {}
      }
      Object item = queue.firstElement ();
      queue.removeElement (item);
      return item;
   }
}
```

The `remove()` method removes an element from the queue, blocking if none is available. This task is fairly simple at first glance; however, it is complicated by multithreading and by the fact that we wish threads to block if the queue is empty. This method first waits for the queue to become nonempty; it then extracts the first element in the queue, removes it from the queue, and returns the item.

To protect against multiple threads accessing the queue at once, we synchronize on the `Vector` of elements before attempting to remove an object. We then sit in a loop which waits for the queue to become nonempty; inside this loop we call `queue.wait()`. This is a very useful method: it causes the current thread to wait until another thread calls the `notify()` method on the queue. In the `add()` method we will call `notify()` when we add an element to the queue, thus waking a sleeping thread. Once we exit the loop, the queue is nonempty and we are also synchronized on it, so no other thread can access the queue. We can then safely extract the first element from the queue and return it.

The `wait()` method is particularly important because it releases synchronization on the queue until the call returns. If this did not occur, then no other thread could add elements to the queue to wake the sleeping thread. To call either `wait()` or `notify()`, a thread must be synchronized on the target object.

```
public void add (Object item) {
   synchronized (queue) {
      queue.addElement (item);
      queue.notify ();
   }
}
```

Adding an object to the queue is simply a matter of appending it to the `Vector` of elements. We then call `queue.notify()`; if threads are waiting for the queue to become nonempty, then this will wake one of them.

```
public boolean isEmpty () {
   return queue.isEmpty ();
}
```

The `isEmpty()` method is simply a matter of querying whether the `Vector` is empty.

17.2 Class QueueOutput-Stream

This class is a `MessageOutput` that, instead of writing messages to an `Output-Stream`, inserts them into a queue that is specified in the constructor. This class extends `MessageOutput` and implements a `send()` method that inserts the message into the queue (Figure 17.2).

Figure 17.2   Class QueueOutputStream

We will use queues and message streams so that we can temporarily store messages in a memory queue; we will build the queue with a `QueueOutputStream` and read messages from it with a `QueueInputStream`.

```
import java.io.*;

public class QueueOutputStream extends MessageOutput {
   // public QueueOutputStream (Queue q) ...
   // public void send () ...
}
```

This class extends `MessageOutput` and implements the `send()` method to place messages in a queue. A `ByteArray-OutputStream` is used to buffer message data. The message queue is specified in the constructor. (Figure 17.3)

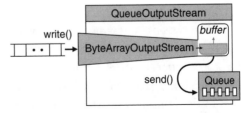

Figure 17.3   Internals of the QueueOutput-Stream class

```
protected ByteArrayOutputStream byteO;
protected Queue q;

public QueueOutputStream (Queue q) {
  super (new ByteArrayOutputStream ());
  byteO = (ByteArrayOutputStream) out;
  this.q = q;
}
```

In the constructor we must first call the superclass constructor; we specify a `Byte-ArrayOutputStream byteO` to buffer the message body. This is the same code that we have seen with the `MessageOutputStream` class. Messages will be placed in the `Queue q`.

```
public void send () {
  byte[] buffer = byteO.toByteArray ();
  byteO.reset ();
  q.add (buffer);
}
```

The `send()` method extracts the current contents of the `ByteArrayOutputStream` and places them into `q`. All the data that have been written to this class will have been stored in `byteO`. Note that there are no headers attached to this byte array; it consists simply of the data that have been written to this class. We know the length of the data because all arrays keep internal counts of their lengths.

Several `QueueOutputStreams` can be attached to a single `Queue`, allowing us to multiplex the results of several threads into a single queue of messages in a coherent manner. This allows, for example, the results of multiple concurrent transactions to be routed into a single queue without mutual interference.

This class has no support for the targeted `send()` method and so inherits the default implementation.

17.3 Class QueueInput-Stream

This class is a `MessageInput` which, instead of reading messages from an `Input-Stream`, extracts them from a queue (Figure 17.4). The queue *must* contain messages in the form of byte arrays; for example, a queue of messages written with a `QueueOutputStream`.

Figure 17.4 ClassQueueInputStream

Calling `receive()` will extract a message from the queue. The caller is then able to read from this message by reading from the `QueueInputStream` using the regular `InputStream` methods. If the queue becomes empty, then calling `receive()` will block until another message is added to the queue.

```
import java.io.*;

public class QueueInputStream extends MessageInput {
   // public QueueInputStream (Queue q) ...
   // public void receive () throws IOException ...
}
```

This class extends `MessageInput-Stream` and implements the `receive()` method. The class is constructed with a `Queue` from which it will remove messages; we will use a `ByteArrayInput-Stream` to permit reading from these messages (Figure 17.5).

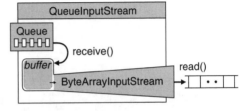

Figure 17.5 Internals of the QueueInput-Stream class

```
   protected Queue q;

   public QueueInputStream (Queue q) {
      super (null);
      this.q = q;
   }
```

In the constructor we must call a valid superclass constructor. The only constructor for `MessageInput` takes an `InputStream` as a parameter. In this case, we pass `null` as a parameter; initially no messages have been received, so no data can be read. Messages will be removed from the `Queue q`.

```
   byte[] buffer;

   public void receive () throws IOException {
      buffer = (byte[]) q.remove ();
      in = new ByteArrayInputStream (buffer);
   }
```

We provide a simple implementation of the `receive()` method that extracts the next message from the buffer and sets the `in` variable of the `FilterInputStream` superclass to refer to a new `ByteArrayInputStream` constructed from this buffer. All subsequent `read()` calls to this stream will read from this `ByteArrayInputStream`, allowing the caller to read from the new message.

In a manner similar to the `MessageInputStream`, several `QueueInputStreams` can be attached to a single `Queue`, allowing several threads to process transactions concurrently.

17.4 Filling a Queue

Queue streams can be used to either queue input coming from a communications channel or to queue output going to a communications channel. Here, we will look at queuing input coming from a communications channel and discuss some of the associated benefits (Figure 17.6).

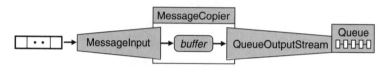

Figure 17.6 Filling a message queue

We will place messages into a queue, and so we will use the `QueueOutputStream` class. The messages which we will be inserting into the queue will be coming from a `MessageInput` attached to some communications channel.

```
void fillQueue (MessageInput from, Queue q) {
   QueueOutputStream to = new QueueOutputStream (q);
   MessageCopier c = new MessageCopier (from, to);
   c.start ();
}
```

The `fillQueue()` method uses the `MessageCopier` that we developed in the previous chapter. We create a new `QueueOutputStream` directed into the specified `Queue q` and then start a `MessageCopier` which copies messages from the `MessageInput from` into the new `QueueOutputStream to`.

This simple method actually has several important uses. Note that several `MessageCopiers` can be attached to a single queue. This allows us to multiplex several message input channels into a single queue for processing. This is helpful because the message processing which occurs on the far end of the queue is entirely insulated from the input to the queue.

Another benefit is that in a real application, the `MessageCopier` thread will be the only thread which reads from the raw `InputStream`. Although several threads may be reading from the queue, these operations will all access byte arrays. As a result, the `MessageCopier` will be the only thread that can experience an `IOException` as a result of a failure in the underlying communications channel (Figure 17.7).

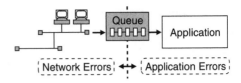

Figure 17.7 The message queue hides input communications problems

We can thus write an application that does not need to be able to handle communications failures occurring wherever a `read()` call occurs. Instead, we can write most of the code to only handle errors of incorrect message formats and other programmer errors, and leave the communications failure handling to a variant of the `Message-Copier` thread which performs appropriate error checking. If an application suite is suitably debugged, message format errors should not occur, and so all of the error handling will be in this one class.

17.5 Emptying a Queue

Here we will look at emptying a `Queue` into a `MessageOutput` (Figure 17.8). Again, we use the `MessageCopier` class to perform the task of relaying messages.

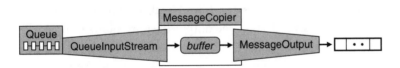

Figure 17.8 Emptying a message queue

We will be extracting messages from a `Queue`, so we will use a `QueueInputStream`. We write the messages out to the specified `MessageOutput`.

```
void emptyQueue (MessageOutput to, Queue q) {
  QueueInputStream from = new QueueInputStream (q);
  MessageCopier c = new MessageCopier (from, to);
  c.start ();
}
```

To copy messages out of the queue, we start a `MessageCopier` that extracts messages from the `Queue q` using a `QueueInputStream from` and inserts them into the `MessageOutput to`.

This is another simple method which has a couple of uses that are similar to those of the previous example. Several `MessageCopiers` can be attached to a single `Queue`. This can be useful when there are multiple streams to a remote host, or if there are multiple remote hosts that can service messages. Multiple streams to a host can help with bandwidth and redundancy if they can be routed through different paths. With multiple streams to different hosts, load can be more evenly shared. Additionally, new requests to one particular host can be delayed until a response to an earlier request has been received, while others can keep going.

The `MessageCopier` thread, again, will be the only one which actually directly accesses the `OutputStream`, and so is the only place where a communications error can cause an exception (Figure 17.9). This means that all output code can essentially ignore exceptions; it is safe to assume that they will not happen. This simplifies application writing because all

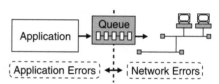

Figure 17.9   The message queue hides output communications problems

exception handling and cleanup can be deferred to a variant of the `MessageCopier`. In particular, an attempt can be made to reopen the connection and no other code need be aware of this; pending transmissions will build up in the queue until a new connection is made or the application decides to terminate.

The queue provides several shielding benefits other than against communications errors. The actual process of transmitting a message down a socket is not instantaneous; network problems may cause significant delays. The output queuing allows us to shield interactive applications from these delays. While the `MessageCopier` thread will delay, the `send()` method of attached `QueueOutputStreams` will always return very quickly because it just needs to shuffle buffers in memory. This is a particular benefit for interactive applications, although one should be aware of buffer sizes and the latency that may occur if they build up.

17.6 Wrapping up

In the previous chapter, we introduced the concept of message streams. In this chapter we have extended this concept to allow us to route these messages through queues; this gives us a very simple mechanism for combining several message streams into one, or splitting one into many. It also allows us to centralize the main error-handling code of our application to shield most threads from delays and errors in the communications channel.

While these message streams allow us to direct several message channels into a single queue, they do not provide any information to assist in reversing this process; it is not possible to determine the origin of a message when it is extracted from the queue. In the next chapter we will develop some multiplexing streams that add additional headers to messages. These headers will allow us to specify the origin of each message in a stream.

chapter 18

Multiplexing message streams

Up to this point, we have been mostly concerned with developing simple message streams that do not add significant function to regular streams. They are, however, a necessary basis for creating a communications library that will make developing tools for serious networked applications considerably easier. In this and the next chapter we develop some useful higher level classes.

This chapter is concerned with the development of message streams that can actually multiplex messages for several applications down a single stream connection in a completely transparent manner. This is achieved by adding a label to the header of every message that indicates the origin of the message.

The purpose of multiplexing is not to route between different clients; we will address that issue in the next chapter. Instead, multiplexing will enable several independent components of a client to communicate down a single network connection. Specifically, an example at the end of the chapter demonstrates how a simple collaborative tool with a white-

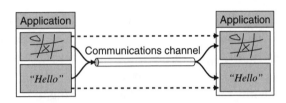

Figure 18.1 Multiplexing two tools down one stream

board and text-based chat can operate across a single communications channel (Figure 18.1). Neither the whiteboard nor the text-chat is aware of the other's existence.

18.1 Class MultiplexOutput-Stream

This class extends `MessageOutput` and attaches to another `MessageOutput`, not a plain `OutputStream`. This lets us multiplex messages down any message stream, whether a `QueueOutputStream` or a `MessageOutputStream`. In effect, this is equivalent to a `FilterOutputStream` which can attach to any underlying `OutputStream` connection; it lets us build powerful communication layers independently of the underlying transport.

This class adds a multiplexing header to the start of every message it sends; all messages sent by this class will thus be sent down the attached `MessageOutput` with a multiplexing label automatically prefixed (Figure 18.2). The multiplexing label is a `String`

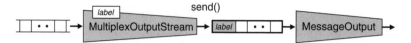

Figure 18.2   Class MultiplexOutputStream

that must be chosen manually and is specified in the constructor, so a `Multiplex-OutputStream` is used only for routing with one specific label.

In essence, we have added a labeling mechanism to the attached `MessageOut`; at the far end of the communications link, this label can be examined to determine the origin of the message.

At the end of this chapter, we will use this class to multiplex several tools down a single connection. A `MultiplexOutputStream` will be used to identify the source of every message—whether it is from a whiteboard or a chat tool (Figure 18.3). At the receiving end, we can examine this label and determine whether to hand the message to the whiteboard or chat tool for processing.

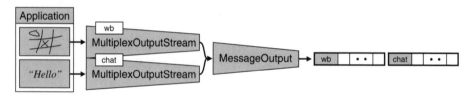

Figure 18.3   Using the MultiplexOutputStream class

```
import java.io.*;

public class MultiplexOutputStream extends MessageOutput {
    // public MultiplexOutputStream (MessageOutput o, String label) ...
    // public void send () throws IOException ...
    // public void send (String[] dst) throws IOException ...
}
```

This class is a `MessageOutput` that attaches to an existing `MessageOut` and adds a routing label to every message; this label is specified in the constructor. We must provide implementations of the `send()` methods.

```
    protected MessageOutput o;
    protected ByteArrayOutputStream byteO;
    protected String label;

    public MultiplexOutputStream (MessageOutput o, String label) {
```

```
      super (new ByteArrayOutputStream ());
      byteO = (ByteArrayOutputStream) out;
      this.o = o;
      this.label = label;
   }
```

In the constructor, we call the superclass constructor and direct all data to be written to a new `ByteArrayOutputStream`. For convenience, we keep a local reference to this `ByteArrayOutputStream` in `byteO`; we keep a reference to the attached `Message-Output` in `o`. The label to be added to messages is specified by `label`.

```
public void send () throws IOException {
   synchronized (o) {
      o.writeUTF (label);
      byteO.writeTo (o);
      o.send ();
   } byteO.reset ();
}
```

The `send()` method sends the message that has been queued up in `byteO`. We synchronize on the attached `MessageOut`, write the header, write the stored message, and then send it using the `send()` method of the attached stream. The header that is added by this class consists of just the multiplexing label; the `send()` method of the attached stream will subsequently attach its own headers.

```
public void send (String[] dst) throws IOException {
   synchronized (o) {
      o.writeUTF (label);
      byteO.writeTo (o);
      o.send (dst);
   }
   byteO.reset ();
}
```

While this class provides no direct support for the targeted send methods, it may be attached to a stream that does support them. We must therefore provide this implementation that calls the appropriate method of the attached stream. If the attached stream does not support targeting, then an exception will be thrown, as usual.

This class is very simple in nature; all it does is write a header at the start of every message. We could obviously do this manually before sending a message; however, this class has the advantage that it is completely transparent to the caller. Indeed, the caller does not know that it is using anything other than a simple message stream.

18.2 Class MultiplexInput-Stream

This is the corresponding input end of a multiplexed stream. The class attaches to a `MessageInput` and extracts the multiplexing header from each message that is received (Figure 18.4). This is the equivalent of a `FilterInputStream`; it adds additional function on top of an existing message stream.

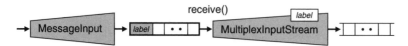

Figure 18.4   Class MultiplexInputStream

The multiplexing label that is read from each message is made publicly accessible to allow the message to be correctly processed.

This class is the delabeling mechanism that lets us examine the origin of each message that we receive (Figure 18.5). We can use this information to determine how to process each message.

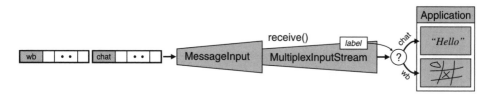

Figure 18.5   Using the MultiplexInputStream class

```
import java.io.*;

public class MultiplexInputStream extends MessageInput {
  public String label;

  // public MultiplexInputStream (MessageInput i) ...
  // public void receive () throws IOException ...
}
```

This class extends the `MessageInput` class and attaches to an existing `Message-Input`. It receives messages from the attached stream and extracts a multiplexing label from each message. The label of each received message is made publicly readable in the `label` variable. We implement the `receive()` method to perform this operation.

The `label` variable will be valid until the next message is received, from which time it will indicate the origin of the subsequent message.

```
protected MessageInput i;

public MultiplexInputStream (MessageInput i) {
    super (i);
    this.i = i;
}
```

The constructor calls the superclass constructor, attaching to the specified `Mes-sageInput i`. All `read()` calls made to this class will thus be passed on to `i`; we make a local copy of `i` for convenience. Reading from this class will thus read from the body of the most recently received message; this is the correct behavior for a `MessageInput`.

```
public void receive () throws IOException {
    i.receive ();
    label = i.readUTF ();
}
```

This method calls the `receive()` method of the attached stream, which accepts the next message from its communications channel. We then read a `String` from this stream; this removes the header that was attached by the `MultiplexOutputStream` that wrote the message. The header is accessible through the `label` variable.

The `MultiplexOutputStream` class operates by inserting a label at the start of every message; we must therefore read this label immediately upon receipt.

This class itself does no actual demultiplexing of the message stream; all it does is to strip off the header that was attached by a `MultiplexOutputStream`. The header is then available to other classes for further processing. We will see next how to use this to actually route the messages.

18.3 Class Demultiplexer

This is an example of a class that extracts messages from a `MultiplexInputStream` and routes them to a `MessageOutput` which is determined by the message label (Figure 18.6). Methods are provided to register and deregister message streams for receiving messages addressed by a particular label.

This is essentially a demultiplexing `MessageCopier`. It completes the set of classes needed to multiplex and demultiplex multiple message streams across a single

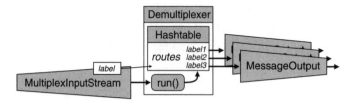

Figure 18.6   Class Demultiplexer

communications channel. The class receives multiplexed messages, takes the label from each message and delivers the message to the currently registered address for receiving messages with that label.

```
import java.io.*;
import java.util.*;

public class Demultiplexer extends Thread {
   // public Demultiplexer (MultiplexInputStream i) {
   // public void register (String label, MessageOutput o) {
   // public void deregister (String label) {
   // public void run () {
}
```

This class is a `Thread`, much like the `MessageCopier`. It attaches to a `Multiplex-InputStream` and maintains a list of routes in an internal `Hashtable`. Destinations can be registered and deregistered with the `register()` and `deregister()` methods. When the thread is started, the `run()` method proceeds to deliver messages appropriately.

```
protected MultiplexInputStream i;
protected Hashtable routes;

static private int plexerNumber;
static private synchronized int nextPlexerNum () { return plexerNumber ++; }

public Demultiplexer (MultiplexInputStream i) {
   super ("Demultiplexer-" + nextPlexerNum ());
   this.i = i;
   routes = new Hashtable ();
}
```

The variable `plexerNumber` and the method `nextPlexerNum()` are used to assign a unique name to each `Demultiplexer` thread. The constructor calls the superclass constructor with that name.

Messages are read from the `MultiplexInputStream i`; the `Hashtable routes` maintain a routing table. This `Hashtable` maps label names to message streams, thus allowing us to easily determine the appropriate destination for a particular message.

```
public void register (String label, MessageOutput o) {
   routes.put (label, o);
}
```

To register a MessageOutput to receive messages with a specific label, we simply place an entry in the Hashtable which maps the label name label to the destination MessageOutput o.

This method replaces any existing entry with the new registration, so only the most recently added destination will receive messages.

```
public void deregister (String label) {
   routes.remove (label);
}
```

Deregistering a label involves removing it from the Hashtable.

```
public void run () {
   try {
      while (true) {
         i.receive ();
         MessageOutput o = (MessageOutput) routes.get (i.label);
         if (o != null) {
            byte[] message = new byte[i.available ()];
            i.readFully (message);
            synchronized (o) {
               o.write (message);
               o.send ();
            }
         }
      }
   } catch (IOException ex) {
      ex.printStackTrace ();
   }
}
```

The run() method is called when this thread is started. We loop, receiving messages from the MultiplexInputStream. For each message that is received, we look up the label in the routes Hashtable. If there is a destination registered for this label, the destination message stream is extracted from the Hashtable, and the message is written to this stream and sent.

Note that if there is no registered destination we simply discard the current message by calling receive() again.

In most common situations involving this class, the destination streams will be QueueOutputStreams that route into an intermediate queue pending processing by a tool. Another useful destination is a DeliveryOutputStream, which we shall look at next.

18.4 Class DeliveryOutput-Stream

Delivering into queues and expecting the client application to be actively trying to receive messages (requiring an explicit receive thread) is sometimes unnecessary for a small application. This class is a `MessageOutput` that actively delivers messages to a recipient. It performs this delivery, calling the `receive()` method of its target whenever a message is to be delivered, instead of writing the message to a stream.

Thus, when a message is sent to a `DeliveryOutputStream` it is immediately presented to the recipient for processing (Figure 18.7).

Figure 18.7   Class DeliveryOutputStream

The cost of using this stream is that the demultiplexing thread must wait for the recipient to process a message before it can proceed with delivering further messages. Also, if the delivery process fails and a `RuntimeException` is thrown, then the delivery thread will terminate. This could be overcome with an appropriate `try ... catch` statement; however, we defer this safeguard to the client.

```
import java.io.*;

public class DeliveryOutputStream extends MessageOutput {
  // public DeliveryOutputStream (Recipient r) ...
  // public void send () ...
}
```

This `MessageOutput` attaches to an object that implements the `Recipient` interface. Messages are intermediately stored in a `ByteArrayOutputStream` and delivered to the recipient immediately upon `send()` being called, using a `ByteArrayInputStream` (Figure 18.8).

```
  protected ByteArrayOutputStream byteO;
  protected Recipient r;

  public DeliveryOutputStream (Recipient r) {
    super (new ByteArrayOutputStream ());
    byteO = (ByteArrayOutputStream) out;
```

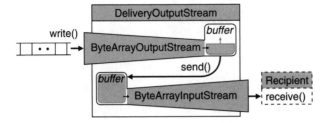

Figure 18.8   Internals of the DeliveryOutputStream class

```
    this.r = r;
}
```

The `Recipient r` will receive messages that are sent to this class. The constructor calls the superclass constructor with a new `ByteArrayOutputStream byteO`; all `write()` calls will thus be directed into this storage buffer.

```
public void send () {
    byte buffer[] = byteO.toByteArray ();
    ByteArrayInputStream bI = new ByteArrayInputStream (buffer);
    r.receive (new DataInputStream (bI));
    byteO.reset ();
}
```

When a message is to be sent we extract it from the `ByteArrayOutputStream` as a byte array `buffer`. We then simply call the recipient's `receive()` method with a new `ByteArrayInputStream` constructed from this buffer. For convenience, we automatically attach a `DataInputStream` to this stream.

18.5 *Interface Recipient*

The `Recipient` interface is a very simple interface that declares a `receive()` method to be called whenever a message needs delivery.

```
import java.io.*;

public interface Recipient {
    public void receive (DataInputStream in);
}
```

The message is delivered in the form of a `DataInputStream` from which the contents can be read in the usual manner.

18.6 A simple collaborative tool

Multiplexed streams can be used to allow multiple tools to communicate down a single communications channel, yet not interfere with each other. As far as any individual tool is concerned, it has a direct message-stream link to a corresponding tool at the far end of the stream.

As an example, we will multiplex two virtual message streams down a single physical connection. We build a very simple collaborative tool with a whiteboard and a text-based chat. We open two frames; the whiteboard of the first tool is connected to the whiteboard of the second tool through a multiplexed message stream; similarly, the text-based chats are attached through a multiplexed message stream. Whatever is written or drawn in the first tool is mirrored in the other, and vice versa (Figure 18.9).

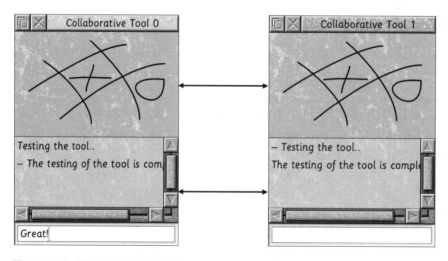

Figure 18.9 The CollabTool interface

The whiteboards and chatboards could each be given different physical connections to the corresponding component on the remote end; however, instead we use `MultiplexOutputStreams` attached to a common carrier. The components are unaware of the fact that they are sharing the communication channel with other components; this is hidden behind the abstraction of a `MessageOutput`.

18.6.1 Class CollabTool

This is the main class that sets up the communications for this example. As described, we create two tools, each with a whiteboard and a chatboard. These tools communicate by multiplexing messages across a single piped stream.

```
import java.io.*;
import java.awt.*;

public class CollabTool extends Frame {
    // public CollabTool (InputStream i, OutputStream o) ...
    // static public void main (String args[]) ...
}
```

This class comprises a single collaborative tool that is a frame that contains a whiteboard and a chatboard. The constructor requires an InputStream and an OutputStream over which the components will communicate; it creates all necessary message streams attached to these. The main() method creates two CollabTool objects that communicate over a pair of connected piped streams.

```
protected static int id = 0;

public CollabTool (InputStream i, OutputStream o) {
    super ("Collaborative Tool " + (id ++));
    Whiteboard wb = new Whiteboard ();
    Chatboard cb = new Chatboard ();
    setLayout (new GridLayout (2, 1));
    add (wb);
    add (cb);
    resize (200, 300);

    MessageOutputStream mO = new MessageOutputStream (o);
    MessageInputStream mI = new MessageInputStream (i);

    cb.setMessageOutput (new MultiplexOutputStream (mO, "chat"));
    wb.setMessageOutput (new MultiplexOutputStream (mO, "wb"));

    Demultiplexer d = new Demultiplexer (new MultiplexInputStream (mI));
    d.register ("chat", cb.getMessageOutput ());
    d.register ("wb", wb.getMessageOutput ());
    d.start ();
}
```

In the constructor for this class, we create a Whiteboard and a Chatboard that will communicate over multiplexed streams attached to the supplied InputStream i and OutputStream o. The communications streams for a single direction are shown in Figure 18.10.

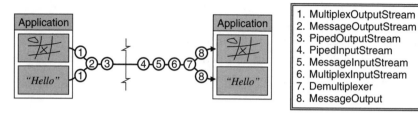

Figure 18.10   The CollabTool communications streams

We first call the superconstructor with an appropriate title for the frame, and then create and lay out the collaborative components consisting of the `Whiteboard wb` and `Chatboard cb`.

We then set up the communications streams; these consist of the `MessageOutput-Stream mO` and the `MessageInputStream mI`, which communicate over the supplied streams `o` and `i`.

We next assign outbound communications streams to the two tools; these are each multiplexed streams that communicate over `mO`. The `Chatboard` is assigned the label *chat*, and the `Whiteboard` is assigned the label *wb*. Every message that is sent by either of these tools will be automatically tagged with the appropriate header before being sent over `mO`. These labels will allow a receiving `CollabTool` to route the messages appropriately.

We finally create a `Demultiplexer d` that processes incoming messages. In this case, both of the tools provide a method `getMessageOutput()` that returns an appropriate message stream to which messages can be sent, so we simply register the appropriate streams and start the `Demultiplexer` to route incoming messages. The `Demultiplexer` examines the label on each incoming message, and simply forwards the message appropriately.

```
static public void main (String args[]) throws IOException {
    PipedOutputStream lO = new PipedOutputStream ();
    PipedInputStream rI = new PipedInputStream (lO);

    PipedOutputStream rO = new PipedOutputStream ();
    PipedInputStream lI = new PipedInputStream (rO);

    new CollabTool (lI, lO).show ();
    new CollabTool (rI, rO).show ();
}
```

The `main()` method creates a pair of piped streams for communicating from the first tool to the second, and vice versa. We then create two `CollabTools` attached to these streams and call their `show()` methods to display them.

In this example, we make no use of Queues. Were it more complex, we might consider using a Queue on the output streams to shield the collaborative components from the communications channel. We will see an example of this in a later chapter.

18.6.2 Class Chatboard

This class implements a simple text-based chat. There is a text output area which displays past messages, and a text input area for the user to enter messages. In the context of the CollabTool class, this will communicate directly with another Chatboard in another frame; in a later chapter, we will reuse this as the basis for a multiuser networked chat application.

```
import java.io.*;
import java.awt.*;

public class Chatboard extends Panel implements Runnable {
    // public Chatboard () { ...
    // public void setMessageOutput (MessageOutput o) { ...
    // public MessageOutput getMessageOutput () { ...
    // public boolean action (Event e, Object arg) { ...
    // public void run () { ...
}
```

The Chatboard is a simple GUI component; we extend the Panel class to be able to contain the text entry and display fields. The CollabTool class will call the set-MessageOutput() method of this class, specifying a message stream over which user messages can be transmitted. Messages that are received from a remote tool will be sent to the message stream returned by the getMessageOutput() method. This stream is a QueueOutputStream that inserts messages into a queue for subsequent processing.

We override the action() method to catch the event that occurs when the user enters a message. We also implement the Runnable interface and provide a run() method that extracts messages from the incoming message queue and displays them (Figure 18.11).

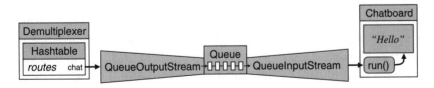

Figure 18.11 The Chatboard communications streams

```
protected TextArea output;
protected TextField input;
protected Queue q;
protected Thread exec;

public Chatboard () {
   setLayout (new BorderLayout ());
   add ("Center", output = new TextArea ());
   output.setEditable (false);
   add ("South",
   input = new TextField ());
   q = new Queue ();
   exec = new Thread (this);
   exec.start ();
}
```

In the constructor, we set up the simple user interface. We create a `TextArea` output that will display messages and a `TextField` input into which the user can enter messages. We lay these out in a simple `BorderLayout` with the entry box at the bottom. We create a `Queue` q for incoming messages, and start a thread `exec` that will extract and display messages that are inserted into it.

```
protected MessageOutput o;

public void setMessageOutput (MessageOutput o) {
   this.o = o;
}
```

This method is called by the `CollabTool` to specify a message stream over which the `Chatboard` can send its messages. As far as this class is concerned, it is simply a `MessageOutput`; the fact that the `CollabTool` class provides a multiplexed message stream is hidden.

```
public MessageOutput getMessageOutput () {
   return new QueueOutputStream (q);
}
```

This method returns a stream that can accept incoming messages. In this case, we return a stream that inserts the messages into q, for subsequent removal by the `exec` thread.

Note that this is just one possible implementation of this method; we will see an alternative that uses the `Whiteboard` class. The advantage of using a queue like this is that, if the processing of a message may take a long time, the `CollabTool` can keep on routing messages while another thread takes care of the slow processing. Obviously this is not the case for this class, but it serves as an example of a possible implementation.

```
public boolean action (Event e, Object arg) {
    if (e.target == input) {
        try {
            o.writeUTF (input.getText ());
            o.send ();
        } catch (IOException ex) {
            ex.printStackTrace ();
        }
        output.appendText (input.getText () + "\n");
        input.setText ("");
        return true;
    }
    return super.action (e, arg);
}
```

This method is called when the user enters a message in the text field input. We send this message over the message stream o, and then append the text to the display region.

```
public void run () {
    QueueInputStream qI = new QueueInputStream (q);
    while (true) {
        try {
            qI.receive ();
            String msg = qI.readUTF ();
            output.appendText ("-- " + msg + "\n");
        } catch (IOException ex) {
            ex.printStackTrace ();
        }
    }
}
```

This method is called by the exec thread and takes care of displaying incoming messages. We attach a QueueInputStream to our queue of messages q and then proceed to extract messages from the queue. For every message that we extract, we read a String and display it.

18.6.3 Class Whiteboard

This is a simple Whiteboard example that provides a surface on which the user can scribble. When the user releases a mouse button, the scribble is transmitted, to be displayed on a remote Whiteboard.

```
import java.io.*;
import java.awt.*;

public class Whiteboard extends Canvas implements Recipient {
    // public Whiteboard () ...
```

```
// public void setMessageOutput (MessageOutput o) ...
// public boolean mouseDown (Event e, int x, int y) ...
// public boolean mouseDrag (Event e, int x, int y) ...
// public boolean mouseUp (Event e, int x, int y) ...
// public MessageOutput getMessageOutput () ...
// public void receive (DataInputStream dI) ...
}
```

The Whiteboard class extends Canvas to provide a basic GUI drawing-surface. The CollabTool class will call the setMessageOutput() method with an appropriate message stream over which we will communicate. We override the mouseDown(), mouseDrag(), and mouseUp() methods to implement the basic scribbling facility.

In this case, unlike the Chatboard class, we will use a DeliveryOutputStream to deliver messages immediately. The getMessageOutput() method returns a DeliveryOutputStream with this as the target; we must therefore implement the Recipient interface, and provide a receive() method that can handle messages as they arrive (Figure 18.12).

Figure 18.12   The Whiteboard communications streams

```
public Whiteboard () {
  setBackground (new Color (255, 255, 204));
}
```

In our constructor we simply choose an off-white background color.

```
protected MessageOutput o;

public void setMessageOutput (MessageOutput o) {
  this.o = o;
}
```

The CollabTool class will call this method with an appropriate MessageOutputStream o over which we will communicate.

```
public boolean mouseDown (Event e, int x, int y) {
  transmit (x, y);
  return super.mouseDown (e, x, y);
}
```

```
// protected void transmit (int x, int y) ...
```

This method is called whenever the user clicks on the Whiteboard. We pass the mouse coordinates on to the transmit() method, which takes care of packaging up a series of coordinates to be transmitted as a scribble to a remote Whiteboard.

```
public boolean mouseDrag (Event e, int x, int y) {
   scribble (x, y);
   transmit (x, y);
   return super.mouseDrag (e, x, y);
}
```

```
// protected void scribble (int x, int y) ...
```

This method is called when the user drags the mouse over the canvas; we call the scribble() method to draw the latest segment onto the screen, followed by the transmit() method to transmit the coordinates.

```
public boolean mouseUp (Event e, int x, int y) {
   scribble (x, y);
   transmit (x, y);
   try {
      o.send ();
   } catch (IOException ex) {
      ex.printStackTrace ();
   }
   return super.mouseUp (e, x, y);
}
```

This method is called when the user finally releases a mouse button; we draw the last segment to the screen with the scribble() method, transmit the last coordinates with our transmit() method, and then actually send the message that we have been building up by calling send(). The scribble is thus only actually transmitted when the user releases the mouse button.

```
protected int oX, oY;

protected void transmit (int x, int y) {
   try {
      o.writeInt (x);
      o.writeInt (y);
   } catch (IOException ex) {
      ex.printStackTrace ();
   }
   oX = x;
   oY = y;
}
```

This method simply writes the coordinates x and y to the message stream o that was provided by the `CollabTool`. As the user drags the mouse on the canvas, the `mouseDrag()` method will be called; this calls the `transmit()` method, so a list of x and y pairs will build up as the body of a message. The `mouseUp()` method calls the `send()` method to actually transmit the message.

As far as this method is concerned, it is writing to a `MessageOutput`; it is unaware that this is actually multiplexed over a common carrier with another tool. The multiplexed channels are completely independent, so the communications of one tool will not affect those of any other. In this case, the user could transmit messages using the `Chatboard` at the same time as scribbling; the `Chatboard` messages would not interfere with the `Whiteboard` messages.

We keep a copy of the most recently transmitted coordinates in oX and oY; we will use these to draw the segment to the screen.

```
protected void scribble (int x, int y) {
   Graphics g = getGraphics ();
   g.drawLine (oX, oY, x, y);
   g.dispose ();
}
```

This method draws the most recent segment to the screen; this is a line between the previously transmitted coordinates oX and oY, and the new coordinates x and y. The `getGraphics()` method returns a graphics context suitable for drawing to the screen; we draw the line and then release the graphics context by calling its `dispose()` method.

```
public MessageOutput getMessageOutput () {
   return new DeliveryOutputStream (this);
}
```

The `CollabTool` class calls this method to obtain a message stream suitable for receiving incoming `Whiteboard` messages. We return a `DeliveryOutputStream` that immediately delivers every message that we receive to our `receive()` method.

```
public void receive (DataInputStream dI) {
   Graphics g = getGraphics ();
   try {
      int x0 = dI.readInt (), y0 = dI.readInt ();
      while (dI.available () > 0) {
         int x1 = dI.readInt (), y1 = dI.readInt ();
         g.drawLine (x0, y0, x1, y1);
         x0 = x1;
         y0 = y1;
      }
   } catch (IOException ex) {
      ex.printStackTrace ();
   }
```

```
        g.dispose ();
    }
```

This method is called whenever a message is delivered for the `Whiteboard`. We read the sequence of scribble coordinates and draw the segments to the screen.

Note that every message that we receive can be treated as a completely separate stream, so the `available()` method will return only the number of bytes remaining in the current message.

In the context of this example, the following events will lead up to this method being called: The remote `Whiteboard` will transmit a sequence of coordinates when the user releases the mouse button. A multiplexing header will be attached to the message and it will be written into the remote `PipedOutputStream`. The receiving `Demulti-plexer` will extract a message from its `PipedInputStream`; it will look up its routing tables and find the appropriate destination stream. In this case, it is a `DeliveryOutput-Stream` attached to the `Whiteboard`. The `Demultiplexer` will write the message to our `DeliveryOutputStream` and `send()` the message; the `DeliveryOutputStream` will then create a `ByteArrayInputStream` from the message and pass it directly to our `receive()` method.

This example collaborative tool is obviously fairly simple. In a more realistic example, each tool would have a whiteboard, a tic-tac-toe game, a text-based chat, and whatever other components would be useful; these could all communicate independently over the same underlying communications channel. Because our demultiplexer supports dynamic registration and deregistration, we can even add and remove components from the tool at runtime.

18.7 Wrapping up

With the addition of the multiplexing streams, we have developed a powerful set of tools for peer-to-peer networked applications. This type of application is characterized by applications communicating with other applications of the same type. In the example given, a whiteboard communicates with another whiteboard, and a text tool communicates with another text tool; similarly, a tic-tac-toe game would communicate with another tic-tac-toe game. The most important characteristic of these applications is, however, that there is a direct link between peer applications. In this case, the link between tools is a multiplexed stream; however, this effectively provides a direct link.

In many cases it is not possible to establish peer-to-peer connections between clients; especially in the context of the Web, where applets can only connect back to the delivering host. In the next chapter we will develop some streams that allow us to route between clients in a peer-to-peer manner, even though the clients are connected only to a single central server. Our multiplexing streams will be able to operate transparently in conjunction with this, so we can use all of these tools across the World Wide Web.

chapter 19

Routing message streams

Multiplexing and message encapsulation are very useful technologies for peer-to-peer interapplication communication. Making the transition from one-to-one communications to one-to-many communications makes them even more useful.

In this chapter we will look at the message stream technology required to shift from one-to-one communications, to server-based one-to-many communications. This consists of routing streams that allow us to specify the recipients of a message, and a server-based router that interprets the routing commands to actually route the messages between multiple clients (Figure 19.1).

In this manner, we will be able to use the multiplexing and message streams that we have developed thus far and apply them to the common situation of multiple users connecting to a central server. This situation is exemplified by the Web, where multiple clients will connect to a single central server to collaborate with each other.

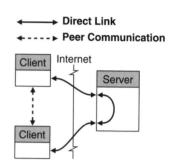

Figure 19.1 Server routing between clients

19.1 Class RoutingOutput-Stream

The streams that we develop here are very similar to the multiplexed streams of the previous chapter. Unlike multiplexed streams, however, the message target is specified when the `send()` method is called and so is not fixed for a particular stream.

When this stream sends a message, a header is attached that specifies the list of recipients. The receiving end must extract this list and route the message accordingly (Figure 19.2).

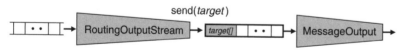

Figure 19.2   Class RoutingOutputStream

At the point of reception and redistribution, the routing list should be removed and the message should be delivered to each specified recipient. Usually a central server will do this, relaying messages to each recipient's network connection.

This class implements the targeted `send()` methods of `MessageOutput`; these allow the recipients of a message to be specified when it is sent. The default `send()` method is a broadcast; the message should go to all users registered at the receiving end.

```java
import java.io.*;

public class RoutingOutputStream extends MessageOutput {
  // public RoutingOutputStream (MessageOutput o) ...
  // public void send () throws IOException ...
  // public void send (String[] dst) throws IOException ...
}
```

The `RoutingOutputStream` class is a `MessageOutput` that attaches to an existing `MessageOutput` and overrides the default implementations of the `send()` methods to attach appropriate routing headers before sending messages to the attached stream.

```java
protected MessageOutput o;
protected ByteArrayOutputStream byteO;
public RoutingOutputStream (MessageOutput o) {
   super (new ByteArrayOutputStream ());
   byteO = (ByteArrayOutputStream) out;
   this.o = o;
}
```

In the constructor, we call the superclass constructor and direct all data into the `ByteArrayOutputStream byteO`. We keep a reference to the `MessageOutput o`; this is used to actually transmit messages when `send()` is called.

```java
public void send () throws IOException {
   synchronized (o) {
      o.writeInt (-1);
      byteO.writeTo (o);
      o.send ();
   }
   byteO.reset ();
}
```

This `send()` method performs a broadcast. We attach a header which consists of the integer -1; this indicates to a corresponding `RoutingInputStream` that the subsequent message should be broadcast. We then send the encapsulated message to the attached stream.

```java
public void send (String[] dst) throws IOException {
   if (dst == null)
      send ();
   else {
      synchronized (o) {
         o.writeInt (dst.length);
         for (int i = 0; i < dst.length; ++ i)
```

```
            o.writeUTF (dst[i]);
        byteO.writeTo (o);
        o.send ();
    }
    byteO.reset ();
  }
}
```

This `send()` method attaches a header to the message consisting of a list of all the target names. If the target list is `null` then we call the broadcast `send()` method; otherwise we send a header consisting of an integer indicating the number of recipients, followed by the names of the recipients. We then send the encapsulated message to the attached stream. Note that we call the undirected `send()` method of the attached message stream; the routing has been handled by this class, and so does not need to be passed on.

This class is similar to the `MultiplexOutputStream` class, except that multiple targets can be specified and the targeting is explicit in the call to `send()`. We can attach another filtered message stream to this; a `MultiplexOutputStream` for example, and the targeted `send()` method of the other stream will call this method, so the routing information will be correctly added.

19.2 Class RoutingInput-Stream

This class is the corresponding routing message decapsulator; it attaches to an existing `MessageInputStream` and extracts the routing header from every message that is received. This routing information is made available to the caller to assist in routing the message correctly (Figure 19.3).

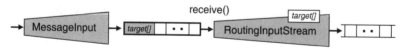

Figure 19.3   Class RoutingInputStream

Like the `MultiplexInputStream`, this class does not perform any actual routing itself; another class must perform this function. We will develop a `Router` to do this, much like the `Demultiplexer` of the last chapter.

Effectively, this class receives messages from a `MessageInput`, takes the recipient list from each message and presents both the message and the list to the caller.

```java
import java.io.*;

public class RoutingInputStream extends MessageInput {
   public String[] target;

   // public RoutingInputStream (MessageInput i) ...
   // public void receive () throws IOException ...
}
```

This class is very similar to the `MultiplexInputStream`; it is a `MessageInput` that attaches to another `MessageInput`. The routing information for each message that is received is made available in the `target` variable.

```java
   protected MessageInput i;

   public RoutingInputStream (MessageInput i) {
      super (i);
      this.i = i;
   }
```

The constructor attaches to an existing `MessageInput` i. All `read()` method calls will thus be passed directly onto i. We keep a local reference to i for convenience.

```java
   public void receive () throws IOException {
      i.receive ();
      int n = i.readInt ();
      if (n < 0)
         target = null;
      else {
         target = new String[n];
         for (int j = 0; j < n; ++ j)
            target[j] = i.readUTF ();
      }
   }
```

When this method is called, we first call the `receive()` method of the attached stream. When this call returns, a message has been received from the underlying communications channel. We then strip off the routing header from the message. If the number of recipients is less than zero, then this is a broadcast and so we set the `target` variable to `null`. Otherwise, we create a new array to hold the recipient list and read the names from the attached stream.

With a `RoutingOutputStream` and a `RoutingInputStream` attached over a communications channel, we have the facility to pass routing information with every message that we send. This can be used to easily implement server-based multiuser applications such as a collaborative environment or web-based chat program.

The setup required to implement such a system is simply to attach a `Routing-OutputStream` to the client's outbound channel and a `RoutingInputStream` to the server's inbound channel. The server will process the routing information to forward incoming messages to the correct targets.

19.3 Class Router

This class is a message copier that receives messages from a `RoutingInputStream` and resends them to the specified message recipients, using an internal routing table.

To perform the server routing we must assign names to each client and register message output streams for each such client name. The choice of names is an application-level issue that is not addressed here; we simply provide a means to register and deregister client names. Typically, clients will choose or be assigned a name when they log onto the system.

This class receives messages, examines the attached recipient list and delivers a copy of the message to each named person (Figure 19.4). If the recipient list specifies a broadcast, then a copy is delivered to each registered client.

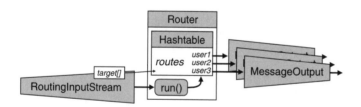

Figure 19.4   Class Router

```
import java.io.*;
import java.util.*;

public class Router extends Thread {
    // public Router (RoutingInputStream i) {
    // public void register (String client, MessageOutput o) {
    // public void deregister (String client) {
    // public void run () {
}
```

This class is a `Thread`, just like the `Demultiplexer` class. Messages are read from a `RoutingInputStream` and routed according to an internal routing `Hashtable`. Clients can be registered and deregistered with the `register()` and `deregister()` methods.

```
protected RoutingInputStream i;
protected Hashtable routes;

static private int routerNumber;
static private synchronized int nextRouterNum () { return routerNumber ++; }

public Router (RoutingInputStream i) {
   super ("Router-" + nextRouterNum ());
   this.i = i;
   routes = new Hashtable ();
}
```

The `nextRouterNum()` method and `routerNumber` variable are used to assign unique names to `Router` threads. The constructor calls the superclass constructor with an appropriate name; we then create a new routing table `routes` and keep a reference to the input stream `i`.

```
public void register (String client, MessageOutput o) {
   routes.put (client, o);
}
```

This method inserts an entry in the routing table for the destination `client`; all messages targeted to this address will be sent to the `MessageOutput o`.

```
public void deregister (String client) {
 routes.remove (client);
}
```

To deregister a client we just remove the entry from the routing table.

```
public void run () {
   try {
      while (true) {
         i.receive ();
         byte[] buffer = new byte[i.available ()];
         i.readFully (buffer);
         if (i.target == null)
            broadcast (buffer);
         else
            multicast (i.target, buffer);
      }
   } catch (IOException ex) {
      ex.printStackTrace ();
   }
}
```

```
// protected void broadcast () throws IOException ...
// protected void multicast (String[] dst) throws IOException ...
```

When the `Router` is started, the `run()` method is called. We loop, receiving messages and routing them appropriately. If the message is to be broadcast then the recipient list will be `null`, and so we call the `broadcast()` method. Otherwise, we call the `multicast()` method with the recipient list. If an exception occurs we exit the loop and display the exception.

```
protected void broadcast (byte[] buffer) {
    Enumeration e = routes.elements ();
    while (e.hasMoreElements ()) {
        MessageOutput o = null;
        synchronized (routes) {
            if (e.hasMoreElements ())
                o = (MessageOutput) e.nextElement ();
        }
        if (o != null) {
            try {
                synchronized (o) {
                    o.write (buffer);
                    o.send ();
                }
            } catch (IOException ex) {
                ex.printStackTrace ();
            }
        }
    }
}
```

The `broadcast()` method simply loops through all clients and transmits the message to the registered `MessageOutput` for each client. This method is complicated somewhat by multithreading.

We determine all the client `MessageOutputs` by getting the `Enumeration` `e` that corresponds to all values in the routing table. While there are more values in `e`, we extract the next `MessageOutput` and send a copy of the message.

We synchronize on the routing table before removing the next element, because another thread could otherwise deregister the last client between our calling `has-MoreElements()` and calling `nextElement()`. This is a peculiarity of the `Hashtable` enumerator. We could, of course, synchronize this whole method on the routing table, but that would tie up the routing table for an excessive amount of time.

```
protected void multicast (String[] dst, byte[] buffer) {
    for (int j = 0; j < dst.length; ++ j) {
        MessageOutput o = (MessageOutput) routes.get (dst[j]);
        if (o != null) {
            try {
                synchronized (o) {
```

```
            o.write (buffer);
            o.send ();
        }
    } catch (IOException ex) {
        ex.printStackTrace ();
    }
}
}
}
```

The `multicast()` method is somewhat simpler. For each recipient in the list, we determine the registered `MessageOutput`, and send a copy of the message.

This `Router` gives us the facility to easily route targeted messages at a server. This routing mechanism builds on top of the existing message streams, and permits the development of fairly complex applications with comparative ease.

This `Router` routes messages only from a single input stream. A server that makes use of this class must either attach one `Router` to every client connection or multiplex all client messages into a single `MessageInput` attached to a single `Router`. In either case, there must be an active reading thread for every client connection.

19.4 Wrapping up

These routing streams allow us to implement complex client/server systems that make use of all of the message stream classes that we have looked at so far.

Implementing an application that consists of distinct components communicating in a peer-to-peer fashion is easier than implementing a monolithic application that has all function operating over a single communications channel. A given component of the peer-to-peer system needs only understand how to communicate with another instance of itself; this simplifies protocols and shields different components from failures within each other.

The most common problem with peer-to-peer applications is that it is frequently not possible for applications to directly peer. In some cases, such as the Web, it is not possible for clients to directly connect. Even where this is possible, there is a problem with the massive number of peer connections required. A small system with ten clients would require forty-five connections for every client to have a direct connection to every other client.

The routing streams which we have just developed allow us to write applications that operate in a peer-to-peer fashion, despite the fact that they are operating in a client/server environment. This is a powerful facility, which we shall use in the following chapters to develop a generic client and server system for easy development of collaborative applications.

chapter 20

A generic message server

At the start of this part of the book, we developed a simple chat system with a multi-threaded server, using classes available in the API. The application had limitations, however, that can be removed by using the message streams that we have developed in the subsequent chapters. In particular, the server required knowledge of the format of client messages; in the example, they were simply UTF-format strings.

In this chapter, we build a generic server that uses these message stream classes. The message streams abstract specific message formats into a generic *message*, which has the significant consequence that one server can serve arbitrary clients; the server needs no knowledge of particular client message formats, and can rely simply on the message streams encapsulation. We make use of queuing streams to buffer data to clients, and routing streams to accomplish routing between clients.

The result is a much more sophisticated server. In the next chapter, we will develop the generic client to use with this server. Together, these classes can effectively form the networking layer for many different applications.

20.1 Class GenericServer

The server follows the same model of multithreading that the simple chat server used earlier. There are two classes; the main server is GenericServer, which accepts connections from clients and creates a new handler for each one. It also keeps a list of all currently connected clients (Figure 20.1). The handler, GenericHandler, does all the work of processing client communications.

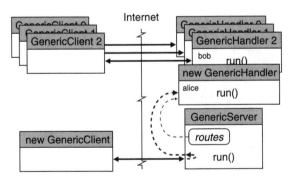

Figure 20.1 The GenericServer framework

```
import java.io.*;
import java.net.*;
import java.util.Hashtable;
```

```
public class GenericServer extends Thread {
  // public GenericServer (int port) throws IOException...
  // public void run () ...
  // public static void main (String args[]) throws IOException ...
}
```

The GenericServer class is a Thread that is responsible for accepting new connections from clients. The port that it listens on is specified in the constructor; a ServerSocket begins listening on this port, and when the thread is started the run() method takes care of accepting new connections.

```
protected ServerSocket s;
protected Hashtable routes;

public GenericServer (int port) throws IOException {
  super ("GenericServer");
  s = new ServerSocket (port);
  routes = new Hashtable ();
}
```

The constructor for the server is fairly simple. We call the superclass constructor with an appropriate name for the thread, create a ServerSocket s that listens on the specified port port, and then create the Hashtable routes. This Hashtable is used by client handlers to maintain a registry of the users currently connected to the server.

```
public void run () {
  try {
    while (true) {
      Socket socket = s.accept ();
      GenericHandler handler = new GenericHandler (routes,
        socket.getInputStream (), socket.getOutputStream ());
      handler.start ();
    }
  } catch (IOException ex) {
    ex.printStackTrace ();
  }
}
```

We follow the same basic multithreaded model as in the simple chat server; the main server sits in a loop accepting connections, and creates a new handler for each client. These handlers execute in separate threads and handle all client communications.

```
public static void main (String args[]) throws IOException {
  if (args.length != 1)
    throw new IOException ("Syntax: GenericServer <port>");
  GenericServer server = new GenericServer (Integer.parseInt (args[0]));
  server.start ();
}
```

The `main()` method takes a port number as a command line argument. It creates a new server that will accept client connections to this port, and starts the server thread.

20.2 Class GenericHandler

The `GenericHandler` class is responsible for handling client connections. When a client connects to the server, a new `GenericHandler` is created to process the client (Figure 20.2). The client initially transmits its username and then proceeds to communicate using the standard message stream methods.

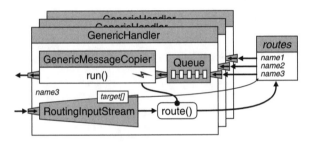

Figure 20.2   Class GenericHandler

The client's handler verifies that the username is not currently in use, and then proceeds to relay messages from the client to the other connected users.

We keep the communications generalized by using the message streams developed in previous chapters, so the handlers need not have knowledge of exactly what comprises the messages that they are passing.

```
import java.io.*;
import java.util.*;
public class GenericHandler extends Thread {
  // public GenericHandler (Hashtable routes, InputStream i,
    OutputStream o) ...
  // public void run () ...
}
```

The `GenericHandler` class extends `Thread` in order that client messages can be processed in a separate thread to the main server. The constructor accepts the streams over which to communicate, and a `Hashtable routes` that will be used to maintain a registry of the currently connected users.

```
  protected Hashtable routes;
  protected InputStream i;
  protected OutputStream o;
```

```
static private int handlerNumber;
static private synchronized int nextHandlerNum () { return
  handlerNumber ++; }

public GenericHandler (Hashtable routes, InputStream i, OutputStream o) {
  super ("GenericHandler-" + nextHandlerNum ());
  this.routes = routes;
  this.i = i;
  this.o = o;
}
```

The constructor takes three parameters. The first is a reference to the server's routing table `routes`, the other two are the streams `i` and `o` attached to the client socket; these are created by the server when the client is accepted.

```
protected String name;

public void run () {
  try {
    DataInputStream dI = new DataInputStream (i);
    name = dI.readUTF ();
    accept (name);
  } catch (IOException ex) {
    ex.printStackTrace ();
  } finally {
    try {
      o.close ();
    } catch (IOException ex) {
      ex.printStackTrace ();
    }
  }
}

// protected void accept (String name) throws IOException ...
```

The `run()` method is called when the handler thread is started, and is responsible for accepting a client connection, verifying the name and relaying client messages.

We first read the client's name `name` from the `InputStream`; note that this occurs before the message streams are set up, and so is performed with the usual `DataInputStream` class. After reading the name, we call the `accept()` method that accepts the connection and processes client messages.

We surround the body of this code with a `try ... catch ... finally` clause that displays any `IOExceptions` that occur, and ensures that the socket connection is closed when this thread terminates.

```
protected MessageOutput myself;

protected void accept (String name) throws IOException {
  Queue q = new Queue ();
  boolean registered = true;
```

```
    synchronized (routes) {
      if (routes.containsKey (name))
        registered = false;
      else
        routes.put (name, myself = new QueueOutputStream (q));
    }
    try {
      new DataOutputStream (o).writeBoolean (registered);
      o.flush ();
      if (registered)
        execute (q);
    } finally {
      if (registered)
        routes.remove (name);
    }
  }

  // protected void execute (Queue q) throws IOException ...
```

This method is responsible for verifying that the client's name is not in use and routing client messages.

We first create a `Queue` `q` that will hold messages that are to be delivered to the client. Other clients will write messages into this queue, and a separate thread will be responsible for actually delivering these messages to the client.

We synchronize on the `routes` `Hashtable` and check to see whether the username is currently in use. If the name is in use, then we set the `registered` flag to `false`; we otherwise insert the client into the `Hashtable`. What we actually insert into the `Hashtable` is a `QueueOutputStream` that places messages into the client's `Queue` `q`, pending actual delivery. We keep a reference to this in the variable `myself`; we will later use this to ensure that the client does not send messages back to itself.

We next write a `boolean` value to the client, indicating whether registration was successful (whether the name was accepted). Again, we use a plain `DataOutputStream` for this operation. If registration was successful, then we call the `execute()` method to relay client messages; we otherwise just exit the method. We use a `try ... finally` clause to ensure that the client is deregistered when the `execute()` method terminates, regardless of how this occurs. This ensures that no other handlers will try to send us messages after we leave, and that we do not leave a stale client name in `routes`.

In the earlier chapter on queues, we saw that one reason to use a queue is that it insulates the sender from the actual output stream. In this case, when one client is sending a message to another client, it won't have to deal with problems with the second client's network connection. Each client is responsible for forwarding its own messages from the queue to the output stream, so if there is a problem with a network connection, only that client is affected.

```
protected void execute (Queue q) throws IOException {
  MessageInput qI = new QueueInputStream (q);
  MessageOutput mO = new MessageOutputStream (o);
  GenericMessageCopier c = new GenericMessageCopier (this, qI, mO);
  try {
    c.start ();
    route ();
  } finally {
    c.stop ();
  }
}
```

The `execute()` method is run after the client has been successfully registered with the server, and is responsible for processing messages from the client, as well as relaying messages to it.

We create a `QueueInputStream` qI that reads from the client's outbound `Queue` q, and a `MessageOutputStream` mO that writes to the client's network connection. We then start a `GenericMessageCopier` c that relays messages from the `Queue` to the client. This `GenericMessageCopier` c will thus transmit the messages that are inserted by other clients of the server. We start the `GenericMessageCopier` thread and call the `route()` method to process messages from the client.

Again, we use a `finally` clause to perform cleanup when the `route()` method terminates; in this case, this requires stopping the `GenericMessageCopier` thread. Note that we have several nested layers of `try ... finally` clauses leading up to this point. The `run()` method ensures that we close the network connection when client processing finishes; the `accept()` method ensures that we deregister the client if appropriate, and this method ensures that we stop the `GenericMessageCopier`.

```
protected void route () throws IOException {
  MessageInputStream mI = new MessageInputStream (i);
  RoutingInputStream rI = new RoutingInputStream (mI);
  while (true) {
    rI.receive ();
    byte[] buffer = new byte[rI.available ()];
    rI.readFully (buffer);
    if (rI.target == null)
      broadcast (buffer);
    else
      multicast (rI.target, buffer);
  }
}

// protected void broadcast (byte[] buffer) throws IOException ...
// protected void multicast (String[] dst, byte[] buffer) throws
//      IOException ...
```

The `route()` method is responsible for processing messages from the client. This consists of determining whether a message is to be broadcast to all clients or multicast to a selected list. We create a `MessageInputStream mI` attached to the client's Input-Stream `i`. We attach a `RoutingInputStream rI` to this that will strip the routing list from incoming messages; we then sit in a loop waiting for messages to arrive.

We accept messages with a call to the `receive()` method of `rI`. We then check to see if there is a target list associated with the routing stream. If there is no list, we call the `broadcast()` method to pass the message along to all the clients; otherwise, there is a list of targets, and we call the `multicast()` method to pass the message to just those named clients.

```
protected void broadcast (byte[] buffer) throws IOException {
   Enumeration e = routes.elements ();
   while (e.hasMoreElements ()) {
      MessageOutput o = null;
      synchronized (routes) {
         if (e.hasMoreElements ())
            o = (MessageOutput) e.nextElement ();
      }
      send (buffer, o);
   }
}

// protected void send (byte[] buffer, MessageOutput o) throws
      IOException ...
```

The `broadcast()` method is responsible for sending messages to all clients in the `routes` Hashtable.

We get an `Enumeration e` of the members of the `Hashtable`. We extract each client's `MessageOutput` from this `Enumeration`, and send the message using our `send()` method.

Remember that when a client registers with the `routes Hashtable`, we map its name to a `QueueOutputStream`. This output stream is therefore available to receive messages from all clients. When we write a message into a client's `Queue`, it will eventually be picked up by the client's `GenericMessageCopier`, which will actually deliver the message to the network.

```
protected void multicast (String[] dst, byte[] buffer) throws IOException {
   for (int j = 0; j < dst.length; ++ j) {
      MessageOutput o = (MessageOutput) routes.get (dst[j]);
      send (buffer, o);
   }
}
```

The `multicast()` method is called when the routing output stream contains a list of targets. This method simply sends the message to every client named in the array `dst`.

This method is simpler than the `broadcast()` method; we can simply loop through all of the elements of the target list and send the message to the corresponding `MessageOutput`.

```
protected void send (byte[] buffer, MessageOutput o) throws IOException {
   if ((o != null) && (o != myself)) {
      synchronized (o) {
         o.write (buffer);
         o.send ();
      }
   }
}
```

The `send()` method writes the message in the buffer `buffer` to the specified `MessageOutput` o. We ensure that o is not `null`, and is not `myself`; this protects against sending any client's messages back to itself. We then synchronize on o and send the message.

20.3 Class GenericMessage-Copier

The `MessageCopier` class which was developed in the message streams chapter is used when we want to relay messages from a `MessageInput` to a `MessageOutput`. Typically, it relays messages from a `Queue` to a network connection, thereby shielding clients from interacting with the actual network.

The `GenericMessageCopier` class is an extension to the `MessageCopier` class that has a small amount of error-recovery capability built in. The constructor accepts a reference to another thread in addition to the raw message streams. If an exception is encountered while relaying messages to the client, the other thread is stopped (Figure 20.3).

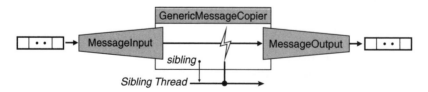

Figure 20.3   Class GenericMessageCopier

In the case of the GenericHandler class, this will cause the main routing method to terminate and so all appropriate cleanup and deregistration will occur. This allows us to handle network problems in a very clean and simple manner.

```
import java.io.*;

public class GenericMessageCopier extends MessageCopier {
    // public GenericMessageCopier (Thread sibling, MessageInput i,
        MessageOutput o) ...
    // public void run () ...
}
```

We extend the MessageCopier class and provide a constructor that accepts a Thread parameter sibling to be stopped should an exception be encountered. The run() method will relay messages from the MessageInput i to the MessageOutput o.

```
    protected Thread sibling;

    public GenericMessageCopier (Thread sibling, MessageInput i,
        MessageOutput o) {
      super (i, o);
      this.sibling = sibling;
    }
```

The constructor takes three parameters; a Thread sibling, to be stopped in the case of an exception, and the two message streams i and o. We pass the streams to the superclass constructor.

```
    public void run () {
      try {
        copy ();
      } catch (IOException ex) {
        ex.printStackTrace ();
        sibling.stop ();
      }
    }
```

In the run() method, we simply call the copy() method that is inherited from the superclass. The copy() method loops, reading messages in from i and writing them out to o. In the case of an IOException, we print the exception's stack trace and then stop the Thread sibling. Note that this is not a finally clause, so if the MessageCopier thread is explicitly stopped, then this clause will not be executed.

20.4 Wrapping up

Alone, this server does not serve much purpose. It demonstrates the use of the message stream classes and some robust error-handling; however, above and beyond this it is nothing more than a router. The purpose of this server is, however, just that: it is a generic framework for a collaboration server that can serve arbitrary clients who communicate using message streams.

In the next chapter, we will look at a `GenericClient` class that complements this server. It provides a framework for client applications that can connect to a central `GenericServer` and then communicate with each other using the message stream classes. The goal of the `GenericServer` and `GenericClient` classes is to remove all need to handle low-level networking issues from applications development. Instead, development can focus on application-level protocols and important issues of function rather than implementation.

As it stands, the `GenericServer` class can serve arbitrary client applications without a need for modification. At the end of the next chapter, however, some extensions are proposed to provide additional function.

chapter 21

Building a generic client

In the previous chapter we developed a server that performs message routing between named clients. Because the message stream classes encapsulate data inside a generic message, the server can route data in a manner that is independent of the actual clients. We can thus use the unmodified GenericServer class as a router for many different client applications.

In this chapter we will develop the corresponding GenericClient class that provides a foundation for a wide variety of different client applications. The Generic-Client class performs the initial network connection and stream setup. User-created clients must implement a Client interface; they can then register with the Generic-Client class and communicate with other users through a central server.

Registering a tool with the GenericClient establishes outbound and incoming message streams that are automatically multiplexed across the connection to the server. Using these streams, tools can communicate through the server in a peer-to-peer fashion, independently of any other tools that may also be communicating through the server.

An example of the use of these classes is provided at the end of the chapter in the form of a networked chat program. The chat provides both text-based chat facility and a crude whiteboard, but the features can be easily upgraded by simply registering new components to the GenericClient framework.

21.1 Class GenericClient

This class performs the network and stream setup for any client that wishes to communicate through a GenericServer (Figure 21.1). Upon creation, it opens a socket

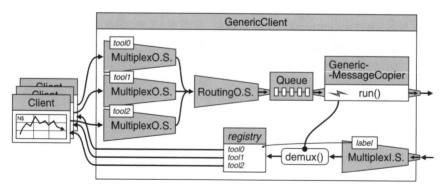

Figure 21.1   Class GenericClient

connection to the specified server and attempts to register a requested username. If the connection attempt is successful, client tools can be registered and will obtain streams for communication. If unsuccessful, then an exception will be thrown. Other than the usual exceptions that can occur during a network setup (*Connection refused*, etc.) a *Name in use* IOException will be thrown if the server refuses the requested name.

Incoming messages are delivered through the Client interface, and a Queue is used to buffer all outbound communications. If a communications exception occurs, then only the part of the GenericClient that is transferring messages from the Queue to the network connection will be affected, and so the GenericClient can shut down gracefully. As a result, client tools can essentially ignore all IOExceptions that may occur when writing out data. If a connection breaks, then all clients will be notified through the Client interface and can terminate normally.

This class is similar to the Demultiplexer class that we looked at earlier. Where it differs is that it will itself perform the network connection setup, and instead of registering message streams to accept the demultiplexed messages you must register Clients. The GenericClient can thus provide more function for the clients, including the assignment of message output streams and notification of broken connections.

```
import java.io.*;
import java.net.*;
import java.util.*;

public class GenericClient extends Thread {
    // public GenericClient (String hostName, int hostPort, String name) throws
        IOException ...
    // public void run () ...
    // public void register (String mx, Client c) ...
    // public void deregister (String mx) ...
}
```

We extend the Thread class; this allows us to perform the stream demultiplexing in a separate thread to the caller. The server address and client username are specified in the constructor. When this Thread is started, the run() method will be called, and this will proceed to demultiplex incoming messages.

Client tools can be registered and deregistered with the register() and deregister() methods. A String identifier must be provided for the multiplexing streams; each tool should be assigned an appropriate name. This will allow messages to be transparently routed to the peer tools of other clients connected to the server.

```
    protected Queue q;
    protected Hashtable registry;
    protected MessageOutput messageO;

    static private int clientNumber;
```

```
static private synchronized int nextClientNum () { return clientNumber ++; }

public GenericClient (String hostName, int hostPort, String name) throws
    IOException {
    super ("GenericClient-" + nextClientNum ());
    connect (hostName, hostPort);
    logon (name); registry = new Hashtable ();
    q = new Queue ();
    QueueOutputStream qO = new QueueOutputStream (q);
    messageO = new RoutingOutputStream (qO);
}

// protected void connect (String hostName, int hostPort) throws
//     IOException ...
// protected void logon (String name) throws IOException ...
```

Creating a `GenericClient` performs all of the network connection and streams setup to prepare for clients to register (Figure 21.2). We first call the superclass constructor with an appropriate thread name; this is not usually necessary, but is sometimes useful for debugging. We then connect to the specified host using the `connect()` method; this may throw an `IOException` if the server cannot be reached. We then attempt to register our username using the `logon()` method; this may throw an `IOException` if either the network connection fails or the username is already in use.

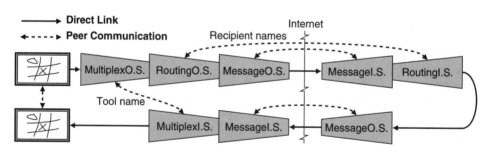

Figure 21.2 Streams within the GenericClient/Server framework

At this point if an exception has not been thrown, then we have successfully connected to the server. We create a new `Hashtable registry`; this will map from the multiplex labels to registered client tools. We create a new `Queue q` to hold outgoing messages and a `RoutingOutputStream messageO` that writes routed messages into `q`.

Every client that registers to the server will receive a stream that multiplexes down `messageO`, so their messages will enter `q` for subsequent delivery. Because `messageO` is a `RoutingOutputStream`, the clients will be able to use the targeted `send()` methods to route messages to specific users.

```
protected InputStream i;
protected OutputStream o;

protected void connect (String hostName, int hostPort) throws IOException {
   Socket s = new Socket (hostName, hostPort);
   i = s.getInputStream ();
   o = s.getOutputStream ();
}
```

This method attempts to open a connection to the server residing on the specified port hostPort of the specified host hostName. If a problem arises, then an exception will be thrown; otherwise we extract an InputStream i and an OutputStream o over which to communicate.

```
protected void logon (String name) throws IOException {
   try {
      DataOutputStream dO = new DataOutputStream (o);
      dO.writeUTF (name);
      dO.flush ();
      DataInputStream dI = new DataInputStream (i);
      boolean registered = dI.readBoolean ();
      if (!registered)
         throw new IOException ("Name in use");
   } catch (IOException ex) {
      try {
         o.close ();
      } catch (IOException ex2) {
      }
      throw ex;
   }
}
```

This method attempts to log onto the server using the specified name name. We write the name to the server with a DataOutputStream and await a response with a DataInputStream. The server responds with a boolean value; if false is returned, then the requested name is already in use, and so we throw an appropriate exception.

We surround the body of this method with a try ... catch clause to ensure that we close the server connection if there is a problem. If an IOException arises, then we close the server connection (ignoring any exception that this may cause) and re-throw the original exception. Thus, we will close the server connection if there is a problem writing to or reading from the server, or if the name is already in use.

```
public void run () {
   QueueInputStream qI = new QueueInputStream (q);
   MessageOutputStream mO = new MessageOutputStream (o);
   GenericMessageCopier c = new GenericMessageCopier (this, qI, mO);
   try {
      c.start ();
      demux ();
```

```
      } catch (IOException ex) {
        ex.printStackTrace ();
      } finally {
        c.stop ();
        closedown ();
      }
    }

  // protected void demux () throws IOException ...
  // protected void closedown () ...
```

A new thread enters here when the `start()` method is called. This thread is responsible for demultiplexing the messages that arrive in from the server. We first set up a thread that relays messages from the message queue q out through the network connection to the server.

We attach a `QueueInputStream qI` to q; this lets us read messages from the internal queue. We then attach a `MessageOutputStream mO` to o; this lets us write messages out to the server. We then create a new `GenericMessageCopier` that reads messages from `qI` and writes them out to `mO`; the `GenericMessageCopier` will thus take all client messages and actually send them to the server.

The main body of this method starts the `GenericMessageCopier` c and subsequently proceeds to demultiplex messages that arrive in from the server.

We surround this body with a `try ... catch ... finally` clause that lets us clean up if a problem is encountered. If an `IOException` is encountered in this thread (the demultiplexer) then we display the exception, and the `finally` clause will be executed to shut down. If an `IOException` is encountered in the `GenericMessageCopier` thread, then it will stop this thread, which will also cause the `finally` clause to be executed. Remember that the `GenericMessageCopier` class takes a reference to another thread that it should stop if it encounters a problem.

We are thus guaranteed that if a problem is encountered with the network connection, then our `finally` clause will be executed. We first stop the `GenericMessage-Copier` thread and then call the `closedown()` method to close the client down.

If a client wishes to manually close the connection, then all it need do is call this thread's `stop()` method. Doing so will cause the `finally` clause to be executed and the connection to be shut down.

```
  protected void demux () throws IOException {
    MessageInputStream mI = new MessageInputStream (i);
    MultiplexInputStream xI = new MultiplexInputStream (mI);
    while (true) {
      xI.receive ();
      Client c = (Client) registry.get (xI.label);
      if (c != null) {
        try {
```

```
            c.receive (new DataInputStream (xI));
        } catch (RuntimeException ex) {
            ex.printStackTrace ();
        }
    }
  }
}
```

This method performs the demultiplexing of incoming messages. We attach a `MessageInputStream` mI to i; this lets us read messages that are relayed to us by the server. We attach a `MultiplexInputStream` xI to mI to strip the multiplexing headers that were attached by another `GenericClient`. Note that routing headers from the `RoutingOutputStream` will have been stripped by the server, and so we will receive messages with just the multiplexing header attached.

The body of this method consists of receiving messages from xI and determining the appropriate target by looking up the multiplexing label in `registry`. If a client tool has been registered for the message target then we pass the message on to its `receive()` method for appropriate processing. If the client expects to process messages quickly, then it can process the message immediately; otherwise, it would be appropriate for it to place messages in a queue for processing in a separate thread (Figure 21.3).

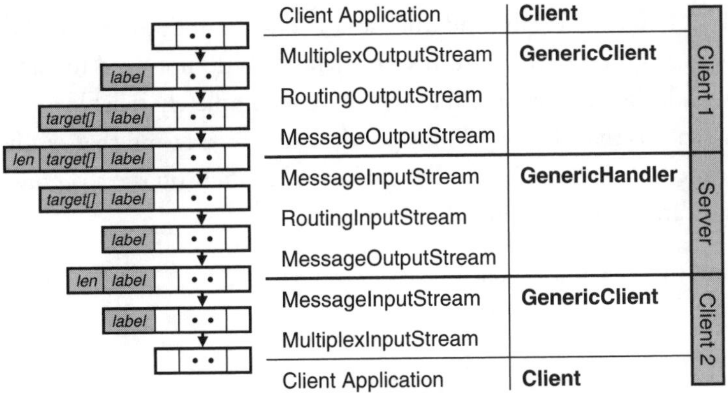

Figure 21.3 Stages of encapsulation between Client tools

Note that we wrap the `MessageInputStream` xI in a `DataInputStream` when we pass it to the client. This may seem redundant, because after all, the `MessageInput-Stream` class is itself a subclass of `DataInputStream`. By wrapping it like this, however, we prevent clients from casting the stream to a `MessageInput` and calling inappropriate methods thereof. Instead, we restrict clients to using only the usual methods of `DataInputStream`.

We also catch any `RuntimeExceptions` that are thrown by the `receive()` method; this protects the `demux()` method from unexpected client exceptions that may occur at runtime. We simply display any such exceptions and continue processing.

```
protected void closedown () {
  try {
    o.close ();
  } catch (IOException ex) {
    ex.printStackTrace ();
  }
  synchronized (registry) {
    Enumeration e = registry.keys ();
    while (e.hasMoreElements ()) {
      deregister ((String) e.nextElement ());
    }
  }
}
```

This method is called by the `finally` clause of the `run()` method to close the client framework down. We first close the network connection by closing the raw `Output-Stream` o. We then loop through all of the currently registered clients, calling their `disconnected()` methods.

Remember that this `GenericClient` and the `GenericMessageCopier` are the only classes that directly access the network streams, so client tools do not need to handle network failures. Instead, they can assume that they have a completely reliable message transport layer. This means that they need only consider `IOExceptions` that result from messages that were incorrectly built by another client, and can rely on the `discon-nected()` method to indicate disconnection.

```
public void register (String mx, Client c) {
  synchronized (registry) {
    deregister (mx);
    registry.put (mx, c);
    c.setMessageOutput (new MultiplexOutputStream (messageO, mx));
  }
}
```

This method registers the `Client` c with the specified multiplexing label mx.

We synchronize on `registry` to ensure that no other client can register simultaneously. We next call the `deregister()` method to disconnect any client that is already registered with the multiplexing label mx; if there is no such client then this will have no effect.

We can finally register the new client tool in `registry` and assign it a new message stream over which to communicate. We assign it a `MultiplexOutputStream` attached to `message0`; remember that `message0` is a `RoutingOutputStream` attached to our message queue. Clients can thus make use of the targeted `send()` methods; every message that they send will be multiplexed with the tool name, routed as specified by the `send()` method, placed in the queue and finally delivered to the network by the `GenericMessageCopier`.

```
public void deregister (String mx) {
    synchronized (registry) {
        Client oC = (Client) registry.get (mx);
        if (oC != null)
            oC.disconnected ();
        registry.remove (mx);
    }
}
```

This method deregisters any client with the specified multiplexing label `mx`.

We synchronize on `registry` to ensure mutual exclusion. We can then determine if there is a client with the specified label; if so, we call its `disconnected()` method, informing it that it has been disconnected. We can then remove it from the `Hashtable`.

21.2 Interface Client

This interface must be implemented by any client tools that wish to attach to the `GenericClient`. The interface specifies a method for the `GenericClient` to set the message stream over which the client tool should communicate, another for the `GenericClient` to supply messages to the client, and another by which the `GenericClient` can inform the client that it has been disconnected (Figure 21.4).

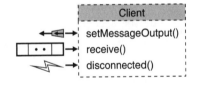

Figure 21.4 Interface Client

```
import java.io.*;

public interface Client {
    public void setMessageOutput (MessageOutput o);
    public void receive (DataInputStream i);
    public void disconnected ();
}
```

The setMessageOutput() method assigns the client a message stream over which it can subsequently communicate with its peers on the server. This stream supports the targeted send() methods so the client can direct messages to specific users.

The receive() method will be called with every message that arrives for the client; the contents of the message can be read from the DataInputStream i. The stream will contain data only from a single message; subsequent messages will be delivered through subsequent calls to receive().

The disconnected() method will be called when the client has been disconnected. As we have already seen, this can result from several possible causes: the network may have failed, the GenericClient may have been stopped, the client may have been deregistered, or another client may have been registered in its place. In all cases, the disconnected client should cease communicating over the message stream that it was formerly assigned.

21.3 A GenericClient example

This class builds on the example that we used to demonstrate the multiplexed streams earlier in the book. We adapt the Chatboard and Whiteboard classes to implement the Client interface; the major difference from the earlier classes is the addition of a disconnected() method.

The main chat application class is simpler than in the demultiplexing example because all the stream setup is performed by the GenericClient class. In fact, all we need do is start the GenericClient, create the components and register them; all the rest is taken care of for us automatically.

We don't need to make any changes to the GenericServer to support this client; we can just start the server and connect as many client tools as we desire.

21.3.1 Class GenericChat

This is the main chat application (Figure 21.5) . It requires a server name and port, and a username to be specified on the command line. It connects to the specified server, registers with the desired name, and opens a frame with a text-chat region and whiteboard. All the users connected to the server can then communicate through these tools (Figure 21.6).

It is important to realize that the chat framework does not know any details about the components. We could subsequently add games and new tools, and the framework would remain unchanged.

```java
import java.io.*;
import java.awt.*;

public class GenericChat extends Frame {
    // public GenericChat (GenericClient c) ...
    // public boolean handleEvent (Event e) ...
    // static public void main (String args[])
    //     throws IOException ...
}
```

This class extends the Frame class; when executed, the main() method opens a window with a text-chat and a whiteboard.

```java
protected GenericClient c;

public GenericChat (GenericClient c) {
    super ("Generic Chat");
    this.c = c;
    ChatboardClient cb = new ChatboardClient ();
    WhiteboardClient wb = new WhiteboardClient ();
    setLayout (new GridLayout (2, 1));
    add (wb);
    add (cb);
    resize (200, 300);

    c.register ("chat", cb);
    c.register ("wb", wb);
}
```

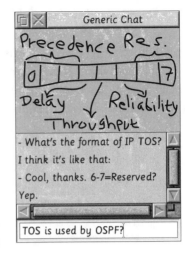

Figure 21.5 The GenericChat interface

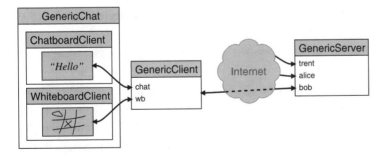

Figure 21.6 Class GenericChat

To create an instance of the GenericChat class we must provide an instance of the GenericClient that is already connected to the server. The GenericChat constructor will then create its tools and register them with the GenericClient.

We first call the superclass constructor with an appropriate title for the window; we then create a ChatboardClient and a WhiteboardClient, lay them out, and register them with the GenericClient. Registering these tools automatically assigns them multiplexed message streams over which to communicate.

```
public boolean handleEvent (Event e) {
    if (e.id == Event.WINDOW_DESTROY) {
        c.stop ();
        hide ();
        return true;
    } else {
        return super.handleEvent (e);
    }
}
```

In the handleEvent() method, we can test for a user attempting to close the window. If this happens, we close down our connection and hide the window. To close the connection we simply call the stop() method of the GenericClient; this stops the thread, causing the appropriate cleanup to be performed and the clients to be deregistered.

```
static public void main (String args[]) throws IOException {
    if (args.length != 3)
        throw new RuntimeException ("Syntax: GenericChat <host> <port>
            <name>");

    GenericClient c = new GenericClient (args[0], Integer.parseInt
        (args[1]), args[2]);
    new GenericChat (c).show ();
    c.start ();
}
```

The main() method is responsible for connecting to the server, registering the chosen name, and creating the chat window.

We first verify that the correct number of arguments has been supplied, throwing an explanatory exception if not. We then create a new GenericClient c that connects to the specified server with the specified username. If a connection cannot be made or the name is already in use, this will throw an IOException and halt the application. Otherwise, we create a new GenericChat that registers some clients. We finally start the GenericClient; this causes two threads to start, one which relays client messages to the server, and another which relays server messages to the clients.

This application is very powerful for its simplicity. It provides real-time multiuser collaboration across a network. The application can be embedded in a Web page as an applet, or run as a standalone application. More importantly, however, it can be easily extended by simply registering more clients. We do not need to change the server or the client framework to add new clients; all the clients will run seamlessly together. We can modify the format of messages for one client and this will have no effect on other clients. Additionally, as we will see, our clients can be very simple. We do not need to cater for communications problems; any connection failure will be reported through the `disconnected()` method. Despite this, the communications all operate through the standard message streams interface.

21.3.2 Class ChatboardClient

This class extends the `Chatboard` that we developed earlier in the multiplexed streams chapter and implements the necessary additions to implement the `Client` interface.

```
import java.io.*;
import java.awt.*;

public class ChatboardClient extends Chatboard implements Client {
   // public void receive () ...
   // public void disconnected () ...
}
```

We extend the basic `Chatboard` class and implement the `Client` interface. This means that we must provide the `setMessageOutput()`, `receive()`, and `disconnected()` methods. In fact, we inherit the `setMessageOutput()` method from the original, so we need to implement only two methods.

We have no need to perform any initialization upon creation, so we omit any constructors. We will thus be assigned a default constructor that takes no parameters.

```
   protected MessageOutput o;

   public void receive (DataInputStream dI) {
      if (o == null)
         o = super.getMessageOutput ();
      try {
         byte[] buffer = new byte[dI.available ()];
         dI.readFully (buffer);
         o.write (buffer);
         o.send ();
      } catch (IOException ex) {
         ex.printStackTrace ();
      }
   }
```

The Chatboard class that we are extending extracts messages from a Queue. As a result, when we receive messages from the GenericClient class we must place them directly into the Queue. We call the superclass getMessageOutput() method; this returns a QueueOutputStream o that writes messages into the message queue. We read the message into a buffer, write this to o, and send() the message. It will thus be placed in the queue for subsequent processing.

```
public void disconnected () {
   input.setEditable (false);
   exec.stop ();
}
```

This method is called when we are disconnected from the server. We set the Text-Field input to be uneditable; this will prevent the user from entering any further messages. The input variable is inherited from the superclass, as is the text entry box for the chat. We also stop the exec thread that reads messages from the queue.

Obviously, if we had not implemented the original Chatboard with message streams, we would need to provide more implementation here. It is, however, a comparatively simple task to add networked operation to other applications, even those that were not implemented initially with networking in mind.

Additionally, in this case, the use of a Queue is probably unnecessary; the tool is sufficiently simple that processing messages will not take long. A Queue would become necessary if the client may take a long time to process a message. This delay in the receive() method would stall the GenericClient thread, and would therefore stall the processing of messages for other client tools.

21.3.3 Class WhiteboardClient

This class is the corresponding Client extension of the earlier Whiteboard class.

```
import java.io.*;
import java.awt.*;

public class WhiteboardClient extends Whiteboard implements Client {
   // public void disconnected () ...
}
```

The implementation of this class is essentially identical to that of the Whiteboard class; we implement the Client interface, but the superclass has already defined appropriate setMessageOutput() and receive() methods. We must therefore only provide an implementation of the disconnected() method.

```
public void disconnected () {
    setForeground (Color.red);
}
```

If we are disconnected from the server, we set our foreground color to red, to indicate that the whiteboard is no longer connected.

21.4 Extending the generic classes

From this example, it should be apparent that we can very easily develop significant networked applications using just the message-streams based communications library. The GenericServer and GenericClient classes can provide a basis for many server-based collaborative applications, and this basis hides much of the complexity associated with networking.

In many cases, however, we may require further function that is not provided by these classes alone; in such cases we can frequently just extend these classes and add in the extra function. This section discusses a few of the extension and optimization options that may be useful.

21.4.1 Message source identification

One facility that we do not provide is an indication of the source of a message. This might be useful if, for example, a chat had the ability to reply to a specific user. It would obviously be fairly easy for the client tools to manually insert their username into every message that they send; however, we can also automate this task.

There are two primary ways to achieve this: the first option is for clients that need source identification to use a stream that automatically adds their username to each message. The MultiplexOutputStream class in fact provides just this function; client tools can attach a MultiplexOutputStream onto the front of their assigned message streams, using their username as a label. Upon receipt of a message, this name can then be extracted using a MultiplexInputStream.

We can alternatively automate this task by extending the GenericHandler class to automatically add the client username to messages that it forwards, and extending the GenericClient class to extract this name and present it with the messages upon receipt (Figures 21.7 and 21.8).

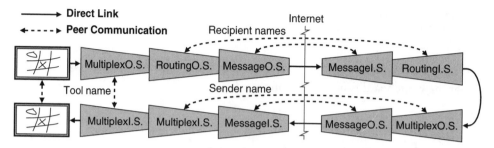

Figure 21.7   Streams within the GenericSourceIDClient/Server framework

```java
import java.io.*;
import java.util.*;

public class GenericSourceIDHandler extends GenericHandler {
   public GenericSourceIDHandler (Hashtable routes, InputStream i,
      OutputStream o) {
      super (routes, i, o);
   }

   protected void send (byte[] buffer, MessageOutput o) throws IOException {
      if ((o != null) && (o != myself)) {
         MultiplexOutputStream mO = new MultiplexOutputStream (o, name); // new
         mO.write (buffer);
         mO.send ();
      }
   }
}
```

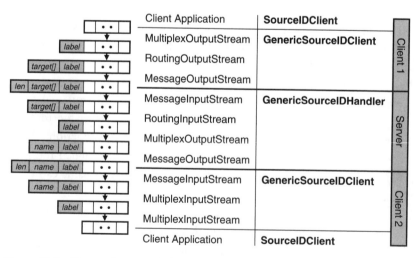

Figure 21.8   Stages of encapsulation between SourceIDClient tools

This class is a modification of the `GenericHandler` class that adds the username as a header onto every message that it forwards from its client. We override the `send()` method that sends the message `buffer` to the message output stream `o` and use a `MultiplexOutputStream` to add the username as a header onto the message before sending it (Figure 21.9).

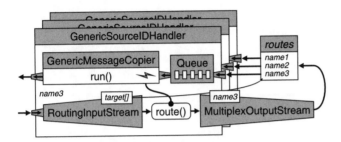

Figure 21.9   Class GenericSourceIDHandler

In addition to defining this `GenericSourceIDHandler` class, we must also subclass the `GenericServer` class to use this modified handler instead of the default `Generic-Handler` class and use the following `GenericSourceIDClient` class.

```java
import java.io.*;

public class GenericSourceIDClient extends GenericClient {
    public GenericSourceIDClient (String hostName, int hostPort, String name)
        throws IOException {
      super (hostName, hostPort, name);
    }
    protected void demux () throws IOException {
        MessageInputStream mI = new MessageInputStream (i);
        MultiplexInputStream nI = new MultiplexInputStream (mI); // new
        MultiplexInputStream xI = new MultiplexInputStream (nI);
        while (true) {
          xI.receive ();
          Client c = (Client) registry.get (xI.label);
          if (c != null) {
            try {
              if (c instanceof SourceIDClient)
                ((SourceIDClient) c).receive (new DataInputStream (xI),
                  nI.label);
              else
                c.receive (new DataInputStream (xI));
            } catch (RuntimeException ex) {
              ex.printStackTrace ();
            }
          }
        }
    }
  }
}
```

The `GenericSourceIDClient` class is a modification of the `GenericClient` class that should be used in conjunction with a `GenericSourceIDHandler`. This class strips the username from incoming messages and presents this, along with the message, to registered client tools.

We override the `demux()` method to attach a `MultiplexInputStream nI` onto the client's input stream; this extracts the username that was attached by the `Generic-SourceIDHandler` class (Figure 21.10). We then attach the `MultiplexInputStream xI` onto this; this extracts the multiplexing target for the message, as attached by the `GenericClient` class.

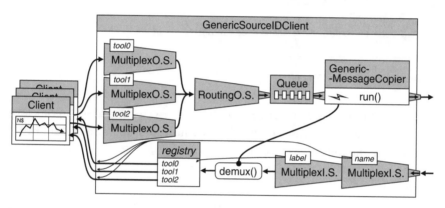

Figure 21.10   Class GenericSourceIDClient

We can then route messages in the usual manner; however, for every message that we route, we check to see whether the target client is a `SourceIDClient` or a normal `Client`. `SourceIDClient` is an extension of the `Client` interface that defines an additional `receive()` method by which we can specify the source of a message. If the client implements this interface, then we call the new `receive()` method, specifying the origin of the message; otherwise we call the conventional `receive()` method. This new class is thus backwards compatible with clients that do not need to know the origins of messages.

```
public interface SourceIDClient extends Client {
   public void receive (DataInputStream i, String from);
}
```

Clients that wish to know the origins of messages can implement the `Source-IDClient` interface. In addition to implementing the `Client` methods, they must implement a new `receive()` method that includes the username of each message's sender. The `GenericSourceIDClient` will then indicate the origin of every message received using this method. The original declaration of the `receive()` method can be ignored; it must be implemented, but the body of the method can be left empty.

21.4.2 Naming registry

Another facility that is not present is a method for clients to determine which users are currently logged onto the server. There are obviously many ways to achieve this; however, possibly the simplest is to assign a special multiplex channel for the server to transmit the names of users as they join and leave.

If a client application is interested in keeping track of names, then it can register a client to process these messages (Figure 21.11).

```
import java.io.*;
import java.util.*;

public class GenericRegistryHandler extends GenericHandler {
   // public GenericRegistryHandler (GenericServer g, InputStream i,
        OutputStream o) ...
   // protected void accept (String name) throws IOException ...
}
```

This is an extension to the `GenericHandler` class that announces the names of new users as they join. We override the `accept()` method to announce the new users when they join, and to announce their leaving when their connections close down. We must also send the new users a list of the currently connected users.

```
   public GenericRegistryHandler (Hashtable routes, InputStream i,
        OutputStream o) {
     super (routes, i, o);
   }
```

The constructor just calls the superclass constructor; there is no other setup necessary.

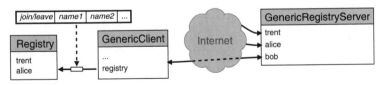

Figure 21.11   The GenericRegistryServer framework

```
protected void accept (String name) throws IOException {
    Queue q = new Queue ();
    boolean registered = true;
    synchronized (routes) {
        if (routes.containsKey (name))
            registered = false;
        else {
            announce (true); // new
            myself = new QueueOutputStream (q);
            listUsers (); // new
            routes.put (name, myself);
        }
    }
    try {
        new DataOutputStream (o).writeBoolean (registered);
        o.flush ();
        if (registered)
            execute (q);
    } finally {
        if (registered) {
            routes.remove (name);
            announce (false); // new
        }
    }
}

// protected void announce (boolean isJoin) throws IOException ...
// protected void listUsers () throws IOException ...
```

We modify the `accept()` method to call the `announce()` and `listUsers()` methods when a new user joins; the `announce()` method announces to current clients that a new user has joined, and the `listUsers()` method sends a list of the current clients to the new user. We must also modify the `finally` clause to announce the user's leaving when the connection is closed.

In the call to `announce()`, we specify `true` if the user is joining and `false` if the user is leaving.

```
protected void announce (boolean isJoin) throws IOException {
    Queue q = new Queue ();
    QueueOutputStream qO = new QueueOutputStream (q);
    MultiplexOutputStream xO = new MultiplexOutputStream (qO, "registry");
    xO.writeBoolean (isJoin);
    xO.writeUTF (name);
    xO.send ();
    broadcast ((byte[]) q.remove ());
}
```

The purpose of this method is to fabricate a message that indicates that a user has joined, and then to broadcast this message to all connected clients.

We will create this message in the Queue q, using the QueueOutputStream q0. We attach a MultiplexOutputStream x0 to q0, identifying the target as the client's registry tool. We then write a message into this stream consisting of a boolean value that indicates whether the user is joining or leaving, followed by its name. When we send the message using the send() method, the message is created and placed into the Queue q. We can then extract the message and broadcast it using the broadcast() method.

```
protected void listUsers () throws IOException {
    MultiplexOutputStream o = new MultiplexOutputStream (myself, "registry");
    o.writeBoolean (true);
    Enumeration e = routes.keys ();
    while (e.hasMoreElements ()) {
        String theName = (String) e.nextElement ();
        o.writeUTF (theName);
    }
    o.send ();
}
```

This method sends a list of the current users to the new client.

We attach the MultiplexOutputStream o to the client's own message stream myself; we can thus simply write the message, consisting of the boolean value true and a list of the current user names, and send this. The message will be automatically placed in the user's outbound message queue by the QueueOutputStream myself.

This message will be subsequently transmitted to the client by its Generic-MessageCopier thread. The GenericClient will receive this message and direct it to the client's registry tool.

It is up to interested clients to register a Client with the name registry that can process these messages, and thereby keep up with the current users of the server. This tool will be quite simple; it will receive messages that consist of a boolean followed by one or more names, and either add or remove these names from an internal list.

We can combine this registry with the previous source identification classes, and thereby keep up with both the current users of the server and the source of each message. Obviously to use this class as-is, we must also provide a GenericRegistryServer class that uses this handler.

21.4.3 Optimizing these classes

These classes are obviously wide open for optimization. When we combine the functions of multiple streams, we end up copying data through multiple buffers before actually transmitting them. The classes, as described, are distinctly not optimized, mainly for the purpose of explanation.

One obvious place for optimization is the output streams that are used by clients of the GenericHandler. All data written by the clients go through a multiplexed stream, to a routing stream, to a queue stream, and into a queue. We could make this path more efficient by defining a GenericMessageStream that performs all of these functions in a single class, building up the message in a ByteArrayOutputStream, attaching headers, and placing it directly into a queue for processing.

We can similarly optimize the route from the queue to the network connection by defining a class that takes buffers directly from the queue and sends them to the network.

On the server side, we can hardwire many of the operations that are currently performed by the message stream classes and increase performance in this manner. Another optimization would involve removing the use of Strings to identify clients for multicast messages. Instead, the server could assign integer identifiers to clients, thus making the process of routing multicasts more efficient.

These optimizations are probably best left to a production stage, when an application is finalized, if they are to be used at all. Machines are generally sufficiently powerful that some extra buffer copying on the client-side will not adversely affect operation. If a server has to support significant load, then optimizations are obviously in order.

The optimizations described here are just the tip of the iceberg when it comes to server-side optimizations. Garbage collection and memory allocation cause a significant impact on performance. A highly-optimized Java server must attempt to minimize these problems. This can be done in a variety of ways.

Typically, instead of always creating new objects for new messages and connections, we would create a queue of reusable objects. When we need a new buffer, we attempt to reuse an old buffer that has sufficient capacity. Similarly, instead of creating new Generic-Handlers we would keep a queue of past handlers and declare methods that let us reuse these for new connections.

There are other implementation-related optimizations possible: it is more efficient to access a variable that is local to a method than to access a class' instance variable. As a result, it may be useful to use a temporary local variable where an instance variable is accessed repeatedly.

Optimizations like this get messy, and are left as an exercise, if necessary. If performance is a significant issue, it may be best to choose another language for the server. The GenericServer class described here can be duplicated in about 1000 lines of C++, although true Java compilers will obviously make this route less advantageous.

21.5 Wrapping up

The message streams that we have introduced here are extremely powerful tools for the development of networked applications. We can produce extensible collaborative tools with a minimum of effort, and these tools can be dynamically introduced to a continually running server.

The `GenericServer` and `GenericClient` classes can support a wide variety of different applications in a generic manner, and as demonstrated, can be extended to include additional function with a minimum of effort.

On the CD accompanying this book, we have included an example chat application that uses these classes with the naming extensions described, to provide real-time collaboration across the Web. The chat classes are located in the `prominence.chat` package. Obviously, the tools are somewhat limited; however, they are very easily extensible.

The remainder of this part of the book introduces a simple cryptography API to assist in the development of secure Internet applications. These classes may be combined with the message streams to provide secure message-based communications, although performance issues must be considered.

The cryptography API will round out our treatment of Java streams and we hope will give the reader some insight into the power and extensibility of the stream communications paradigm.

chapter 22

A cryptographic framework

In this and the following chapters we will look at a simple set of cryptographic streams that will provide us with some tools to help in the development of secure Internet applications. It is extremely important to have an understanding of the theory behind cryptography before embarking on the development of a secure application.

For the unfamiliar, an introduction to cryptography is provided at the start of this book, and the cryptography appendix provides more details about the topic. We will assume henceforth that the reader is familiar with concepts such as symmetric encryption, cryptographic hash functions, stream ciphers, and so forth.

In this chapter, we provide an overview of the cryptographic framework that we will develop; this framework includes support for hash functions and symmetric block encryption. In the next chapter, we develop streams that use this framework to provide encryption and authentication facilities across communications channels; following this, we will actually develop the encryption classes and in the following chapter, the hash classes. The last chapter is concerned with key generation and the appropriate use of these classes.

It is important to stress the importance of an *a priori* understanding of the field of cryptography, because there are a great many pitfalls into which the uninitiated can fall. For example, cryptanalytical theory currently holds that an attack on DES may require upwards of 8,796,093,022,208 computations. This may seem like it could take a long time; however, for a high-tech attacker this may take less than a day. Worse still, is that if the users of a system insist on picking passwords that are easy to remember—and hence easy to guess—then an attack may only take a few minutes, even for less stalwart opponents than the NSA.

22.1 Encryption algorithms

The encryption algorithms that this framework supports are all of the symmetric variety. Symmetric algorithms use the same key to encrypt data as to decrypt it; this key must be a secret that is shared between the sender and recipient (Figure 22.1). Typically, this will be a secret password known only to two people (or to a client and a server). It is imperative that this password not be guessable, because otherwise anyone who can guess the password will be able to decrypt the secret communications.

Asymmetric algorithms, on the other hand, use a different key to encrypt data and to decrypt it. One key, the public key, may be publicly distributed and anyone may have access to it. The important feature about these algorithms is that only those with access to the other key, the private key, can actually decrypt data that is encrypted with the

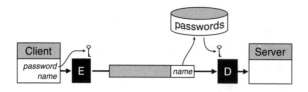

Figure 22.1   Symmetric encryption

public key (Figure 22.2). This type of algorithm is more powerful than a symmetric encryption algorithm; however, there are several important factors that limit its usefulness in Java.

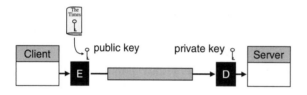

Figure 22.2   Asymmetric encryption

Typically, asymmetric encryption requires access to a library that supports big numbers (1024 bits long and beyond). The JDK 1.0.2 API does not include such a library,* and it would be beyond the scope of this book to develop one. Additionally, without using native methods, asymmetric encryption can be extremely slow: the negotiation phase of an SSL implementation can take tens of seconds, even though there is not much data being encrypted.

DES is considered to be a fairly fast algorithm; the Java implementation that we provide—not the fastest in the world, by any means—encrypts on a 166 MHz Pentium at about the same rate as an assembler implementation on a 6 MHz 80286. Using a JIT compiler improves the situation, but the same machine still encrypts about six times slower than with optimized C, or at about the same speed as an assembler implementation on a 33 MHz 80486 (Figure 22.3).

	Pentium 166MHz			Ultra Sparc 167MHz
	Microsoft Internet Explorer 3.0 + JIT	**Netscape Navigator 3.0 + JIT**	**Sun JDK 1.0 (1.1)**	**Sun JDK 1.0 (1.1)**
DES	160 kB/s	130 kB/s	10 kB/s (31)	10 kB/s (15)
TripleDES	50 kB/s	40 kB/s	3 kB/s (9)	3 kB/s (5)
SHS	1540 kB/s	1020 kB/s	60 kB/s (159)	60 kB/s (98)

Figure 22.3   Speed of some algorithms

---

* JDK 1.1 has introduced a class `java.lang.Bignum`.

For encryption, we will therefore work with symmetric algorithms and assume that users can be trusted to choose good passwords. This is adequate for systems where public-access security is not paramount. If security is more important, then it is probably advisable to license suitable technology from a trusted source. Readers are advised to verify any code that they choose to use; implementation errors are a common cause of weak security in an otherwise secure system.

As part of this framework, we will also examine cryptographically secure hash algorithms and look at the password and key generation issues that are involved in implementing a secure Internet application.

22.2 Overview

The framework that we will develop is fairly general; however, for reasons of brevity, we must keep it somewhat limited. The following classes make up the top level of the framework:

22.2.1 Crypt

This class is simply a repository of useful functions. Encryption tends to require a lot of transformation functions that convert arrays of bytes into arrays of integers, and so forth. This class provides a useful set of such methods.

22.2.2 Cipher

This is the superclass for all ciphers. A cipher, in this case, is an encryption algorithm. We will develop an implementation of DES, the data encryption standard, and some variants, including DES-CBC and triple-DES. The encryption algorithms that we consider are all block algorithms; i.e., they encrypt a small block of data at a time. We will also look at extending these to support chaining, which strengthens the algorithms when encrypting streams of data.

22.2.3 Hash

This is the superclass for all hash functions; a hash function computes a digest from a large message. We will develop an implementation of SHS, the secure hash algorithm.

We will also develop a SHS-MAC variant that uses a `Cipher` to provide a means of authentication.

22.2.4 CipherOutputStream and Cipher-InputStream

These classes provide a streams interface to the encryption functions that we develop. These are encrypted filter streams that attach to existing streams, so we can provide a secure link across any available communications channel. Because we have a generic `Cipher` class, we can use many different encryption algorithms in the cipher stream framework.

22.2.5 HashOutputStream and HashInput-Stream

These classes provide a streams interface to hash functions. Again, these are filter streams, so we can add message authentication to any existing communications channel. We use the generic `Hash` class to allow for an extensible library of hash functions.

22.3 Class Crypt

This class provides a variety of useful methods for manipulating arrays of bytes. Encryption algorithms almost invariably operate on arrays of data, and these methods will be used fairly frequently to convert bytes to integers, longs to bytes, and so forth.

We will just describe the methods here and not their implementation.

```
public class Crypt {
    // public static final boolean equals (byte[] a, byte[] b) ...
    // public static final void zero (byte[] a, int ao, int l) ...
    // public static final void fill (byte a, byte[] b, int bo, int l) ...
    // public static final void intToBytes (int a, byte[] b, int bo) ...
    // public static final void intsToBytes (int[] a, int ao, int l, byte[] b,
    //     int bo) ...
    // public static final int bytesToInt (byte[] a, int ao) ...
    // public static final void bytesToInts (byte[] a, int ao, int[] b, int bo,
    //     int l) ...
    // public static final void longToBytes (long a, byte[] b, int bo) ...
    // public static final long bytesToLong (byte[] a, int ao) ...
```

```
// public static final String bytesToHex (byte[] a) ...
// public static final String longToHex (long a) ...
}
```

All of the methods are static and final; being static means that they are class methods and so we do not need to create an instance of Crypt to make use of them. Declaring that they are final allows a compiler to perform some optimizations; because it is guaranteed that no subclass can override these methods, they can sometimes be optimized and in-lined. Technically, all static methods are final; however, the explicit declaration serves the purposes of clarity.

```
public static final boolean equals (byte[] a, byte[] b) {
   if (a.length != b.length)
     return false;
   else {
     for (int i = 0; i < a.length; ++ i)
       if (a[i] != b[i])
         return false;
     return true;
   }
}
```

This method determines whether the two-byte arrays a and b are equal. They must have the same length and the same contents to be equal.

```
public static final void zero (byte[] a, int ao, int l) {
   fill ((byte) 0, a, ao, l);
}
```

This method zeroes l bytes of array a, starting from offset ao.

```
public static final void fill (byte a, byte[] b, int bo, int l) {
   for (int i = 0; i < l; ++ i)
     b[bo + i] = a;
}
```

This method fills l bytes of array b with the value a, starting from offset bo.

```
public static final void intToBytes (int a, byte[] b, int bo) {
   b[bo] = (byte) (a >> 24);
   b[bo + 1] = (byte) (a >> 16);
   b[bo + 2] = (byte) (a >> 8);
   b[bo + 3] = (byte) (a);
}
```

This method writes the integer a as its four component bytes into array b, starting at offset bo. The integer is written high-byte first.

```
public static final void intsToBytes (int[] a, int ao, int l, byte[] b,
   int bo) {
```

```
    for (int i = 0; i < 1; ++ i)
        intToBytes (a[ao + i], b, bo + (i << 2));
}
```

This method writes 1 integers from array a as bytes into the byte array b. The integers are taken from offset ao of array a, and written from offset bo in array b.

```
public static final int bytesToInt (byte[] a, int ao) {
    return (a[ao] << 24) + ((a[ao + 1] & 0xff) << 16) +
        ((a[ao + 2] & 0xff) << 8) + (a[ao + 3] & 0xff);
}
```

This method takes four bytes from array a at offset ao, and returns the corresponding integer.

```
public static final void bytesToInts (byte[] a, int ao, int[] b, int bo,
        int 1) {
    for (int i = 0; i < 1; ++ i)
        b[bo + i] = bytesToInt (a, ao + (i << 2));
}
```

This method performs the reverse operation of the intsToBytes() method, reading 1 integers from the byte array a starting at offset ao, writing them into the integer array b starting at offset bo.

```
public static final void longToBytes (long a, byte[] b, int bo) {
    b[bo] = (byte) (a >> 56);
    b[bo + 1] = (byte) (a >> 48);
    b[bo + 2] = (byte) (a >> 40);
    b[bo + 3] = (byte) (a >> 32);
    b[bo + 4] = (byte) (a >> 24);
    b[bo + 5] = (byte) (a >> 16);
    b[bo + 6] = (byte) (a >> 8);
    b[bo + 7] = (byte) (a);
}
```

This method writes the long a as eight bytes into array b, starting at offset bo.

```
public static final long bytesToLong (byte[] a, int ao) {
    return ((a[ao] & 0xffL) << 56) | ((a[ao + 1] & 0xffL) << 48) |
        ((a[ao + 2] & 0xffL) << 40) | ((a[ao + 3] & 0xffL) << 32) |
        ((a[ao + 4] & 0xffL) << 24) | ((a[ao + 5] & 0xffL) << 16) |
        ((a[ao + 6] & 0xffL) << 8) | (a[ao + 7] & 0xffL);
}
```

This method reads eight bytes from array a, starting from offset ao, and returns the corresponding long.

```
public static final String bytesToHex (byte[] a) {
    StringBuffer s = new StringBuffer ();
```

```
   for (int i = 0; i < a.length; ++ i) {
      s.append (Character.forDigit ((a[i] >> 4) & 0xf, 16));
      s.append (Character.forDigit (a[i] & 0xf, 16));
   }
   return s.toString ();
}
```

This method converts an array of bytes into a hexadecimal String; the result will consist of two hexadecimal digits for every byte of the input; leading zeroes will be preserved.

```
public static final String longToHex (long a) {
   byte[] b = new byte[8];
   longToBytes (a, b, 0);
   return bytesToHex (b);
}
```

This method converts a long into a hexadecimal String sixteen digits long.

22.4 Class Cipher

This is the generic superclass of all ciphers; it declares the basic methods to encipher and decipher data. The class is oriented towards ciphers that encrypt data in blocks, and provides methods that encrypt large amounts of data by making repeated calls to the single-block encryption methods (Figure 22.4).

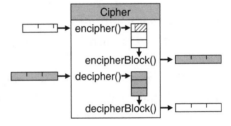

Figure 22.4   Class Cipher

```
public abstract class Cipher {
   // public byte[] encipher (byte[] plain, int off, int len) ...
   // public byte[] encipher (byte[] plain) ...
   // public byte[] decipher (byte[] cipher, int off, int len) ...
   // public byte[] decipher (byte[] cipher) ...
   // public abstract int blockSize ();
   // public abstract void encipherBlock (byte[] plain, int po,
        byte[] cipher, int co);
   // public abstract void decipherBlock (byte[] cipher, int co,
        byte[] plain, int po);
}
```

The basic interface to this class is through the encipher() and decipher() methods that encrypt and decrypt blocks of data, and the blockSize() method that returns the size of block operated on by the encryption algorithm. The default implementations of the `encipher()` and `decipher()` methods make use of the `encipherBlock()` and `decipherBlock()` methods to encrypt data in units of the encryption block size.

Actual implementations of this class must provide implementations of the `block-Size()`, `encipherBlock()`, and `decipherBlock()` methods.

```
public byte[] encipher (byte[] plain, int off, int len) {
   int n = blockSize ();
   byte[] cipher = new byte[((len + n - 1) / n) * n];
   int i;
   for (i = 0; i < len - n + 1; i += n)
      encipherBlock (plain, off + i, cipher, i);
   if (i < len) {
      byte[] last = new byte[n];
      System.arraycopy (plain, off + i, last, 0, len - i);
      Crypt.fill ((byte) 0x55, last, len - i, n - len + i);
      encipherBlock (last, 0, cipher, i);
   }
   return cipher;
}
```

This method encrypts `len` bytes of the array `plain` starting from index `off`, and returns the encrypted result.

We first create a buffer `cipher` to hold the resulting encrypted data. This buffer must be large enough to hold the plaintext and must also be a multiple of the encryption block size. We then encrypt the plaintext in chunks of the block size; we use the `encipherBlock()` method to encrypt from the plaintext buffer into the ciphertext buffer.

If the plaintext itself is not a multiple of the block size, then we must encrypt the last partial chunk separately. We create a small buffer that is the size of one block, copy the remaining data into this and fill the rest of the buffer with the byte `0x55` (although there is nothing magical about this value). We can then use the `encipherBlock()` method to encrypt this last block.

Note that this implementation is just one option for encrypting a large amount of data, and may be overridden by a subclass. This implementation always returns a ciphertext array that is a multiple of the encryption block size. There are algorithms (ciphertext stealing) that allow us to produce a result that is the same size as the input. This might be more appropriate for some situations where we don't want the padding that the preceding implementation introduces.

```
public byte[] encipher (byte[] plain) {
   return encipher (plain, 0, plain.length);
}
```

This method encrypts the entire byte array `plain` using the `encipher()` method.

```
public byte[] decipher (byte[] cipher, int off, int len) {
  int n = blockSize ();
  byte[] plain = new byte[len];
  for (int i = 0; i < len; i += n)
    decipherBlock (cipher, off + i, plain, i);
  return plain;
}
```

This method decrypts a block of `len` bytes of encrypted data `cipher` starting from index `off`, returning the plaintext result. The length of the encrypted data *must* be a multiple of the block size; this corresponds to the `encipher()` implementation that pads the ciphertext to be a multiple of the block size. Obviously, if we provided an alternative `encipher()` method we must also override this method.

Because the ciphertext is a multiple of the block size, we can just create a plaintext buffer `plain` and decrypt the ciphertext blocks using the `decipherBlock()` method. This method cannot determine whether the `encipher()` method padded the data, so the caller must be able to determine the correct length of `plaintext`.

```
public byte[] decipher (byte[] cipher) {
  return decipher (cipher, 0, cipher.length);
}
```

This method decrypts the entire byte array `cipher` using the `decipher()` method.

```
public abstract int blockSize ();
```

This method must be implemented by every encryption algorithm, and should indicate the block size, in bytes, operated on by the algorithm. A block size of one indicates an algorithm that encrypts one byte at a time.

```
public abstract void encipherBlock (byte[] plain, int po, byte[] cipher,
  int co);
```

This method should encrypt one block of data from offset `po` of byte array `plain` into byte array `cipher` at offset `co`. The implementation of this method must be capable of encrypting data in-place; i.e., `plain` and `cipher` may be the same array.

```
public abstract void decipherBlock (byte[] cipher, int co, byte[] plain,
  int po);
```

This method should decrypt one block of data from offset `co` of byte array `cipher` into byte array `plain` at offset `po`.

This class provides us with a generic template for various encryption algorithms. This is tailored toward encrypting large chunks of data at a time. It is not well suited to encrypting many messages that are smaller than the encryption block size, although the block size for DES is eight bytes, so this is generally not a particular problem. Cipher-text stealing would allow us to produce a ciphertext that is exactly the same size as the plaintext; however, it requires that the encryption algorithm be operating in a chaining mode (such as DES-CBC).

We will not ordinarily use this class directly; the encryption streams that we develop in the next chapter take a `Cipher` object and use it to to provide an encrypted communications channel. With these classes, we can then add security to applications that communicate using the normal stream classes.

22.5 Class Hash

This class is the generic superclass for all hash functions. Hash functions are used to compute message digests; a message digest is, as the name suggests, a *summary* of the message. The hash function has several important properties; it should be impossible to recreate a message from its digest, and it should also be computationally infeasible to find two different messages which have the same digest. A digest is in essence, a unique abstract of the message. Significant research has been performed to verify that these properties hold for cryptographic hash algorithms (Figure 22.5).

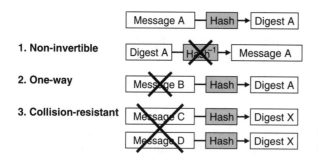

Figure 22.5 Properties of a crypto-graphic hash function

A hash function can be used to ensure that a message is not corrupted during trans-mission. To transmit a message you first compute the message digest, and then transmit both the message and its digest. When the message is received, you again compute a digest of the received message. If the received digest and the computed digest match, then you can be sure that the message is not corrupt.

By itself, this does not protect against deliberate alteration; a malicious user could modify a message and simply send along a digest for this new message. To overcome this we use a MAC, or message authentication code. A MAC is a hash algorithm that uses a secret key to prevent such tampering. Only the sender and the intended recipient know this key, and so only they can compute the message digests.

The Hash class is a generic superclass for cryptographic hash functions and provides a standard interface for computing message digests (Figure 22.6).

Figure 22.6   Class Hash

```
public abstract class Hash {
   // public abstract byte[] digest (byte[] text, int off, int len);
   // public byte[] digest (byte[] text) ...
   // public abstract int digestSize ();
}
```

The basic interface to all hash functions is that you can provide a message and the hash algorithm will compute a digest. This function is provided by the digest() method, which returns a digest of the supplied message. The digestSize() method allows the caller to determine the size of hash that is returned by a particular algorithm.

```
public abstract byte[] digest (byte[] text, int off, int len);
```

This method returns a digest from the subarray of text consisting of len bytes, from offset off. The digest is an array of bytes that is typically much smaller than the original message; however, the properties of hash functions ensure that it is extremely unlikely that any two messages will produce the same digest.

```
public byte[] digest (byte[] text) {
   return digest (text, 0, text.length);
}
```

This method computes a digest for the whole array text using the previous method.

```
public abstract int digestSize ();
```

This method returns the digest size returned by this algorithm. The MD5 hash algorithm returns 16 (16 bytes, 128 bits); the SHS algorithm that we implement returns 20 (20 bytes, 160 bits).

Using this generic class, we can implement HashInputStream and HashOutput-Stream classes that transparently ensure the integrity of a communications channel.

22.6 Wrapping up

The classes that we have described here provide just the framework for a simple encryption library. We must now add the streams classes that make these classes usable by general networked applications, and then provide actual implementations of the encryption algorithms.

In the next chapter, we develop the `CipherInputStream` and `CipherOutputStream` classes that provide security for streams-based communications, and the `HashInputStream` and `HashOutputStream` classes that provide integrity for streams-based communications. Following this, we provide implementations of DES, SHS, and a few derivatives.

chapter 23

Cryptographic streams

In this chapter we develop the streams that accompany the cryptographic framework. We develop two pairs of stream classes; one pair to provide security, the other pair to provide integrity and authentication.

The CipherOutputStream and CipherInputStream classes use a Cipher object to encrypt a communications channel; this lets us transmit sensitive information over a public network such as the Internet. The HashOutputStream and HashInputStream classes use a Hash object to add an integrity check to a communications channel; this will let us verify that transmitted data have not been corrupted or tampered with in transit.

23.1 Class CipherOutput-Stream

This class is a filtered OutputStream that attaches to an existing OutputStream and encrypts all data written to it. The Cipher that is used to perform the encryption is specified in the constructor. This class operates by storing in a buffer all the data that are written to it, and only encrypting and sending these data when the flush() method is called (Figure 23.1).

Figure 23.1   Class CipherOutput-Stream

This is similar to the operation of the MessageOutputStream class, except that instead of relying on an explicit call to send() we send the data whenever the stream is flushed. Using the flush mechanism means that we can encrypt a communications channel in a way that is completely transparent to the caller. The corresponding Cipher-InputStream provides a similar transparent interface to the decryption process.

```
import java.io.*;

public class CipherOutputStream extends FilterOutputStream {
    // public CipherOutputStream (OutputStream o, Cipher c) ...
    // public void flush () throws IOException ...
    // public void close () throws IOException ...
}
```

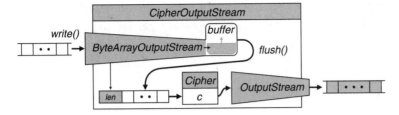

Figure 23.2   Internals of the CipherOutputStream class

The `CipherOutputStream` class is a filtered output stream; the constructor accepts the `OutputStream` to which to attach and the `Cipher` with which to encrypt. We override the `flush()` and `close()` methods appropriately (Figure 23.2).

```
protected ByteArrayOutputStream byteO;
protected OutputStream o;
protected Cipher c;

public CipherOutputStream (OutputStream o, Cipher c) {
   super (new ByteArrayOutputStream ());
   byteO = (ByteArrayOutputStream) out;
   this.o = o;
   this.c = c;
}
```

In the constructor we accept an `OutputStream o` over which we will send encrypted data and a `Cipher c` with which we will perform the encryption. We call the superclass constructor with a new `ByteArrayOutputStream byteO` that allows us to easily buffer all the data that are written to us, pending encrypting and sending.

```
public void flush () throws IOException {
   writeEncrypted ();
   o.flush ();
}

// protected void writeEncrypted () throws IOException ...
```

When the `flush()` method is called, we use the `writeEncrypted()` method to encrypt and write out the data that we have buffered, and then we flush `o` to ensure that the data we have written are sent in a timely manner.

```
public void close () throws IOException {
   flush ();
   o.close ();
}
```

We must also override the close() method to flush and close the attached stream. Remember that we have attached the FilterOutputStream superclass to byteO, and so the default implementation of close() will attempt to close byteO; the correct operation of this method is to close o.

```
protected void writeEncrypted () throws IOException {
    if (byteO.size () > 0) {
        byte[] b = byteO.toByteArray ();
        byteO.reset ();

        byte[] plain = new byte[b.length + 4];
        Crypt.intToBytes (plain.length, plain, 0);
        System.arraycopy (b, 0, plain, 4, b.length);

        byte[] cipher = c.encipher (plain);
        o.write (cipher);
    }
}
```

This method encrypts and sends the data that we have buffered. If we have no data buffered then we simply do nothing; we otherwise extract the buffered data, encrypt them and send them. The extra copying in this method serves to just insert the buffer length at the beginning of the buffer before we encrypt it.

Remember that the Cipher class may have to pad the plaintext to be a multiple of the block size before it can encrypt it. After padding the message, it does not actually include any information that indicates how much padding has been added. We must therefore manually precede the message by an integer that indicates how many valid data follow.

We have two options for sending this value: we can either transmit it in plaintext separately from the encrypted data, or we can actually encrypt it and send it as part of the encrypted message. The latter is obviously the preferred choice because it divulges less information. Be aware, however, that traffic analysis can actually reveal most of this information to any eavesdropper who cares to listen, regardless of whether we encrypt the messages or not.

We call the toByteArray() method of byteO to extract the contents of the buffer into b. We then create a new buffer plain that will contain both the buffer length and the contents of the buffer. We write the buffer length into this array using the intToBytes() method, and then copy the buffer data in using the arraycopy() method. We can finally encrypt this entire plaintext buffer, which includes the buffer length, and write the result to the attached stream. The recipient can then decrypt this data and easily determine how much padding has been added.

23.1.1 Transmission granularity

There are, in fact, several alternatives to waiting for a `flush()` call before encrypting and transmitting the entire buffer. One option would be to add a threshold size so that the buffer is automatically transmitted when it reaches a certain size. Another option would be to transmit the buffer continuously in units of the encryption block size. This has the advantage that the time involved in encrypting the data is spread out over the duration of a message being sent; the receiver can be decrypting the message while the sender is still encrypting later blocks. On the other hand, encrypting a large block in one go is slightly more efficient.

The major problem with continually sending data is that unless we are using a non-padding `Cipher` we encounter a problem with flushing. When `flush()` is called, we must send all of the buffered data immediately, whether or not we have a full encryption block. To send this data we must add some padding bytes. The problem is how to tell the receiver that these bytes are padding and not part of the normal message.

The usual way to overcome this problem is to make the last byte of every block indicate the amount of padding that has been added to the block. The receiver can thus discard the padding bytes from every block that is received. This process has the disadvantage of wasting a byte from every block, although it actually need not be terribly inefficient; we could use some other larger block size than that of the encryption algorithm.

23.2 Class CipherInput-Stream

The `CipherInputStream` class is the corresponding class that decrypts stream data. It attaches to an `InputStream` and decrypts data from it; data must be in the format that is written by `CipherOutputStream`. The `Cipher` that performs the decryption is specified in the constructor (Figure 23.3).

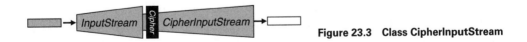

Figure 23.3   Class CipherInputStream

This class transparently performs the decryption; there is no need to explicitly call any `receive()` method or the equivalent. Whenever `read()` is called, the class checks

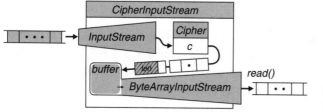

Figure 23.4 Internals of the CipherInputStream class

to see whether more data must be decrypted; if so, it reads and decrypts a new chunk of data from the attached stream (Figure 23.4).

```
import java.io.*;

public class CipherInputStream extends InputStream {
  // public CipherInputStream (InputStream i, Cipher c) ...
  // public int read () throws IOException ...
  // public int read (byte[] b, int o, int l) throws IOException ...
  // public int available () throws IOException ...
  // public long skip (long n) throws IOException ...
  // public void close () throws IOException ...
}
```

This class is a filtered `InputStream`; we do not directly subclass `FilterInput-Stream` because none of the default method implementations are useful. Instead, we must implement all of the methods of `InputStream` ourselves.

```
  protected ByteArrayInputStream byteI;
  protected DataInputStream dataI;
  protected Cipher c;

  public CipherInputStream (InputStream i, Cipher c) {
    dataI = new DataInputStream (i);
    this.c = c;
    byte[] nothing = new byte[0];
    byteI = new ByteArrayInputStream (nothing);
  }
```

The `InputStream` i from which we must decrypt data, and the `Cipher` c that performs this decryption, are both specified in the constructor. We attach a `DataInput-Stream` to i so that we can make use of the `readFully()` method.

When we must decrypt some new data, we read them from the `DataInputStream` `dataI` and decrypt them using the `Cipher` c. All of the relevant methods in this class check first, before reading any data from `byteI`, to see if the buffer is actually empty. If it is, then we must decrypt some more data and replace `byteI` with a `ByteArray-InputStream` that reads from the new data. Because we initially set `byteI` to read from an empty array, the first call to `read()` will automatically cause a block of data to be decrypted.

```
public int read () throws IOException {
   if (byteI.available () == 0)
      readEncrypted ();
   return byteI.read ();
}

// protected void readEncrypted () throws IOException ...
```

This method reads a single byte from `byteI`. We first check, however, to see if `byteI` is empty; if it is then we must decrypt some more data, and so we call the `readEncrypted()` method.

```
public int read (byte[] b, int o, int 1) throws IOException {
   if (byteI.available () == 0)
      readEncrypted ();
   return byteI.read (b, o, 1);
}
```

This method reads a subarray of bytes from `byteI`; we again check to see if we must first decrypt more data.

```
public int available () throws IOException {
   return byteI.available ();
}
```

This method returns the number of bytes that are currently available to read without blocking. We just return the amount of data available in `byteI`, without reading and decrypting any more. We cannot easily determine how many valid data are available to read from the attached stream.

```
public long skip (long n) throws IOException {
   if (byteI.available () == 0)
      readEncrypted ();
   return byteI.skip (n);
}
```

This method attempts to skip over the specified number of bytes. We must first, however, check to see whether our buffer is empty; if so, we decrypt some more data. We may obviously skip fewer bytes than requested, as the specification of this method permits.

```
public void close () throws IOException {
   dataI.close ();
}
```

This method closes the attached stream dataI.

```
protected void readEncrypted () throws IOException {
   int n = c.blockSize ();
   byte[] b = new byte[((4 + n - 1) / n) * n];
   try {
      dataI.readFully (b);
   } catch (EOFException ex) {
      return;
   }
   byte[] d = c.decipher (b);
   int l = Crypt.bytesToInt (d, 0);

   if (l <= b.length) {
      byteI = new ByteArrayInputStream (d, 4, l - 4);
   } else {
      b = new byte[((l - b.length + n -1) / n) * n];
      dataI.readFully (b);
      byte[] d2 = c.decipher (b);
      b = new byte[l - 4];
      System.arraycopy (d, 4, b, 0, d.length - 4);
      System.arraycopy (d2, 0, b, d.length - 4, l - d.length);
      byteI = new ByteArrayInputStream (b);
   }
}
```

This method reads a chunk of encrypted data from dataI, decrypts it, and makes it available to read from byteI. This is significantly complicated by the fact that we actually encrypt the size of each chunk, and so must decrypt one block of data before we can determine how much more we should read and decrypt.

To determine the size of the chunk, we must first decrypt four bytes of data. We therefore create a buffer b that can hold at least four bytes; the calculation that we use creates an array that is at least four bytes long, and is also a multiple of the encryption block size.

We attempt to fill this from the attached stream using the readFully() method. If this method throws an EOFException then we have reached the EOF and can just return; the read() call from byteI will subsequently indicate EOF. Otherwise, once we have read b, we can then decrypt it into d and find out l, the amount of valid data that we encrypted. There are subsequently two major cases to handle.

In the first case, we have decrypted all of the data that were written in this chunk. We can simply reassign byteI to read from the remainder of the decrypted data in d and return.

Otherwise, we must decrypt more data. We create a new buffer b to hold the remainder of the chunk. Again, this must be a multiple of the encryption block size. We read this buffer from dataI and decipher it into d2. We must then join the remaining data from d with the new data in d2. We copy both of these buffers into a new buffer b, using the `arraycopy()` method, and reassign `byteI` to read from this decrypted data.

This method is complicated by the fact that our `Cipher` function c could equally operate with a block size of one, three, eight, or eighty bytes, and so we must be prepared for any possibility. The fundamental idea behind the encrypted streams is simple, however: we buffer up data, and when it is time to send it, we encrypt it along with the length and send it. To receive this, we decrypt the length, and then read and decrypt the remaining data.

Note that we could perform the decryption as blocks arrive, and not wait to read an entire chunk every time. This would, however, make the code somewhat more complex.

23.3 Class HashOutput-Stream

This class is similar in nature to the `CipherOutputStream`, but considerably simpler in implementation. We attach to an `OutputStream` and use a hash function to provide message integrity and authenticity. The hash function is specified by a `Hash` object that is supplied in the constructor (Figure 23.5).

Figure 23.5 Class HashOutput-Stream

Again, we store up data in a buffer; when `flush()` is called we compute a digest of the buffer and then transmit both the buffer and digest. The corresponding `Hash-InputStream` reads the message and digest, recomputes a digest of the message and verifies that both digests match. Like the encrypted streams, this mechanism is transparent to the caller.

```
import java.io.*;

public class HashOutputStream extends FilterOutputStream {
    // public HashOutputStream (OutputStream o, Hash h) ...
    // public void flush () throws IOException ...
    // public void close () throws IOException ...
}
```

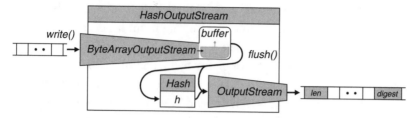

Figure 23.6   Internals of the HashOutputStream class

This class follows the model of the `CipherOutputStream` very closely. We extend `FilterOutputStream`, and buffer up all data that are written to us in a `ByteArray-OutputStream`. When `flush()` is called, we compute a digest and then write out both the message and its digest. Like the encryption class, we must also transmit the size of the message along with the message (Figure 23.6).

```
protected ByteArrayOutputStream byteO;
protected DataOutputStream dataO;
protected Hash h;

public HashOutputStream (OutputStream o, Hash h) {
  super (new ByteArrayOutputStream ());
  byteO = (ByteArrayOutputStream) out;
  dataO = new DataOutputStream (o);
  this.h = h;
}
```

In the constructor, we create the `ByteArrayOutputStream byteO` that will buffer all of the data that are written to us. We attach a `DataOutputStream dataO` to the `OutputStream o`; we will use this to write the message and digest.

```
public void flush () throws IOException {
  writeHashed ();
  dataO.flush ();
}

// protected void writeHashed () throws IOException ...
```

When `flush()` is called, we call the `writeHashed()` method to actually write the message and digest to `dataO`. We then flush the stream to ensure that any buffers are cleared.

```
public void close () throws IOException {
  flush ();
  dataO.close ();
}
```

When `close()` is called, we must first flush any buffered data, and then close the attached stream `dataO`.

```
protected void writeHashed () throws IOException {
   if (byteO.size () > 0) {
      byte[] b = byteO.toByteArray ();
      byteO.reset ();
      dataO.writeInt (b.length);
      dataO.write (b);
      byte[] hash = h.digest (b);
      dataO.write (hash);
   }
}
```

This method writes the message and digest to the attached stream `dataO`. We first extract the buffered data into `b`, and then reset `byteO`. We send the size of the message first, followed by the body of the message, which is the buffered data, followed by the digest as computed by `h`.

A corresponding `HashInputStream` can then verify this digest to ensure that the message has not been corrupted or tampered with.

23.4 Class HashInputStream

This class provides the corresponding integrity-checking reading class for a hashed stream. It attaches to an `InputStream` and verifies the data that arrive on this stream, using a hash function (Figure 23.7).

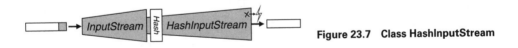

Figure 23.7   Class HashInputStream

To the user, a `HashOutputStream` connection to a `HashInputStream` looks just like a buffered connection; nothing is sent until `flush()` is called, but then whatever has been sent can be read unmodified from the `HashInputStream`. Behind the scenes, the `HashInputStream` actually reads the messages and digests that are written by the `HashOutputStream` and verifies that each message matches its digest. If a `read()` call encounters a corrupt message, then an appropriate `IOException` is thrown (Figure 23.8).

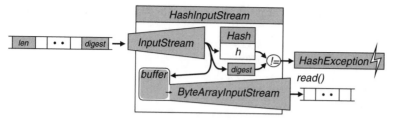

Figure 23.8 Internals of the HashInputStream class

```
import java.io.*;

public class HashInputStream extends InputStream {
    // public HashInputStream (InputStream i, Hash h) ...
    // public int read () throws IOException ...
    // public int read (byte[] b, int o, int l) throws IOException ...
    // public int available () throws IOException ...
    // public long skip (long n) throws IOException ...
    // public void close () throws IOException ...
}
```

This class is a filtered stream, although it actually subclasses InputStream. It reads messages and digests from the attached stream, and it checks the integrity of each message using a Hash specified in the constructor. If a message is successfully read, then it is made available for reading through an internal ByteArrayInputStream; otherwise, an appropriate exception is thrown.

```
protected ByteArrayInputStream byteI;
protected DataInputStream dataI;
protected Hash h;

public HashInputStream (InputStream i, Hash h) {
    dataI = new DataInputStream (i);
    this.h = h;
    byte[] nothing = new byte[0];
    byteI = new ByteArrayInputStream (nothing);
}
```

In the constructor, we create a new DataInputStream attached to the InputStream i; we will use this to read messages and digests. Every read() call first checks to see whether byteI is empty and reads a new message if necessary. To ensure that the first call to read() will read a new message we initially attach byteI to an empty buffer.

This class actually reads from byteI, so when we insert a message into byteI, then it actually becomes readable directly from this HashInputStream class. We precede every relevant call with a check to see whether we need to receive a new message, and do so if necessary. In this manner, if a read() method is called and there are no data in byteI, then we receive a new message, check the digest, and place the message in byteI. The read() method will then be able to read from this new message.

```
public int read () throws IOException {
   if (available () == 0)
      readHashed ();
   return byteI.read ();
}

// protected void readHashed () throws IOException ...
```

This method reads a single byte. We first check to see whether byteI is empty; if so, then we use the readHashed() method to read and verify a new message. We then call the read() method of byteI; this will read from the current message stored there.

```
public int read (byte[] b, int o, int 1) throws IOException {
   if (available () == 0)
      readHashed ();
   return byteI.read (b, o, 1);
}
```

This method reads a subarray of bytes. Again, we first check and receive a new message if necessary, and then subsequently read() from byteI.

```
public int available () throws IOException {
   return byteI.available ();
}
```

This method returns the number of bytes that are currently available to be read from byteI.

```
public long skip (long n) throws IOException {
   if (available () == 0)
      readHashed ();
   return byteI.skip (n);
}
```

This method attempts to skip n bytes. If byteI is currently empty, then we read a new message so that the skip() call can actually skip some data.

```
public void close () throws IOException {
   dataI.close ();
}
```

This method closes the attached stream dataI.

```
protected void readHashed () throws IOException {
   int n;
```

```
      try {
        n = dataI.readInt ();
      } catch (EOFException ex) {
        return;
      }
      byte[] buffer = new byte[n];
      dataI.readFully (buffer, 0, n);
      byte[] digest = new byte[h.digestSize ()];
      byte[] newDigest = h.digest (buffer);
      dataI.readFully (digest);
      if (!Crypt.equals (digest, newDigest))
        throw new HashException (h.getClass().getName() +
            " digest check failed.");
      byteI = new ByteArrayInputStream (buffer);
    }
```

This method reads a new message from `dataI` and then verifies that it is not corrupt by checking the received digest against one computed from the received message.

To read a message, we first read `n`, the size of the following message. If an EOF-Exception is encountered, then we have reached the EOF and can return immediately; a subsequent call to read from `byteI` will return EOF.

We next read the message body into the buffer `buffer` and the message digest into the buffer `digest`. We can then compute a new digest for the message `newDigest` and verify that the message has been accurately received.

If the digests do not match, then we throw a `HashException` to indicate the problem; we include the class-name of the hash function in the detail message of this exception. Otherwise, we can reassign `byteI` to read from this new message.

23.5 Class HashException

This class is a simple `IOException` that can be thrown if a message fails its digest check. These exceptions are thrown by methods of the `HashInputStream` class.

```
import java.io.*;

public class HashException extends IOException {
  public HashException () {
  }

  public HashException (String detail) {
    super (detail);
  }
}
```

A `HashException` can either be created with no detail message or with a detail message that describes the cause of the exception. This class follows the structure of all normal exception classes.

23.6 Wrapping up

These streams provide a very convenient interface to encryption and hashing techniques. They allow us to add security and integrity checking beneath any existing application that uses the streams interface. As we have seen, we can use the streams interface to produce complex applications, so the ability to add security to any stream channel is a very powerful one.

In the next chapter we will provide an implementation of the DES symmetric encryption algorithm. We obviously cannot provide a significant insight into the internal workings of the encryption beyond what is provided in the appendix, however we do extend this to implement TripleDES and DES-CBC. In the subsequent chapter we will implement the SHS secure hash standard, and in the last chapter we will discuss certain password and key management issues that are involved in using encryption algorithms.

chapter 24

Encryption algorithms

This chapter is concerned with actually implementing and using encryption algorithms. We focus on the DES algorithm; alternatives such as IDEA and RC5 follow the same model. We also discuss derivatives, including EDE (triple-DES) and DES-CBC; these allow us to enhance the security of block encryption algorithms such as DES.

A tenet of the cryptographic community is that a new algorithm is very definitely not necessarily a good algorithm. The DES encryption algorithm has been around since the 1970s and so has been subject to significant amounts of cryptanalysis, yet no public results have shown a significant weakness in the algorithm. Advances in analysis techniques and computational power have rendered the small key size somewhat vulnerable, but the algorithm appears to be fundamentally sound. IDEA, on the other hand has a 128-bit key length—over twice as long as DES—but has been around only since the 1990s and so has not been subject to the same degree of cryptanalysis as DES. IDEA is both faster than DES and has a more secure key length, however the paranoid may wish to wait for further cryptanalytical results. We don't provide an implementation of IDEA here, however it is similar to DES in that it is a sequence of bit-manipulation operations, and sample code is freely available.

24.1 Class DES

This class is an implementation of DES, the data encryption standard. There are some fairly involved transformations and permutations required to implement DES; we have separated these into a DEA class. This nomenclature should not be misconstrued as a mirror of the relationship between DES and DEA; DES and DEA are essentially the same thing, the data encryption standard or data encryption algorithm.

The DES class is a high-level implementation of DES: it makes use of methods of the DEA class to actually perform the low-level DES transformations (Figure 24.1). This

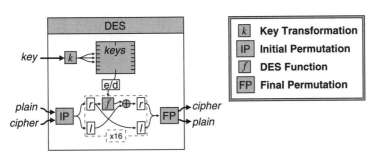

Figure 24.1 Class DES

class inherits from the `Cipher` class and implements the block encryption and decryption methods `encipherBlock()` and `decipherBlock()`. These methods will be called by the default `encipher()` and `decipher()` methods of the `Cipher` class.

Because this encryption algorithm extends the `Cipher` class, we can use instances of this class with the `CipherOutputStream` and `CipherInputStream` classes to provide a DES-encrypted communications channel.

```
public class DES extends Cipher {
  // public DES (long key) ...
  // public void encipherBlock (byte[] plain, int po, byte[] cipher, int co) ...
  // public void decipherBlock (byte[] cipher, int co, byte[] plain, int po) ...
  // public int blockSize () ...
}
```

We extend the `Cipher` class, and so inherit the default implementations of the `encipher()` and `decipher()` methods. These methods make use of the `encipherBlock()` and `decipherBlock()` methods to encrypt and decrypt data in amounts of the encryption block size, and so we need only implement methods that encrypt and decrypt a single block of data at a time.

```
  protected long keys[];

  public DES (long key) {
    keys = DEA.makeKeys (key);
  }
```

DES uses a 56-bit key to generate a *key schedule* that is used in the encryption process. The key schedule is a 16-entry array of 48-bit values that are derived from the initial key.

The constructor accepts the 56-bit encryption key, and we compute and store the derived key schedule in the keys array. The key is actually specified as a 64-bit `long` value; every eighth bit is a *parity* bit that we can discard. The parity bits are used elsewhere to ensure that a key has been communicated correctly.

We must use the same key to decrypt data as to encrypt it, so the key must be a secret that is shared by only the sender and recipient. We will discuss the generation of keys later in this book.

```
  public void encipherBlock (byte[] plain, int po, byte[] cipher, int co) {
    long plainText = Crypt.bytesToLong (plain, po);
    long cipherText = encrypt (plainText);
    Crypt.longToBytes (cipherText, cipher, co);
  }

  // public final long encrypt (long w) ...
```

DES encrypts data in 64-bit blocks. This is most efficiently implemented by actually using `long` values, rather than arrays of bytes. We therefore use the `bytesToLong()` method of the `Crypt` class to convert the plaintext sub-array of bytes into a single `long` value. We can then use the `encrypt()` method, which encrypts a `long` value. We finally use the `longToBytes()` method to expand the encrypted result of this method into a series of eight bytes in the specified target array `cipher`.

```
public void decipherBlock (byte[] cipher, int co, byte[] plain, int po) {
   long cipherText = Crypt.bytesToLong (cipher, co);
   long plainText = decrypt (cipherText);
   Crypt.longToBytes (plainText, plain, po);
}

// public final long decrypt (long w) ...
```

Deciphering a block of data follows the same form as encrypting a block. We first concatenate the eight bytes of ciphertext into a single `long` value. We pass this through the `decrypt()` method, which returns the corresponding plaintext. We can then expand this value into the output plaintext array.

```
public int blockSize () {
   return 8;
}
```

DES operates in blocks of 64 bits, so we must return the corresponding block size of eight bytes. This is used by the `encipher()` and `decipher()` methods to determine how much data to process per block using the `decipherBlock()` and `encipher-Block()` methods.

```
public final long encrypt (long w) {
   long[] keys = this.keys;
   long x = DEA.initialPerm (w);
   int l = (int) (x >>> 32);
   int r = (int) x;
   for (int i = 0; i < 16; ++ i) {
      int tmp = DEA.desFunc (r, keys[i]) ^ l;
      l = r;
      r = tmp;
   }
   long y = ((long) r << 32) | ((long) l & 0xffffffffL);
   return DEA.finalPerm (y);
}
```

This method performs the actual DES encryption. To encrypt a block of data w we must first pass w through an initial permutation; this produces a permuted value x. We then divide x into two halves; and run these through sixteen rounds of the DES encryption function. This function involves an expansion, an S-box substitution, and a P-box permutation; each round uses a different key from the key schedule. After sixteen rounds, we join the two halves again and run the result through a final permutation to produce the encrypted result. There is nothing more to DES than, essentially, bit-twiddling; however, it has stood up to years of analysis.

We actually make this method `public` because it is very useful for other code to be able to encrypt 64-bit chunks using this interface to the encryption algorithm.

For reasons of efficiency, we declare this method as `final` and use a local copy of the key schedule. The compiler can perform more optimizations with these declarations.

```
public final long decrypt (long w) {
   long[] keys = this.keys;
   long x = DEA.initialPerm (w);
   int l = (int) (x >>> 32);
   int r = (int) x;
   for (int i = 15; i >= 0; -- i) {
      int tmp = DEA.desFunc (r, keys[i]) ^ l;
      l = r;
      r = tmp;
   }
   long y = ((long) r << 32) | ((long) l & 0xffffffffL);
   return DEA.finalPerm (y);
}
```

Decrypting DES remarkably involves exactly the same process, except that the key schedule is used in reverse. The `decrypt()` method is therefore identical to the `encrypt()` method, except that we loop backwards through the keys.

24.2 Class DEA

This class provides the low-level bit-twiddling functions that are used by the DES class.

```
public final class DEA {
   // public static final long[] makeKeys (long key) ...
   // public static final long initPerm (long x) ...
   // public static final int desFunc (int x, long k) ...
   // public static final long finPerm (long x) ...
}
```

The signature of this class is fairly straightforward; all the methods are `static` and correspond to the various stages of the encryption algorithm. We will not discuss these steps in detail; an understanding of the internals of the algorithm is not necessary to be able to use it.

```
public static final long[] makeKeys (long key) {
```

```
      long reduced = perm (key, keyReducePerm);
      int l = (int) (reduced >> 28);
      int r = (int) (reduced & 0xfffffff);
      long[] keys = new long[16];
      for (int i = 0; i < 16; ++ i)
        keys[i] = perm (rotate (l, r, keyRot[i]), keyCompressPerm);
      return keys;
   }

   public static final long initialPerm (long x) {
      return perm (x, initPerm);
   }

   // This combines the expansion function, pBox and sBox
   // Based on optimizations by David A. Barrett
   // (barrett@asgard.boulder.Colorado.EDU)
   public static final int desFunc (int x, long k) {
      int p = x >>> 27;
      int q = (p & 3) << 4;
      int r = x << 5;
      p |= r;
      r = sBoxP[0][(int) ((k >> 42) ^ p) & 0x3f]; p >>>= 4;
      r |= sBoxP[7][(int) ((k >> 0) ^ p) & 0x3f]; p >>>= 4;
      r |= sBoxP[6][(int) ((k >> 6) ^ p) & 0x3f]; p >>>= 4;
      r |= sBoxP[5][(int) ((k >> 12) ^ p) & 0x3f]; p >>>= 4;
      r |= sBoxP[4][(int) ((k >> 18) ^ p) & 0x3f]; p >>>= 4;
      r |= sBoxP[3][(int) ((k >> 24) ^ p) & 0x3f]; p >>>= 4;
      r |= sBoxP[2][(int) ((k >> 30) ^ p) & 0x3f]; p >>>= 4;
      r |= sBoxP[1][(int) ((k >> 36) ^ (p | q)) & 0x3f];
      return r;
}

   public static final long finalPerm (long x) {
      return perm (x, finPerm);
   }

   // protected static final long perm (long k, int p[]) ...
   // protected static final long rotate (int l, int r, int s) ...

   // protected static final int keyReducePerm[] ...
   // protected static final int keyCompressPerm[] ...
   // protected static final int keyRot[] ...
   // protected static final int initPerm[] ...
   // protected static final int finPerm[] ...
   // protected static final int sBoxP[][] ...
```

The makeKeys() method generates a key schedule for the specified key key (Figure 24.2).

The initPerm() method performs the initial permutation, and the finalPerm() method performs the final permutation. The desFunc() method performs one round of the main encryption function; this implementation uses a special table that combines

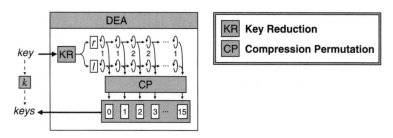

Figure 24.2   DES key-schedule generation

the expansion permutation, S-Box substitution, and P-Box permutation (Figure 24.3). This is significantly faster than explicitly performing the three steps separately, which is how the algorithm is defined.

```
protected static final long perm (long k, int p[]) {
   long s = 0;
   for (int i = 0; i < p.length; ++ i)
      if ((k & (1L << p[i])) != 0)
         s |= 1L << i;
   return s;
}

protected static final long rotate (int l, int r, int s) {
   return ((long) (((l << s) & 0xfffffff) | (l >>> (28 - s))) << 28) |
      ((r << s) & 0xfffffff) | (r >> (28 - s));
}
```

This class makes use of a perm() function that performs a generalized permutation operation, and a rotate() method that returns a long value that consists of l and r each rotated left s bits and then joined into a single 64-bit value.

```
protected static final int keyReducePerm[] = {
   60, 52, 44, 36, 59, 51, 43, 35, 27, 19, 11, 3, 58, 50,
   42, 34, 26, 18, 10, 2, 57, 49, 41, 33, 25, 17, 9, 1,
   28, 20, 12, 4, 61, 53, 45, 37, 29, 21, 13, 5, 62, 54,
   46, 38, 30, 22, 14, 6, 63, 55, 47, 39, 31, 23, 15, 7
};
```

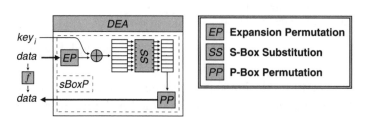

Figure 24.3   One round of DES encryption

```
protected static final int keyCompressPerm[] = {
    24, 27, 20, 6, 14, 10, 3, 22, 0, 17, 7, 12,
    8, 23, 11, 5, 16, 26, 1, 9, 19, 25, 4, 15,
    54, 43, 36, 29, 49, 40, 48, 30, 52, 44, 37, 33,
    46, 35, 50, 41, 28, 53, 51, 55, 32, 45, 39, 42
};

protected static final int keyRot[] = {
    1, 2, 4, 6, 8, 10, 12, 14, 15, 17, 19, 21, 23, 25, 27, 28
};

protected static final int initPerm[] = {
    57, 49, 41, 33, 25, 17, 9, 1, 59, 51, 43, 35, 27, 19, 11, 3,
    61, 53, 45, 37, 29, 21, 13, 5, 63, 55, 47, 39, 31, 23, 15, 7,
    56, 48, 40, 32, 24, 16, 8, 0, 58, 50, 42, 34, 26, 18, 10, 2,
    60, 52, 44, 36, 28, 20, 12, 4, 62, 54, 46, 38, 30, 22, 14, 6
};

protected static final int finPerm[] = {
    39, 7, 47, 15, 55, 23, 63, 31, 38, 6, 46, 14, 54, 22, 62, 30,
    37, 5, 45, 13, 53, 21, 61, 29, 36, 4, 44, 12, 52, 20, 60, 28,
    35, 3, 43, 11, 51, 19, 59, 27, 34, 2, 42, 10, 50, 18, 58, 26,
    33, 1, 41, 9, 49, 17, 57, 25, 32, 0, 40, 8, 48, 16, 56, 24
};

protected static final int sBoxP[][] = {
    { 0x00808200, 0x00000000, 0x00008000, 0x00808202,
      0x00808002, 0x00008202, 0x00000002, 0x00008000,
      0x00000200, 0x00808200, 0x00808202, 0x00000200,
      0x00800202, 0x00808002, 0x00800000, 0x00000002,
      0x00000202, 0x00800200, 0x00800200, 0x00008200,
      0x00008200, 0x00808000, 0x00808000, 0x00800202,
      0x00008002, 0x00800002, 0x00800002, 0x00008002,
      0x00000000, 0x00000202, 0x00008202, 0x00800000,
      0x00008000, 0x00808202, 0x00000002, 0x00808000,
      0x00808200, 0x00800000, 0x00800000, 0x00000200,
      0x00808002, 0x00008000, 0x00008200, 0x00800002,
      0x00000200, 0x00000002, 0x00800202, 0x00008202,
      0x00808202, 0x00008002, 0x00808000, 0x00800202,
      0x00800002, 0x00000202, 0x00008202, 0x00808200,
      0x00000202, 0x00800200, 0x00800200, 0x00000000,
      0x00008002, 0x00008200, 0x00000000, 0x00808002 },
    { 0x40084010, 0x40004000, 0x00004000, 0x00084010,
      0x00080000, 0x00000010, 0x40080010, 0x40004010,
      0x40000010, 0x40084010, 0x40084000, 0x40000000,
      0x40004000, 0x00080000, 0x00000010, 0x40080010,
      0x00084000, 0x00080010, 0x40004010, 0x00000000,
      0x40000000, 0x00004000, 0x00084010, 0x40080000,
      0x00080010, 0x40000010, 0x00000000, 0x00084000,
      0x00004010, 0x40084000, 0x40080000, 0x00004010,
      0x00000000, 0x00084010, 0x40080010, 0x00080000,
      0x40004010, 0x40080000, 0x40084000, 0x00004000,
      0x40080000, 0x40004000, 0x00000010, 0x40084010,
```

```
      0x00084010, 0x00000010, 0x00004000, 0x40000000,
      0x00004010, 0x40084000, 0x00080000, 0x40000010,
      0x00080010, 0x40004010, 0x40000010, 0x00080010,
      0x00084000, 0x00000000, 0x40004000, 0x00004010,
      0x40000000, 0x40080010, 0x40084010, 0x00084000 },
    { 0x00000104, 0x04010100, 0x00000000, 0x04010004,
      0x04000100, 0x00000000, 0x00010104, 0x04000100,
      0x00010004, 0x04000004, 0x04000004, 0x00010000,
      0x04010104, 0x00010004, 0x04010000, 0x00000104,
      0x04000000, 0x00000004, 0x04010100, 0x00000100,
      0x00010100, 0x04010000, 0x04010004, 0x00010104,
      0x04000104, 0x00010100, 0x00010000, 0x04000104,
      0x00000004, 0x04010104, 0x00000100, 0x04000000,
      0x04010100, 0x04000000, 0x00010004, 0x00000104,
      0x00010000, 0x04010100, 0x04000100, 0x00000000,
      0x00000100, 0x00010004, 0x04010104, 0x04000100,
      0x04000004, 0x00000100, 0x00000000, 0x04010004,
      0x04000104, 0x00010000, 0x04000000, 0x04010104,
      0x00000004, 0x00010104, 0x00010100, 0x04000004,
      0x04010000, 0x04000104, 0x00000104, 0x04010000,
      0x00010104, 0x00000004, 0x04010004, 0x00010100 },
    { 0x80401000, 0x80001040, 0x80001040, 0x00000040,
      0x00401040, 0x80400040, 0x80400000, 0x80001000,
      0x00000000, 0x00401000, 0x00401000, 0x80401040,
      0x80000040, 0x00000000, 0x00400040, 0x80400000,
      0x80000000, 0x00001000, 0x00400000, 0x80401000,
      0x00000040, 0x00400000, 0x80001000, 0x00001040,
      0x80400040, 0x80000000, 0x00001040, 0x00400040,
      0x00001000, 0x00401040, 0x80401040, 0x80000040,
      0x00400040, 0x80400000, 0x00401000, 0x80401040,
      0x80000040, 0x00000000, 0x00000000, 0x00401000,
      0x00001040, 0x00400040, 0x80400040, 0x80000000,
      0x80401000, 0x80001040, 0x80001040, 0x00000040,
      0x80401040, 0x80000040, 0x80000000, 0x00001000,
      0x80400000, 0x80001000, 0x00401040, 0x80400040,
      0x80001000, 0x00001040, 0x00400000, 0x80401000,
      0x00000040, 0x00400000, 0x00001000, 0x00401040 },
    { 0x00000080, 0x01040080, 0x01040000, 0x21000080,
      0x00040000, 0x00000080, 0x20000000, 0x01040000,
      0x20040080, 0x00040000, 0x01000080, 0x20040080,
      0x21000080, 0x21040000, 0x00040080, 0x20000000,
      0x01000000, 0x20040000, 0x20040000, 0x00000000,
      0x20000080, 0x21040080, 0x21040080, 0x01000080,
      0x21040000, 0x20000080, 0x00000000, 0x21000000,
      0x01040080, 0x01000000, 0x21000000, 0x00040080,
      0x00040000, 0x21000080, 0x00000080, 0x01000000,
      0x20000000, 0x01040000, 0x21000080, 0x20040080,
      0x01000080, 0x20000000, 0x21040000, 0x01040080,
      0x20040080, 0x00000080, 0x01000000, 0x21040000,
      0x21040080, 0x00040080, 0x21000000, 0x21040080,
      0x01040000, 0x00000000, 0x20040000, 0x21000000,
      0x00040080, 0x01000080, 0x20000080, 0x00040000,
      0x00000000, 0x20040000, 0x01040080, 0x20000080 },
```

```
  { 0x10000008, 0x10200000, 0x00002000, 0x10202008,
    0x10200000, 0x00000008, 0x10202008, 0x00200000,
    0x10002000, 0x00202008, 0x00200000, 0x10000008,
    0x00200008, 0x10002000, 0x10000000, 0x00002008,
    0x00000000, 0x00200008, 0x10002008, 0x00002000,
    0x00202000, 0x10002008, 0x00000008, 0x10200008,
    0x10200008, 0x00000000, 0x00202008, 0x10202000,
    0x00002008, 0x00202000, 0x10202000, 0x10000000,
    0x10002000, 0x00000008, 0x10200008, 0x00202000,
    0x10202008, 0x00200000, 0x00002008, 0x10000008,
    0x00200000, 0x10002000, 0x10000000, 0x00002008,
    0x10000008, 0x10202008, 0x00202000, 0x10200000,
    0x00202008, 0x10202000, 0x00000000, 0x10200008,
    0x00000008, 0x00002000, 0x10200000, 0x00202008,
    0x00002000, 0x00200008, 0x10002008, 0x00000000,
    0x10202000, 0x10000000, 0x00200008, 0x10002008 },
  { 0x00100000, 0x02100001, 0x02000401, 0x00000000,
    0x00000400, 0x02000401, 0x00100401, 0x02100400,
    0x02100401, 0x00100000, 0x00000000, 0x02000001,
    0x00000001, 0x02000000, 0x02100001, 0x00000401,
    0x02000400, 0x00100401, 0x00100001, 0x02000400,
    0x02000001, 0x02100000, 0x02100400, 0x00100001,
    0x02100000, 0x00000400, 0x00000401, 0x02100401,
    0x00100400, 0x00000001, 0x02000000, 0x00100400,
    0x02000000, 0x00100400, 0x00100000, 0x02000401,
    0x02000401, 0x02100001, 0x02100001, 0x00000001,
    0x00100001, 0x02000000, 0x02000400, 0x00100000,
    0x02100400, 0x00000401, 0x00100401, 0x02100400,
    0x00000401, 0x02000001, 0x02100401, 0x02100000,
    0x00100400, 0x00000000, 0x00000001, 0x02100401,
    0x00000000, 0x00100401, 0x02100000, 0x00000400,
    0x02000001, 0x02000400, 0x00000400, 0x00100001 },
  { 0x08000820, 0x00000800, 0x00020000, 0x08020820,
    0x08000000, 0x08000820, 0x00000020, 0x08000000,
    0x00020020, 0x08020000, 0x08020820, 0x00020800,
    0x08020800, 0x00020820, 0x00000800, 0x00000020,
    0x08020000, 0x08000020, 0x08000800, 0x00000820,
    0x00020800, 0x00020020, 0x08020020, 0x08020800,
    0x00000820, 0x00000000, 0x00000000, 0x08020020,
    0x08000020, 0x08000800, 0x00020820, 0x00020000,
    0x00020820, 0x00020000, 0x08020800, 0x00000800,
    0x00000020, 0x08020020, 0x00000800, 0x00020820,
    0x08000800, 0x00000020, 0x08000020, 0x08020000,
    0x08020020, 0x08000000, 0x00020000, 0x08000820,
    0x00000000, 0x08020820, 0x00020020, 0x08000020,
    0x08020000, 0x08000800, 0x08000820, 0x00000000,
    0x08020820, 0x00020800, 0x00020800, 0x00000820,
    0x00000820, 0x00020020, 0x08000000, 0x08020800 }
};
```

The DEA class includes several arrays of magic numbers; these are used by the encryption algorithm to perform permutations and substitutions.

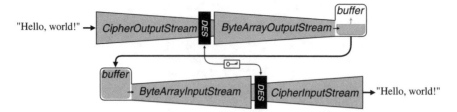

Figure 24.4 Using DES encryption

During the key schedule generation process, we use the key reduction permutation `keyReducePerm` that reduces the key from 64 bits to 56 bits by stripping the parity bits, the key rotation table `keyRot` that specifies the amount by which each half of the key is rotated at each round, and the key compression permutation `keyCompressPerm` that selects 48 of the remaining 56 bits.

For the actual encryption, we use an initial permutation `initPerm` that is a straight permutation of the 64 data bits, a final permutation `finPerm` that is the inverse of the initial permutation, and the array `sBoxP` which combines DES' expansion permutation, S-Boxes, and P-Box into a single table. This is an optimization developed by David A. Barrett that greatly speeds up the execution of this class.

In a straight implementation of DES, the expansion permutation expands the right half of the data from 32 to 48 bits, the S-Boxes replace each 6-bit sub-block of this with 4-bits from a lookup table, and the P-Box performs a straight permutation on the resulting 32 bits. The S-boxes provide DES with most of its strength; they implement a nonlinear function and are designed to protect against many cryptanalytical attacks. We greatly speed this class up by combining these parts of the algorithm into a single table that performs exactly the same function. Of course, many more possibilities for optimization remain.

24.3 Using the DES class

The DES class is an implementation of the Cipher class, and so we can use instances of this class in the cipher streams that we developed in the previous chapter (Figure 24.4). The cipher streams can be used by any application that uses the streams interface, so we will only demonstrate with code fragments.

The following fragment of code writes the message *Hello, world!* into a `ByteArray-OutputStream`, using a `CipherOutputStream` to encrypt the transmission.

```
ByteArrayOutputStream byteO = new ByteArrayOutputStream ();
long key = 0x0123456789abcdefL;
DES des = new DES (key);
CipherOutputStream cipherO = new CipherOutputStream (byteO, des);
DataOutputStream dataO = new DataOutputStream (cipherO);
dataO.writeUTF ("hello, world!");
dataO.flush ();
```

We create a `ByteArrayOutputStream byteO` that will be the communications channel for this example. We then create a `CipherOutputStream cipherO` that attaches to this, and that uses an instance of the DES class as an encryption algorithm. We use an arbitrary key `key` for the DES class.

Any data that we wish to be encrypted can now be sent to this `CipherOutput-Stream`. In this case, we attach a `DataOutputStream` and send the message *Hello, world!* Remember that our `CipherOutputStream` class will buffer all data until `flush()` is called. We flush the `DataOutputStream`; this flushes the attached `CipherOutput-Stream`, which causes the data to be encrypted and transmitted.

The following fragment of code decrypts the message by constructing a `Byte-ArrayInputStream` from the previously encrypted data, and reading from this using a `CipherInputStream`.

```
byte[] message = byteO.toByteArray ();
ByteArrayInputStream byteI = new ByteArrayInputStream (message);
CipherInputStream cipherI = new CipherInputStream (byteI, des);
DataInputStream dataI = new DataInputStream (cipherI);
System.out.println (dataI.readUTF ());
```

We extract the encrypted data from `byteO` and create a `ByteArrayInputStream byteI` that lets us read from this. We attach a `CipherInputStream` so that we can decrypt the data, and then we can read our message back using a `DataInputStream`.

Note that we use the same instance of the DES class to decrypt the data as we used to encrypt it. We could alternatively use a different instance, as long as we use the same key.

As should be clear from this example, the entire encryption process is transparent to the application. We must, of course, flush the `OutputStream`; however, we would have to do this anyway if we buffered the output.

Being able to modify the operation of our streams in a manner that is completely transparent to any higher level application is an extremely useful aspect of the generic streams I/O interface provided by the language. It allows us to provide arbitrary levels of encryption and integrity checking on a communications channel, yet hide all of this from applications.

24.4 Class EDECipher

The short length of the DES key is often argued as a weak point in the algorithm. Recent increases in computer speeds and cryptanalytical techniques mean that the comparatively small key space is vulnerable to attack. A simple way to increase the security of an encryption algorithm is to apply the algorithm several times.

Multiple encryption is not as simple as it would seem. Simply encrypting data twice with different keys does not provide twice the security of encrypting data once. If the encryption algorithm is a mathematical group, then encrypting twice will be no stronger than encrypting just once. DES is not a group, but you must, in fact, encrypt data three times to achieve twice the security of encrypting data just once.

The recommended way to perform triple encryption is to encrypt the data with one key, to decrypt it with a second key and to then encrypt it again with a third key. Sometimes the same key is used for the first and third stages, but this is obviously weaker.

Because of the encrypt-decrypt-encrypt form of this encryption, this is referred to as *EDE*. We now develop a `Cipher` that performs EDE encryption using three supplied ciphers (Figure 24.5).

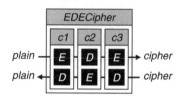

Figure 24.5   Class EDECipher

```
public class EDECipher extends Cipher {
    // public EDECipher (Cipher c1, Cipher c2, Cipher c3) ...
    // public void encipherBlock (byte[] plain, int po, byte[] cipher, int co) ...
    // public void decipherBlock (byte[] cipher, int co, byte[] plain, int po) ...
    // public int blockSize () ...
}
```

The `EDECipher` is an implementation of the `Cipher` class that employs three other `Cipher`s to perform the encryption. As usual, we must provide implementations of the three methods `encipherBlock()`, `decipherBlock()`, and `blockSize()`.

```
    protected Cipher c1, c2, c3;
    public EDECipher (Cipher c1, Cipher c2, Cipher c3) {
        this.c1 = c1;
        this.c2 = c2;
        this.c3 = c3;
    }
```

The three ciphers, `c1`, `c2`, and `c3`, that will be used to perform the encryption and decryption are specified in the constructor.

```
public void encipherBlock (byte[] plain, int po, byte[] cipher, int co) {
   c1.encipherBlock (plain, po, cipher, co);
   c2.decipherBlock (cipher, co, cipher, co);
   c3.encipherBlock (cipher, co, cipher, co);
}
```

The implementation of this algorithm is remarkably simple; we can just apply the three ciphers in sequence. We encrypt with c1, decrypt with c2, and then encrypt with c3.

```
public void decipherBlock (byte[] cipher, int co, byte[] plain, int po) {
   c3.decipherBlock (cipher, co, plain, po);
   c2.encipherBlock (plain, po, plain, po);
   c1.decipherBlock (plain, po, plain, po);
}
```

To decrypt a block, we correspondingly perform the reverse process—decrypt with c3, encrypt with c2, and decrypt with c1.

```
public int blockSize () {
   return c1.blockSize ();
}
```

This particular implementation assumes that the three ciphers have the same block size; typically we will use the same encryption algorithm for c1, c2, and c3. There is, of course, nothing to prevent us from using different algorithms; however, there is less theory about the strength of the cascade that results from this mix. Providing that we use different—and independent—keys for each cipher, then the result of this cascade will be no weaker than any of the algorithms by themselves.

24.5 Class TripleDES

We can use the EDECipher class to trivially implement triple-DES. A common variant of this makes use of the same key for the first and last stage; however, this does reduce security.

```
public class TripleDES extends EDECipher {
   public TripleDES (long k1, long k2) {
      this (k1, k2, k1);
   }
   public TripleDES (long k1, long k2, long k3) {
      super (new DES (k1), new DES (k2), new DES (k3));
   }
}
```

This class extends the `EDECipher` class to implement triple-DES. We simply call the superclass constructor with three new instances of the `DES` encryption class.

We can use this class in place of `DES` in the earlier `CipherStream` example, and we will benefit from an algorithm that, although three times slower, is twice as strong.

24.6 Class CBCCipher

In its basic form, DES operates in ECB mode, or electronic codebook mode; it is a *block* cipher. This means that when you encrypt a block of data, you do not consider any data that have been previously encrypted; you encrypt the block solely based on its contents. As a result, if the same block occurs several times in a particular piece of data, then that block will result in the same ciphertext at each occurrence. Attackers can exploit this if they know, for example, that the second block in every bank transaction is an amount of money. They can simply insert blocks from previous transactions and change the amounts of money that are being transacted without corrupting the syntactic correctness of the message. Another problem is that attackers can also identify structure in messages because of this repetition problem.

The encryption performed by a *stream* cipher, on the other hand, depends on earlier data that have already been encrypted. Replacing a block of ciphertext from a stream cipher will not be possible because it and the subsequent data will not decrypt successfully. Successful decryption of any block depends on the data that have gone before, and if you change this, then the decryption will result in garbage. Similarly, structure in the plaintext will not be observable in the ciphertext of a stream cipher. See the appendix on security for a further discussion of these issues.

We can convert a block cipher into a stream cipher by *chaining* the data: We modify the encryption of every block by data that have been previously encrypted. The cipher-block-chaining mode exclusive-ORs every plaintext with the previous ciphertext block, before encryption.

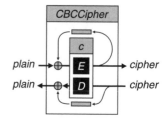

Figure 24.6   Class CBCCipher

This `CBCCipher` class converts a block cipher into a stream cipher by applying CBC to the encryption process (Figure 24.6). In a similar manner to the `EDECipher` class that we just looked at, we attach to an existing `Cipher` and modify its operation accordingly.

```
public class CBCCipher extends Cipher {
   // public CBCCipher (Cipher c) ...
   // public CBCCipher (Cipher c, byte[] iv) ...
   // public void encipherBlock (byte[] plain, int po, byte[] cipher, int co) ...
   // public void decipherBlock (byte[] cipher, int co, byte[] plain, int po) ...
   // public int blockSize () ...
}
```

The CBCCipher class is a Cipher that attaches to an existing block-cipher and applies CBC stream-encryption to it. We can thus easily perform CBC encryption with DES (DES-CBC) or any other Cipher that we implement.

```
protected Cipher c;
protected byte[] oldEncipher, oldDecipher;
protected int bS;
public CBCCipher (Cipher c, byte[] iv) {
   this.c = c;
   bS = c.blockSize ();
   oldEncipher = new byte[bS];
   oldDecipher = new byte[bS];
   if (iv != null) {
      System.arraycopy (iv, 0, oldEncipher, 0, bS);
      System.arraycopy (iv, 0, oldDecipher, 0, bS);
   }
}
```

In this constructor, you specify the Cipher c and an initialization vector iv that will be used to initialize the cipher-block-chaining.

We must keep a record of the last ciphertext block, to perform this process. In this class, we keep the previous ciphertext in the oldEncipher array for encryption and in oldDecipher for decryption. We keep separate ciphertext histories for encryption and decryption, because we wish to be able to use the same Cipher for encrypting data that is going out a communications channel as for decrypting data that is coming in. If we used the same history, then the encryption process would interfere with the decryption process, and vice versa.

```
public CBCCipher (Cipher c) {
   this (c, null);
}
```

This constructor assumes a default initialization vector of 0.

```
public void encipherBlock (byte[] plain, int po, byte[] cipher, int co) {
   for (int i = 0; i < bS; ++ i)
      cipher[co + i] = (byte) (oldEncipher[i] ^ plain[po + i]);
   c.encipherBlock (cipher, co, cipher, co);
   System.arraycopy (cipher, co, oldEncipher, 0, bS);
}
```

To encrypt a block, we exclusive-OR the plaintext with the previous ciphertext block and then encrypt this with the `Cipher` c. We must also keep a copy of this new ciphertext for the purposes of encrypting the next block.

```
public void decipherBlock (byte[] cipher, int co, byte[] plain, int po) {
    c.decipherBlock (cipher, co, plain, po);
    for (int i = 0; i < bS; ++ i) {
        byte o = cipher[co + i];
        plain[po + i] ^= oldDecipher[i];
        oldDecipher[i] = o;
    }
}
```

To decrypt a block, we first decrypt the received block with c; by decrypting it we reverse the encryption that occurred. We are then left with the plaintext that was initially ciphertext exclusive-ORed, and so we must undo this process too. To undo an exclusive-OR operation, you can simple apply the exclusive-OR again, so we just exclusive-OR the decrypted block with the previous ciphertext. We must also keep a copy of the ciphertext to decrypt the next block. We use the temporary variable o because the arrays `cipher` and `plain` may in fact be the same.

```
public int blockSize () {
    return bS;
}
```

The block size of this CBC variant is the same as the original `Cipher`.

This class adds very little overhead to the encryption process; we must simply apply an exclusive-OR before encrypting and again, after decrypting. This significantly strengthens the encryption because we are no longer vulnerable to random block-substitutions or removals.

For all common situations, we strongly advise the use of this variant in place of a normal block encryption algorithm.

24.7 Initialization vectors

We briefly discussed how DES is subject to block-substitution attacks if we don't apply a chaining algorithm. It turns out that it is still vulnerable to an attack on the first block that is sent (or, in fact, any continuous section of blocks from the beginning). The first block that is sent will not be exclusive-ORed (or, in this implementation, will be exclusive-ORed with 0) and so is vulnerable to block-replay. Because the second block depends on this first block, we can actually substitute the start of an encrypted communication stream with an entire sequence of blocks from an earlier conversation.

An initialization vector is a redundant value that is exclusive-ORed with the first block of data that is encrypted. In this case, this is the initial contents of `oldEncipher` and `oldDecipher`. The sender and receiver must agree on a value for this; however, any random value or timestamp will prevent a substitution attack against the beginning of a message. Remember that the purpose of CBC is to ensure that if the same block is encrypted twice, then it will result in different ciphertext each time. The initialization vector ensures that if the same message is encrypted twice, then it will result in a different ciphertext each time.

24.8 Class TripleDESCBC

We can combine EDE with CBC in one of two ways; we can either create an EDE from three CBC ciphers (inner-CBC), or we can create a CBC cipher from one EDE cipher (outer-CBC) (Figure 24.7).

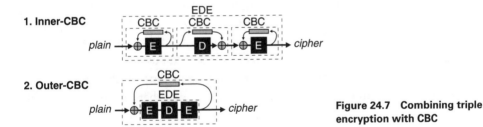

Figure 24.7 Combining triple encryption with CBC

It might appear that inner-CBC would be more secure; after all, we are applying more exclusive-OR operations than the alternative. It turns out, however, that this is not the case, and that outer-CBC is a better option (Figure 24.8).

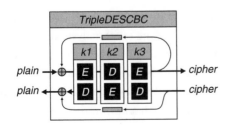

Figure 24.8 Class TripleDESCBC

```
public class TripleDESCBC extends CBCCipher {
   public TripleDESCBC (long k1, long k2) {
      super (new TripleDES (k1, k2));
   }

   public TripleDESCBC (long k1, long k2, long k3) {
      super (new TripleDES (k1, k2, k3));
   }
}
```

This class implements outer-CBC triple-DES; we extend the CBCCipher class and add constructors that take either two or three DES keys. Each of the constructors calls the superclass constructor with a new TripleDES Cipher formed from these keys.

In effect, this class is wrapping CBC-feedback around a single TripleDES Cipher. This TripleDES Cipher is actually an encrypt-decrypt-encrypt Cipher formed from three distinct DES Ciphers.

24.9 Wrapping up

In this chapter we have provided an implementation of DES, and also some of what are effectively filter ciphers that modify the execution of a plain Cipher such as DES. There are many other encryption algorithms available that may be faster and possibly more secure than DES. It turns out that implementing these algorithms is frequently fairly simple. The specifications are publicly available, and there are usually free implementations available from which to work. Some encryption algorithms worth noting include IDEA and RC5; the cryptography appendix covers these and others in a bit more detail.

It is very important, if we ever work from public code, that we verify the implementation. There are usually example plaintext/ciphertext pairs available from official sources that can be used to easily check that an implementation is correct.

Another avenue worth pursuing is a DES variant. Many cryptanalytic attacks on DES require a large amount of precomputed data. If we employ even a slight variant of DES, then this data will be of no use and a cryptanalytical attack will be significantly harder. It is not wise to invent these modifications ourselves; significant work went into the DES specification, and arbitrary changes will probably greatly weaken the encryption. There are, however, variants of DES that have undergone cryptanalysis and appear to be sound. Among these, corrected s^3DES is more secure against linear cryptanalysis than plain DES, and Biham's key-dependent S-Box variant is also worth noting.

The DES class that we developed here requires a 64-bit key (of which it uses 56 bits); however, we have not yet discussed how to generate such a key. In the next chapter we will provide an implementation of SHS, the secure hash standard. We will also develop a derivative that uses DES to generate a message authentication code. These classes will provide integrity checks for messages that are transmitted in plaintext; however, we will also be able to use the SHS class to generate keys for encryption algorithms. This, and other key-generation issues are discussed in the final chapter of this part of the book.

chapter 25

Hash algorithms

The TCP transport protocol uses internal CRC checks to ensure that data are not accidentally corrupted during transmission; however, if an application is genuinely concerned with security then the Internet protocols are easily subverted. The concepts of integrity and authentication are that a message can be verified to be intact, and that a message can be verified to have come from a particular sender.

Encrypting a communications channel provides partial authentication; only two people will share the encryption key and so if an encrypted message is received successfully, then you can be fairly sure of the sender. Without chaining, however, the message will be vulnerable to block substitution attacks. Even CBC is vulnerable to attacks; to flip bits in any particular block, you need only flip the corresponding bits of the previous block. The altered block will of course decrypt to garbage; however, this does provide an attacker with some undesirable control.

To combat this problem, we use a hash function. Such a function takes a long message and computes a small digest. This digest can be transmitted along with the message. To verify that the message has been received successfully, the recipient can recompute a digest from the message and verify that this matches the original digest that accompanied the message.

An important property of a cryptographically secure hash algorithm is that it should be *computationally infeasible* to find two messages that hash to the same digest. With such an algorithm, we can either send this digest on an encrypted channel or in plaintext; it is not possible to reproduce a message from its digest and it is not possible to produce a new message with the same digest. As a result, if the message is changed then the digests will not match. Of course, an attacker can simply replace both a message and its digest; we will discuss this problem later.

25.1 Class SHS

This class implements SHA, the secure hash algorithm specified by SHS, the secure hash standard. This is a hash function that computes a 160-bit digest from a message of arbitrary length.

This class is a subclass of the Hash class that we developed earlier; this lets us use the SHS class to provide integrity checking on any streams-based communications channel (Figure 25.1).

```
public class SHS extends Hash {
    // public byte[] digest (byte[] text, int off, int len) ..
    // public int digestSize () ...
}
```

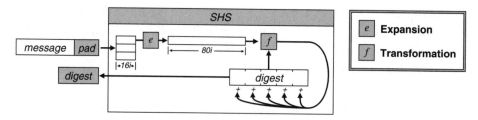

Figure 25.1   Class SHS

The `Hash` class declares two methods that must be defined by a subclass, `digest()` and `digestSize()`. The `digest()` method computes a digest of the specified message, and the `digestSize()` method indicates how large the digest will be.

```
public byte[] digest (byte[] text, int off, int len) {
   byte[] message = pad (text, off, len);
   int[] data = new int[80];
   int[] digest = { h0, h1, h2, h3, h4 };

   for (int i = 0; i < message.length; i += 64) {
     Crypt.bytesToInts (message, i, data, 0, 16);
     transform (digest, data);
   }

   byte[] result = new byte[20];
   Crypt.intsToBytes (digest, 0, 5, result, 0);
   return result;
}

// protected byte[] pad (byte[] text, int off, int len) ...
// protected final void transform (int[] digest, int[] data) ...

protected static final int h0 = 0x67452301;
protected static final int h1 = 0xEFCDAB89;
protected static final int h2 = 0x98BADCFE;
protected static final int h3 = 0x10325476;
protected static final int h4 = 0xC3D2E1F0;
```

This method returns a digest of the specified byte array `text`. The digest is computed from `len` bytes of the array, starting from index `off`.

SHA operates on blocks of 64 bytes at a time, and specifies the manner by which a message should be padded to be a multiple of this block size. We use the `pad()` method to perform this padding; this method returns a new array `message` that consists of the original message with appropriate padding (Figure 25.2).

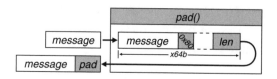

Figure 25.2   SHS padding function

To compute a digest we loop through the padded message, copying every 64 bytes from `message` to `data` and then using the `transform()` method to actually perform the SHS block-step.

The algorithm uses integer values during computation; this is very efficient on most computers. It builds up a 20-byte digest in the `digest` array, operating on data from the `data` array. The initial values for the `digest` array are provided by the algorithm specification.

Once this is complete, we can return an array of bytes corresponding to the digest.

```
protected byte[] pad (byte[] text, int off, int len) {
    int padLen = (len + 9 + 63) & ~63;
    byte[] paddedText = new byte[padLen];
    System.arraycopy (text, off, paddedText, 0, len);
    paddedText[len] = (byte) 0x80;
    Crypt.longToBytes ((long) len << 3, paddedText, padLen - 8);
    return paddedText;
}
```

This method pads the specified text to be a multiple of the hash block size. We do this by creating a new array `paddedText` that is the correct size, copying the original message into it, appending a byte 128 to the message and inserting the original message length into the last eight bytes of the padded message. By inserting the original message length at the end, we ensure that no two different messages can actually result in the same padded message.

```
protected final void transform (int[] digest, int[] data) {
    int a = digest[0];
    int b = digest[1];
    int c = digest[2];
    int d = digest[3];
    int e = digest[4];

    for (int i = 16; i < 80; ++ i) {
        int tmp = data[i - 3] ^ data[i - 8] ^ data[i - 14] ^ data[i - 16];
        data[i] = (tmp << 1) | (tmp >>> 31);
    }
    for (int i = 0; i < 80; ++ i) {
        int temp = ((a << 5) | (a >>> 27)) + e + data[i];
        if (i < 20)
            temp += ((b & c) | (~b & d)) + k1;
        else if (i < 40)
            temp += (b ^ c ^ d) + k2;
        else if (i < 60)
            temp += ((b & c) | (b & d) | (c & d)) + k3;
        else
            temp += (b ^ c ^ d) + k4;
        e = d;
        d = c;
```

```
        c = ((b << 30) | (b >>> 2));
        b = a;
        a = temp;
    }

    digest[0] += a;
    digest[1] += b;
    digest[2] += c;
    digest[3] += d;
    digest[4] += e;
}

protected static final int k1 = 0x5A827999;
protected static final int k2 = 0x6ED9EBA1;
protected static final int k3 = 0x8F1BBCDC;
protected static final int k4 = 0xCA62C1D6;
```

This method performs the body of the SHA digest. We expand the 16 `int` values in the `data` array into 80 by applying various exclusive-OR and shift operations. Note that the shift operation was an addendum to correct a flaw in the original algorithm, and so the test cases provided in the original specification are no longer valid to test this implementation.

To compute a digest, the algorithm applies various arithmetic and logical operations to the digest and the 80 elements of `data`. Again, it uses some *magic* constants during this computation. The resulting digest is returned to the `digest` array for processing by the next block of data.

```
public int digestSize () {
    return 20;
}
```

This algorithm produces a 160-bit digest, which is represented by 20 bytes.

Like many cryptographic algorithms, SHA consists of a series of seemingly magic bit-twiddling operations. There are actually goals for these operations; they are not just provided at random. A principle goal is the *avalanche* effect, so that at the end, changing any bit in the plaintext has an equal chance of affecting any bit in the output.

25.2 Using the SHS class

The `SHS` class is an implementation of the `Hash` class, and so we can use it with the hash streams that we developed earlier to add an integrity check to any application that uses a streams-based communications channel.

The following fragment of code demonstrates the transmission of a simple message using a `HashOutputStream` that automatically adds a digest to the end of the message.

```
// OutputStream o ...
HashOutputStream hashO = new HashOutputStream (o, new SHS ());
DataOutputStream dataO = new DataOutputStream (hashO);
dataO.writeUTF ("hello, world!");
dataO.flush ();
```

We attach the `HashOutputStream hashO` to an existing `OutputStream o`, using the `SHS` class to compute digests. We can then use a `DataOutputStream` to send to this stream, just as to any normal stream. When we `flush()` the stream, the digest will be computed and the message sent.

The corresponding fragment to read a message back follows:

```
// InputStream i ...
HashInputStream hashI = new HashInputStream (i, new SHS ());
DataInputStream dataI = new DataInputStream (hashI);
System.out.println (dataI.readUTF ());
```

A `HashInputStream hashI` is attached to the `InputStream i`; it verifies all data that are read using the supplied `SHS` hash class. We can read from this stream in a completely transparent manner; were the message integrity to be violated, the `read()` call would throw an appropriate `HashException`.

25.3 Class HashMAC

An obvious problem with using a hash algorithm like SHS to provide integrity in the presence of hostility is that, although an error will be detected if just a small part of a message is changed, an attacker would be quite capable of simply computing a new digest and replacing the digest as well.

To combat this problem, we need a MAC, or message authentication code. This is a hash algorithm that uses a key to compute the digest. Unless the attacker knows this key, it will not be able to compute the new digest (Figure 25.3).

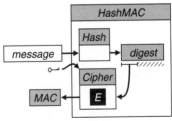

Figure 25.3 Class HashMAC

```
public class HashMAC extends Hash {
    // public HashMAC (Hash h, Cipher c) ...
    // public byte[] digest (byte[] text,
        int off, int len) ...
    // public int digestSize () ...
}
```

This class is a `Hash` that takes an existing hash algorithm and encryption algorithm, and combines them to form a MAC. We use the hash algorithm to compute a digest of the message in the usual manner, but then we encrypt this digest with the encryption algorithm.

If the sender and receiver have a shared secret key for this encryption algorithm, then an attacker will not be able to forge a digest and break the integrity checking.

```
protected Hash h;
protected Cipher c;
public HashMAC (Hash h, Cipher c) {
  this.h = h;
  this.c = c;
}
```

The code simply takes an existing `Hash` h and `Cipher` c, and provides an implementation of the `digest()` method.

```
public byte[] digest (byte[] text, int off, int len) {
  byte[] hash = h.digest (text, off, len);
  return c.encipher (hash, 0, Math.min (hash.length, c.blockSize ()));
}
```

The `digest()` method computes a digest of the message using h and then encrypts the result with c.

You will note that we don't encrypt the entire digest; we simply encrypt the first block and discard the rest. If we assume that the attacker does not know our key, then the 160-bit length is unnecessary; it simply provides an attacker with more plaintext/ciphertext pairs with which to work.

Remember that an attacker can easily compute the message digest. If we consider this digest to be a piece of plaintext, then the MAC that an attacker can observe is the ciphertext. It can then use this plaintext and corresponding ciphertext to attempt to break the encryption key. This type of attack requires vast quantities of plaintext/ciphertext pairs; the less information that we leak, the more secure our application.

```
public int digestSize () {
  return c.blockSize ();
}
```

The digest size of this `Hash` is equal to the block size of the encryption algorithm.

Using this type of MAC we can safely transmit messages in plaintext, thus saving the expense of encrypting the entire message, yet the receiver can still verify that the message has not been tampered with during transmission. The hash algorithm operates considerably faster than the encryption algorithm, so where appropriate it is always more efficient to transmit nonsensitive information in plaintext and just use a MAC for integrity checking than to encrypt the entire message.

One thing to note, however, is that if we use a block-cipher in ECB mode (electronic codebook mode, i.e., no chaining), then there is nothing to stop an attacker from repeating an entire message along with a digest. Using a CBC-mode encryption algorithm for the MAC prevents this because the encryption of every digest depends on previous messages. Of course, if the same initialization vector (IV) is used for every conversation, then an entire conversation can be repeated. The best solution is to use a different IV for every conversation, or to initiate with a challenge/response sequence.

A challenge/response sequence is a very simple phase that you can use to initialize CBC encryption algorithms with initialization values. A new client sends an encrypted random value r to the server; the server then responds with the value $r + 1$, or some other computed value, and the client verifies the response. An attacker cannot defeat this because it cannot decrypt r and return $r + 1$, and it cannot repeat an old message because the sender will observe an erroneous response.

25.4 Wrapping up

In the previous chapter, we saw how to implement secure communications channels using encryption techniques. In this chapter, we saw how to implement communications channels with integrity checking using hash techniques. In addition, we saw how to combine hash functions and encryption to provide plaintext integrity checking in the presence of hostility.

Sometimes we wish to also provide integrity checking for ciphertext. While many of the attacks that can be mounted on a ciphertext (block substitution, etc.) result in a corruption of the stream, it would be useful to provide automatic integrity checking so that we do not have to check every message for validity. The simplest way to do this is to wrap encryption around a hashed stream; the hash algorithm will thus automatically verify message integrity.

We can actually perform this process slightly more efficiently if we create new classes that combine the two functions. We encrypt each message and send the corresponding ciphertext; we then compute a digest of the plaintext, and send this. We need not encrypt the digest because it does not leak any information. Upon reading this message, we decrypt it and recompute the digest; this should match the digest that came with the ciphertext.

An important prerequisite for the use of these classes is the generation of good keys. In the following chapter we will look at generating keys and some of the issues involved in writing applications that authenticate clients to a central server.

chapter 26

Using encryption

Up to this point, we have ignored the problem of key generation. The DES algorithm requires a 56-bit key and we have taken this for granted by using fixed constants. There are generally two situations where we will need to generate a key: the first occurs when a user types in a password. We need to convert the string of characters into a key suitable for the encryption process. The second occurs when a server is generating a sequence of session keys for clients. A session key is a key that is used for a single conversation; typically a user will authenticate with a password, and then receive a different key to encrypt the subsequent conversation. We use session keys to limit the damage that can be caused by an attacker breaking a particular key; if the session key is broken, then only one conversation will be exposed.

In this chapter, we will discuss all of these issues. The first is generating a key from a password; we will make use of the SHS algorithm to perform this process. The second is generating a sequence of session keys; we will make use of the DES algorithm to perform this process. The final issue is that of user authentication, and we will combine password and session key generation for this.

26.1 Generating password keys

Generating a key from a password is very easy; we can simply apply a cryptographically secure hashing algorithm to generate a digest from the password (Figure 26.1). Because of the properties of the hashing algorithm—you cannot recreate a password from its digest and you cannot feasibly create another password that hashes to the same digest—this digest is a perfectly appropriate key. Under certain systems—UNIX without shadow passwords, for example—this

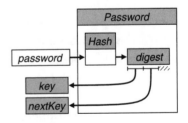

Figure 26.1 Generating keys from passwords

digested key is publicly readable (UNIX passwords use some extra techniques for security. Until recently, this was not considered a significant security threat.

Usually the digest will be longer than the required key length; however, we can just select the desired number of bits from the digest. Performing some exclusive-OR operations to reduce the digest will not improve security.

```
long keyFromPassword (String password) {
    byte[] passwordBytes = new byte[password.length () * 2];
    for (int i = 0; i < password.length (); ++ i) {
        char c = password.charAt (i);
```

```
    passwordBytes[i * 2] = (byte) (c >> 8);
    passwordBytes[i * 2 + 1] = (byte) c;
  }
  SHS hash = new SHS ();
  byte[] keyBytes = hash.digest (passwordBytes);
  return Crypt.bytesToLong (keyBytes, 0);
}
```

The `keyFromPassword()` method converts the supplied string `password` into an array of bytes and computes a digest of this. Note that in this case, we are considering the full sixteen bits of each character, so we produce two bytes from each character. In most situations this will be unnecessary, but it does not affect the security of the system.

```
long nextKeyFromPassword (String password) {
  byte[] passwordBytes = new byte[password.length () * 2];
  for (int i = 0; i < password.length (); ++ i) {
    char c = password.charAt (i);
    passwordBytes[i * 2] = (byte) (c >> 8);
    passwordBytes[i * 2 + 1] = (byte) c;
  }
  SHS hash = new SHS ();
  byte[] keyBytes = hash.digest (passwordBytes);
  return Crypt.bytesToLong (keyBytes, 8);
}
```

This method is very similar to the previous method, except that it returns the second 64-bit value from the message digest. We can use this for two purposes, either as a second key for two-key Triple-DES or as an initialization vector for DES-CBC.

Bear in mind, when using plaintext passwords, the ease with which simple passwords can be guessed. This method *will* convert a one-character password into a 64-bit key, but this will take someone mere moments to guess. The security appendix discusses the problems of choosing good passwords in more detail.

In particular, with respect to these two methods, it should be noted that unless the password string contains more than 64 bits worth of randomness, then there will probably be a one-to-one mapping between the keys returned by `keyFromPassword()` and the keys returned by `nextKeyFromPassword()`. Algorithms which require two independent keys, such as tripleDES, will thus not provide increased strength using these keys unless appropriately strong passwords or pass-phrases are used. At least, against a very smart attacker.

26.2 DES keys

The `keyFromPassword()` method returns a 64-bit value. The DES encryption algorithm requires only 56 bits; the other bits can be used as a parity check. We will see how this is useful when we look at password authentication with a server later in this chapter. See Figure 26.2.

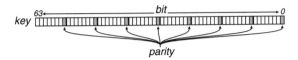

Figure 26.2   DES parity bits

The DES parity bits are the low bit in each of the eight bytes of the key. We can easily compute parity for any key by using the exclusive-OR operation (Figure 26.3).

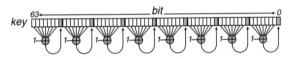

Figure 26.3   Computing the DES parity bits

```
long paritySet (long key) {
   long pKey = (key >> 1) ^ (key >> 2) ^ (key >> 3) ^ (key >> 4) ^ (key >> 5)
      ^ (key >> 6) ^ (key >> 7);
   return (key | 0x0101010101010101L) ^ (pKey & 0x0101010101010101L);
}
```

This method performs the exclusive-OR operations necessary to compute parity in the low bit of every byte in the supplied key. Remember that this does not affect the encryption process, which simply discards these parity bits; instead, we can use these bits to ensure that a key has survived transmission. We will see this use of the parity bits in the authentication protocols that we look at later.

```
boolean isParity (long key) {
   return (key == paritySet (key));
}
```

This method verifies that the key is the same after parity is set, and is therefore correct. There is only a one-in-256 chance that a corrupt key will pass this test.

26.3 Weak keys

There are certain keys that are known to be weak when used with DES. For example, if all of the bits in a key are zero, then the resulting DES key schedule will be all zero, which will weaken the algorithm. There are two approaches to dealing with weak keys.

One approach is to completely ignore weak keys because the likelihood of generating one at random is miniscule. Another approach is to simply reject passwords that generate weak keys, and to verify that no session key is a weak key. This is probably the appropriate approach given the simplicity of the solution.

Here is a list of DES's weak keys, semiweak key pairs, and possibly weak keys (hexadecimal, with parity):

```
0101010101010101 |  1f1f1f1f0e0e0e0e  |  e0e0e0e0f1f1f1f1  |  fefefefefefefefe

01fe01fe01fe01fe     fe01fe01fe01fe01  |  1fe01fe00ef10ef1     e01fe01ff10ef10e
01e001e001f101f1     e001e001f101f101  |  1ffe1ffe0efe0efe     fe1ffe1ffe0efe0e
011f011f010e010e     1f011f010e010e01  |  e0fee0fef1fef1fe     fee0fee0fef1fef1

1f1f01010e0e0101  |  011f1f01010e0e01  |  1f01011f0e01010e  |  01011f1f01010e0e
e0e00101f1f10101  |  fefe0101fefe0101  |  fee001f01fef10e01  |  e0fe1f01f1fe0e01
fee0011ffef1010e  |  e0fe011ff1fe010e  |  e0e01f1ff1f10e0e  |  fefe1f1ffefe0e0e
fe1fe001fe0ef101  |  e01ffe01f10efe01  |  fe01e01ffe01f10e  |  e001fe1ff101fe0e
01e0e00101f1f101  |  1ffee0010efef001  |  1fe0fe010ef1fe01  |  01fefe0101fefe01
1fee01e0ef1fe10e  |  01fee01f01fef10e  |  01e0fe1f01f1fe0e  |  1ffefe1f0efefe0e
e00101e0f10101f1  |  fe1f01e0fe0e01f1  |  fe011fe0fe010ef1  |  e01f1fe0f10e0ef1
fe0101fefe0101fe  |  e01f01fef10e01fe  |  e0011ffef1010efe  |  fe1f1ffefe0e0efe
1ffe01e00efe01f1  |  01fe1fe001fe0ef1  |  1fe001fe0ef101fe  |  01e01ffe01f10efe
0101e0e00101f1f1  |  1f1fe0e00e0eef1f1  |  1f01fee00e01fef1  |  011ffee0010efef1
1f01e0fe0e01f1fe  |  011fe0fe010eef1fe  |  0101fefe0101fefe  |  1f1ffefe0e0eefefe
fefee0e0fefef1f1  |  e0fefee0f1fefef1  |  fee0e0fefef1f1fe  |  e0e0fefef1f1fefe
```

26.4 Class X9_17KeyGen

In the authentication schemes that we will look at next, we will see that the server must be able to generate a series of session keys. These must be random; it would be very bad if a client could connect to the server repeatedly, determine the session key generation algorithm and guess what session keys would be generated for future clients.

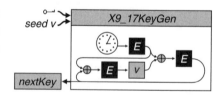

Figure 26.4   Class X9_17KeyGen

ANSI has a specification X9.17 that uses the DES encryption algorithm to produce random 64-bit values for just this purpose (Figure 26.4).

```
public class X9_17KeyGen {
  protected DES des;
  protected long v;

  public X9_17KeyGen (long key, long seed) {
    des = new DES (key);
```

```
      v = seed;
  }

  public long nextKey () {
     long t = des.encrypt (System.currentTimeMillis ());
     long r = des.encrypt (t ^ v);
     v = des.encrypt (t ^ r);
     return r;
  }
}
```

This class implements the X9.17 key generation standard. To seed the generator we must specify a key `key` and a seed `seed`. The administrator can type in a sequence of random data when the server is started and the earlier `keyFromPassword()` methods can be used to produce these values. Alternatively, the programmer can use another mechanism for obtaining random values; see the appendix on security for a few suggestions.

The process of producing a session key involves encrypting the current time, computing the key `r` from this, and updating the internal seed `v` based on this key value.

26.5 Password authentication

Authenticating a client to a server is an extremely common problem. The usual situation is that there is a user with a username and a password, and there is a server with a list of passwords for its users. The client cannot simply send the server the password, because then an eavesdropper would be able to capture the password. Instead, we must use an authentication protocol.

An extremely simply and effective protocol is the following: the user sends its name to the server in plaintext. The server looks up the user's password in its user database. It then generates a session key, encrypts this with the user's password and sends this back to the user. The user must decrypt this key using his or her own password. The client and server now share a session key that can be used for the remainder of the conversation (Figure 26.5).

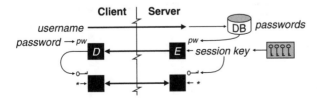

Figure 26.5 Authenticating a client to a server

An eavesdropper cannot learn from this conversation because no meaningful data have been sent. Without the user's secret key, the server's response cannot be decoded, and because the session key is essentially random data, there is no plaintext/ciphertext being leaked to the eavesdropper.

An additional stage to this protocol consists of a challenge/response phase that allows the client to determine that an intruder is not replaying an earlier conversation. The client picks a random number, encrypts it with the session key and transmits it to the server; the server decrypts this and responds with a value that is computed from the client's challenge. If the response is correct, then the client knows that it has a live connection to the server.

The following two classes implement this authentication protocol.

26.5.1 Class AuthServer

The `AuthServer` class provides an implementation of the server side of this authentication protocol (Figure 26.6). The server maintains a list of usernames and passwords; when a client connects, it transmits its username in plaintext. The server generates a session key, encrypts this with the user's password, and sends this key back to the client. This completes the initial phase of authentication; the server then awaits a challenge from the client. When the challenge is received, the server replies with the computed response, and then suitable encrypted streams are passed to an appropriate client handler. An example `AuthHandler` class is described later in this chapter.

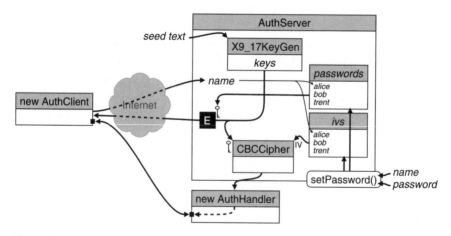

Figure 26.6 Class AuthServer

To generate secure session keys, this server requires some initial random data. These are provided in the form of a string that is passed to the server constructor. It is up to the user to provide an appropriate random string when the server is started; see the appendix on cryptography for further information on issues related to random data.

User passwords are stored in internal data structures; we provide a method that lets user passwords be assigned, but we do not provide methods to persistently store these passwords. Such a mechanism would obviously depend upon the server situation.

We will make use of the key-from-password methods that we described earlier; we assume that they are located in a class called `Password`.

```java
import java.io.*;
import java.net.*;
import java.util.*;

public class AuthServer {
    // public AuthServer (String seedText) ...
    // public void setPassword (String user, String password) ...
    // public void authenticate (InputStream i, OutputStream o) throws
    //     IOException ...
    // public static void main (String args[]) throws IOException ...
}
```

The `AuthServer` class implements an authenticating secure server. The key-generation seed text is specified in the constructor, and user passwords are specified with the `setPassword()` method. The `authenticate()` method accepts a connection attached to the specified streams; authentication is performed with the attached client, followed by a challenge/response phase. If the challenge/response is successful, a handler is created with encrypted streams to the client.

```java
protected X9_17KeyGen keys;
protected Hashtable passwords, ivs;
public AuthServer (String seedText) {
    keys = new X9_17KeyGen (Password.keyFromPassword (seedText),
        Password.nextKeyFromPassword (seedText));
    passwords = new Hashtable ();
    ivs = new Hashtable ();
}
```

In the constructor, we create a new key generator `keys` using the specified seed text `seedText` to initialize the generator. We then create a new `Hashtable passwords` that holds user password keys, and a new `Hashtable ivs` that holds the user initialization vectors.

```java
public void setPassword (String user, String password) {
    passwords.put (user, new Long (Password.keyFromPassword (password)));
    byte[] iv = new byte[8];
```

```
Crypt.longToBytes (Password.nextKeyFromPassword (password), iv, 0);
    ivs.put (user, iv);
}
```

The setPassword() method associates the username user with the specified password password. We create a key using the keyFromPassword() method, and insert this in the passwords Hashtable. This key is the user's encryption key, and will be used to encrypt session keys. We then create another key using the nextKeyFromPassword(). We place the key in an eight-byte array and insert it in the Hashtable ivs; we will use it to initialize a CBC cipher. We will discuss this in more detail after the authenticate() method.

Note that we don't store the password in plaintext on the server; doing so is both unnecessary and a security risk. Is is never necessary to store passwords in plaintext; if we store a user database in a file, then we should store these encoded values. Remember, a hash function is one-way, so even if an intruder can read these values then he cannot determine the user's actual password. Access to the password file obviously gives an intruder control over all communications to the system, but the one-way property means that he will not also be able to determine users' plaintext passwords. Such information would be a very useful basis for guessing users' passwords on other systems.

Obviously the password file must be kept secure and inaccessible to users on the system, however it is equally important to keep the IV file secure. Remember that unless the users choose very strong passwords, then there will probably be a one-to-one mapping between the password keys and the IV's. If an intruder can gain access to the IV file, then with some effort he could then recover the password file.

```
public void authenticate (InputStream i, OutputStream o) throws IOException {
    String user = new DataInputStream (i).readUTF ();
    long sessionKey = DES.paritySet (keys.nextKey ());
    new DataOutputStream (o).writeLong (encodeKey (user, sessionKey));
    o.flush ();
    Cipher sessionDES = new CBCCipher (new DES (sessionKey),
        (byte[]) ivs.get (user));
    byte[] temp = new byte[8];
    new DataInputStream (i).readFully (temp);
    long challenge = Crypt.bytesToLong (sessionDES.decipher (temp), 0);
    Crypt.longToBytes (challenge + 1, temp, 0);
    o.write (sessionDES.encipher (temp));
    try {
        new DataInputStream (i).readFully (temp);
        long complete = Crypt.bytesToLong (sessionDES.decipher (temp), 0);
        if (complete != challenge + 2)
            throw new AuthException ("Incorrect password.");
    } catch (EOFException ex) {
        throw new AuthException ("Challenge/response failed.");
    }
```

```
        InputStream sessionI = new CipherInputStream (i, sessionDES);
        OutputStream sessionO = new CipherOutputStream (o, sessionDES);
        accept (user, sessionI, sessionO);
    }

    // protected void accept (String name, InputStream i, OutputStream o) ...
    // protected long encodeKey (String user, long key) throws AuthException ...
```

The `authenticate()` method authenticates a user connected to the streams i and o, and then calls the `accept()` method to start a new handler to communicate over the encrypted channel.

We first read the client's name user from i and generate a session key sessionKey using our key-generator keys. We then encrypt this key with the user's password, using the `encodeKey()` method, and transmit this back to the client. The `encodeKey()` method encrypts the key with the user's password key, as stored in the passwords Hashtable. Note that we correctly set the parity in the session key so the client will easily be able to tell if the key has decrypted successfully.

We then create a new `Cipher sessionDES` that performs DES encryption in CBC mode. We use sessionKey as the key for DES, and use the value in the ivs Hashtable as an initialization vector for the cipher-block chaining.

The challenge/response phase follows; we read a long value from the client into the temp array, decrypt this using sessionDES and respond with one plus the client's challenge, again encrypted with sessionDES. A more complex function is unnecessary because an intruder will not be able to decrypt the client's challenge to compute the appropriate response.

If this response was correct, then we await one final counter-response from the client. Remember that at this stage, the server has no assurance that the client has the correct password; if the password is incorrect, then the client will not be able to decode server transmissions, although that may not become immediately apparent to the server. As a result, we require validation that the client can indeed communicate with us. There are two mechanisms that we can use to achieve this result.

If, as is the case with the AuthClient class, the client sends the current time as the challenge, then if we assume that the client and server clocks are relatively synchronized, we can simply validate the client's challenge. There is only a one in five-million chance that an incorrect challenge from the client will decrypt to fall within a given century, so allowing a fair degree of skew between client and server clocks, we can simply validate the client's challenge and assume an incorrect password if there is a large enough disparity.

Instead, however, in this case we require the client to counter respond with one plus our response. If the challenge/response phase failed, then the client will close the socket connection, we will encounter an EOFException and can then throw an appropriate

`AuthException`. We otherwise read and decrypt a `long` value from the client and ensure that this is correct, throwing an appropriate `AuthException` otherwise.

We can finally set up encrypted streams to communicate with the client; we create an encrypted `InputStream sessionI` and an encrypted `OutputStream sessionO` that use this `Cipher` to communicate with the user. We then call the `accept()` method which creates a handler attached to these streams.

Because we are using a different session key for each conversation with the user, we don't need to use a random initialization vector to prevent replay attacks. Even if a client has exactly the same conversation twice, the different session keys will produce completely different results. Instead, we use an initialization vector that is constructed from the user's password. This provides us with a small amount of increased security over using no initialization vector, although this is not very significant.

Our challenge/response sequence prevents an intruder from replaying an old conversation: if the intruder attempts to masquerade as the client, then the counter-response will fail and the server will observe the deception. Note that the intruder could not understand the conversation in any case, but this allows the server to identify deceit immediately.

```
protected void accept (String name, InputStream i, OutputStream o) {
   new AuthHandler (name, i, o).start ();
}
```

This method creates and starts a new `AuthHandler` that will communicate over the supplied secure streams `i` and `o`. The `AuthHandler` class is responsible for all subsequent communications with the client; its implementation will depend upon the particular application in question.

```
protected long encodeKey (String user, long key) throws AuthException {
   if (!passwords.containsKey (user))
      throw new AuthException ("User not registered.");
   Long password = (Long) passwords.get (user);
   DES des = new DES (password.longValue ());
   return des.encrypt (key);
}
```

This method encrypts a session key `key` with the user `user`'s password. We first check to see whether the user has a password; if not, then we throw an appropriate exception. Otherwise, we extract the user's password key `password`, and use this to DES-encrypt the session key.

```
public static void main (String args[]) throws IOException {
   if (args.length < 2)
      throw new RuntimeException ("Syntax: AuthServer <port> {seed text}");
```

```
ServerSocket server = new ServerSocket (Integer.parseInt (args[0]));
StringBuffer seed = new StringBuffer ();
for (int i = 1; i < args.length; ++ i)
   seed.append (args[i]).append (' ');
AuthServer auth = new AuthServer (seed.toString ());
while (true) {
   Socket s = server.accept ();
   try {
      auth.authenticate (s.getInputStream (), s.getOutputStream ());
   } catch (IOException ex) {
      ex.printStackTrace ();
      s.close ();
   }
 }
}
```

In the `main()` method, we create a new `AuthServer` that accepts client connections, authenticates the clients, and creates handlers to communicate with them in a secure manner.

Command-line parameters specify the server's port and also the text that is used to seed the server's key generation. We create a `ServerSocket socket` that listens on the specified port, and then append all of the remaining command-line parameters into the `StringBuffer seed`. We then create an `AuthServer auth` with this seed text.

We finally sit in a loop, accepting client connections, and passing these on to `auth` for authentication. If there is a problem authenticating a single user, then we just display the exception and keep going.

Note that we don't specify any user passwords in this method; it is obviously also necessary to load in a user database from storage.

An important point of security worth noting is that specifying seed text on the command-line like this is not necessarily a good idea. On many systems, it is possible to determine commands that are being run by other users, and it may also be possible to observe their command-line parameters. In this case, other users would be able to determine the server's session-key generation seed. Instead, it would be more appropriate to read the seed-text from `System.in` and thus hide the seed text from unauthorized observation.

26.5.2 Class AuthClient

The `AuthClient` class provides the client-side of this authentication protocol. The constructor accepts a server address, and a username and password. It connects to the server, authenticates the user, performs a challenge/response phase, and finally returns encrypted communications streams that can be used to securely communicate with the server (Figure 26.7).

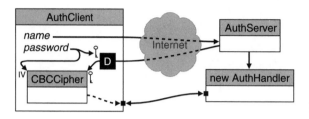

Figure 26.7   Class AuthClient

```
import java.io.*;
import java.net.*;

public class AuthClient {
  // public AuthClient (String server, int port, String user, String password)
  //    throws IOException ...
  // public InputStream getInputStream () ...
  // public OutputStream getOutputStream () ...
}
```

The AuthClient constructor accepts the server and user information; it automatically connects to the server and authenticates the client. If there is a problem, then an appropriate exception is thrown. The getInputStream() and getOutputStream() methods can subsequently be used to obtain secure streams to the server.

```
protected InputStream i;
protected OutputStream o;

public AuthClient (String server, int port, String user, String password)
    throws IOException {
  Socket s = new Socket (server, port);
  OutputStream out = s.getOutputStream ();
  new DataOutputStream (out).writeUTF (user);
  out.flush ();
  InputStream in = s.getInputStream ();
  long encKey = new DataInputStream (in).readLong ();
  DES keyDes = new DES (Password.keyFromPassword (password));
  long key = keyDes.decrypt (encKey);
  if (!DES.isParity (key)) {
    s.close ();
    throw new AuthException ("Incorrect password.");
  }
  byte[] iv = new byte[8];
  Crypt.longToBytes (Password.nextKeyFromPassword (password), iv, 0);
  Cipher sessionDES = new CBCCipher (new DES (key), iv);
  long challenge = System.currentTimeMillis ();
  byte[] temp = new byte[8];
```

```
      Crypt.longToBytes (challenge, temp, 0);
      out.write (sessionDES.encipher (temp));
      new DataInputStream (in).readFully (temp);
      long response = Crypt.bytesToLong (sessionDES.decipher (temp), 0);
      if (response != challenge + 1)
         throw new AuthException ("Challenge/response failed.");
      Crypt.longToBytes (response + 1, temp, 0);
      out.write (sessionDES.encipher (temp));
      o = new CipherOutputStream (out, sessionDES);
      i = new CipherInputStream (in, sessionDES);
   }
```

The constructor performs all the work of client authentication. We create a `Socket` s and connect to port `port` of the specified server `server`.

We initially transmit the username `user` in plaintext, and await the encrypted session key response `encKey`. We next create a new DES `Cipher keyDes` using the password as a key, and decrypt the actual session key `key`.

If the DES parity of the received key is incorrect, then the password was incorrect, and we throw an appropriate exception. There is less than a half percent chance (one in 256) that an incorrect password would pass this test, and even if an incorrect password did pass the test, the session key would not be correct, and so communications would remain unintelligible.

We create a CBC-mode DES cipher `sessionDES` using the key `key` and an initialization vector that is derived from the user's password. We now perform the challenge/response phase which consists of encrypting the current time with `sessionDES` and transmitting this to the server. We await the server's response which must decrypt to be one plus the value which we transmitted, or else the challenge/response has failed and either an intruder was present or our password was actually incorrect. The final stage of this phase is to respond to the server with one plus its response, again encrypted with `sessionDES`.

We can finally create the encrypted communications streams `i` and `o` using `sessionDES` and return.

Our challenge/response phase prevents an intruder from replaying an earlier conversation with the server; if the intruder attempts to masquerade as the server, he will not be able to provide the appropriate response to our challenge and will be discovered. Note that if the server initiated the challenge/response sequence, then we could not identify such a deception.

Another point worth noting is that this protocol is only as secure as the system on which it is running. If an intruder could control our perception of time, then they could reset the clock and replay an earlier conversation. Such a situation could arise if a workstation were to receive its time from a network time protocol that does not include appropriate authentication techniques. Pay attention to the security of your systems as much as to the security of your applications.

```
public InputStream getInputStream () {
    return i;
}
```

This method returns the encrypted stream i from the server.

```
public OutputStream getOutputStream () {
    return o;
}
```

This method returns the encrypted stream o to the server.

A client can use this class to connect and authenticate to a server, and subsequently communicate in a secure fashion across a public network.

Before using this code in a critical environment, it is important to take several precautions: You should be familiar with encryption and authentication in general, as well as with recent advancements in the field. You should verify that this code does indeed function and provide security as claimed. And finally, you should be aware of other potential security weaknesses in your environment: if your operating system does not provide memory security, then another user on the same machine could observe session keys in memory.

With such issues in mind, code such as this can be used to provide much-needed security for Internet applications. Currently this encryption is not tremendously fast; however, it is frequently the case that only some information need be encrypted, and the rest transmitted in plaintext.

26.6 Using the authentication classes

We can use these authentication classes for many purposes, including authentication of users before granting them access to sensitive data or just providing a secure communications environment. In this example, we apply the authentication classes to a familiar environment: a networked chat program.

26.6.1 Class AuthChat

This class implements the client side of a networked chat. It makes use of the Auth-Client class to establish a secure communications channel to the server, and provides the usual text-based chat interface.

```
import java.io.*;
import java.awt.*;

public class AuthChat extends Frame implements Runnable {
    public AuthChat (String title, String server, int port, String username,
        String password) throws IOException {
    public void run () {
    public boolean handleEvent (Event e) {
    public static void main (String args[]) throws IOException {
}
```

The constructor for this class accepts a title for the Frame, title, the server name server and port port, and the client's username username and password password. A new thread executes in the run() method to receive data from the server, and the handleEvent() method processes user input. The main() method creates a new Auth-Chat with the appropriate parameters.

```
    protected DataInputStream i;
    protected DataOutputStream o;
    protected TextArea output;
    protected TextField input;
    protected Thread listener;

    public AuthChat (String title, String server, int port, String username,
            String password) throws IOException {
        super (title);
        AuthClient conn = new AuthClient (server, port, username, password);
        this.i = new DataInputStream (conn.getInputStream ());
        this.o = new DataOutputStream (conn.getOutputStream ());
        setLayout (new BorderLayout ());
        add ("Center", output = new TextArea ());
        output.setEditable (false);
        add ("South", input = new TextField ());
        pack ();
        show ();
        input.requestFocus ();
        listener = new Thread (this);
        listener.start ();
    }
```

The constructor performs authentication and network setup before laying out the user interface. We first construct an AuthClient conn that connects to the specified server and authenticates with the specified user information. If authentication fails, then an appropriate exception will be thrown; we can otherwise communicate securely through the encrypted streams i and o that are returned by auth.

We finally lay out the simple user interface and start a `Thread listener` that receives data from the server.

```
public void run () {
   try {
      while (true) {
         String line = i.readUTF ();
         output.appendText (line + "\n");
      }
   } catch (IOException ex) {
      ex.printStackTrace ();
   } finally {
      listener = null;
      input.hide ();
      validate ();
      try {
         o.close ();
      } catch (IOException ex) {
         ex.printStackTrace ();
      }
   }
}
```

The `listener` thread enters the `run()` method and receives data from the server in the form of UTF `Strings`. We loop, receiving such `Strings` and displaying them in the output region `output`. When an `IOException` is encountered we hide the input region `input` and close the server connection.

```
public boolean handleEvent (Event e) {
   if ((e.target == input) && (e.id == Event.ACTION_EVENT)) {
      try {
         o.writeUTF ((String) e.arg);
         o.flush ();
      } catch (IOException ex) {
         ex.printStackTrace();
         listener.stop ();
      }
      input.setText ("");
      return true;
   } else if ((e.target == this) && (e.id == Event.WINDOW_DESTROY)) {
      if (listener != null)
         listener.stop ();
      hide ();
      return true;
   }
   return super.handleEvent (e);
}
```

User input generates `Events` that are passed to the `handleEvent()` method. We simply transmit every `String` that the user enters, and flush the communications stream. If an exception is encountered, then we stop the `listener` `Thread` which causes the `finally` clause to perform the appropriate cleanup. If the user tries to close the frame, then we again stop `listener`, and hide the frame.

```
public static void main (String args[]) throws IOException {
    if (args.length != 4)
        throw new RuntimeException ("Syntax: AuthChat <host> <port> <name>
            <password>");
    new AuthChat ("AuthChat " + args[0] + ":" + args[1], args[0],
        Integer.parseInt (args[1]), args[2], args[3]);
}
```

The `main()` method simply verifies the command-line parameters, and then starts a new `AuthChat` that connects to the specified server with the specified user information.

26.6.2 Class AuthHandler

This is an example implementation of the `AuthHandler` class that implements a simple broadcast-chat.

```
import java.io.*;
import java.util.*;

public class AuthHandler extends Thread {
    // public AuthHandler (String name, InputStream in, OutputStream out) ...
    // public void run () ...
}
```

The `AuthHandler` class is a `Thread` that processes input from the user whose name is specified in the constructor, and communicates over the encrypted streams that are provided in the constructor.

```
protected String name;
protected DataInputStream i;
protected DataOutputStream o;

public AuthHandler (String name, InputStream in, OutputStream out) {
    this.name = name;
    i = new DataInputStream (in);
    o = new DataOutputStream (out);
}
```

The `AuthServer` class performs authentication with the user and then provides the username `name` as well as the encrypted streams `in` and `out` to a new instance of this `AuthHandler` class. The `AuthHandler` is subsequently responsible for communicating with the user.

```
protected static Vector handlers = new Vector ();

public void run () {
   try {
      broadcast (name + " has joined.");
      handlers.addElement (this);
      while (true) {
         String msg = i.readUTF ();
         broadcast (msg);
      }
   } catch (IOException ex) {
      ex.printStackTrace ();
   } finally {
      handlers.removeElement (this);
      try {
         o.close ();
      } catch (IOException ex) {
         ex.printStackTrace();
      }
   }
}

// protected static void broadcast (String message) ...
```

The `run()` method is responsible for processing the user's input. We register with the static `Vector` handlers which maintain a list of all the current users, and then proceed to read `Strings` from the user and broadcast them with the `broadcast()` method. When an `IOException` is encountered, we display the exception and the `finally` clause deregisters us and closes the connection to the client.

```
protected static void broadcast (String message) {
   synchronized (handlers) {
      Enumeration e = handlers.elements ();
      while (e.hasMoreElements ()) {
         AuthHandler c = (AuthHandler) e.nextElement ();
         try {
            synchronized (c.o) {
               c.o.writeUTF (message);
            }
            c.o.flush ();
         } catch (IOException ex) {
            c.stop ();
         }
      }
   }
}
```

The `broadcast()` method simply loops through all of the `AuthHandlers` that are registered in the `handlers Vector`, and transmits the specified message `message`. If an exception is encountered, then we stop the afflicted `AuthHandler`; its `finally` clause will then automatically take care of cleaning up and deregistering.

26.7 Wrapping up

We hope that these chapters have provided both useful code and some insight into the field of cryptography; it is a fascinating and useful subject.

JDK 1.1 introduces a new security API, `java.security`, that provides a standard cryptographic framework for Java applications. In the initial release, this includes just support for digital signatures, message digests, and key management. Future releases should also support encryption and ACLs. The framework is built around the concept of a *Security Package Provider* (SPP). This allows vendors to plug their own cryptographic implementations into the standard Java cryptographic framework. The default SPP, provided by Sun, implements DSS, MD5, SHA, and some key and certificate management functions that are of immediate use with digitally signed applets. If you wish to employ encryption, then you must still use your own encryption API. However, the new `Bignum` class should assist custom implementations of public-key cryptosystems.

There are many legal issues related to cryptography with which you should become familiar before you release a product that contains cryptographic code. Many of the algorithms are patented and are subject to licensing restrictions. Furthermore, the use and export of cryptography is subject to legal restrictions that vary from country to country. For example, US ITAR (International Traffic in Arms Regulations) prevents us from including cryptographic code on the accompanying CD-ROM. Similarly, a license is required to export any application that includes cryptographic algorithms. Consult the cryptographic literature, federal authorities, or an ITAR attorney if you wish to find out more about this matter. Currently, in the US in particular, this aspect of the law is actively undergoing change. There are several ongoing lawsuits, and control over cryptography may soon transfer from the State Department to the Commerce Department. In the meantime there is much legally uncharted cryptographic water.

These encryption classes conclude the applications section of this book; the remainder of the book covers some of the new APIs that are being released for Java. The object serialization classes are an obvious extension to the stream classes that let us transmit Java objects to communications streams, just as the data stream classes let us transmit Java primitives. Another technology, the RMI framework, provides a remote method invocation facility that greatly simplifies networked applications programming. Both of these make up the future networking options part of the book.

PART IV

Future networking options

As we have seen from the first two sections, the Java language API comes equipped with a diversity of networking options. But new technologies are currently being developed which will further expand the options available to programmers. This section introduces two of these technologies with examples: object serialization and remote method invocation. At the time of this writing, the APIs for these technologies have not been finalized, so there may be some minor changes. At the end of this section is a brief description of other APIs currently being developed at JavaSoft.

Chapter 27: Object serialization and persistence   Object serialization is a new technology that allows complete objects to be transmitted down a stream, just as the data stream classes allow primitive values to be transmitted. The ObjectInputStream and ObjectOutputStream classes are filter streams derived from the data stream classes. The ObjectOutputStream class transmits an object graph for an object being sent. This graph contains a record of all fields of the object, including reference types. The ObjectInputStream decodes this graph, and creates an exact replica of the object when it is read from the stream. Persistence is a side-effect of object serialization, and can be used to keep the state of objects while they are stored in an inactive state, such as in a file. We demonstrate the use of these streams with examples, and discuss the issues surrounding this technology.

Chapter 28: Remote method invocation   The remote method invocation API provides a framework for creating distributed objects across a network, and follows the same basic concept as RPC (remote procedure call). This provides a high level alternative to communicating with streams and sockets. Using this new API, it is possible to access objects on remote machines as if they are normal local objects. Internally, RMI uses TCP/IP, but to the programmer it appears as a normal method call, despite the fact that the affected object may be on a completely different computer, halfway around the world. In this chapter, we first describe the high level view of the RMI model, then demonstrate the technique with an example. Perforce, we must keep this example small because the API is undergoing continuous revision.

Chapter 29: Future APIs   As the language progresses, there are many new APIs that will be available as part of the core language distribution. This chapter documents some of the changes to the existing networking API and lists the most important of the future APIs.

chapter 27

Object serialization and persistence

In this chapter, we take a look at a new set of stream classes available with the language API that allow complete `Objects` to be written to communications channels without much effort on the part of the programmer. These streams allow the programmer to send an `Object` to a stream as easily as an integer. This facility is extremely powerful. You are not restricted to just sending data types such as a `Color` or a `Vector`. You can, for example, transmit an entire applet, and it will be successfully recreated by the recipient.*

Internally, this process is achieved by the streams' creating an object graph that describes the structure of an object, and all objects to which it refers. This structure is transmitted along with all of the object variables, so that the object, and *all* objects to which it refers, can be faithfully recreated when it is read from the stream.

At the time of writing, the serialization process is undergoing continuous revision. The final specification should be available with the release of JDK 1.1; however, because of its changing nature, we provide just a high level overview of serialization in this chapter.

27.1 Overview

An inherent characteristic of networked applications is the need to send data back and forth between two applications, possibly on remote machines. This is usually achieved in three stages, which we have already implemented in some form using streams and sockets. These stages are, in sequence, packing up the data into a form that can be sent over some communications channel (marshaling), delivering the data, and unpacking the data into the original form at the other end (unmarshaling). See Figure 27.1.

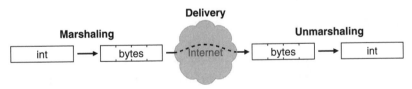

Figure 27.1   Data communications

27.1.1 Marshaling

Marshaling is the process of breaking data down into bytes so that they can be sent over a communications channel such as TCP. In earlier chapters, we did this by breaking

---

* Sending active AWT Components is properly supported only in JDK 1.1.

down integers into 4 bytes and writing the bytes to an `OutputStream`. Marshaling of the Java primitive types is handled for us by the `DataOutputStream` class, which does exactly this. If we want to send more complex data represented in whole objects, then we have to break down the object manually into a form that can be reconstructed on the other end. If the object refers to other objects, this process can be very complex.

The new Java API provides a streaming facility to accomplish this at a high level, taking the complexity out of the hands of the programmer but allowing for all the flexibility of passing objects. *Object serialization* is the term used for marshaling actual objects so that they can be transmitted and later unmarshaled with all fields, even other reference types, intact.

27.1.2 Delivery

The delivery stage is the process of actually sending the data across the network. We have seen this before with streams and sockets. The Java object serialization implementation uses streams to connect to any available transport mechanism.

27.1.3 Unmarshaling

Unmarshaling refers to the unpacking of the data after they have been delivered. The serialization process reduces data into byte streams, but it retains enough information to reconstruct the data after delivery. The trick to successful automated transmission of objects is the computing of a graph that describes the structure of all references held by the object, so that unmarshaling can succeed in exactly recreating the original data.

27.1.4 Marshaling objects

Marshaling primitive types is fairly easy, but if there is a need to send reference types, it quickly becomes quite difficult. Transporter accidents on *Star Trek* are one example of the problems that can be encountered during this process when unmarshaling is not successful, and the movie *The Fly* shows what can happen if the stream becomes corrupt. Objects typically have multiple fields, and may refer to many other objects. To faithfully reconstruct the object after delivery, all fields and outside references must be tracked and kept to ensure correct reconstruction. A graph structure representing object relationships is created in the Java object serialization model. This is done automatically for the programmer by the stream classes `ObjectOutputStream` and `ObjectInputStream`, and it automatically handles self-referential objects, or *cycles* in the graph (Figure 27.2).

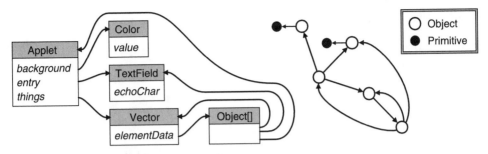

Figure 27.2   An applet and part of its object graph

27.1.5 The object streams

The marshaling and unmarshaling processes are achieved using the object streams, and the delivery occurs when these streams are attached to an underlying communications channel such as a file or a socket. Using these streams is actually quite easy, but a lot of behind-the-scenes work is being done to compute the graph and access internal class variables (Figure 27.3).

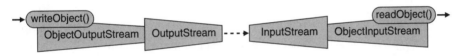

Figure 27.3   The Object streams

27.2 Class ObjectOutput-Stream

The `ObjectOutputStream` class extends `DataOutputStream`, and has all the methods of the superclass. As a `FilterOutputStream`, it attaches to an existing `OutputStream` in the usual manner (Figure 27.4).

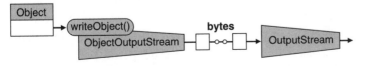

Figure 27.4   Class ObjectOutputStream

27.2.1 Methods

When primitive types are being sent, the methods of DataOutputStream should be used. For example:

```
ObjectOutputStream out = new ObjectOutputStream (socket.getOutputStream ());
int number = 42;
out.writeInt (number);
```

In this example, we send an integer using the writeInt() method, which ObjectOutputStream inherits from DataOutputStream.

In addition to the various methods of DataOutputStream, the ObjectOutput-Stream class provides several other methods that are related to the serialization process. The method of most interest is, however, the writeObject() method.

void writeObject(Object o) throws IOException   The writeObject() method is responsible for serializing objects and sending them to the stream. This method is used to send whole objects.

```
int[] array = new int[10];
out.writeObject (array);
```

In this example, we send an array of integers using the writeObject() method. Objects of any type can be sent; here is an example of sending a Color.

```
Color whiteish = new Color (240, 240, 240);
out.writeObject (whiteish);
```

The ObjectOutputStream can send *all* of the fields of an object, including private and protected fields that are not publicly accessible; only fields marked transient or static will not be sent.

27.2.2 IOException

Certain objects may refuse to be serialized, for security reasons, and will throw a java.io.NoAccessException (java.io.NotSerializableException under JDK 1.1) if such an attempt is made. In particular, when you serialize an object, any private fields will be exposed. This presents a security risk, because these fields can be extracted from the transmission byte stream. For this reason, the JDK 1.1 release of object serialization requires that all objects explicitly declare permission to be serialized. The default operation will be to refuse to serialize an object unless it declares permission.

The mechanism for declaring permission to be serialized under JDK 1.1 is to implement the java.io.Serializable interface; there are no methods to be implemented as the object streams automatically extract all instance data. Alternatively, a class can implement the `java.io.Externalizable` interface and provide implementations of the `writeExternal()` and `readExternal()` methods that manually serialize an instance. If you subclass a serializable object, then the new class is transitively serializable; this behavior can be overridden by implementing the `readObject()` and `writeObject()` methods. These methods can also be used to modify the default serialization behavior. Most of the core API classes that you would expect support serialization by implementing the `java.io.Serializable` interface; this includes classes such as `java.lang.String`, `java.awt.Rectangle`, and the `java.awt.Components`, but not classes such as `java.io.InputStream` or `java.net.Socket`.

There are several other `IOExceptions` that can be thrown by the `writeObject()` method. If an exception occurs during serialization, then the data that have been written thus far by the `ObjectOutputStream` are useless.

27.3 Class ObjectInput-Stream

The `ObjectInputStream` class extends `DataInputStream`, and thus has all the methods of the superclass. As a `FilterInputStream`, the constructor attaches to an existing `InputStream`, from which all data will be read. Primitive types are read in the normal way, but there are new methods for dealing with reference types. See Figure 27.5.

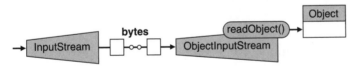

Figure 27.5 Class ObjectInputStream

27.3.1 Methods

For example, to read the integer we wrote to the stream before, we use the `readInt()` method which `ObjectInputStream` inherits from `DataInputStream`.

```
ObjectInputStream in = new ObjectInputStream (socket.getInputStream ());
int temp;
temp = in.readInt ();
```

This simply reads four bytes and reconstructs an integer.

In addition to the methods of `DataInputStream`, the `ObjectInputStream` also provides various methods related to the deserialization process. These include methods to resolve unknown class files and so forth. Again, however, the method of most interest is the `readObject()` method.

Object readObject() throws IOException, ClassNotFoundException   The `read-Object()` method is responsible for deserializing objects from a communications stream.

```
Color col;
col = (Color) in.readObject ();
```

This example reads the `Color` object. It's that simple! The `readObject()` method returns an `Object` that we must cast to the appropriate type.

27.3.2 IOException

The `readObject()` method may throw various `IOExceptions` if there is a problem with the deserialization process.

27.3.3 ClassNotFoundException

A `ClassNotFoundException` will be thrown if the class files for an object cannot be located.

27.4 Class DateServer

Here we present a simple example using object streaming in place of manual marshaling and transmission of data. This is a server that uses an `ObjectOutputStream` to send a `Date` object to every client that connects (Figure 27.6).

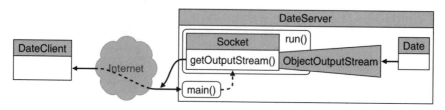

Figure 27.6   Class DateServer

```
import java.net.*;
import java.io.*;
import java.util.Date;

public class DateServer extends Thread {
    // public DateServer (Socket s) throws IOException ...
    // public void run () ...
    // public static void main (String args[]) throws IOException ...
}
```

This class combines the server and handler in a single class, as we have seen before. The `main()` method accepts new connections on a port specified at the command line. We create a new instance of the `DateServer` class to handle every connection that we receive; the server simply sends the current date and time to the client.

```
protected ObjectOutputStream out;

public DateServer (Socket s) throws IOException {
    OutputStream o = s.getOutputStream ();
    BufferedOutputStream bO = new BufferedOutputStream (o);
    out = new ObjectOutputStream (bO);
}
```

The constructor for this class accepts a `Socket s` that the handler will process.

We obtain an `OutputStream o` from s. We attach a `BufferedOutputStream bO` to this, and an `ObjectOutputStream out` to this. This stream will allow us to send any data, including whole objects, with all the hard work hidden from the programmer.

```
public void run () {
    try {
        out.writeObject (new Date ());
        out.close ();
    } catch (IOException ex) {
        ex.printStackTrace ();
    }
}
```

In the `run()` method, we send a `Date` object using the `writeObject()` method of `ObjectOutputStream`, then close the stream.

If we were using a `DataOutputStream`, we would have to separate all the fields of `Date` that we wanted to send, and then send each one as a primitive type. We would also have to remember the ordering so that we could correctly reconstruct the data at the other end. Additionally, if the `Date` class had any private or protected fields, then we could not send a complete representation. The `ObjectOutputStream` class can access all of these internal fields of an object.

```
public static void main (String args[]) throws IOException {
    if (args.length != 1)
        throw new RuntimeException ("Syntax: DateServer <port>");
```

```
        System.out.println ("Starting on port " + args[0]);
        ServerSocket server = new ServerSocket (Integer.parseInt (args[0]));
        while (true) {
            System.out.println ("Waiting");
            Socket client = server.accept ();
            System.out.println ("Accepted from " + client.getInetAddress ());
            DateServer c = new DateServer (client);
            c.start ();
        }
    }
```

This server should look familiar; we listen on a port, and instantiate a new handler for each client that connects. The handler creates an object stream for the response, then writes the date using the `writeObject()` method of `ObjectOutputStream`.

27.5 Class DateClient

This is the corresponding `DateClient` for the `DateServer` class. We connect to a server and read the `Date` that it transmits (Figure 27.7).

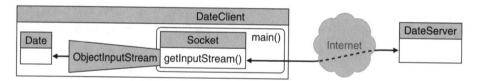

Figure 27.7   Class DateClient

```
import java.io.*;
import java.net.*;
import java.util.Date;

public class DateClient {
    public static void main (String args[]) throws IOException,
        ClassNotFoundException {
        if (args.length != 2)
            throw new RuntimeException ("Syntax: DateClient <host> <port>");
        Socket s = new Socket (args[0], Integer.parseInt (args[1]));
        ObjectInputStream in = new ObjectInputStream (s.getInputStream ());
        Date when = (Date) in.readObject ();
        in.close ();
        System.out.println (when);
    }
}
```

The client code resides completely in the `main()` method. We get a `Socket s` to the server, then attach an `ObjectInputStream in` to the socket's input stream. We are expecting a `Date` object, so we read in the object using the `readObject()` method of `ObjectInputStream` and cast this to a `Date`. Note that we must handle the exceptions that can be thrown by the `readObject()` method; in this case, we just pass them on.

If we had done the marshaling manually, then we would have to know exactly in what order to expect the fields of the `Date` object.

27.6 More detail

The object streams are easy to use, but there is a lot of complexity behind the scenes. During the serialization process, a graph structure of the object and all its references is created. This graph does record keeping for deserialization. Multiple references to the same object are counted so that multiple copies of that object are not created during deserialization. When the object is read with `ObjectInputStream`, a local copy is made; the copy of the object located at the origin of streaming will be unaffected by changes made to the deserialized object.

When the object graph is created, all fields are included except those marked `static` or `transient`. It is important to note that `private` fields are included, so private fields that should not be sent should be labeled `private transient`. There may be some cases where it does not make sense to transport object fields, and these should be labeled `transient`. An example is an operating system file descriptor that is transient by nature.

27.7 Persistence

Persistence refers to the ability to store active objects and reactivate them later with their previous state intact. Object serialization allows for persistence since the object can be streamed to a file and then reconstructed at a later date. Object persistence can be very important to the design of object-oriented applications. For example, a customer object could be shared among applications. This makes sense—this is the way we treat objects in the real world. It would be nice if we could let the customer object *sleep* until an application needs to access it. Once the access is complete, any changes will be committed, and it can be placed back in storage. Normal databases can perform the same basic function, of course, but if the objects can be stored in a serialized form, all fields and classes to which the object refers will automatically be reconstructed when the object *wakes up*. This allows for far more complexity in object relationships with little more programmer effort.

27.8 Using object streams for persistence

In this example, we create a simple application to keep track of a list of favorite colors. This example is contrived, but is meant to show the main concepts and techniques involved in creating persistent objects. We keep a list of Colors in a Vector, and provide a means for storing and retrieving them from a file. The Vector is automatically serialized before streaming to the file, so we can read it back into an application with a single call.

27.8.1 Class FavoriteColors

We will demonstrate object persistence with a simple application that makes use of a persistent Vector object. We will store this Vector in a file, so that changes made by this application will be permanent.

The general procedure is to collect the Vector from a file, do our processing, and then return it to storage. In this case, we will use a Vector of Color objects (Figure 27.8).

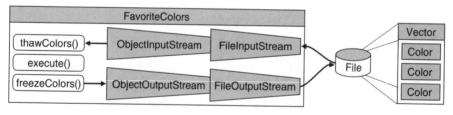

Figure 27.8 Class FavoriteColors

```
import java.io.*;
import java.util.*;
import java.awt.Color;
```

```
public class FavoriteColors {
    // public FavoriteColors(String fileName) throws IOException,
    //    ClassNotFoundException ...
    // public void execute () throws IOException ...
    // public static void main (String args[]) throws IOException,
    //    ClassNotFoundException ...
}
```

When you create an instance of this class, it automatically loads a Vector of Color objects from the file specified on the command line; it creates a new Vector if the file does not exist. The execute() method allows this Vector to be examined and modified. When the user is finished, the Vector is written back to the file.

```
protected String fileName;
protected Vector colors;

public FavoriteColors (String fileName) throws IOException,
    ClassNotFoundException {
    this.fileName = fileName;
    colors = thawColors ();
}

// protected Vector thawColors () throws IOException,
//    ClassNotFoundException ...
```

In the constructor, we load the Vector of Color objects colors with the thaw-Colors() method. This method loads in the Vector from the specified file fileName, or creates a new Vector if the file does not exist.

```
protected Vector thawColors () throws IOException, ClassNotFoundException {
    try {
        FileInputStream file = new FileInputStream (fileName);
        ObjectInputStream objectIn = new ObjectInputStream (file);
        Vector result = (Vector) objectIn.readObject();
        objectIn.close ();
        return result;
    } catch (FileNotFoundException ex) {
        System.out.println ("New file.");
        return new Vector ();
    }
}
```

The thawColors() method is responsible for collecting a Vector that is stored in a file. We assume that either the file does not exist, or that it contains a Vector that was stored in a serialized form using the writeObject() method of ObjectOutputStream.

We first create the FileInputStream file, attached to the specified file file-Name; if this file does not exist, then a FileNotFoundException will be thrown. We then create an ObjectInputStream objectIn attached to this. We can then read in the `Vector` as a whole object using the `readObject()` method of `ObjectInput-Stream`, and cast this to a `Vector`. We close the input stream and return the result, or if the file did not exist, then we return a new, empty `Vector`.

We simply pass on any other exceptions that may occur.

```
public void execute () throws IOException {
   ASCIIInputStream in = new ASCIIInputStream (System.in);
   while (true) {
      System.out.println ("Enter 1 to list colors, 2 to add a color,
         3 to quit:");
      int temp = in.readInt ();
      switch (temp) {
      case 1:
         for (int i = 0; i < colors.size (); ++ i)
            System.out.println (colors.elementAt (i));
         break;
      case 2:
         System.out.println ("Enter the color value in hex (#ff00ff):");
         String color = in.readWord ();
         if (color.startsWith ("#"))
            color = color.substring (1);
         colors.addElement (new Color (Integer.parseInt (color, 16)));
         break;
      case 3:
         freezeColors ();
         return;
      }
   }
}
```

```
// protected void freezeColors () throws IOException ...
```

The `execute()` method polls for user input based on a simple menu. We use the `ASCIIInputStream` class that we developed in Chapter 6 to read user input. The options that are presented include listing the contents of the `Vector`, adding a `Color` to the `Vector`, and quitting.

When the user adds a `Color`, we simply read a word (any continuous sequence of non-whitespace characters) and parse this as a hexadecimal value. We can then create a new `Color` from this value and add it to the `Vector`.

Listing the `Vector` is self-explanatory, and when we quit, we use the `freeze-Colors()` method to return the `Vector` to persistent storage.

```
protected void freezeColors () throws IOException {
   FileOutputStream file = new FileOutputStream (fileName);
   ObjectOutputStream objectOut = new ObjectOutputStream (file);
   objectOut.writeObject (colors);
   objectOut.close ();
}
```

The freezeColors() method is responsible for putting the Vector into persistent storage. We first create a FileOutputStream file that writes to the specified file file-Name. We then attach an ObjectOutputStream objectOut to this, and stream the colors Vector to the file using the writeObject() method. The Vector and its components are automatically serialized by the stream, and we achieve persistent storage in the file. Finally, we close the object stream which closes the file.

Any application could read in the Vector, modify it, and then store it again. Persistence is significant because we can keep the state of an object without having it always in memory. Multiple applications could access the same object as needed, and the object would always be current. Because we use the standard writeObject() and read-Object() methods, we don't need to agree on a low level Vector encoding format.

```
public static void main (String args[]) throws IOException,
    ClassNotFoundException {
  if (args.length != 1)
    throw new RuntimeException ("Syntax: FavoriteColors <colorFile>");
  FavoriteColors faves = new FavoriteColors (args[0]);
  faves.execute ();
}
```

The main() method simply verifies that a filename has been specified, creates a new FavoriteColors object, and executes this with the execute() method.

27.9 Wrapping up

The object streams are an extremely important addition to the Java I/O library. Instead of manually breaking objects up into their component pieces, the programmer can instead automatically serialize entire complex objects. The fact that you can serialize a complete applet and recreate it in a remote machine has remarkable implications. In addition, because the object stream classes leverage off the standard streams interface, this technology can be applied to a wide variety of applications.

Object persistence is a side effect of object serialization, and proves to be useful and convenient for a whole range of applications. Obviously it is possible to manually store objects; however, the ability to store arbitrary complex objects is very much more convenient.

In the next chapter, we take a look at another use for serialization, but this time even more details are hidden from the programmer.

chapter 28

Remote method invocation

The Java remote method invocation (RMI) framework provides all the underlying layers necessary for Java objects to communicate with each other using normal method calls, even if the objects are running in virtual machines on opposite sides of the world. As long as the runtime systems can communicate via TCP/IP (for example, two computers on the Internet), client/server applications can be developed without streams and sockets (Figure 28.1).

Figure 28.1   Remote method invocation

This allows the programmer to avoid complex communication protocols between applications, and instead adopt a higher level method-based protocol. RMI is an alternative to the more low level streams/socket communication, and the specific implementation is hidden from programmers.

28.1 *The basic architecture*

The whole purpose of the Java remote method invocation implementation is to provide a framework for Java objects to communicate via their methods, *regardless of their location*. This means that a client should be able to access a server on the local machine or on the network as if they were executing in the same runtime system. From the programmer's point of view, the networking detail necessary for client/server applications disappears; any communication setup is performed automatically, without assistance from the programmer.

To create a class that will be remotely accessible, we first define an interface which declares those methods that we wish to make public. Parameters and return values may be of any type; data transfer is handled by object streams automatically. The class must implement this interface, plus any other interfaces and methods it needs for its own local use. A *stub* and *skeleton* are then generated automatically using `rmic`, a tool available in the Java RMI distribution. The stub is a class that automatically translates remote method calls into network communication setup and parameter passing. The skeleton is a corresponding class that resides on the same virtual machine as the remote object, and which accepts these network connections and translates them into actual method calls on the object (Figure 28.2).

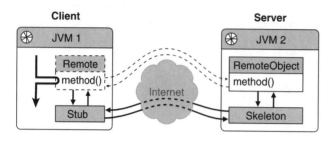

Figure 28.2 The RMI architecture

The final setup involved in using RMI is that the remote object must then be registered with a naming service that allows clients to address the object by name. This is similar to the ports of TCP; the port number of a server is its address on a machine. Similarly, remote objects running on a particular machine can be addressed with the machine address and a name for the particular remote object in question.

When a client wishes to make calls to a remote object, it must first look up the object in the naming service. This returns a remote reference to the object which automatically informs the object that it has a remote client. Among other things, this prevents the object from garbage being collected when there are still remote references to it (Figure 28.3).

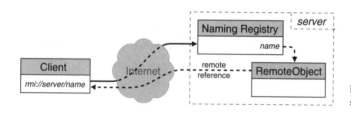

Figure 28.3 The naming service

Locating the remote object in this manner also tells the client where to find the stub class; this class is subsequently downloaded if it is not available locally. Once the client has the stub, it has all the information necessary to invoke methods of the remote object; the RMI framework takes care of all further low level communications work. The client is able to make method calls on the object as if it were making calls to the object locally.

Tracing the method call in Figure 28.2, the client appears to invoke the method on the remote object directly, as shown by the dotted lines. The call is actually being passed to the stub, which handles all of the details of the communication setup, as well as transmitting the call and parameters to the skeleton. The skeleton then makes the actual method call on the remote object. The return value is finally sent back from the skeleton to the stub, which then returns the result to the client as if the method call had been made locally. Exceptions, of course, are passed back, as well as correct results.

If the remote object has been set up correctly, then all of this work is transparent to both the remote object and the client. This does not mean that objects may be turned into remote objects without prior knowledge and intent; specific interfaces must be implemented and specific class files must be generated. It also does not mean that any method of the remote object may be invoked; only those methods declared in the remote interface are accessible to clients. However, bearing these differences in mind, the RMI framework is an extremely powerful mechanism because it allows networked applications to be developed as if everything is just a method call away.

28.1.1 The remote object

A remote object is any object that has been set up to accept method calls from another object running in a remote Java virtual machine. This is achieved with two parts; an interface describing the methods of the object, and an implementation of this interface.

Defining the remote interface An interface must be written for the remote object defining all methods that should be public. This interface must extend `java.rmi.Remote`, an interface which identifies that a reference is to a remote object (Figure 28.4).

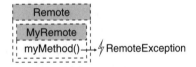

Figure 28.4   The remote interface

For example, to write a simple remote object with one method, the interface would look like this:

```
import java.rmi.Remote;
import java.rmi.RemoteException;

public interface MyRemote extends Remote {
   public Object myMethod (String s) throws RemoteException;
}
```

Here, we declare an interface which can be implemented by any remote object, and which declares a single remotely accessible method `myMethod()` that takes a `String` parameter and returns an `Object`. Note that all methods declared in a remote interface must declare that they can throw exceptions of type `java.rmi.RemoteException`. A method may, of course, declare that it can throw other exceptions in addition.

Implementing the RemoteObject

The remote object implementation must extend `java.rmi.server.RemoteObject` or a subclass, and implement any of the remote interfaces that it wishes to support. The `RemoteObject` subclasses provide implementations of the `java.rmi.Remote` interface from which all remote

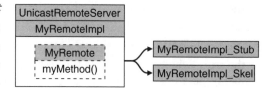

Figure 28.5   The remote object implementation

interfaces must extend. In practical use, `java.rmi.server.UnicastRemoteServer` (`java.rmi.server.UnicastRemoteObject` under JDK 1.1) is most likely to be used; this provides an implementation of all the behavior of a typical remote object (Figure 28.5).

An implementation of the simple interface shown above should look something like this:

```
import java.rmi.server.UnicastRemoteServer;
import java.rmi.RemoteException;

public class MyRemoteImpl extends UnicastRemoteServer implements MyRemote {
   public MyRemoteImpl () throws RemoteException {
   }
   public Object myMethod (String s) {
      return s;
   }
}
```

We extend the `java.rmi.UnicastRemoteServer` class and implement the remote interface that we just declared. Note that the constructors for the superclass `Unicast-RemoteServer` may throw exceptions of type `RemoteException`, so we must also declare a constructor that throws exceptions of this type.

28.1.2 The stub and skeleton

Stub and skeleton objects must then be generated with the `rmic` tool. This tool takes the remote object class file as a parameter, and generates a class file for each of the stub and the skeleton. If the remote object classes are to be accessible over a network, then these files should be placed in a directory accessible by the networking protocol, such as a publicly readable HTML directory.

28.1.3 Marshaling, delivery, and unmarshaling

The generated client stub and remote object skeleton automatically perform the necessary communication for RMI. They are responsible for marshaling the data, delivery, and unmarshaling the data at the other end. Typical methods have reference types as parameters and return values. The Java RMI model uses the object serialization classes discussed in the last chapter to accomplish this task. This is a low level aspect of the RMI model, and is hidden from the programmer. Remember that object passing is always by copy, as it was when we used the object streams directly.

28.1.4 RemoteException

`RemoteException` is the superclass of all exceptions that can occur in the RMI runtime. This exception is thrown whenever a remote method invocation fails. All methods in a remote interface must throw this exception.

28.1.5 The naming mechanism

Clients can invoke methods on remote objects only if they have a reference to the object. A simple name server is provided in the RMI model for this purpose. Remote objects register themselves using the `java.rmi.Naming` class, which uses a URL-based naming scheme (Figure 28.6). An implementation of a naming registry is supplied with the RMI distribution. Under JDK 1.0 this is provided by the

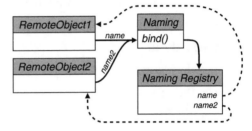

Figure 28.6   Registering with the naming service

`java.rmi.registery.RegistryImpl` class. Under JDK 1.1 it is provided by the `rmiregistry` command. It requires no subclassing, and is run before the remote object or clients are started.

Clients use the `java.rmi.Naming` class to look up and obtain remote references to objects. The address of the remote object is specified with a URL that indicates the remote machine and the name of the object on the machine. When an object registers itself with the registry, it specifies a name by which it can be referenced. Remote clients will connect to the registry and locate the object based on this name. (Figure 28.7).

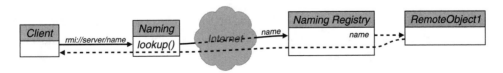

Figure 28.7   Locating a remote object with the naming service

28.2 An example

This example demonstrates remote method invocation with the same date server from the last chapter done with RMI. We start with a checklist of the steps necessary to create the application, then show the result of each step.

28.2.1 Checklist of steps

To create the date server application, we need to execute the following steps. This is a general task list that can be used when implementing any application that uses RMI:

- Define the remote interface.
- Implement the remote interface.
- Register the remote object in the name server registry.
- Generate the stub and skeleton using rmic.
- Write a client.
- Start the registry.
- Start the server.
- Run the client.

28.2.2 Interface DateServer

The first step is to write an interface which describes all the methods we want the client to be able to invoke. In this case, we have only one method to make public, and it will return a Date object.

```
import java.rmi.Remote;
import java.rmi.RemoteException;
import java.util.Date;

public interface DateServer extends Remote {
   public Date getDate () throws RemoteException;
}
```

We extend the Remote interface so that our object can have remote behavior. The getDate() method is declared to throw RemoteException, which can occur during any problem with the remote method invocation.

28.2.3 Class DateServerImpl

The second step is to write an implementation for the remote object interface. We extend `UnicastRemoteServer` (`UnicastRemoteObject` under JDK 1.1) and implement `DateServer`. All remote object implementations must extend the `RemoteObject` class or one of its subclasses. `UnicastRemoteServer` is provided in the RMI API, and is a subclass of `RemoteObject` intended for use in a client/server setting. This class automatically prepares to accept RMI connections for remote method calls.

```
import java.rmi.server.UnicastRemoteServer;
import java.rmi.server.StubSecurityManager;
import java.rmi.RemoteException;
import java.rmi.Naming;
import java.util.Date;

public class DateServerImpl extends UnicastRemoteServer implements DateServer {
   // public DateServerImpl () throws RemoteException ...
   // public Date getDate () ...
   // public static void main (String args[]) ...
}
```

We extend the `UnicastRemoteServer` class and implement the remote interface that we have defined. We must provide a constructor that throws `RemoteException` (this type of exception can be thrown by the superclass constructor), and implement the methods of the remote interface.

For this example, we also declare a `main()` method that creates an instance of this class and registers it with the RMI naming registry.

```
public DateServerImpl () throws RemoteException {
   }
```

For this class, we simply pass on the `RemoteExceptions` that can occur in the superclass constructor. Typical problems include if the networking cannot be set up to receive remote method calls.

```
public Date getDate () {
   return new Date ();
   }
```

The implementation of the `getDate()` method of the `DateServer` interface simply creates and returns a new `Date` object.

```
public static void main (String args[]) throws Exception {
   System.setSecurityManager (new StubSecurityManager ());
   DateServerImpl dateS = new DateServerImpl ();
   Naming.bind ("DateServer", dateS);
   }
```

The `main()` method sets a new security manager, creates a new `DateServerImpl` `dates`, and registers this object with the naming service `java.rmi.Naming`. We declare that this method may throw exceptions of type `Exception`, as a catch-all for the many exceptions that can be thrown by the remote object and naming registry.

By default, applications do not have a security manager, and so code has unlimited access to resources. This is a dangerous default situation with RMI because if a remote client hands back a handle to a remote object, then the server will try to load in the stub for this remote object. A user could place arbitrary code in this stub, and could thus gain undesired access to the server's resources. To indicate your awareness of this situation, you must explicitly set a security manager that permits the loading of stub objects; the `StubSecurityManager` (`java.rmi.RMISecurityManager` under JDK 1.1) is one such class. The `StubSecurityManager` class is available in the RMI API, and should be set before the remote object is created. In a production system, you might want to create your own `SecurityManager` that would run the client code within a restricted environment.

The `dates` object is then registered with the naming service that is provided by the `java.rmi.Naming` class. The `bind()` method is a static method of `Naming`. The first parameter specifies the name that we wish to give the object; remote clients will look the object up by this name. The second parameter is the remote object itself. If an object is already registered locally with this name, then the `bind()` method will throw an `AlreadyBoundException`. We could use the `rebind()` method to overcome this.

After we have registered this object, remote clients can get a reference to it by making a connection to the registry running on this machine, and making a request for the object that is registered with the name *DateServer.*

28.2.4 *Generating the stub and skeleton*

To generate the stub and skeleton, first we compile the `DateServerImpl` class and then we use `rmic` with the date server implementation class name as the parameter:

```
rmic DateServerImpl
```

Two class files will be generated, one for the stub and one for the skeleton. The stub should be placed in a directory accessible by the Web server for clients to access, or else should be supplied with the client code, alongside the remote interface.

```
DateServerImpl_Skel.class
DateServerImpl_Stub.class
```

The `DateServerImpl_Stub` class will be used by the client machine, and the `DateServerImpl_Skel` class will be used by the server machine.

28.2.5 Class DateClient

The client is very simple; it looks up the date server in the naming service, collects a reference to it, makes a call to its getDate() method, prints the result, and then quits.

```
import java.rmi.server.StubSecurityManager;
import java.rmi.Naming;
import java.util.Date;

public class DateClient {
   public static void main (String args[]) throws Exception {
      if (args.length != 1)
         throw new RuntimeException ("Syntax: DateClient <hostname>");
      System.setSecurityManager (new StubSecurityManager ());
      DateServer dateServer = (DateServer) Naming.lookup
         ("rmi://" + args[0] + "/DateServer");
      Date when = dateServer.getDate ();
      System.out.println (when);
   }
}
```

The client has only a main() method. It first sets the StubSecurityManager (java.rmi.RMISecurityManager under JDK 1.1), since the default for applications is to have no security manager. Remember, when we bind the remote object we download its stub class, and this could contain malicious code.

The lookup() method of Naming is then used to collect a reference to the remote DateServer object. A URL with the protocol field rmi is used to name this object. (Under JDK 1.1, it is not necessary to use the rmi protocol field. Instead, a URL of the form //servername/objectname can be used.) The URL specifies two things: the machine on which the remote object resides, and the name with which the object has been bound on that machine. In this case, the host is specified on the command line (localhost is useful for testing) and the name of the object is DateServer. As we will see next, the registry must be running on that machine for this lookup() call to succeed.

Behind the scenes, the Naming class connects to the registry that is running on the specified host and then queries it for the object matching the specified name.

The object returned by this call is a *remote reference* that implements whatever remote interfaces have been implemented by the actual object. We must therefore cast the result to the expected remote interface; note that the client specifies the remote interface name, and *not* the remote implementation class-name. As a result, only the methods declared in the remote interfaces will be accessible.

When the reference to the remote object (through its interface) has been obtained, calls can be made to its methods. In this case, we make a call to the getDate() method and print the response. When we make this local method call, the local stub connects to the remote skeleton, which calls the remote object method, obtains a result, and streams this back down to the stub. The result is then displayed.

28.2.6 Running the application

To run the example, first start the registry on the server machine:

```
java java.rmi.registry.RegistryImpl
```

This registry is then accessible to remote clients in order to look up remote objects on this machine (under JDK 1.1, just run the `rmiregistry` command). Next, start the server on the same machine:

```
java DateServerImpl
```

When we run this class, an instance of the `DateServerImpl` class is created and registered with the local registry. Note that the registry must be running on the server machine before this registration can occur. Finally, run the client on any machine:

```
java DateClient localhost
```

When we run the client, we must specify the name of the host that is hosting the date server object. This first connects to the remote registry, obtains a reference to the remote object, and then calls its `getDate()` method; this returns the current date on the server machine. Very useful if your watch is slow.

28.3 Wrapping up

The RMI framework handles all of the low level details required for invisible networking with remote objects, and provides a simple way to create complex client/server applications. The steps and example discussed in this chapter show the general technique, and this model can be followed for all client/server applications.

At the time of this writing, the RMI specification is still in beta release, so some minor changes to the API may yet be made. For this reason, we have restricted ourselves to covering usage of the RMI in fairly general terms. The RMI specification has already been through several major changes up to this point; however, it should be finalized with the final 1.1 release of the JDK.

Obviously, RMI provides for a different style of networking than that supported by streams and sockets, and both styles have their uses. Streams and sockets are obviously necessary to interact with existing applications, and are also useful when the programmer desires full control over a client/server system. It is comparatively easy to build systems that automatically roll over to a standby server if the main server dies; similarly, UDP and TCP can be combined, so that the protocol in use depends on the data being transmitted. Such control is not as easy using RMI; however, on the other hand, RMI provides a much higher level interface to networking. This has the advantage that the programmer can define a much cleaner, higher level application protocol, and all communication details are taken care of transparently.

Which style of network programming you choose should depend on the application that you are targeting. While streams and sockets may be more familiar and provide more control, the remote method invocation framework is an extremely powerful and useful facility to have available.

chapter 29

Future APIs

The release of JDK 1.1, the next major overhaul of the Java language and environment, brings with it many changes and upgrades that are relevant to Java network programmers. The purpose of this chapter is to list some of the changes that it brings, of which RMI and object serialization are but two. There are some changes to the existing networking API, and there will be a host of new APIs, some of which will ship with JDK 1.1, and the rest of which will arrive over the course of time. Up-to-date information will, as always, be available from JavaSoft's website: `http://www.javasoft.com/`

29.1 Networking changes

Changes to the networking APIs are relatively minor, and will not affect existing code. The most significant change is the addition of a `MulticastSocket` class that provides easy Java access to IP multicasting; other changes include support for socket options, a new set of socket exception classes, and facility for subclassing the `Socket` and `ServerSocket` classes.

29.1.1 Socket options

TCP and UDP support various optional socket parameters that govern how the socket behaves. JDK 1.1 provides Java support for accessing these options. These are discussed later, along with changes to each of the relevant socket classes.

29.1.2 IP Multicast

JDK 1.1 provides support for Java applications to make use of IP multicast. Multicast is much like UDP, except that instead of sending a packet to a single destination, you send a packet to a *multicast group* and the underlying network protocols attempt to transport the packet to all interested recipients; the sender does not even need to know who the recipients are. As with UDP, multicast is packet based and does not guarantee reliability; packets may be lost, duplicated, or reordered, and successful delivery may be different for different recipients.

A multicast group is simply an IP address that falls into IP class D (224.xx.xx.xx–239.xx.xx.xx). Recipients express an interest in receiving packets addressed to a particular multicast group, and the underlying network protocols take care of announcing this interest to relevant routers on the network. To send a packet to a multicast group, a client simply inserts a packet into the network with the appropriate target address; a sender need not be a member of the group, and does not know who will receive the packet. Some multicast addresses are officially assigned to particular applications and there are proposals for the dynamic assignment of multicast addresses, but within an organization it is usually possible to use internally assigned addresses.

Multicast is currently not widely deployed on the Internet, and so it is not possible to have a multicast conversation with just anyone on the Internet. The MBone is an experimental multicast framework that transports multicast packets through IP *tunnels* between multicast-enabled *islands*. Owing to its popularity, the MBone is now fairly widely deployed, at least in academia, so it is possible to use multicast between members of the MBone. It is usually also possible to enable multicast within a LAN, or to use multicast between machines on a multicast-enabled network such as Ethernet. It is expected that multicast will be widely deployed on the Internet in the future.

Multicast packets include a time-to-live (TTL) field that limits how far a packet will be propagated across a network. The exact meaning of the field depends on the routing protocol in use and how the multicast routers have been configured. With DVMRP, the routing protocol of the MBone, a packet sent with a TTL of 63, by default, will not be forwarded through any IP tunnels. This allows an organization to have a multicast conversation that will not be broadcast to the Internet at large. With appropriate administration, an internal network can be further partitioned. It is important to use the TTL field appropriately to prevent unnecessary Internet traffic.

The MulticastSocket class is discussed later in this chapter.

29.2 Changes to class Socket

The Socket class has been altered so that it can be subclassed in order to add extended socket function to an existing Socket class. Some examples of potentially useful functions include authentication, encryption, and compression; the authentication client/ server classes that we developed earlier would be more appropriately added as an extension of the normal Socket classes. Support has also been added for binding a Socket to different local network interfaces, in addition to support for the following socket options.

void setSoTimeout(int timeout) throws SocketException This method sets a timeout in milliseconds after which a blocking socket operation will automatically abort. This is useful if you wish to only wait a certain length of time for a client to respond with some data, or only wait a certain length of time for a new socket connection to arrive. This method is supported by all sockets, both client-side and server-side.

If a timeout occurs, then an InterruptedIOException will be thrown.

int getSoTimeout() throws SocketException This method returns the current socket timeout value; a value of 0 indicates that there is no timeout, i.e., any socket operations will block indefinitely (the default).

void setTcpNoDelay(boolean on) throws SocketException This method controls the use of Nagle's algorithm over a socket connection. Nagle's algorithm is used to make TCP more efficient by delaying the writing of small amounts of data until either enough data has been buffered so that a large packet can be sent or there is no unacknowledged data en route to the server.

Nagle's algorithm makes normal unbuffered communications much more efficient, but it can introduce an unacceptable delay for certain applications; Nagle is turned on by default.

boolean getTcpNoDelay() throws SocketException This method returns whether Nagle's algorithm is currently enabled.

void setSoLinger(boolean on, int val) throws SocketException This method allows a client to set a maximum linger timeout on a TCP socket. TCP guarantees to successfully deliver all data transmitted to a socket. This means that when a socket is closed the network connection is not immediately terminated; it will remain open while all unsent data is transmitted. Setting a linger value means that the operating system will only wait for the specified time after closing a socket before closing down the network connection. If data has not been successfully transmitted the network connection is aborted.

When a socket connection is closed naturally, there is usually a four-minute period during which an identical connection cannot be recreated (from the same client port to the same server port).* This delay is required to protect against *wandering duplicate* packets on the network; these are packets which were delayed and then retransmitted. If an old connection is closed, and a new identical connection is established before the delayed packet times out, then the delayed packet could arrive successfully and be inserted into the conversation. A linger timeout should not in general be used, because if a connection is aborted because of a timeout, then the normal safeguard will be bypassed.

int getSoLinger() throws SocketException This method returns the current linger setting, or −1 if the option is disabled.

---

* Client sockets are assigned random port numbers, so the linger delay does not prevent a client from opening another connection to the same server.

29.3 Changes to class ServerSocket

The ServerSocket class has been modified in order that it too can be subclassed and bound to different local addresses; other changes include support for the setSoTimeout() and getSoTimeout() methods.

29.4 Changes to class DatagramSocket

The DatagramSocket class has been extended to support binding to different local addresses and the setSoTimeout() and getSoTimeout() methods.

29.5 Class MulticastSocket

The MulticastSocket class extends the DatagramSocket class and adds support for IP multicast. As a result, it provides all the methods of DatagramSocket including the new setSoTimeout() and getSoTimeout() methods. In addition it provides methods to control group membership and a send() method that allows the TTL of a multicast packet to be specified.

void joinGroup(InetAddress mcastaddr) throws IOException This method announces interest in the specified multicast group mcastaddr. Network protocols will propagate this interest to the relevant routers, so that packets sent to the multicast group mcastaddr will become available to read through this socket. Remember that you do not need to be a member of a group in order to send packets to it. You only need to join the group if you wish to receive such packets.

void leaveGroup(InetAddress mcastaddr) throws IOException This method is used to leave the specified multicast group mcastaddr.

void send(DatagramPacket p, byte ttl) throws IOException This method sends the DatagramPacket p to its destination address, which should be a multicast IP address, and provides an option to specify the TTL for the packet. The default `send()` method assumes a TTL of 1, which will restrict the packet to just the attached network.

void setInterface(InetAddress inf) throws SocketException   This method sets the network interface to be used for multicast packets sent through this socket; this is useful for multihomed hosts.

InetAddress getInterface() throws SocketException   This method returns the current network interface used for multicast packets.

29.5.1 Sending multicast packets

Sending a packet to a multicast group follows exactly the same model as sending a normal datagram packet, except that a TTL can be specified when a packet is sent. The following code fragment demonstrates the process of sending a multicast packet:

```
MulticastSocket socket = new MulticastSocket();
DatagramPacket packet = new DatagramPacket (data, data.length,
   InetAddress.getByName (multicastGroup), multicastPort);
socket.send (packet, (byte) 63);
```

We first create a `MulticastSocket` packet; we will not be receiving packets, so we don't specify a port number. We next create a `DatagramPacket` packet addressed to the specified multicast group `multicastGroup` and port `multicastPort` (e.g., group `224.3.4.5`, port `5000`). We finally send the packet into the network with the specified time-to-live; in this case, we choose 63 which will restrict the packet to just our own multicast island.

29.5.2 Receiving multicast packets

Receiving a multicast packet involves one more step than receiving a normal datagram packet; we must explicitly announce interest in a multicast group before waiting for packets to arrive. The following code fragment demonstrates receiving a multicast packet.

```
MulticastSocket socket = new MulticastSocket (multicastPort);
socket.joinGroup (InetAddress.getByName (multicastGroup));
byte buffer[] = new byte[65536];
DatagramPacket packet = new DatagramPacket ();
socket.receive (packet);
InetAddress fromAddr = packet.getAddress ();
```

```
int fromPort = packet.getPort ();
int length = packet.getLength ();
byte data[] = packet.getData ();
// ...
socket.leaveGroup (InetAddress.getByName (multicastGroup));
socket.close ();
```

As before, in order to receive packets we must create a multicast socket and bind it to a specific port. We next announce interest in a particular multicast group; in this case, group `multicastGroup`. We create a `DatagramPacket packet` into which we will receive a packet from the network. We then call `receive()`, which blocks until a datagram packet arrives. We can then use the usual methods of the `DatagramPacket` class to extract information about the sender and the contents of the datagram. We leave the multicast group and close the socket when we are finished.

29.6 Socket exceptions

The final extension to the `java.net` API of importance to this book is the addition of some new exception classes that subclass `SocketException` and allow for more fine-grained handling of networking exceptions. These include the following:

BindException   This exception indicates that the requested local port or address could not be bound. Typically, this occurs when a server socket is created and the requested port is already in use or is a system port.

ConnectException   This exception indicates that the connection attempt was refused because there was no server listening on the specified port of the remote machine.

NoRouteToHostException   This exception indicates that the remote host could not be reached, typically because of a network problem.

29.7 I/O changes

The classes of the `java.io` package have been augmented by a suite of *character stream* classes that represent character-oriented communications channels. These classes parallel the basic byte-oriented stream classes in many ways, but are derived from classes called `Reader` and `Writer` that abstractly represent connections from and to character-oriented communications channels. These classes allow Java programs to easily interoperate with different character devices by providing automatic encoding translation. This allows textual input to be automatically translated from its local encoding to Unicode; similarly, Unicode output can be easily translated back to the local character encoding.

29.8 New APIs

Several new APIs are currently under development by JavaSoft and various industry partners; the official public release of each is expected to be staggered over the course of 1997. Most of these new developments do not have specifications at the time of this writing, but they have been announced in general terms.

29.8.1 Media

The new Media API will provide developers with a rich set of tools for using multimedia in applications and applets. The media framework will allow for synchronization of streaming media such as video and audio. Animation effects will be included, along with two- and three-dimensional transformations. Telephony will be part of this API, and will allow integration between computers and telephony, for use in Java-enabled handheld devices and such.

29.8.2 JDBC

The JDBC is a standard SQL database access interface.

29.8.3 Commerce

The commerce API will allow developers to create applications and applets that can handle secure cash transactions. Both lump-sum and metered payment models will be provided.

29.8.4 Security

The security API will provide a framework for including digital signatures, encryption, and authentication in applications and applets.

29.8.5 CORBA 2.0 IDL to Java Compiler

This API will allow developers to create CORBA 2.0 compliant objects. CORBA is effectively a cross-platform, cross-language form of remote method invocation. Because of its cross-language nature, the definition of interfaces is much more complex than with RMI.

29.8.6 Server

This API is intended to assist in creating next-generation Web server attachments. Codename Jeeves is an extensible Java-only web server which allows *servlet* extensions to be added to the server at runtime.

29.8.7 Management

The management API will allow developers to create applets that can manage enterprise networks over Intranets.

29.8.8 Java Beans

This is a codename for an API that will allow developers to plug existing component objects (such as Microsoft's OLE/COM/ActiveX, OpenDoc, and Netscape's Live-Connect) into Java applications.

PART V

Appendices

These appendices provide further background context useful to better apply the techniques and code supplied in the body of the book. An in-depth survey of networking technologies is included first, to provide context for networked applications development. An overview of cryptography offers further information about the principles of cryptograpy, including encryption and authentication algorithms.

Appendix A: Networking   This chapter continues on from the earlier introduction to networking. Future technologies such as IPv6, as well as modern infrastructural technologies such as ATM and SONET, are discussed in detail. Also provided are thorough descriptions of the worldwide telco WAN, as well as the architecture and administration of the Internet.

Appendix B: Cryptography   Cryptography is a popular topic for good reason. Encryption and authentication allow applications to securely tunnel sensitive information across insecure public networks, such as the Internet, without fear of third-party tampering or snooping. This appendix discusses current protocols and algorithms, and provides a small review of what is coming up in the field.

Appendix C: Tables   There is much tabular information that bears relevance to networking and the Java language; this appendix contains a few such tables of data, including the ASCII character set, Unicode block allocations, well known UNIX networking services, and the formats of typical HTTP requests and responses.

Appendix D: Classes from this book   This appendix provides a quick references to the classes that we developed in this book. Most of these classes are supplied on the accompanying CD-ROM as both `.java` and `.class` files.

appendix A

Networking

Networking is a fascinating and multifaceted subject. This appendix covers networks from LAN to WAN and B-ISDN. It focuses on in-depth discussion of networking issues including IP routing, Internet architecture, and telco WAN technologies.

A.1 Overview of networks

A network is simply a collection of interconnected information devices which speak the same data transmission protocol. The actual choice of protocols and physical interconnection facilities used for a given network depends on a variety of factors, including the geographic span of the network and the applications that it is designed to support.

A.1.1 Network classification

Computer networks are typically classified based on geographic area and the protocols they utilize to transport data. The two standard size-based designations are *local area network* (LAN) and *wide area network* (WAN). Common protocol-based network classifications include IPX/SPX (Novell), AppleTalk, and TCP/IP. Some physical networks run more than one protocol; for example, a LAN may simultaneously run IPX/SPX and TCP/IP. Networks which simultaneously run a set of parallel protocols are usually referred to as *heterogeneous*.

A.1.2 LAN and WAN

LAN and WAN are dissimilar technologies. LAN was developed primarily by computer networking researchers. WAN was developed by phone company (telco) engineers and standards organizations. As a result, the two implement similar functionality in fundamentally different ways. Since the Internet is comprised of LAN and WAN components, it is important to consider both when trying to understand how the Internet works. It turns out that the Internet behaves very much, but not exactly, like a large LAN, even though it is technically a WAN. Interestingly, modern technologies such as asynchronous transfer mode (ATM) contain characteristics of both technologies. (Figure A.1).

- *Examples of LANs*   Ethernet, Token Ring, AppleTalk, Novell (IPX/SPX)
- *Examples of WANs*   X.25, ISDN, Frame Relay

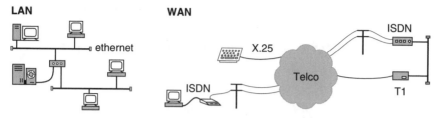

Figure A.1   LAN and WAN

A.1.3 Data switching technologies

Every network must have a method for packaging and routing data. The Internet is based on a data routing scheme known as *packet switching*. A packet-switched system divides a body of data up into small discrete units of varying size (packets) that get to their common destination independently, possibly via different network routes. This architecture ensures that if the primary route that the data are using becomes unserviceable for some reason, then another route can be established dynamically. Similarly, when routes become congested, the network can react by establishing alternative routes, thereby distributing load more evenly.

The standard phone system, technically known as the *plain old telephone service* (POTS) or *public switched telephone network* (PSTN), utilizes a different data delivery methodology known as *circuit switching*. In a circuit-switched system, a dedicated, pre-allocated route is established to carry an entire data session. Circuit-switched telco networks (with the exception of X.25) do not typically implement any advanced services such as flow control, error checking, or data formatting. For the purposes of computer networking, the phone system is therefore usually used as a transport substrate for the wide-area components of packet-switched networks such as the Internet, which provide these services.

A fairly new technology called *cell switching* will eventually replace circuit and packet switching, especially for wide-area data transport. A cell-switched system utilizes packets of fixed size with headers of fixed length. Asynchronous transfer mode (ATM) is an example of such a system. ATM represents a compromise between the synchronous circuit-switched model popular with phone companies and the packet-switched system preferred by computer networkers. Cell switching is the preferred technology for the B-ISDN (a.k.a. the Information Superhighway) because of its superior bandwidth interface granularity, which means that it supports many data transfer rates (Figure A.2).

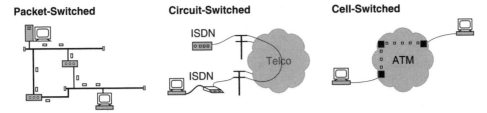

Figure A.2   Data switching technologies

A.2 Local area networks

Local area networks, or LANs, are physically relatively small, usually spanning a mile or less. LAN technologies are usually characterized by shared media access, which means that every device on the LAN essentially shares the same transmission wire.

LANs, due to their physical and media access characteristics, typically have a large amount of bandwidth compared to WAN. Standard Ethernet, for example, has an upper speed limit of 10 Mbps. FDDI is on the order of 100 Mbps.

- *Common LAN technologies*   Ethernet (10 Mbps, Fast is 100 Mbps), Token Ring (4 Mbps, 16 Mbps), FDDI (100 Mbps), LocalTalk (230 Kbps)

A.2.1 Common LAN topologies

The physical organization of a LAN is known as its *topology*. There are three common network topologies. The simplest is a bus or chain, in which all machines are connected to a common cable. A ring topology is similar to a bus, but the ends of the cable connect to form a ring. A star topology consists of a hub which connects separately to each networked node. How exactly the nodes share access to the common network medium—their *media access*—is determined by the *datalink* specification. Traditional LANs provide any-to-any connectivity (i.e., any machine can communicate with any other machine on the LAN) and a *broadcast* mode that allows each station to send a frame that will be picked up by every other station on the LAN (Figure A.3).

A.2.2 Ethernet

Ethernet is the most popular LAN technology in place today. Ethernet is a physical and datalink specification that spans several types of cabling and several related data framing

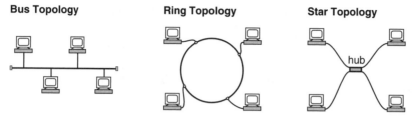

Figure A.3 Common LAN topologies

protocols in the 802.*x* family. Ethernet media access control allows any station on the network to try to transmit at any time, even though this may produce collisions when several transmit at one time. This media access mechanism is called *carrier sense multiple access with collision detection* (CSMA/CD). CSMA/CD identifies collisions, and allows each station to have adequate access to the common channel.

Each node on an Ethernet has an Ethernet interface card, usually called the *network adapter* or *network interface card* (NIC). Each NIC has a special hardware address, assigned in such a way as to guarantee uniqueness, even across vendors. The NIC connects to the network cabling and picks up packets from the wire that have its address as their destination. The NIC also picks up packets addressed to the broadcast address, which is a special address that is received by all NICs.

Ethernet cabling comes in three flavors. Old installations used a bulky inflexible cable known as *thicknet*. Second-generation Ethernets typically used a cheaper, thin coax cable which was usually deployed in a chain for connecting stations. This type of cabling is officially known as 10-base-2, but is generally referred to as *thinnet*. Modern Ethernet installations use a type of cable designated 10-base-T or *unshielded twisted-pair* (UTP), arranged in a star topology around a hub. UTP is rated from category one through category five, with category five (cat 5) as the highest rating. Cat 5 UTP is standard for Ethernet cabling in modern facilities.

A *hub* is a device with multiple ports, each of which is connected to a node on the network via a 10-base-T link in a star topology. Typically, a hub acts as a concentrator, which brings all of the links together into one channel, connected to the other nodes. For Ethernets, a star topology is superior to a chain because there is only one station on a given cable leg, which results in fewer collisions. Hubs are called *smart* if they are remotely manageable with an administrative protocol called *simple network management protocol* (SNMP). Hubs can frequently be chained together, allowing a single large Ethernet to be created (Figure A.4).

Bridges are devices that sit between LANs or subsections of the same LAN. Bridges maintain datalink hardware address tables in memory and forward frames that have destinations on the other side of the bridge. Bridges operate at the datalink layer, the

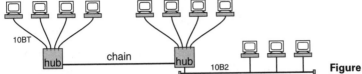

Figure A.4 Ethernet hubs

second layer of the network stack introduced at the beginning of this book, and usually connect homogeneous networks.

A *switching hub*, or *switch*, is a fairly new type of hub that actively forwards frames directly from a transmitting station to a receiving station, thereby avoiding collisions completely. Switches essentially act as bridges which partition each station into its own network. Switches may also provide network-layer routing, in which case they act as routers (Figure A.5).

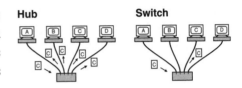

Figure A.5 A switching hub

A *router* is a network device that is connected to two or more networks and forwards packets between the networks based on their network protocol destination addresses. In the case of a small LAN, a router usually serves as the gateway between the LAN and the Internet. Such a router picks up packets on its inside interface that have destinations

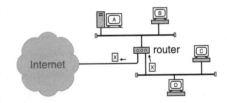

Figure A.6 An IP router

outside of the local subnet, and forwards them to the outside interface, which is usually the endpoint of a WAN link such as a T-1. It also forwards packets that appear on its outside interface to its appropriate inside interface (Figure A.6).

Routers can also sit between different LANs in the same network complex, or between parts of a wide area enterprise network. In this case, the routers' interfaces may be ethernets or WAN link endpoints. This allows traffic on a large network to be effectively partitioned.

High speed Ethernet In addition to the standard 10-Mbps Ethernet, 100-Mbps Fast Ethernet is available over Category 5 UTP. Also, Gigabit Ethernet, which is capable of speeds of 1 Gbps, is on the way. Gigabit Ethernet is expected to see immediate deployment in the backbones of larger Ethernet installations.

A.3 Wide area networking

Wide area networking (WAN) comes into play in the context of geographically large networks. WAN generally makes use of the public phone system infrastructure provided by phone companies.

Internet WAN is built over the top of the phone system. Traditionally, computer data networks and protocols have borne very little resemblance to telco digital voice and data networking protocols. The Internet therefore developed by using dedicated high speed phone lines as the basic wide area transport links for normal IP communications.

Telco WAN links have historically been expensive, leased point-to-point links from LANs to the Internet backbone. As the Internet has become more popular, more demand for connectivity has begun to appear. As a result, ISPs and phone companies have started offering intermediate and more affordable bandwidth solutions, such as Frame Relay and ISDN.

A.3.1 Telco WAN background

In general, the world's phone network is a point-to-point mesh or cloud, depending on the exact service in question. In other words, when a call is placed, the call is assigned a temporary direct link to the destination. This architecture is opposite in design philosophy to LANs, which share a common transmission media, and support LAN broadcast and multicast. This difference is a natural one: the phone system was designed to accommodate telephone calls from one subscriber to another within a huge subscriber base, whereas LANs were originally intended to move computer data among a relatively small number of machines.

The telco switching fabric is based on bearer channels of fixed capacity. These bearer channels, which contain enough bandwidth for a single phone call, are allocated across the long distance network as calls are placed. Long distance calls are aggregated into larger high speed channels, called *trunks*, for transport across the telco backbone. Trunks themselves are aggregated into even higher speed trunks across the backbone as well (Figure A.7).

Figure A.7 Aggregated bearer channels

Each channel or trunk is placed into next trunk level by a process called *time division multiplexing* (TDM). Every second, a timeslice sample of each channel is bundled into a trunk frame at a particular time slot. At every phone switch on the route to the destination the call is mapped out of its time slot and into the corresponding slot of the next trunk en route to the next backbone switch. At the last switch in the route, the call is demultiplexed out of the trunk and presented as a continuous stream to the remote end of the connection.

Demultiplexing is the act of extracting component channels from a higher level channel, and is used to unpack a high speed trunk into its component calls. Demultiplexing an entire trunk within the backbone in order to route a few bearer channels is an expensive process in terms of performance. In a completely synchronized hierarchy there is no need for this sort of wholesale demultiplexing within the backbone.

In the context of telco, synchronization means that a given channel always falls in the same time slot within each level of the multiplexing hierarchy. Synchronization is useful because in a truly synchronized multilevel system, switches may simply route calls directly into and out of high speed trunks based

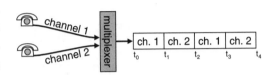

Figure A.8   Time-division multiplexing

on their respective time slots. Otherwise, to route a particular call channel, the switch has to demultiplex high speed trunks to get to their lower level component trunks and then demultiplex these into the actual calls (Figure A.8).

A.3.2   The legacy phone network

The term *plesiochronous digital hierarchy* (PDH) is sometimes used to describe currently implemented telco network technologies, because they do not scale from lowest to highest level in a truly synchronous fashion.

A single phone channel, such as that needed for a standard voice conversation, is an 8-bit value sampled at the rate of 8,000 samples per second. These numbers are based on the minimum amount of data per second needed to digitally represent a human voice with decent quality, and form the basis for the architecture of the entire phone network. Eight thousand 8-bit samples per second produces a bearer channel with a bandwidth of 64 Kbps. Telcos refer to this type of connection as a DS-0.

DS-0s are allocated by the phone network as needed to carry voice transmissions. Those DS-0s with an endpoint not serviced by the local phone switch are multiplexed into higher bandwidth trunk lines. Of course, since the phone system is circuit-switched, there is no dynamic routing of each individual DS-0 slice or frame. Instead, the entire path is preallocated by the phone network during a call setup phase.

A.3.3 DS-0s, DS-1s, and DS-3s

DS-0s carry 64 Kbps. The next step up from a DS-0 is a DS-1, usually referred to as a T-1, which consists of 24 multiplexed DS-0s. The T-1 is the standard dedicated Internet WAN connection, and can carry approximately 1.5 Mbps of traffic. The next standard step up from a T-1 is a DS-3, or T-3, which multiplexes 28 T-1s for a total of 672 simultaneous individual DS-0s. T-3s have a bandwidth of approximately 43 Mbps (Figure A.9).

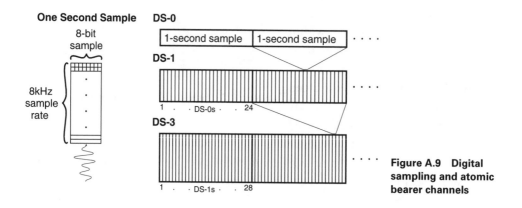

Figure A.9   Digital sampling and atomic bearer channels

The biggest problem with the PDH is that it is not synchronous. At the T-3 level it is impossible to extract a given DS-0 without first demultiplexing the entire T-3 down to T-1s. This results in slow switching times. As a response to this problem, a new technology called *synchronous optical network/synchronous digital hierarchy* (SONET/SDH), was developed. SONET/SDH is a synchronous framing standard, data rate standard, and switching system that can attain speeds on an order of magnitude greater than PDH.

A.3.4 The B-ISDN

The Broadband-Integrated Services Digital Network (B-ISDN), sometimes referred to as the *Information Superhighway*, is the proposed world information infrastructure designed to carry every sort of data from video and voice to file transfer. The interface to the B-ISDN is intended to be flexible enough to accommodate time-dependent (iso-chronous) services such as realtime multimedia, as well as data transfer of all sorts. SONET/SDH is extremely fast, but it has severe limitations for application as the switching fabric for the B-ISDN. The major problem with SONET/SDH for this purpose is that it does not offer enough interface bandwidth granularity, and therefore cannot accommodate many data rates. SONET/SDH is, however, excellent as a framing format and transport technology, and is in fact used for this purpose in the B-ISDN.

ATM is a data transport specification that contains circuit-switched and packet-switched elements, and as such offers the best of both worlds. ATM is primarily run over fiber, but it can be run over copper cabling as well. Early adopters are already utilizing ATM as a LAN technology, as well as a WAN technology, to reduce interface problems between LAN and WAN. B-ISDN implemented with ATM as its switching fabric is extremely granular, and therefore flexible for many data rates and service types.

A.3.5 Common WAN links

The following list outlines the WAN interfaces commonly used for Internet connectivity, along with their associated bandwidth. Note that there are other types of WAN interfaces which are not listed because they are not usually used outside of telco. The latency of each link, which is the total amount of time a frame of information takes to traverse the link, is included. The problem with a high-latency link, such as a satellite link, is that although its bandwidth may be high, there is always a large delay, or lag, between data being sent and data actually arriving.

When using a telco WAN link for an Internet connection, it is important to remember that both a phone company and an Internet service provider (ISP) come into play. The phone company provides a line to the ISP, which then provides some type of Internet interface. Typically, the telco line is leased, and the ISP interface contains some sort of lease plus bandwidth usage component. The telco link may be point-to-point between the subscriber and the ISP, such as in the case of a T-1, or it may go into a telco cloud, as with Frame Relay.

POTS POTS stands for *plain old telephone service*. Even though the telco system's backbone has been digital for years, most subscribers unfortunately still have an analog phone line to their businesses and residences. The limited geographic range of the digital alternative, N-ISDN, the high price of digital phones, and the relatively high cost of digital subscriber interface installation prevent digital from gaining real penetration into the POTS subscriber base. POTS is sometimes also called the public switched telephone network (PSTN).

Serial Line Internet Protocol (SLIP) and Point-to-Point Protocol (PPP) both use the analog phone system interface as the transport layer for an Internet link. SLIP/PPP connections are temporary links over standard serial phone lines between a modem on the user's end and a modem bank and terminal server at the ISP. These connections are asynchronous, generally of low quality, and of comparatively high latency. These connections do, however, have the redeeming quality of being inexpensive (Figure A.10).

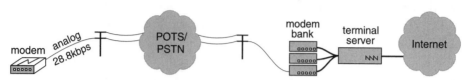

Figure A.10   POTS data communications

DS-0   A DS-0 is the atomic digital telco bearer channel. A DS-0 is allocated for every call and contains 64 Kbps of bandwidth. DS-0s are used as the building blocks for other digital interfaces such as N-ISDN and T-1.

N-ISDN BRI: 64 or 128 Kbps   Narrowband Integrated Services Digital Network (N-ISDN) is the forerunner of the proposed B-ISDN or Information Superhighway. N-ISDN, which is usually simply called ISDN, is a standard designed to provide a digital subscriber interface over the copper wires which make up the majority of the installed subscriber loop infrastructure. ISDNs were originally positioned in the market as integrated digital voice and video, hence the name *Integrated Services Digital Network*. ISDN went nowhere until it was discovered as a cost-effective way to transport data. ISDN comes in two interface levels, PRI and BRI.

ISDN Basic Rate Interface (BRI) consists of two DS-0 bearer (B) channels and a 16 Kbps signalling (D) channel. Latency is high. ISDN BRI is becoming popular because of increasingly simple setup and low cost. ISDN is available only within 18,000 feet of an ISDN-enabled phone switch. This is usually not a problem in urban areas, but most rural areas cannot take advantage of this service (Figure A.11).

Figure A.11   ISDN BRI

ISDN Primary Rate Interface (PRI) is a high-bandwidth version of the BRI which runs over T-1. It consists of 23 64-Kbps B channels and one 64-Kbps D channel. PRIs are usually used to concentrate multiple incoming BRIs.

Frame Relay   Frame Relay (FR) is a packet-switched telco network which may be likened to a modern version of the old X.25 telco data network. FR uses endpoint equipment similar to T-1, and may in fact be upgraded to T-1 or transported over T-1.

FR allocates physical bandwidth in the network only when data are being sent or received, so FR circuits are referred to as *virtual circuits* (VCs). VCs employ a DataLink Connection Identifier (DLCI) to identify the circuit's path through the network. In the case of switched virtual circuits (SVCs), the network has to set up this connection

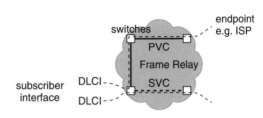

Figure A.12   Frame relay circuits

identifier dynamically, which adds to transport latency. A permanent virtual circuit (PVC), on the other hand, keeps a permanently assigned DLCI to avoid the call setup overhead. FR PVCs therefore behave like dedicated circuits in this respect (Figure A.12).

Because the FR network is a shared cloud, available capacity at any given time is not guaranteed. Committed information rates (CIRs), which guarantee the subscriber a minimum amount of bandwidth, may be purchased from providers to circumvent this problem. FR bandwidth varies, but is typically offered with an interface of 56 Kbps.

Switched 56 digital data service   Switched 56 provides subscribers a fairly low cost, but high latency access so that they do not have to buy leased lines. Switched 56 service requires the same equipment as a T-1, and usually may be upgraded to T-1 service or frame relay. Bandwidth is 56 Kbps.

T-1   T-1 is AT&T's name for a DS-1 formatted signal, which is a multiplexed aggregate of 24 DS-0s. T-1s are conventionally used as wide area transport service (WATS) lines for incoming and outgoing 800 numbers and other rotating phone exchanges. T-1s are dedicated point-to-point circuits, which means that they permanently connect their endpoints. This type of connection from a telco is typically referred to as a leased line, because the line bandwidth is always available (and billable), even if it is not being used to full capacity. Since T-1 is a point-to-point dedicated circuit, telco bills it by the mile, making such a network of dedicated lines very expensive.

T-1 is a high-quality connection, with a nominal bandwidth of 1.544 Mbps and low latency. T-1 is fairly expensive and requires a CSU/DSU for both ends of the line, plus local telco and ISP setup and monthly fees.

Fractional T-1   A fractional T-1, or *fractional,* is some subset of the full T-1 bandwidth of 24 DS-0 channels. Fractionals are available in increments of 64 Kbps. The exact increments are based on the telco provider. Not all telcos will lease fractionals, and ISPs do not automatically offer matching service levels for a given telco. The actual usable bandwidth for the fractional is less than the number of DS-0s because of some signaling overhead.

Fractional T-1s use the same CSU/DSU for both ends of the line, plus the same additional setup as a full T-1.

T-3   T-3 is AT&T's name for a DS-3 formatted signal. The DS-3 multiplexes 28 T-1s for an approximate total bandwidth of 43 Mbps. Usually DS-3s are used by providers to carry backbone traffic.

SMDS   Switched multimegabit data service is a relatively new addition to high speed telco networking services. SMDS is a broadband, multiaccess, packet-switched network service designed to bridge LANs over WAN. SMDS supports connection with ATM, Frame Relay, SMDS Interface Protocol (SIP), or Data Exchange Interface (DXI).

ADSL   Asynchronous digital subscriber link (ADSL) and a family of related technologies are beginning to be embraced as alternatives to ISDN over the copper subscriber loop. ADSL can drive 1.5 Mbps over a distance of 18,000 feet. At a distance of 12,000 feet, ADSL can drive 6.1 Mbps. The wire gauge has an effect and can diminish the range.

Very high speed digital subscriber line (VDSL), a related technology, has been shown to deliver 50 Mbps for up to 1,000 feet in tests.

Cable   Cable companies are starting to deliver packet-based services to subscribers, including video on demand (VOD) and TCP/IP transport. Cable-based packet bandwidth varies widely, but by most estimates falls in the 35 Mbps range.

Some cable-based efforts are focused on setting up parallel, high-performance cable backbone segments which function in parallel to the Internet. These alternative networks are intended as high speed backbones for business use.

Satellite   Satellite Internet links are already available in some places, with some offerings of bandwidth of roughly 400–500 Kbps. Unfortunately, at this time satellite links are downstream only and display high latency. Typically, a modem, or similar technology, must be used for the upstream link.

A.3.6 Future Internet: ATM

Asynchronous transfer mode (ATM) is a relatively newly adopted standard (1988) that forms the switching and multiplexing fabric for the B-ISDN. ATM is a cell-based technology designed to compromise between the needs of time-sensitive data such as real-time video and multimedia, and data transfer applications.

ATM is intended to support traffic with widely different characteristics, as well as to integrate with current standards. ATM therefore contains facilities to transport voice, video, X.25, and data packets.

ATM virtual circuits and routing ATM routing takes place between ATM switches. Much like the legacy phone network, ATM switches set up a path at the beginning of data transfer. The switches set up virtual path identifiers (VPIs) and virtual channel identifiers (VCIs). VPIs identify a circuit path within the ATM network; VCIs identify a channel within a given VPI. This arrangement

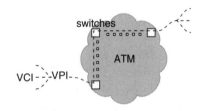

Figure A.13 Asynchronous transfer mode

allows hosts to multiplex multiple applications streams (VCIs) into one virtual path. The network uses the VPIs to route cells, but ignores the VCIs, which are used only by the hosts that are party to the connection (Figure A.13).

ATM is called *asynchronous* because it is not synchronous in the telco sense of the word. ATM uses a multiplexing scheme known as *statistical time division multiplexing* (STDM) instead of the TDM used in SONET/SDH. STDM is a sophisticated procedure that allocates circuit bandwidth in the network based on the amount of bandwidth a particular connection (VPI) requests. This request, including peak and average utilization and maximum burst duration, is made as the VPI is being set up.

The ATM cell An ATM cell is 53 bytes long. The header makes up five bytes of this cell and contains a general flow control (GFC) field, a payload type identifier (PTI) field, a cell loss priority (CLP) field, VPI and VPC fields, and a header error control (HEC) field.

The ATM stack The ATM stack consists of three layers: the physical layer, the ATM layer, and the ATM adaption layer (AAL). The physical layer defines the transport used, and includes SONET/SDH. The ATM layer defines routing, switching, and multiplexing. The AAL is used to encapsulate application types to assign their data timing priorities (Figure A.14).

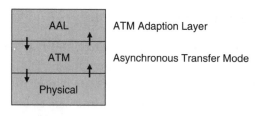

Figure A.14   The ATM stack

The AAL consists of service classes A, B, C, D, and X, where A is voice and D is connectionless packets. B and C are intermediate levels. D allows circuit-oriented ATM to operate in a connectionless, low-priority data-transport mode.

- *Class A*   Constant-rate circuit emulation (e.g., voice)
- *Class B*   Variable-rate circuit (e.g., audio and video)
- *Class C*   Connection-oriented data transfer (e.g., TCP/IP)
- *Class D*   Connectionless (e.g., SMDS, UDP, IP)
- *Class X*   User-regulated, connection-oriented, best-effort delivery

IP over ATM ATM can encapsulate IP traffic by using AAL classes C-X. However, address binding is extremely difficult. ATM does not support broadcasting, so IP cannot use ARP to discover hardware addresses. In addition, nodes do not know their physical addresses. Eventually, IP will be widely implemented over ATM, but these and other problems need to be solved.

LAN emulation In order to bring ATM to the LAN environment, it will have to interoperate with older networking technologies already in place. For this reason, ATM must have an emulation layer to provide older technologies with services such as connectionless data sending and LAN multicast and broadcast services.

The ATM Forum is proposing a standard which defines a client/server LAN interface to an ATM network. The ATM Forum's solution consists of a LAN emulation client (LEC), which is a proxy ATM station located on both the LAN and the ATM networks, and a LAN emulation server (LES), which provides MAC-to-ATM address resolution. When a station on the LAN tries to transmit to a station on the ATM network or vice versa, the LES resolves the address translation and the LEC acts as a gateway.

ATM problems   The ATM specification is still under development. It remains to be seen whether ATM switches will be able to provide full versions of complex services such as STDM.

A.4 The Internet

The Internet is the global IP-based network over which the Web and other popular information systems operate. Now, more and more, the Internet is being used commercially for both public and private purposes. Publicly, the Web provides advertising and customer support facilities; privately, VPN technologies allow companies to interconnect across the Internet in a secure manner (Figure A.15).

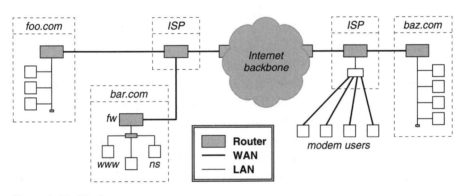

Figure A.15   The Internet

A.4.1 A brief history

The Internet originally grew out of an Advanced Research Projects Agency (ARPA) project to link several research universities. ARPANET, a rudimentary packet-switching network running over dedicated phone lines between UCLA, Stanford, USC-Santa Barbara, and the University of Utah, went online in 1969.

ARPANET was put under the control of the DOD in 1975. On January 1, 1983, TCP/IP was instated as the ARPANET protocol. ARPANET then split into a nonmilitary ARPANET and MILNET, which was integrated with the Defense Data Network. ARPANET became connected to other government and academic networks which were using TCP/IP.

The National Science Foundation (NSF) became involved in 1984. NSF upgraded and expanded backbone links and established the now-familiar set of top-level domains (EDU, COM, MIL, NET, GOV, and ORG). NSF removed itself from direct involvement in May 1995, when the backbone was commercialized.

A.4.2 Administration

The administration of the Internet has been formalized to bring order to a global network that grew from these various beginnings.

ISOC   The governing board of the Internet is the Internet Society, a nonprofit organization made up of a volunteer membership of interested individuals. The ISOC is the parent organization for the IAB.

IAB   The Internet Architecture Board is responsible for long-term architectural and technical direction for the Internet.

IETF   The Internet Engineering Task Force is the body that specifies Internet protocols and makes technical decisions about Internet architecture. The IETF is composed of working groups, which are organized under areas of study. Each working group is organized around a particular engineering problem; they attempt to draft a standard, and cease to exist if and when the standard is adopted. Participation in working groups is completely voluntary and open to interested members of the Internet community on an informal basis.

IESG   The Internet Engineering Steering Group is the IETF's managing body. It is composed of Area Directors, and the IETF chair. IESG creates IETF working groups, assigns them to areas, and approves the standards they propose.

IRTF   The Internet Research Task Force deals with long-term technical research issues under the jurisdiction of the IAB. The IRTF is composed of Research Groups which are assigned different research topics.

IRSG   The Internet Research Steering Group is the managing body for the IRTF, and consists of IRTF Research Group chairs.

IANA   The Internet Assigned Numbers Authority (IANA) assigns port numbers for well-defined services, such as telnet and TCP port 23.

InterNIC The Internet Network Information Center (InterNIC) administers Domain Name Registration (DNS) services. This includes assigning requested domain names and administering the root name servers which define mappings for the top-level domains.

Routing Arbiter The Routing Arbiter, a joint project between Merit and ISI, provides routing coordination for the Internet routing infrastructure. The RA provides routing servers at each NAP, based on entries in the Routing Arbiter Database.

North American Network Operator Group NANOG is a working group with members from ISPs, the peering points, regional networks, the Internet registries, and federal networks. NANOG meetings are held three times a year. Merit hosts many of these meetings.

A.4.3 Current Internet architecture

The Internet is composed of independent routing units called autonomous systems. These systems used to be primarily educational and military networks connected via the National Science Foundation's high speed routing backbone. Today the Internet backbone is largely commercial telco providers, such as MCI, UUNET, and Sprint, that interface at *peering points*, such as MAE-East in Washington, DC.

Autonomous systems An autonomous system (AS) is a self-contained IP routing system. All routers in an AS communicate and route among themselves. As a result, any packet that arrives at an AS that has a destination inside the AS will automatically be routed to the appropriate host without further outside routing.

Internal routing protocols such as RIP and OSPF are used within AS's to perform intra-AS routing. External routing protocols such as BGP are used to route between AS's.

Provider backbones The Internet backbone consists of high speed WAN links, typically T-3 and greater. The term *backbone* is a bit of an anachronism, because with the commercialization of the NSF backbone in May 1995, the original Internet backbone was retired. Today the Internet backbone is comprised of the respective backbones of the service providers that run the commercial regional networks. These provider backbones interconnect at a set number of designated peering points and by direct peering between providers.

Smaller service providers connect directly to the larger commercial providers with smaller WAN links (typically T-1), and even smaller providers buy from them, and so on down to the end consumer.

It is desirable to obtain an Internet connection as close to the top-level providers as possible. Closeness is measured in *hops*, or the number of IP gateways (usually routers) that your traffic must go through to get to the appropriate backbone. Closer connections are faster because they avoid latency incurred in additional router hops (Figure A.16).

Figure A.16 Major peering points

Peering points The peering points include NSF-awarded Network Access Points (NAPs) and other exchanges. The four NSF-awarded NAPs are:

- *MAE-East* MAE-East is located in Washington, DC. MAE-East is a bridged FDDI/Ethernet hybrid with three classes of connection: switched FDDI, shared FDDI, and switched Ethernet.

- *Sprint NAP* The Sprint NAP is located in Pennsauken, NJ. It is a FDDI LAN that supports both shared and dedicated bandwidth.

- *Ameritech Advanced Data Services (AADS) NAP*   The AADS NAP is in Chicago. The AADS NAP uses ATM and supports DS-3, HSSI with ADSU, DS-3 Native ATM, and OC-3c (155 Mbps) SONET interfaces. It serves the Chicago LATA.

- *PacBell NAP*   The PB NAP is located in San Francisco, and spans five LATAs. There are at least 21 network providers connected to the PB NAP. PacBell uses its own proprietary ATM cell relay service as the switching fabric.

- *Other peering points*   Other peering points include FIX-East in Washington, DC, MAE-LA in Los Angeles, MAE-West in San Jose, CA, and CIX and FIX-West in San Francisco. Besides interconnecting at common exchanges, direct peering also occurs between providers on a private basis.

The Routing Arbiter has a presence at the peering points. The RA provides a route server (RS) which coordinates the interconnecting providers by obtaining routing information from each ISP's routers on the NAP and processing the information based on the ISP's routing policy requirements, which are listed by each peering ISP in the Routing Arbiter Database (RADB). The RS then passes the processed routing information to each ISP's router.

The RS does not itself do any routing among the ISP routers. It passes routing information from one ISP system to another with BGP-4's third-party routing function (see page 457), with the next hop pointing to the router that advertises the route to the RS. In this way, the RS sets the routes without actually forwarding any traffic packets.

A.4.4 IP routing protocols

Routing protocols come in two types: distance-vector and link-state. Distance-vector protocols build a routing table based on the distances from each network to the current router, and broadcast it to neighboring routers. A link-state protocol holds a map of the entire network, which is regularly updated, as its routing table. Link-state based routing protocols are generally considered to be superior to distance-vector based protocols, but do not scale as well in the presence of large AS's (Figure A.17).

A.4.5 Interior routing protocols

Within each autonomous system, IP uses interior routing protocols to determine how to route packets.

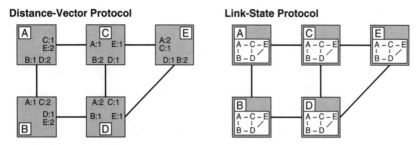

Figure A.17 Distance-vector and link-state routing

RIP   Routing Information Protocol is the simplest routing protocol, and is implemented by the UNIX `routed` daemon. RIP counts the number of hops from source to destination to find the neighboring router to which to send the packet.

IGRP   Cisco's improved version of RIP, IGRP is a sophisticated distance-vector protocol. IGRP does not count hops to determine the shortest path to a given destination. Instead, it calculates based on four metrics: delay, bandwidth, reliability, and load.

OSPF   Open Shortest Path First is a link-state protocol that calculates the shortest path for each packet based on a *shortest path* calculation from information about the entire network. This calculation takes order $n\log(n)$ operations, where n is the number of links in the network. This means that as a network gets bigger, the cost of doing this routing becomes bigger, even faster. This calculation must be performed at every router along a packet's path, which can be very costly; caching is used for efficiency, however router memory can be rapidly exhausted.

A.4.6 Exterior Routing Protocols

Routers in different AS's communicate their routes to each other with an Exterior routing protocol. The routers then internally advertise routes to the other ASs' networks, and networks that the other AS's can reach.

EGP   Exterior Gateway Protocol was one of the original exterior routing protocols used in the Internet. A router using EGP first acquires its neighbors by attempting to handshake with routers listed in a control database. When neighbors have been established, EGP periodically tests for neighbor reachability and network reachability.

Neighbor reachability is a periodic check to determine if a given neighbor is still up and routing. Network reachability periodically requests a list of reachable networks from neighboring AS's.

After EGP acquires routes from connected AS's, it includes those exterior routes that are useful in its interior routing tables.

BGP   Border Gateway Protocol is a modern exterior gateway protocol, widely in service for exterior routing over the Internet. BGP runs over TCP/IP and is designed to scale significantly better than EGP. BGP is based on the concept of *path vectors*, which prevent routing loops. Path vectors announce the entire route to a given network, listing all AS's in the route.

BGP uses open, update, and keep-alive in place of EGP's neighbor acquisition, neighbor reachability, and network reachability functions, respectively.

BGP's current version is BGP-4, although there are many BGP-3 routers still in service. BGP-4 includes support for CIDR (Figure A.18).

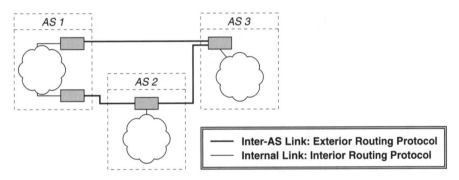

Figure A.18   **Interior and exterior routing protocols**

A.4.7 *CIDR*

Classless Interdomain Routing (CIDR) was devised in the early 1990s to address problems caused by the explosion of hosts connecting to the Internet. The immediate problem this expansion caused was a shortage of Class B networks, of which there are only 16,384. Class B networks can contain a convenient number of hosts, and so are very popular.

CIDR prevents Class B exhaustion by assigning contiguous groups of Class C networks in place of class B networks.

The next serious problem that the Internet faced was the massive growth of routing tables because of the huge number of new networks, especially Class C networks allocated in place of Class B networks. Noncontiguous network assignment also creates routing problems because nonstandard routes have to be advertised as special routing exceptions, and as such take up extra routing entries.

CIDR remedies this situation through a process known as address aggregation. Class C network ranges are partitioned into worldwide continental regions, to be handed out by regional authorities to lower levels. This scheme ensures that routing tables can map all of the traffic from broad provider ranges based on examining very few bits in the address.

This measure helped reduce routing tables, but in the final analysis, only true provider-based address aggregation will provide maximum benefit. The problem with provider-based allocation is that if the provider owns the range of numbers its clients use, then to change providers the client has to renumber all of its networks and hosts, which is not a trivial task.

The third problem is IP address space exhaustion. This will be addressed by IPv6, which contains a much larger address space than IPv4. CIDR helps this problem by encouraging efficient use of addresses by mapping them close together, but the address space will eventually be exhausted anyway.

A.4.8 IP multicast

Multicast makes use of the IP Class D range, which is designated by an initial byte with a value in the range 224–239. Multicast packets have as their destination all hosts who declare interest in a particular multicast address, instead of just one host (interface) on the network, as is the case with traditional unicast IP addresses. This is extremely useful behavior because it allows a single message transmission to reach multiple hosts with minimum network usage. In addition, the sender need not keep track of the list of recipients, because this information is maintained by the low level multicast protocol (Figure A.19).

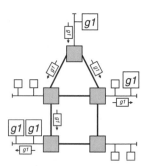

Figure A.19 Multicasting to a group of hosts

Multicast addresses Multicast addresses are officially assigned by IANA. Certain multicast addresses are for general use while others correspond to specific uses, such as MBone channels. Most multicast addresses are officially allocated, while some others are just well known.

Assigned multicast addresses:

- *224.0.0.1* All systems on this subnet
- *224.0.0.2* All routers on this subnet
- *224.0.1.11* IETF audio

MBone and multicast routing The Multicast Backbone (MBone) is an experimental virtual multicast network that tunnels over the Internet. Most IP routers do not yet support multicast, so these tunnels are required to link multicast islands.

When a multicast router receives a multicast packet, it uses the Internet Group Membership Protocol to determine if there are members of that particular multicast group within the networks connected to its other interfaces. If no members are present, the router will not forward the multicast packet. IGMP is transmitted to the router by hosts as they join multicast groups, and updates are passed in the link state database to other routers as in OSPF (Figure A.20).

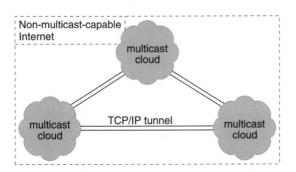

Figure A.20   The MBone

Distance Vector Multicast Routing Protocol, DVMRP, is the routing protocol used in the MBone between routers. DVMRP is a distance vector based protocol. DVMRP updates are sent to all connected multicast routers and over all tunnels connected to the sending router. DVMRP uses a pruning algorithm to cut out transmissions to areas of the network with no members of the current group. Periodic flooding allows new members to join.

Protocol Independent Multicast (PIM) is a newer multicast routing protocol. PIM is protocol-independent because it makes no assumptions about the capabilities of the underlying unicast routing protocol. PIM comes in two variants, dense and sparse. Dense is for use in situations where the number of nodes on a particular network that have joined the group is relatively large. Sparse is for situations where only a few nodes on the network have joined the group. Sparse prevents flooding the entire network with group packets if only a few nodes are listening.

Multicast Open Shortest Path First (MOSPF) is a multicast extension to OSPF, and makes use of a shortest path calculation to determine optimal routes within an AS.

A.4.9 IPv6

IPv6 is the next-generation replacement protocol for IPv4. It solves many of the problems associated with IPv4, especially the lack of sufficient address space.

Addressing IPv6 provides an address space of 128 bits as opposed to IPv4's 32 bits. An IPv6 address may be represented in three ways. The first is the form x.x.x.x.x.x.x.x, where each x is a 16-bit word. It is not necessary to include leading zeros in a field. The second way is a shorthand for representing long strings of contiguous zeros. For example, the address 0000.0000.0000.0000.0000.0000.0000.0001 (the loopback address) can be shortened to ::1. There may be only one shortening of this type in the address.

The third form is for use when interoperating with legacy IPv4. This form allows the first six groups of sixteen to precede the normal Internet *dotted quad*. An example is 0000:0000:0000:0000:0000:FA43.182.34.2.100, which of course can be shortened to ::FA43.182.34.2.100.

IPv6 supports unicast and multicast addresses. The function of broadcast addresses is performed by multicast addresses in IPv6. IPv6 adds *anycast* addresses, which are allocated from the unicast address pool and specify all hosts in a specified group. An anycast address is used for multiple interfaces that are configured to respond to the same IPv6 address. A probable use for these addresses is a group of routers belonging to the same provider.

Address allocation in IPv6 is different from IPv4. Instead of network classes, the address space is divided into unicast and multicast addresses, with subareas reserved for service providers. Roughly 15% of the address space is allocated. The rest is reserved for future use.

Unicast addresses are divided into global provider-based addresses, geographic-based addresses, NSAP addresses, IPX hierarchical addresses, site-local-use addresses, link-local-use address, and IPv4-capable host addresses. Other types may be defined in the future. IPv6 addresses are contiguously bitmaskable, making IPv4 CIDR-like routing possible.

The provider-based address space is assigned to registries, which assign portions to providers, which in turn assign smaller portions to customers.

IPv6 is designed to run over 802.x-based networks such as Ethernet by allowing the globally unique 48-bit hardware address to automatically be used as the organizational IP identifier. Hosts on 802.x networks can therefore use their hardware address to auto-generate their IPv6 address.

IPv6 datagrams   Datagram headers have been simplified in IPv6 to take up less bandwidth and speed up processing during routing. A security extension to IPv6 headers also provides for authentication and encryption possibilities.

IPv6 provides priority levels which enable the sender to prioritize packets coming from the same source. Two classes of traffic, congestion-controlled and noncongestion-controlled, are provided. Congestion-controlled traffic, priority levels 0–7, consists of traffic types such as email and data transfer, which can be backed off under conditions of network congestion. Noncongestion-controlled traffic, priority levels 8–15, consists of traffic types such as video and audio, which does not back off.

Congestion-controlled data can have priority of level 0–7, where 0 is lowest.

0   Uncharacterized

1   Filler (e.g., USENET)

2   Unattended data (e.g., email)

3   Reserved

4   Attended data (e.g., FTP, NFS)

5   Reserved

6   Interactive data (e.g., telnet)

7   Internet control (e.g., routing protocols, SNMP)

IPv6 is still a standards-track proposed IETF standard. Implementation will probably not begin until 1997 at the earliest.

A.5 References

- Christian Huitema, *Routing in the Internet*, Prentice Hall, 1995.
- Routing Arbiter web page, `http://www.ra.net/`.
- Uyless Black, *TCP/IP & Related Protocols*, McGraw-Hill, 1994.
- S. Deering and R. Hinden, "Internet Protocol, Version 6 (IPv6) Specification," RFC 1883, `ftp://ds.internic.net/rfc/rfc1883.txt`.
- S. Deering and R. Hinden, "IP Version 6 Addressing Architecture," RFC 1884, `ftp://ds.internic.net/rfc/rfc1884.txt`.

appendix B

Cryptography

This appendix provides more detail to complement the earlier overview of cryptography. In particular, it provides details of different encryption algorithms and the different modes in which they can operate, as well as issues related to the use of passwords. The appendix concludes with some of the more esoteric fields of cryptology that may be of interest to the reader.

B.1 Streams, blocks, and modes of operation

One rather subtle but very important categorization of encryption algorithms divides them into *stream ciphers* and *block ciphers*. Stream ciphers operate on streams of data, usually a bit or a byte at a time, while block ciphers operate on blocks of data, typically 64 bits. The result of this is that a byte doesn't always encrypt to the same value when encrypted by a stream cipher—it depends on where in the stream the byte occurs, and what comes before it in the stream—while a block will always be encrypted to the same value by a block cipher. This puts a block cipher at a serious disadvantage, since it can make patterns in the plaintext very obvious: if an attacker were watching a series of block-encrypted bank transaction sheets, large parts of the ciphertext would be the same for all sheets, so the attacker could quickly find which parts to modify in order to affect someone's bank balance. (Guessing how to modify it might be more difficult.) Patterns also remain visible in block-encrypted images. While compression of the data seems to solve this problem (indeed it is *always* a good idea to compress plaintext as much as possible before encrypting it for precisely that reason—it removes patterns which could be used as the weak point at which to attack a system), this would seem to illustrate a problem with using block ciphers—why then are some of the most popular encryption algorithms block ciphers? Block ciphers can be turned into stream ciphers in a number of ways; the four most popular are described here, followed by an orthogonal modification called *triple encryption* (Figure B.1).

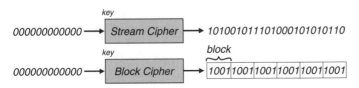

Figure B.1 Stream versus block encryption

B.1.1 Electronic code book (ECB)

This is the normal mode of operation of a cipher; the cipher operates by reading the plaintext in block-sized quantities and encrypting each block independently (Figure B.2). Decryption is straightforward, but ECB has the disadvantage described above—that pattern in the plaintext is often preserved. Also, if an error occurs during transmission, then all of the block hit by the error is corrupted. ECB does have the advantage of supporting random access.

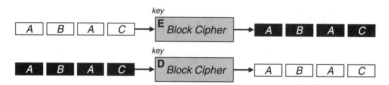

Figure B.2   Electronic code book mode

A problem immediately arises in the question of what to do with the last block—a 64-bit block cipher given 72 bits to encrypt will encrypt the first 64 bits, and then be left with eight bits. If preserving file length is unimportant then these eight bits can be *padded* to 64 bits by appending 56 random bits (or 56 zeros; random bits are somewhat more secure); if length must be preserved, then we can use the last byte in each block to indicate the amount of padding that has been added (Figure B.3). We would thus send 56 bits in our first block and 16 in the second. A 64 bit message would be encoded in two blocks: the last block would contain one byte of data, 48 random bits and a byte with value 56. There are a huge variety of different ways (some of them international standards) of padding messages; this is just one (which will only work for blocks up to 256 bits in size)—check the literature for more.

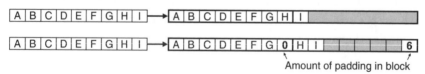

Amount of padding in block

Figure B.3   Padding block ciphers

B.1.2 Cipher block chaining (CBC)

In general, CBC is the mode of choice for cryptographic implementations (Figure B.4). In this mode, the previous block of ciphertext is bitwise XORed with the current block of plaintext before it is encrypted; to decrypt, each ciphertext block is decrypted and then bitwise XORed with the previous ciphertext block.

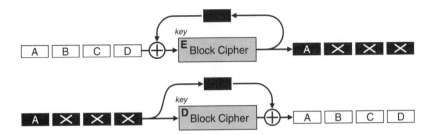

Figure B.4   Cipher block chaining mode

This usually hides patterns (Figure B.5). Transmission errors corrupt all of the affected block and the corresponding bits in the next block. Padding (as with ECB) must be performed.

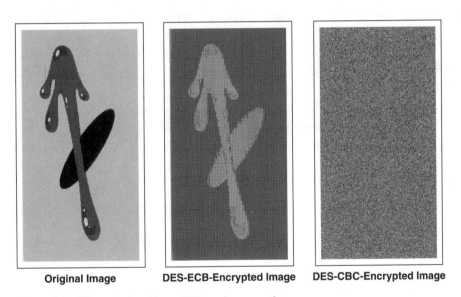

| **Original Image** | **DES-ECB-Encrypted Image** | **DES-CBC-Encrypted Image** |

Figure B.5   Why you should use CBC-mode encryption

The question for CBC is what block is previous to the first block; this is usually answered by the two parties agreeing on an *initialization vector* (IV) in advance, or by the sender transmitting the IV it is using with the message (Figure B.6). CBC supports random read access (with an extra block read), but not random write access.

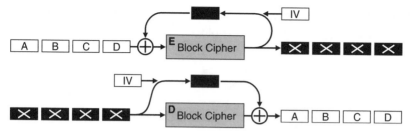

Figure B.6 Initialization vectors

B.1.3 Cipher feed back (CFB)

CFB mode operates on N-bit blocks, where N is less than or equal to the algorithm's real block size B: a B-bit IV is agreed upon (as for CBC), and then encrypted; the N most significant bits of this encrypted block are XORed with the next N bits of plaintext to form the next N ciphertext bits. As well as being transmitted, the N ciphertext bits are then shifted into the IV from the right (so that the N most significant bits of the IV are lost and the $B - N$ least significant bits are shifted N bits to the left). The process is then repeated with the modified IV for the next N bits. To decrypt, we follow the same process except that since the ciphertext needs to be shifted into the IV, the bits are available to shift in *before* XORing with the output of the encryption operation. (Note that for both encryption and decryption modes, the cipher itself is used in *encrypt* mode—no proper decryption is necessary.)

This hides patterns, but if the plaintext is known, an attacker can twiddle bits to change the message meaning safely (although subsequent blocks are corrupted). The IV *must* be changed when encrypting a different message if the same key is being used. Transmission errors corrupt the corresponding plaintext bits and all of the next block. No padding is necessary (Figure B.7).

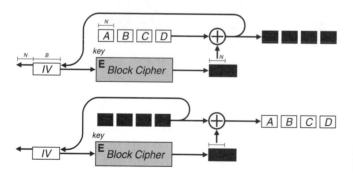

Figure B.7 Cipher feed back mode

B.1.4 Output feed back (OFB)

OFB mode operates on *N*-bit blocks in a similar manner to CFB, the difference being that the *N* bits shifted into the IV are the *N* most significant bits of the just-computed encrypted IV. Thus OFB generates a stream of pseudorandom data independent of the plaintext and XORs it onto the plaintext (Figure B.8).

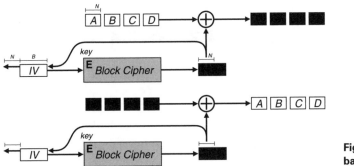

Figure B.8 Output feed back mode

This hides plaintext patterns, but the message is easy to modify in the same way as with CFB. Again, the IV must be changed if another message is being encrypted using the same key. Transmission errors corrupt only the corresponding plaintext bits.

Warning: OFB has been shown to be unsafe when *N* is anything other than the algorithm's real block size (*B*). There is a modification, *counter mode*, which overcomes the problem (see the literature).

B.1.5 Triple encryption

No matter what mode your cipher is running in, you should be able to strengthen it using triple encryption: encrypt the message three times. Interestingly, this is not three times as strong as just encrypting once, and therein lies the reason for using the technique: double encryption, where you encrypt using one key and then again using another key, adds one bit of security to a system in most cryptographers' eyes. (The attack, called *meet-in-the-middle*, involves having two pairs of associated plaintext-ciphertext blocks and enough memory to store one block encrypted by *every possible key*—not very likely for most modern algorithms.) Triple encryption with three different keys defeats the meet-in-the-middle attack, *doubling* the strength of the algorithm. Triple encryption is normally implemented as encrypt-decrypt-encrypt, not encrypt-encrypt-encrypt, as it then has the convenient backward-compatible property that setting all keys the same makes it the same as single encryption. The standard (X9.17) implementation also requires that the first and last keys are identical, rendering it subject to another attack which makes it only as strong as single encryption *but* requires a huge amount of *chosen plaintext*. This requires an attacker to be able to encrypt data using the key which they're trying to break: this is normally nigh-impossible (Figure B.9).

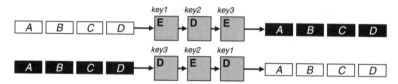

Figure B.9   Triple encryption

Meet-in-the-middle attacks on double encryption with an algorithm, which like IDEA (described later), has a 128-bit key, is almost certainly impossible because of the amount of memory needed. The attacks possible on triple encryption are difficult to mount under normal circumstances, but if you don't want to risk the attack on double encryption, then there's little point in risking the attack on triple encryption: use three independent keys unless you're constrained by standards compliance.

One final point about triple encryption: it is important that the algorithm used doesn't form a group operation, i.e., that encrypting with one key and then encrypting with another key doesn't turn out to be the same thing as encrypting once with a third key. This isn't the case with DES, but it is the case with the Caesar Cipher, for example. (Shifting the alphabet right four places and then shifting it right 13 places is the same as shifting it right 17 places.) It is thought that IDEA doesn't form a group.

B.2 Combining public and symmetric systems

As mentioned in Section 2.3, public key cryptosystems are (so far) much slower than symmetric key cryptosystems. This has resulted in the following popular trick for encrypting a message: pick a random key for a symmetric algorithm, encrypt this using the recipient's public key, and encrypt the message using the symmetric algorithm key. Then transmit both the encrypted symmetric key and the encrypted message to the recipient: the recipient uses its private key to discover the symmetric key and then uses the symmetric key to decrypt the message itself. This trick combines the flexibility of public key systems with the speed of symmetric ones, and is in use in a huge number of applications today, including Phil Zimmerman's pgp (Pretty Good Privacy) program and most popular Web browsers that support secure transactions (Figure B.10).

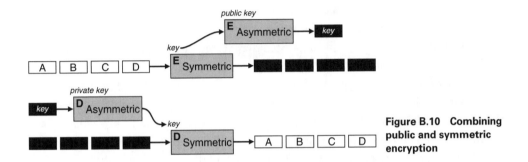

Figure B.10   Combining public and symmetric encryption

Using a random number generator to create these *session keys* for the symmetric algorithm is normal practice (bearing in mind some caveats mentioned in Section B.5), but alternative methods exist—ANSI X9.17 suggests the following:

1 Establish K, a secret key generation key, and V, a seed. These should be taken from a good random number source.

2 Obtain a timestamp T (this need not be tied to a system clock, but could simply comprise a number-of-keys-generated counter).

3 Compute $R \leftarrow E_K(E_K(T) \oplus V)$. This is the next session key.

4 Set $V \leftarrow E_K(E_K(T) \oplus R)$. This new value of V is used when generating the next session key.

X9.17 uses DES (described later) as its encryption algorithm, but others could be used instead; if the required session key is larger than the algorithm's block size, then the algorithm can be iterated, and successive values of R concatenated until the desired key length is obtained.

In the above notation, $E_K(x)$ means x *encrypted using key K*, and $x \oplus y$ means *bitwise exclusive OR of x and y*.

B.3 Key length and system strength

Common in establishing the strength of a system is a notional brute force cryptanalysis of the system: if an attacker tried every possible key to decrypt your message, forge your signature, or break in, how much effort would it take? If no shortcuts exist in the system (this is a very big if), then this is often taken as a rough measure of how secure the system is. The usual measure is in bits; if a system has 80-bit strength, then it would take *at most* 2^{80} simple operations (trial encryptions, guesses, whatever) to break it.

Consider the secret key cipher DES (more recently known as DEA): it has a 64-bit key, so trying to decrypt a DES-encrypted message by guessing keys would take at most 2^{64} (18,446,744,073,709,551,616) tries—however, the warning about shortcuts applies here: in fact, DES automatically discards 8 bits of the key, so by taking this into account it is only necessary to try guessing 2^{56} (72,057,594,037,927,936) keys.

Public and secret key cryptosystem strengths cannot be compared directly, as breaking a public key system consists of computing the secret key from the public key, which is often easier than guesswork. Computationally, breaking a 512-bit RSA takes about the same effort as breaking a 64-bit symmetric algorithm, ditto a 2,000-bit RSA versus a 120-bit symmetric.

It is important to remember that a secured system is only as strong as its weakest link: if you sign a document using a 2,000-bit RSA key, but use a hash function which only produces 64-bit digests, then it would make much more sense for an attacker to try to forge a document with the same digest as your message than for them to try breaking your RSA key.

B.4 Passwords and system security

Passwords, PINs, or pass phrases entered by the user are a common weak link in security systems: users will almost always enter the password on a keyboard, so it has to consist of typeable characters, and might consist of only alphanumeric characters or even just digits. There is a great danger in this, since in a password-controlled environment the bytes of the password often correspond directly to the bytes of the key. Also, while a byte can hold 256 different values, only 97 of these can be typed on most keyboards, there are only 62 alphanumerics (36 if you ignore case), and only 10 digits. Consequently, in order to achieve 64-bit security, a typeable password would have to be at least 10 characters long, an alphanumeric password would have to be at least 11 characters long, a case-insensitive alphanumeric password would have to be at least 13 characters long, and a digits-only password would have to be 20 characters long! An eight-character password using these restrictions would have less than 53, 48, 41, and 27 bits of security respectively.

This problem gets even worse when under analysis it turns out that in plain English text every character is worth only 1.3 bits of security: this is a consequence of the structure of English words and sentences—*q* is almost always followed by *u*, capital letters usually appear only at the beginning of words, *e* occurs often while *z* occurs rarely, and so on. Individual words, at 2.3 bits per character, are slightly better, but still unacceptable. The net result of this is that, given free choice, people often choose passwords which are very easily guessed: the standard UNIX password system, which has a limit of eight characters and uses DES, lends itself to attack by guessing programs such as `Crack`, which have in the past compromised 40 percent of users on academic systems.

Two strategies can be combined to combat this problem in password choice:

- Use a password system which allows long pass phrases and encourage (or force) users to use this facility.

- Encourage (or force, by refusing to accept purely alphanumeric passwords) users to select their password from as wide a range of characters as possible.

B.5 Random numbers

One of the other common weak links in system security is a system's source of random numbers. Whenever a new key is to be created, some random numbers will usually be needed: for DES, 56 bits of random data are padded out to make the 64-bit key; for RSA, at least 1,024 bits of random data are used to generate a pair of huge prime numbers which are then made into a 1,024-bit key pair. A good source for these bits would be coin tosses (where heads translates to 0 and tails to 1, for example); unfortunately few people are willing to toss a coin 1,024 times, and situations arise in the computer where the coin would have to be tossed automatically anyway. There are other physical means of creating random data using feedback or radioactivity, and although some machines have built in hard random number sources such as these, most computers don't. As a result, *pseudorandom* number generators are common in programs: these use a mathematical formula to generate a random-looking sequence of numbers from an initial value, or *seed*. The use of a formula means that the sequence is completely predictable from the seed—indeed, it has to be, since the computer has no unpredictable random number source. This means that the seed still has to be properly random, so we're back to the original problem of finding a good random number source on the computer (Figure B.11). Here are some places to look:

- *User-provided* Ask the user to type random stuff (or move the mouse randomly) and record the time intervals between key presses (or the pointer coordinates).

- *Audio* An unconnected sound sampler (`/dev/audio` on UNIX systems) is often pretty good.

- *Time* The system time, at the highest available resolution, is the oldest (and one of the worst) source of randomness around.

- *System information* Load average, process ID, window number, number of running processes, etc. Early Netscape encryption was broken because it used this information.

- *Hardware status* Disk information (free space, inodes, etc.), network address.

- */dev/random* FreeBSD pools together any randomness it can find and makes it available through `/dev/random`.

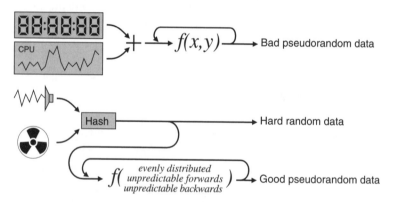

Figure B.11   Random number generators

Once some initial randomness has been recorded, it needs to be compressed into something suitable for use as a seed. (To start with it could look very nonrandom). A hash function is ideal for this purpose.

The function you use to generate the pseudorandom sequence from the seed is also very important, as it may behave in a way which significantly weakens your system. Some functions converge on particular values; some functions have an uneven distribution (e.g., output 0 a lot more frequently than 1); and other functions are *predictable*: if a system were operating using the combined public symmetric system described earlier, it will need to generate a new random key for the symmetric system for every new message the system encrypts. Further, if a flurry of messages went to a single user, that user could end up with a series of keys which form a direct copy of output from the system's pseudorandom number generator. The user might then be able to work out what the generator will produce next or what it has produced previously—neither of these possibilities is at all desirable. A lot of mathematical thought has gone into pseudorandom number generators which are *evenly distributed* and *unpredictable both forwards and backwards*.

B.6 Real algorithms

Before moving on to protocols—how to use cryptography safely—here is some information on a few real algorithms, symmetric ciphers first.

B.6.1 DES/DEA—the Data Encryption Standard

Designed by IBM and introduced in 1977 by the American National Institute of Standards and Technology (NIST, then National Bureau of Standards (NBS)), this is without doubt the most widely used encryption algorithm today. It was recertified in 1987 (despite the National Security Agency's objections that "it seemed increasingly likely that DES would soon be broken") and (despite NBS' claim that it would not be recertified) again in 1992. Many more commercial, international, and financial standards have been based on its use (the name *DEA* comes from the American National Standards Institute's (ANSI) adoption of DES). Some staff at NIST believe it has reached the end of its useful life, but the last two times that it has come up for recertification, businesses have insisted that it remain certified; whether the same will happen in 1998 is open to debate. While the 56-bit key is small relative to current computational power, the algorithm is too entrenched to be abandoned.

The result of its popularity has been to render DES target of a huge amount of cryptanalytic research; the algorithm only really started to fall (publicly) in 1990—to differential cryptanalysis, a technique DES' designers at IBM now claim to have known about since 1974. Since then linear cryptanalysis has found further weaknesses, finally reducing the complexity of an attack on the algorithm to 2^{43} (8,796,093,022,208) known plaintexts, as compared with the brute force keyspace search which requires 2^{56} encryptions. However, the size of the keyspace has long been a cause of concern—even DES' predecessor, Lucifer, had a 112-bit key—to the extent that machines have been proposed with costs as modest as $1,000,000 which would be capable of breaking DES by brute force in 24 hours or less. It is widely believed that major governments have (and have had for some time) the capability to break DES in this manner, but that such capability has not yet fallen into corporate hands.

DES operates at about 2.5 MBps on a 200 MHz Pentium Pro with a C/assembly implementation, and up to 64 MBps in dedicated hardware implementation.

B.6.2 RC4—Rivest Cipher 4

Ron Rivest (of RSA fame) designed this stream cipher for RSA Data Security, Inc. in 1987. The company kept it as a trade secret until 1994, when an anonymous poster sent compatible source to the Cypherpunks mailing list. Despite RSADSI's best efforts, RC4 is now common knowledge (although anyone attempting to sell his or her own implementation risks legal action). No cryptanalytic results exist yet.

The algorithm supports variable key size, is extremely simple to implement, and runs (independent of key size) in excess of 5 MBps on a 200 MHz Pentium Pro.

B.6.3 RC5—Rivest Cipher 5

Another of Rivest's creations (only introduced in 1995), this block cipher has variable number of rounds, block size, and key size. RSADSI claims to have cryptanalysed the 64-bit block version extensively, with good results, but nobody else has studied it. The algorithm is patented.

The 64-bit block, 12-round, 16-byte key version runs at over 6.5 MBps on a 200 MHz Pentium Pro.

B.6.4 IDEA—International Data Encryption Algorithm

Xuejia Lai and James Massey developed this algorithm (originally Proposed Encryption Standard, PES), in 1990, which was subsequently strengthened and released as Improved PES, finally renamed IDEA in 1992. It is patented by Ascom-Tech AG. It rose to fame with Phil Zimmerman as the choice symmetric algorithm in his pgp program.

IDEA is a block cipher with 128-bit key and a 64-bit block. The theoretical basis for its design is solid and seems to have been well implemented: while many have tried to break it, no cryptanalytic result that weakens standard IDEA has yet appeared.

IDEA executes at about 2 MBps on a 200 MHz Pentium Pro, and up to 22 MBps in dedicated hardware implementation.

B.6.5 Skipjack (Clipper/Capstone/Fortezza)

This is one of the more controversial algorithms around; it was created by the NSA during the years 1985–90, is classified and subject to a patent secrecy agreement. The US government plans to implement it solely in tamper resistant hardware in conjunction with some extra logic, the two chips resultant being called Clipper (containing an OFB-only Skipjack implementation) and Capstone (containing Skipjack in ECB, CBC, CFB, and OFB, DSA, SHA, a public key-based key exchange algorithm (see Section B.7), a hard random number source, and an exponentiator). Capstone is now available in a PC card called Fortezza.

The reason for the controversy surrounding Skipjack is not directly to do with Skipjack itself, but with the implementations made available. Both Clipper and Capstone implement a form of *key escrow*, whereby it is possible for the government to decrypt any message encrypted using these chips after obtaining certain information regarding the particular chip in use from two government agencies. These systems are designed to facilitate government eavesdropping (Figure B.12).

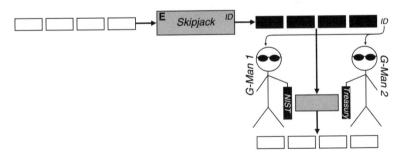

Figure B.12 Key escrow

Skipjack itself is known to be a block cipher with an 80-bit key and 64-bit blocks; the government assembled a panel of respected experts to give the algorithm a clean bill of health, but the experts do not seem to have been given enough time to analyze the algorithm. That said, the NSA plans to use Skipjack in certain areas, so they probably believe that it's secure.

B.6.6 Red Pike

This block cipher is the British Government's answer to Skipjack. It has been proposed as the source of security in a planned overhaul of the British National Health Service's computer network. Like Skipjack, details are thin on the ground.

B.6.7 RSA

RSA is not the first public key encryption algorithm, but it is the earliest one which remains unbroken—almost every variant of the first public key encryption algorithm (by Ralph Merkle and Martin Hellman and based on the knapsack problem,* see Figure B.13) has been broken. Rivest, Adi Shamir, and Leonard Adleman came up with RSA in 1978; its simplicity is probably a significant reason for its popularity, although it also has the advantages of relatively small key size and message expansion compared to other public key systems. (The McEliece public key system deals in key sizes in the tens of kilobytes and produces twice as much ciphertext as it is given plaintext, although it is hundreds of times faster than RSA.)

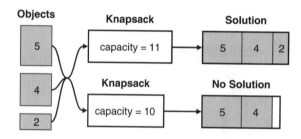

Figure B.13   The knapsack problem

A very brief mathematical treatment of RSA follows; it uses Euler's theorem, a special case of which says that given two distinct primes p and q,

$$x^{(p-1)(q-1)} \equiv 1 \bmod pq \text{ for all } x \text{ satisfying } \gcd(x,pq) = 1$$

---

* The knapsack problem is that of exactly filling a knapsack given a selection of objects you want to pack—mathematically, given a list of numbers, can you select some of them to add up exactly to a specified quantity?

An RSA key pair is created as follows:

- Find large primes p and q.
- Pick e relatively prime to $(p-1)(q-1)$ in the range $1 \le e < (p-1)(q-1)$.
- Compute $d \equiv e^{-1} \bmod (p-1)(q-1)$, so $de \equiv 1 \bmod (p-1)(q-1)$.

The public key now consists of the numbers pq (the modulus) and e (the public exponent), and the private key is the pair pq and d (the private exponent). To encrypt using either key, convert the message into a number (or series of numbers m_1, m_2, ...); to encrypt, the sender exponentiates each number by its exponent modulo the modulus, so for someone sending a message to the owner of the key the ciphertext will be

$$m_1^e \bmod pq, \; m_2^e \bmod pq, \; \ldots$$

To decrypt, the recipient exponentiates by its exponent (again, modulo the modulus), in this case getting

$$(m_1^e)^d \bmod pq, \; (m_2^e)^d \bmod pq, \; \ldots$$

However, the choice of e and d (so that $ed \equiv 1 \bmod pq$) means that

$$(m_i^e)^d = m_i^{ed} = m_i^{k(p-1)(q-1)+1} \text{ (for some } k)$$

so, by Euler's theorem,

$$m_i^{k(p-1)(q-1)+1} = m_i \bullet (m_i^{(p-1)(q-1)})^k \equiv m_i \bullet (1)^k = m_i \bmod pq$$

back to the original message, as desired! (Note that this proof isn't actually complete; the special case where $\gcd(m_i, pq) \ne 1$ isn't covered, but it does work in the end.) See Figure B.14.

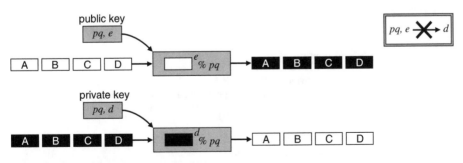

Figure B.14 Public-key encryption with RSA

So why does RSA work? When the two keys are separated, it becomes extremely difficult to work out what the other key is if you have only one of them. Specifically, you first need to work out what the factors of the modulus *pq* are. The factorization problem has received a *lot* of attention over the years. (RSA has been around for almost as long as DES, and people have thought about factorization for much longer than that.) However, it is (and seems likely to remain so) currently many orders of magnitude easier to perform RSA encryption than factorization of the same RSA modulus. (See Section B.8 for more information on factorization difficulty.)

Because RSA works with numbers, the key size is variable. You can have a key as large as you like. Large keys are much more secure, but they're slower too: doubling key size will make an individual encrypt/decrypt operation about six times slower. (But if you were encrypting a stream of data, you could operate on twice as much data at a time.) Generating keys is quite a complicated business, too. There are a few ways of factoring numbers which are relatively fast if the numbers have certain properties, so the modulus shouldn't have those properties. Finding big prime numbers is a slow process anyway; doubling the key size will slow down key generation by a little more than a factor of eight.

Table B.1 gives the timing, in seconds, of some RSA operations on a 200 MHz Pentium Pro system. (Key generation times vary hugely depending on algorithm used; exponentiation is the basic operation of encryption.) C.R.T. exponentiation uses the Chinese Remainder Theorem to speed up secret key operations (only) by a factor of about three. Fermat 5 exponentiation uses the constant 65,537 as the public exponent, which speeds up public key operations (only) by a factor which increases with key size. (Using the same constant for lots of public keys like this is perfectly safe.) Both the Chinese Remainder Theorem and Fermat public exponents are common in RSA implementations. Unlike most block ciphers, hardware implementations of RSA-like algorithms don't tend to be much faster than software; software is also much more flexible. (1,024-bit RSA in hardware has only been available for the last year.) However, hardware can be more secure (by keeping the secret key on a password-controlled RSA smart card, for example).

Table B.1 Speed of various RSA operations

Modulus size (bits)	Generate key	Normal exponentiate	C.R.T. exponentiate	Fermat 5 exponentiate
1,024	3	0.34	0.10	< 0.01
1,536	12	1.09	0.30	0.01
2,048	25	2.05	0.67	0.02

B.6.8 DSA—digital signature algorithm

Recommended by the National Institute of Standards and Technology, this NSA-designed public key algorithm appeared in 1991 as an attempt to create a strong digital signature standard. Much controversy resulted, largely because of industry's existing investment in RSA, and the widely held belief that even if the algorithm were sound (which many questioned because of its source), it was part of a greater conspiracy to discourage use of strong public key techniques for encryption. (DSA was designed so that it could not be used for encryption, although a flaw in the design means that a small amount of encrypted data can be stored in a signature.) DSA was standardized as the Digital Signature Standard.

DSA supports key sizes up to 1,024 bits (which is acceptable), is as fast as RSA for signing, and about 10 times slower for verifying. DSA is claimed to infringe on three patents.

B.6.9 SHA—secure hash algorithm

This hash function appeared from the same source and at the same time as the DSA, to be used as the digest function with DSA. It is a successful-looking attempt to improve on MD4, producing a 160-bit digest and operating at about 4 MBps on a 200-MHz Pentium Pro. No successful cryptanalysis has yet been made, although NIST did make an unexplained modification to strengthen it soon after its initial release.

B.6.10 MD5

Another attempt to improve on the MD4 hash function, this time by MD4's author, Rivest. MD5 produces a 128-bit digest. Some cryptanalytic results suggest that it may be far less strong than intended, particularly with regard to collision resistance (see the section on RIPEMD below). It is fast though, running at 7 MBps on a 200-MHz Pentium Pro.

B.6.11 RIPEMD

RIPEMD was another attempt to improve on MD4; it was produced as part of the European RACE Integrity Primitives Evaluation (RIPE) report in 1995. Since then, successful cryptanalysis of MD4 in late 1995 suggests that both MD5 and RIPEMD are at immediate risk of compromise, so RIPEMD-128 and RIPEMD-160 have been proposed with modifications to make them resistant to the cryptanalytic techniques used in the attack on MD4. (The numbers indicate the size of the digest in bits—RIPEMD-128 should only be used in situations where exactly 128 bits are necessary; in other circumstances 160 bits would always be preferable.) RIPEMD-160 was published in February 1996; its design criteria are public, unlike those of SHA, so in time it may become the preferred hash algorithm. It runs at about 3.7 MBps on a 200-MHz Pentium Pro.

B.6.12 BBS—Blum, Blum, Shub PRNG

This pseudorandom number generator is excellent for cryptographic purposes: its authors have proven that if you look at this generator's output for a while and can reliably guess what it will output next or what it output just before you started watching, then you can break the RSA public cipher just as fast. Since RSA doesn't really look as if it's in danger of being broken, the BBS generator is generally regarded as *unpredictable forwards and backwards*. This makes it an excellent algorithm for turning a little bit of seed data into an infinite stream of independent session keys.

1 Pick large primes p and q, both congruent to 3 mod 4. Let $n = pq$.

2 Get a seed x in the range $0 < x < n$ and set $x_0 \leftarrow x^2$ mod n.

3 To obtain random bits, set $x_i \leftarrow x_{i-1}^2$ mod n, and output the $\lfloor \log_2 \log_2 n \rfloor$ least significant bits of x_i.

To ensure maximal length sequences, it's necessary to keep hold of p and q and ensure some more properties on x_0, which means that you have secrets to keep.

The algorithm isn't extremely fast (about 54 Kbps with a 512-bit modulus on a 200-MHz Pentium Pro), but it is secure.

B.7 Protocols

A protocol is simply a sequence of instructions intended to achieve something among a group of communicating parties. The *something*, in the security context, is often either the establishment of trust in one or more party's credentials, or the transfer of some secret information—often, but not always by any means: protocols exist for proving one person possesses some information without his or her having to reveal it, allowing distrustful people to generate random numbers that they both trust, payment of digital cash, etc. The protocol may merely be designed so as to prevent the participants from cheating on each other, or it may be there to protect them from others; it is very important to establish its goal and what it requires beforehand (who should trust whom, what secrets they share, etc.).

The literature of cryptographic protocols uses two central characters—Alice and Bob, the communicating parties (sometimes joined by Carol, et al.)—and evil Eve the eavesdropper, Trevor the trustworthy, Malcom the malicious attacker, and many others.

The protocols here don't specify which algorithms to use; however, when a number of cryptographic systems are linked together in a protocol, attackers will always attack the weakest point, so balance is essential. This was illustrated to a small extent in the protocols in the Capstone chip: a checksum was used to prevent users from forging session keys which the government wouldn't be able to decrypt; the checksum turned out only to be 16 bits long, so it is possible to forge a session key in about forty minutes by trying random keys until luck demands that the checksum adds up correctly.

B.7.1 A simple protocol

This protocol is designed to allow Alice to recognize Bob. It assumes that at some stage in the past, Bob gave Alice his name and a password. The protocol goes as follows:

- Bob tells his name and password to Alice. If the password is correct, Alice believes she's talking to Bob; if the password is wrong, she doesn't (Figure B.15).

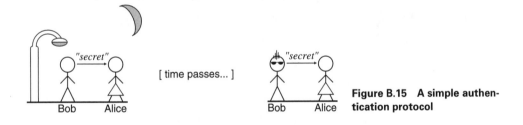

[time passes...]

Figure B.15   A simple authentication protocol

One problem with this protocol is that anyone close enough to hear Bob talking can wander up to Alice later on and successfully pretend to be Bob. Unfortunately it's the protocol which is used to control access to almost every computer system on the Internet. With Alice being the computer, Bob the user, and the Internet being the air they speak through, there are often plenty of people in a position to hear Bob telling his password to Alice.

One of the easiest solutions to this is to use *one-time passwords*: Bob tells Alice (or Alice tells Bob) a list of (say) twenty passwords, and Alice never accepts a password twice. When Bob runs out of passwords, he has to get a new list.

This achieves its goal, but in a computer context, is this goal much use? Once the computer believes Bob is who he says he is, Eve can still hear everything that subsequently passes between them, and Malcom can slip the occasional message in (going in one direction or the other), or block others to disrupt relations between Bob and the computer. Without encryption Eve can eavesdrop, and without signatures Malcom can subtly disrupt communications without anyone noticing.

B.7.2 Otway-Rees authenticated key establishment

This aims to allow Alice and Bob to identify each other and establish a secret key which they can then use for an encrypted conversation.

It assumes that at some stage in the past, Alice and Bob each established a separate secret key with Trevor, so Alice and Trevor share key K_a and Bob and Trevor share key K_b. It needs a symmetric cipher and a process for generating random numbers (Figure B.16).

1. Alice sends Bob a message containing an index number I (which increases every time she uses the protocol), her name, Bob's name, and the same three items plus a random number R_a all encrypted using K_a. So Alice's message might look like this:

   A → B: I, Alice, Bob, $E_{Ka}(I$, Alice, Bob, $R_a)$

2. Bob sends a message to Trevor comprising the message Bob just received from Alice, with an appended K_b-encrypted packet containing another random number (R_b), the index number, and their two names:

   B → T: I, Alice, Bob, $E_{Ka}(I$, Alice, Bob, $R_a)$, $E_{Kb}(I$, Alice, Bob, $R_b)$

3. Trevor creates a session key K_t for Alice and Bob to communicate with, and sends this message to Bob:

   T → B: I, $E_{Ka}(R_a, K_t)$, $E_{Kb}(R_b, K_t)$

4. Bob decrypts his packet from Trevor and sends on to Alice:

   B → A: I, $E_{Ka}(R_a, K_t)$

5. Alice decrypts her packet.

The random numbers and index number serve to prevent anyone from recording one of these conversations to try and replay it while masquerading as Alice, Bob, or

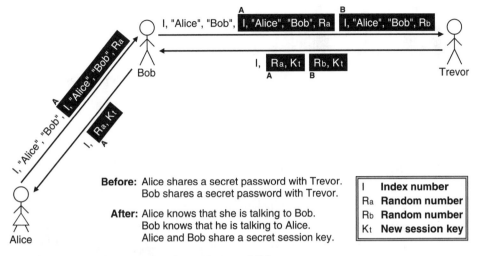

Before: Alice shares a secret password with Trevor.
Bob shares a secret password with Trevor.

After: Alice knows that she is talking to Bob.
Bob knows that he is talking to Alice.
Alice and Bob share a secret session key.

I	Index number
Ra	Random number
Rb	Random number
Kt	New session key

Figure B.16 Otway-Rees authenticated key establishment

Trevor. The index number also allows everyone to keep track of which conversation the messages they receive relate to (in case they are computers having lots of these conversations at the same time). They are assured of each other's identities as well, because only Alice and Trevor could have created the K_a-encrypted messages, and only Bob and Trevor the K_b-encrypted ones. The names have to be sent *in the clear* so that Trevor can work out what keys to use to decrypt the messages he receives.

B.7.3 Key exchange using public key systems

Setting up a session key with a public key cryptosystem is fairly straightforward:

- Alice picks a random session key, encrypts it with Bob's public key, and sends this to Bob (Figure B.17).

The problem here is how Alice gets hold of Bob's public key—unless she trusts the source, it could be doctored by Malcom: say Malcom published his public key with Bob's name on it, then he could intercept the message containing the encrypted key which Alice sent to Bob, decrypt it with his secret key, reencrypt it using Bob's public key, and send it on: this would mean that Alice and Bob thought that everything was fine, but Malcom could see or modify everything they said to each other (Figure B.18).

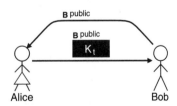

Figure B.17 Key exchange using public key encryption

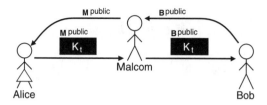

Figure B.18   Public-key distribution problems

A trusted third party could help, although he doesn't need to be accessible during the protocol: if Alice had met Trevor on a previous occasion, she could have obtained his public key. Then Trevor could sign copies of other people's public keys *with their names attached* using his secret key, and leave them in public places: whenever Alice comes across one of these *certificates* she can be sure that it truly belonged to the person it claimed to belong to, since she trusts Trevor's signature. Trevor in this case is often known as a *certification authority* (Figure B.19).

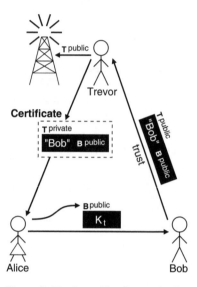

Figure B.19   A certification authority

This type of key distribution is now being used by Microsoft Internet Explorer to certify the origin of potentially dangerous code. When you encounter unprotected executable content on the Web, a certification windows pops up informing you of the author. A trusted third-party certification authority verifies the origin of the code using public key encryption and digital signatures.

B.8   Cryptanalysis

Breaking a system involves either breaking the algorithms in use or finding a weakness in the protocols. For example, in September 1995, the security in Netscape's Navigator 1.1n (provided with SSL, its Secure Socket Layer) was broken in both ways:

- First, because of US export restrictions on cryptography, Netscape wasn't allowed to use a strong encryption algorithm in Navigator because it sold it abroad. The stream cipher in use was RC4 with a *40-bit key*—RC4 would, so far as is currently known, be fine with an 80-bit key, but 40 bits is so small that it means the cipher could actually be attacked directly by a brute force search of the key space. It was broken by a French academic, Damien Doligez, after eight days' work on a network of 120 computers, and subsequently broken by another team after less than 32 hours' of computer time. This crack was taken more as a comment on US export law than anything else. The secure (unexportable) version of Netscape has used 128-bit RC4 since July 1996.

- The second crack was more serious, and made it to the front page of the *New York Times* (September 19, 1995, pp. A1, D21). The Netscape random number generator was seeded very badly, merely using the time, process ID, and parent process ID, all of which (bar microsecond time) are visible to other users of the same computer system, and even if not visible can be guessed quite rapidly by somebody on a different computer. Two postgraduate students at UC Berkeley discovered this and implemented a program to take advantage of it. This program would guess the correct key in less than a minute on a Pentium machine, and guess subsequent keys from the same browser almost instantaneously. Netscape responded extremely quickly to the problem, supplying an improved browser in a matter of days, but this does serve to illustrate the care that must be taken in implementing a secure system. Some say it's also illustrative of the dangers of not releasing your source code and submitting to peer review.

RSA itself was cracked in 1994 in response to a challenge (called RSA-129) laid down by RSA's authors in *Scientific American* in 1977; however, the crack involved factoring a single key of only 129 digits (426 bits), took eight months, and used the cooperating services of 1,600 computers around the Internet (and hence was possibly (at the time) the largest single computation ever made). The total amount of computation expended was estimated at 5,000 MIPS (million instructions per second—an approximate estimate of computer power) years—equivalent to a hundred Pentiums working flat out on the problem for one year. Or a thousand Pentiums for five weeks. Or ten thousand for four days. Since then, RSA-130 (430 bits) was factored in early 1996 using a newer (and currently the best) algorithm; it required only 500 MIPS years of computation. A few important points appear here:

- Advances in mathematical methods can have at least as large an impact as improvements in technology.

- Modern methods of factoring allow the job to be split up across a number of machines to speed up the factorization process.

- Therefore more machines means faster factoring. (At the one-week point, things break down because all of the results have to be pumped into a single supercomputer to be digested into the result.)

- Therefore more money means faster factoring.
- The RSA-129 group only used 0.03 percent of the estimated computing power of machines attached to the Internet.

The preceding points make things look a bit bleak for RSA: the RSA-129 problem was expected to take 40 quadrillion years when it was posed. Arjen Lenstra and his co-conspirators broke that deadline by quite a margin—so why do people still trust RSA? The answer lies in the way that hardware and mathematical techniques have improved over the years since 1977. They have progressed in leaps and bounds, and are expected to continue to do so, *but* RSA keys can get bigger even faster. Table B.2 gives a rough idea of how three factoring algorithms compare: quadratic sieve was the algorithm used to factorize RSA-129, general number field sieve was used on RSA-130, and special number field sieve doesn't actually work on general numbers, so is currently useless—it is included to suggest the possible. The numbers in Table B.2 are logarithms, so the quadratic sieve would need 1,000,000,000,000 (the 12 indicates twelve 0s) times as much computation to factorize a 1,024-bit modulus as it did to factorize RSA-129, and the special number field sieve could factorize a 512-bit modulus a little over twice as fast as the quadratic sieve dealt with RSA-129.

Table B.2 $\log_{10}$ complexity of factoring RSA moduli compared to RSA-129

Bits	512	768	1,024	1,536	2,048
Quadratic sieve	2.1	7	12	20	26
General number field sieve	1.8	6	9	14	18
Special number field sieve	−0.4	2.3	5	9	12

Rivest published an excellent paper on factorization complexity in 1990, estimating resources available to a variety of attackers ranging from individuals through corporations to governments, taking varying levels of mathematical wizardry and technological advances into account to come up with estimates as to what size key was needed to be safe against these attackers. Technology advances since then make his estimates seem a little optimistic, and Bruce Schneier has subsequently published estimates based on assumptions which better reflect today's technology: assume that a dedicated individual can gain access to 10,000 MIPS years, that large companies could get a thousand times more, and that a large government could get a hundred times more than the company. Then assume that computer power (for the same cost) increases by a factor of ten every five years. Finally, assume that the speed of factorization algorithm used by each corresponds to the three listed in Table B.2. Some of Schneier's (1994) estimates appear in

Table B.3; although he made some very pessimistic assumptions—error may have already stepped in with the use of the general number field sieve by Lenstra's group on RSA-130—but 2,048-bit keys are so big that even these estimates suggest they'll be safe for the next twenty years.

Table B.3 Guestimated factoring capability of various agencies over time

Year	Individual	Corporation	Government
2000	1,024	1,280	1,536
2005	1,280	1,536	2,048
2010	1,280	1,536	2,048
2015	1,536	2,048	2,048

B.9 Esoterica

All of the above controversy may turn out to be moot in a few years' time: new technologies threaten to overturn the entire cryptographic world. *Quantum computing* and *molecular computing* compute on previously unheard-of degrees of parallelism, and may bring the existing cryptographic world to an end. The new technologies aren't all bad, however, as *quantum cryptography* (as opposed to cryptanalysis) has been demonstrated already.

B.9.1 Quantum computing

Quantum computing bases its power on the ability of the quantum world to superimpose all possible states of a system; the classic example of this is Schrödinger's cat, which is sealed in a box with a poison gas capsule which is set to release the gas with some probability (triggered, for example, by a radioactive source)—before the box is opened again, the cat may be regarded as neither dead nor alive, but *both*: until someone looks, its state is unknown,

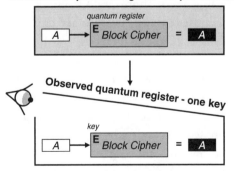

Figure B.20 Quantum cryptanalysis

and could be either. On a much smaller scale, replacing the cat with bits in a quantum computer's register, the bits of the register can hold both values 0 and 1 simultaneously. Hence the register can in fact hold *all* its possible values at one time; it will randomly collapse to a single value when it is observed, much as the cat will randomly become alive or dead when the box is opened. Shor has shown that this ability to hold values simultaneously can be used, for example, in an algorithm for factorization. On a normal computer the problem would take time exponential in the length of the number being factored, while on a quantum computer the problem is quadratic in the length of the target: a quantum factorization engine could factor RSA-129 in seconds! See Figure B.20.

While some of the basic building blocks of quantum computational devices have been demonstrated, there are many currently unsolved problems, including that of setting up the inputs for the quantum computer, controlling errors (which increase in proportion to the time the device has been working on a problem), and stopping the outside world from interfering with (and destroying) the computations. While there is no sign of a near future solution to many of these difficulties, researchers are making progress: an October 1996 result shows how error-correcting codes could be entangled with data in a quantum register *while still permitting useful operations on it*, thus producing an error-tolerant quantum computer.

B.9.2 Molecular computing

Leonard Adleman kickstarted this field in 1994 when he solved a problem in the same domain as factoring using a DNA soup. The problem, the Directed Hamiltonian Graph, is this: given a collection of cities connected by one-way roads, find a route from city A to city B which passes through every other city exactly once (Figure B.21).

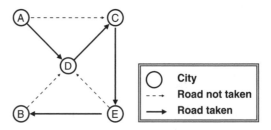

Figure B.21   A directed hamiltonian graph

DNA-enzyme mixes naturally perform pattern matching quite effectively, so Adleman represented each road on the map with a twenty-base DNA string, coded specially such that all of the roads going into each particular city had matching codes at one end: thus if city C had roads coming from A and going to B, there were DNA strings in the mixture with A's code at one end and C's code at the other, and other strings with C's code at one end and B's at the other. Mixing the appropriate enzymes (which join segments of DNA with matching codes) in with the DNA and letting it react for the right amount of time, Adleman ended up with a large collection of joined strings of various lengths. As he states in his paper, the following algorithm will solve the problem:

1 Generate random paths through the graph.

2 Keep only those paths that begin with the starting city and end with the final city.

3 If the graph has *n* vertices, then keep only those paths that enter exactly *n* vertices.

4 Keep only those paths that enter all of the vertices of the graph at least once.

5 If any paths remain, these solve the problem.

The first step has already been performed by the DNA mix; it remains to throw away strings which start or end in the wrong place, or are too short or too long, and finally every string which don't contain every city. The entire process (for a seven-city map) took seven days' work in the laboratory; Adleman believes that the process has linear time complexity, and parts of it could be automated. He speculates that DNA-based computations could reasonably be performed at a thousand times the speed of current supercomputers, at an astonishingly low energy cost.

There is, however, a serious problem: that of translating a cryptographic problem into a molecular computing one (the molecular computer model is radically different to that of digital computers). But Boneh, Dunworth, and Lipton have designed a molecular approach to breaking DES (applicable to any other 64-bit cipher of similar complexity) which they expect would locate the key used for one plaintext-ciphertext pair in four months. (While dedicated DES breaking machines are believed to take twenty-four hours, this compares quite favorably with the Internet attacks on RC4, which would have taken 239 years to break 56-bit RC4.) Much work needs to be done before this scale of procedure could be performed (particularly on the subject of error-resistance), but it shows that molecular computing has remarkable potential.

B.9.3 Quantum cryptography

Quantum cryptography was proposed as early as 1970, with two new approaches in 1990 and 1992. It works today: British Telecom has used it over tens of kilometers of normal optical fiber at communications rates of twenty kilobits per second. Quantum cryptography relies on Heisenberg's *uncertainty principle*: it is impossible to accurately measure the state of a quantum system without disturbing it. In the most successful approach two parties communicate a random session key across an optical fiber as follows:

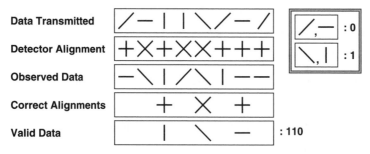

Data Transmitted	/ — │ │ \ / — /
Detector Alignment	+ X + X X + + +
Observed Data	— \ │ / \ │ — —
Correct Alignments	+ X +
Valid Data	│ \ — : 110

/ , — : 0
\ , │ : 1

Figure B.22   Quantum cryptography

1 Alice transmits a series of photons down the fiber, randomly polarizing each photon at one of four angles: horizontal, vertical, or one of the two 45 degree diagonals (Figure B.22).

2 Bob tries to measure the polarization of the photons as he receives them; unfortunately, he has to have his detector aligned either rectilinearly or diagonally, and if the detector is aligned to one basis while a particle is aligned in the other basis (e.g., the particle is diagonally polarized while his detector is rectilinearly aligned), the detector's measurement is useless. This means that if Bob randomly swaps his detector between the two alignments, the chances are that 50 percent of the time he'll get results which he can't trust. What can he do?

3 Bob sends the sequence of alignments he used back to Alice.

4 Now Alice can tell when Bob should have obtained the correct result—i.e., when Bob's detector was aligned in the same basis as Alice's photon. She tells Bob which alignments he got right, and they agree that (say) a vertical and one of the diagonal alignments represent a 0 bit, while a horizontal or (other) diagonal alignment represent a 1.

5 Now Alice and Bob have a shared key: they know which bits from the message were correctly received by Bob, and can start encrypting using it. What about Eve? Eve would have been in much the same situation as Bob; she'd have been trying to detect what way the photons coming from Alice were aligned, and every time she got this wrong, she would actually alter the alignment of that photon. So all Alice and Bob need to do is compare some of the bits which they should have communicated correctly. If the bits are all the same then Eve probably wasn't eavesdropping and they can start encrypting (obviously the bits they compared can't be used as a key), but if there are lots of errors then they have to assume that she was listening in, and try to communicate by some other method.

Alice and Bob will have to communicate a little bit over twice the number of bits that they need for a key to cover for Bob's mistakes and the check bits they compare at the end. Then they can switch to a fast encrypted digital channel afterwards.

As with everything else, there are some teething problems, including the difficulty of differentiating between errors from the system itself and errors caused by Eve, but essentially this already works. The one problem is installing a continuous fiberoptic cable between Alice and Bob. Repeaters obviously cannot be used for the same reason that Eve can't eavesdrop; British Telecom expects a limit of 50 km.

B.9.4 Hardware fault cryptanalysis

A flurry of papers cropped up in September and November 1996 based on a single idea: obtaining keys from a secure or tamperproof hardware key store (such as a smartcard) by inducing hardware faults in the device and analyzing the consequences. Faults may be induced in the hardware by a number of mechanisms, including:

- Running the device at the edge of its operating envelope—too high or low a voltage, temperature, clock rate, etc.
- Use of electromagnetic radiation, e.g., microwaves (or for EPROMS, ultraviolet light).
- Use of localized electrical pulses on EEPROMS.

Following this, something similar to differential cryptanalysis may be used to obtain the original key (Biham, Shamir). Another algorithm—the original in this group of papers—obtains the RSA secret key without having to factor the modulus: the authors (Boneh, Lipton, DeMillo, all associated with Bellcore) say that their algorithm is not significantly affected by key size, and hence might lift even 2000-bit keys from hardware very easily. Bao, Deng, Han, Jeng, Nagir, and Narasimhalu detail an alternative algorithm to do this (Bellcore haven't yet published details). Ross Anderson suggests an idea which uses the parity check in DES keys to lift the key bits directly from the hardware. Biham and Shamir propose an algorithm which can obtain any key in a system which uses memory with asymmetric error probabilities (i.e., an error is far more likely to clear bits then set bits—EEPROMs have this property), in quadratic time—slower than Ross Anderson's attack, but still incredibly fast compared to alternatives. This last one will work with any cryptosystem whatsoever.

Sounds like a bad day for smartcards, and despite the fact that chipcard manufacturers claim to have been aware of this technique for cryptanalysis, most cards seem nevertheless to be vulnerable—seem being the operative word, as to date none of the researchers involved has actually tried their attack: all of the attacks are theoretical, if extremely credible. A number of other items should be noted: the fault models depend on the fault not destroying the hardware, or corrupting internal code, and assume that the hardware is not fault-resistant. Most of the attacks require many identical (i.e., same-keyed) pieces of hardware with identical copies of the key, as the key data will be corrupted in an undefined manner from which they cannot recover. This is obviously a ludicrous situation to be in if, as is most likely, the attacker has one stolen chipcard to work with.

So again: interesting stuff, but don't worry yet.

B.9.5 Timing analysis

Paul Kocher published a paper in early 1996 detailing an attack on an RSA system by timing exponentiation operations: the secret key is inferred from the length of time the RSA system takes to process data chosen by the attacker. This is particularly interesting as the attack should be possible over a network. Kocher shows how many obvious preventative measures (such as modifying the RSA exponentiation stage to run in constant or random time by adding a wait afterwards) won't work because the system's load, power consumption, and other characteristics may change when the exponentiation finishes anyway. However, he also shows how the attack may be foiled completely by using signature blinding (not detailed here; it's well documented in the literature).

This attack isn't just limited to RSA: it may be used against any system whose runtime varies with the key, which includes most, if not all, public key systems, IDEA, some implementations of DES, and many other algorithms. Await further results.

B.10 Encryption in use

Encryption is already widely used on the World Wide Web, and it is worth knowing the technologies that are in use.

Some Web servers provide password-restricted access to certain areas of a web-site through a `.htaccess` file (or equivalent). This file simply lists the hosts that are allowed to access a site, and some username/password pairs that restrict individual access. This does not use encryption; instead, the username and password are encoded and transmitted, and the server accepts or denies the request based on this information. The encoding does not provide encryption, and so passwords are open to snooping.

S-HTTP is a proposed standard for encrypting HTTP transactions. It supports digital signatures, authentication, and encryption. Signatures allow a client to verify a document's authenticity through a third party; authentication simply provides message integrity and sender authenticity for individual transactions. S-HTTP builds on top of HTTP, and as such is restricted to HTTP-based communications. It supports MD2, MD5 and SHS message digests, and various modes of DES and triple-DES, as well as IDEA, RC2, and RC4 for encryption.

Much more popular is Netscape's SSL protocol, or Secure Sockets Layer. Any document with the protocol `https` uses this encryption. SSL provides encryption at the socket layer, and so supports arbitrary communications on top of this. SSL uses RSA public key cryptography and DES or 128-bit RC4 symmetric session encryption. Unfortunately, due to US restrictions, the internationally exported version of Netscape is limited to using 128-bit RSA for key distribution and 40-bit RC4 for encryption. Neither is particularly secure. SSL offers encryption on a channel, reliably using a keyed MAC (SHA or MD5) and authentication through the use of public key encryption. It uses public key certificates that allow servers to securely vouch that they are who they claim to be. SSL is now supported by most popular browsers.

Microsoft's Internet Explorer uses SSL to provide secure transactions, and also uses digital certificates to verify potentially dangerous executable content on the Web. The Active-X technology allows unprotected binaries to be downloaded; their authenticity is guaranteed through digital certificates, so if you trust the author and the certification authority, then you can trust the downloaded code.

This type of digital certification is due to be incorporated into Java so that applets can be downloaded and run in unrestricted environments if the author and certification authority are trusted. This addition should bring about a new generation of extremely powerful downloadable Web content.

appendix C

Tables

This appendix provides a few tables of data that are relevant to Java networking issues.

C.1 Java escaped characters

String and character literals in Java source require the following characters to be encoded with their corresponding escape codes:

Escape code	Meaning
\n	newline (LF)
\r	carriage return (CR)
\t	tab
\"	double quote
\'	single quote
\\	backslash

C.2 The ASCII character set

ASCII is a widely used seven-bit character encoding of the basic Latin alphabet. Some systems support an extended eight-bit form that includes some foreign and accented characters in addition to this regular set.

Dec	Oct	Hex	Char	Dec	Oct	Hex	Char
0	000	0x00	NUL (^@)	17	021	0x11	DC1 (^Q)
1	001	0x01	SOH (^A)	18	022	0x12	DC2 (^R)
2	002	0x02	STX (^B)	19	023	0x13	DC3 (^S)
3	003	0x03	ETX (^C)	20	024	0x14	DC4 (^T)
4	004	0x04	EOT (^D)	21	025	0x15	NAK (^U)
5	005	0x05	ENQ (^E)	22	026	0x16	SYN (^V)
6	006	0x06	ACK (^F)	23	027	0x17	ETB (^W)
7	007	0x07	BEL (^G)	24	030	0x18	CAN (^X)
8	010	0x08	BS (^H)	25	031	0x19	EM (^Y)
9	011	0x09	HT (^I)	26	032	0x1a	SUB (^Z)
10	012	0x0a	LF (^J)	27	033	0x1b	ESC (^[)
11	013	0x0b	VT (^K)	28	034	0x1c	FS (^\)
12	014	0x0c	FF (^L)	29	035	0x1d	GS (^])
13	015	0x0d	CR (^M)	30	036	0x1e	RS (^^)
14	016	0x0e	SO (^N)	31	037	0x1f	US (^_)
15	017	0x0f	SI (^O)	32	040	0x20	SPC ( )
16	020	0x10	DLE (^P)	33	041	0x21	!

Dec	Oct	Hex	Char	Dec	Oct	Hex	Char
34	042	0x22	"	81	0121	0x51	Q
35	043	0x23	#	82	0122	0x52	R
36	044	0x24	$	83	0123	0x53	S
37	045	0x25	%	84	0124	0x54	T
38	046	0x26	&	85	0125	0x55	U
39	047	0x27	'	86	0126	0x56	V
40	050	0x28	(	87	0127	0x57	W
41	051	0x29	)	88	0130	0x58	X
42	052	0x2a	*	89	0131	0x59	Y
43	053	0x2b	+	90	0132	0x5a	Z
44	054	0x2c	,	91	0133	0x5b	[
45	055	0x2d	-	92	0134	0x5c	\
46	056	0x2e	.	93	0135	0x5d	]
47	057	0x2f	/	94	0136	0x5e	^
48	060	0x30	0	95	0137	0x5f	_
49	061	0x31	1	96	0140	0x60	`
50	062	0x32	2	97	0141	0x61	a
51	063	0x33	3	98	0142	0x62	b
52	064	0x34	4	99	0143	0x63	c
53	065	0x35	5	100	0144	0x64	d
54	066	0x36	6	101	0145	0x65	e
55	067	0x37	7	102	0146	0x66	f
56	070	0x38	8	103	0147	0x67	g
57	071	0x39	9	104	0150	0x68	h
58	072	0x3a	:	105	0151	0x69	i
59	073	0x3b	;	106	0152	0x6a	j
60	074	0x3c	<	107	0153	0x6b	k
61	075	0x3d	=	108	0154	0x6c	l
62	076	0x3e	>	109	0155	0x6d	m
63	077	0x3f	?	110	0156	0x6e	n
64	0100	0x40	@	111	0157	0x6f	o
65	0101	0x41	A	112	0160	0x70	p
66	0102	0x42	B	113	0161	0x71	q
67	0103	0x43	C	114	0162	0x72	r
68	0104	0x44	D	115	0163	0x73	s
69	0105	0x45	E	116	0164	0x74	t
70	0106	0x46	F	117	0165	0x75	u
71	0107	0x47	G	118	0166	0x76	v
72	0110	0x48	H	119	0167	0x77	w
73	0111	0x49	I	120	0170	0x78	x
74	0112	0x4a	J	121	0171	0x79	y
75	0113	0x4b	K	122	0172	0x7a	z
76	0114	0x4c	L	123	0173	0x7b	{
77	0115	0x4d	M	124	0174	0x7c		
78	0116	0x4e	N	125	0175	0x7d	}
79	0117	0x4f	O	126	0176	0x7e	~
80	0120	0x50	P	127	0177	0x7f	DEL

C.3 Unicode 2.0 block allocations

Unicode is a sixteen-bit international character encoding standard that supports the alphabets of many different languages in addition to a variety of mathematical and geometric shapes. Groups of characters from different alphabets and different origins are assigned contiguous blocks of the character set; this table lists the Unicode 2.0 block allocations.

Start code	End code	Block name
\u0000	\u007F	Basic Latin
\u0080	\u00FF	Latin-1 Supplement
\u0100	\u017F	Latin Extended-A
\u0180	\u024F	Latin Extended-B
\u0250	\u02AF	IPA Extensions
\u02B0	\u02FF	Spacing Modifier Letters
\u0300	\u036F	Combining Diacritical Marks
\u0370	\u03FF	Greek
\u0400	\u04FF	Cyrillic
\u0530	\u058F	Armenian
\u0590	\u05FF	Hebrew
\u0600	\u06FF	Arabic
\u0900	\u097F	Devanagari
\u0980	\u09FF	Bengali
\u0A00	\u0A7F	Gurmukhi
\u0A80	\u0AFF	Gujarati
\u0B00	\u0B7F	Oriya
\u0B80	\u0BFF	Tamil
\u0C00	\u0C7F	Telugu
\u0C80	\u0CFF	Kannada
\u0D00	\u0D7F	Malayalam
\u0E00	\u0E7F	Thai
\u0E80	\u0EFF	Lao
\u0F00	\u0FBF	Tibetan
\u10A0	\u10FF	Georgian
\u1100	\u11FF	Hangul Jamo
\u1E00	\u1EFF	Latin Extended Additional
\u1F00	\u1FFF	Greek Extended
\u2000	\u206F	General Punctuation

Start code	End code	Block name
\u2070	\u209F	Superscripts and Subscripts
\u20A0	\u20CF	Currency Symbols
\u20D0	\u20FF	Combining Marks for Symbols
\u2100	\u214F	Letterlike Symbols
\u2150	\u218F	Number Forms
\u2190	\u21FF	Arrows
\u2200	\u22FF	Mathematical Operators
\u2300	\u23FF	Miscellaneous Technical
\u2400	\u243F	Control Pictures
\u2440	\u245F	Optical Character Recognition
\u2460	\u24FF	Enclosed Alphanumerics
\u2500	\u257F	Box Drawing
\u2580	\u259F	Block Elements
\u25A0	\u25FF	Geometric Shapes
\u2600	\u26FF	Miscellaneous Symbols
\u2700	\u27BF	Dingbats
\u3000	\u303F	CJK Symbols and Punctuation
\u3040	\u309F	Hiragana
\u30A0	\u30FF	Katakana
\u3100	\u312F	Bopomofo
\u3130	\u318F	Hangul Compatibility Jamo
\u3190	\u319F	Kanbun
\u3200	\u32FF	Enclosed CJK Letters and Months
\u3300	\u33FF	CJK Compatibility
\u4E00	\u9FFF	CJK Unified Ideographs
\uAC00	\uD7A3	Hangul Syllables
\uD800	\uDB7F	High Surrogates
\uDB80	\uDBFF	High Private Use Surrogates
\uDC00	\uDFFF	Low Surrogates
\uE000	\uF8FF	Private Use
\uF900	\uFAFF	CJK Compatibility Ideographs
\uFB00	\uFB4F	Alphabetic Presentation Forms
\uFB50	\uFDFF	Arabic Presentation Forms-A
\uFE20	\uFE2F	Combining Half Marks
\uFE30	\uFE4F	CJK Compatibility Forms
\uFE50	\uFE6F	Small Form Variants
\uFE70	\uFEFF	Arabic Presentation Forms-B
\uFF00	\uFFEF	Halfwidth and Fullwidth Forms
\uFEFF	\uFEFF	Specials
\uFFF0	\uFFFF	Specials

C.4 Modified UTF-8 Encoding

UTF-8 is an efficient encoding of Unicode character strings that recognizes the fact that the majority of text-based communications are in ASCII, and therefore optimizes the encoding of these characters.

Strings are encoded as two bytes that specify the length of the string followed by the encoded string characters. The two-byte length is written in network byte order, and indicates the length of the *encoded* string characters, not just the number of characters in the string.

[lenHI][lenLO]{encoded characters}

The individual characters are encoded according to the following table. ASCII characters are encoded as a single byte; Greek, Hebrew, and Arabic characters are encoded as two bytes; and all other characters are encoded as three bytes. The variant of UTF-8 used by Java has one modification: the character \u0000 is encoded in two bytes, so that no character will be encoded with the byte zero.

Character	Encoding
\u0000	[11000000] [10000000]
\u0001–\u007f	[0][bits 0–6]
\u0080–\u07ff	[110][bits 6–10] [10][bits 0–5]
\u0800–\uffff	[1110][bits 12–15] [10][bits 6–11] [10][bits 0–5]

C.5 Hierarchy of networking exceptions

Listed on page 500 is the inheritance hierarchy of exception classes that are relevant to the I/O, networking, and RMI packages.

```
java.lang.Exception
  ├─ java.io.IOException
  │    ├─ java.io.EOFException
  │    ├─ java.io.FileNotFoundException
  │    ├─ java.io.InterruptedIOException
  │    ├─ java.io.ObjectStreamExceptionπ
  │    │    ├─ java.io.InvalidClassExceptionπ
  │    │    ├─ java.io.InvalidObjectExceptionπ
  │    │    ├─ java.io.NotActiveExceptionπ
  │    │    ├─ java.io.NotSerializableExceptionπ
  │    │    ├─ java.io.OptionalDataExceptionπ
  │    │    ├─ java.io.StreamCorruptedExceptionπ
  │    │    └─ java.io.WriteAbortedExceptionπ
  │    ├─ java.io.SyncFailedExceptionπ
  │    ├─ java.io.UTFDataFormatException
  │    ├─ java.net.MalformedURLException
  │    ├─ java.net.ProtocolException
  │    ├─ java.net.SocketException
  │    │    ├─ java.net.BindExceptionπ
  │    │    ├─ java.net.ConnectExceptionπ
  │    │    └─ java.net.NoRouteToHostExceptionπ
  │    ├─ java.net.UnknownHostException
  │    ├─ java.net.UnkownServiceException
  │    └─ java.rmi.RemoteExceptionπ
  │         ├─ java.rmi.AccessExceptionπ
  │         ├─ java.rmi.ConnectExceptionπ
  │         ├─ java.rmi.MarshalExceptionπ
  │         ├─ java.rmi.NoSuchObjectExceptionπ
  │         ├─ java.rmi.ServerErrorπ
  │         ├─ java.rmi.ServerExceptionπ
  │         ├─ java.rmi.ServerRuntimeExceptionπ
  │         ├─ java.rmi.StubNotFoundExceptionπ
  │         ├─ java.rmi.UnexpectedExceptionπ
  │         ├─ java.rmi.UnknownHostExceptionπ
  │         ├─ java.rmi.UnknownServiceExceptionπ
  │         ├─ java.rmi.UnmarshalExceptionπ
  │         ├─ java.rmi.server.ExportExceptionπ
  │         │    └─ java.rmi.server.SocketSecurityExceptionπ
  │         ├─ java.rmi.server.SkeletonMismatchExceptionπ
  │         └─ java.rmi.server.SkeletonNotFoundExceptionπ
  ├─ java.lang.ClassNotFoundException
  ├─ java.lang.CloneNotSupportedException
  │    └─ java.rmi.server.ServerCloneExceptionπ
  ├─ java.lang.IllegalAccessException
  ├─ java.lang.InstantiationException
  ├─ java.lang.InterruptedException
  ├─ java.lang.RuntimeException
  │    └─ java.lang.SecurityException
  │         └─ java.rmi.RMISecurityExceptionπ
  ├─ java.rmi.AlreadyBoundExceptionπ
  ├─ java.rmi.NotBoundExceptionπ
  └─ java.rmi.server.ServerNotActiveExceptionπ
```

π : JDK 1.1

C.6 Multiplication tables 1 to 6

	1	2	3	4	5	6
× 1	1	2	3	4	5	6
× 2	2	4	6	8	10	12
× 3	3	6	9	12	15	18
× 4	4	8	12	16	20	24
× 5	5	10	15	20	25	30
× 6	6	12	18	24	30	36
× 7	7	14	21	28	35	42
× 8	8	16	24	32	40	48
× 9	9	18	27	36	45	54
× 10	10	20	30	40	50	60
× 11	11	22	33	44	55	66
× 12	12	24	36	48	60	72

C.7 IP address classes

IP addresses are divided into address classes that broadly allocate groups of IP addresses, so that an address that begins with the byte 191, for example, belongs to a class B network. CIDR is now addressing problems such as class B exhaustion by grouping contiguous class C addresses into a single network allocation.

Class	Address range	Allocation
Class A	1–126.xx.xx.xx	16M host network
Class B	128–191.xx.xx.xx	65536 host network
Class C	192–223.xx.xx.xx	256 host network
Class D	224–239.xx.xx.xx	multicast
Class E	240–255.xx.xx.xx	reserved

C.8 Selected well-known UNIX TCP and UDP services

Several UNIX TCP and UDP port numbers are allocated to well-known services such as finger, SMTP (mail) and HTTP (Web); if you connect to TCP port 13 of a UNIX machine that supports the `daytime` service and is not behind a firewall, then it will respond with the current time. This table lists some of these services; the complete table contains thousands of entries.

Port	Protocol	Service	Description
7	TCP/UDP	echo	Echo
9	TCP/UDP	discard	Discard
11	TCP	systat	Active Users
13	TCP/UDP	daytime	Daytime
15	TCP	netstat	Netstat
17	TCP	qotd	Quote of the Day
18	TCP/UDP	msp	Message Send Protocol
19	TCP/UDP	chargen	TTYTST Source Character Generator
20	TCP	ftp-data	File Transfer (Data)
21	TCP	ftp	File Transfer (Control)
23	TCP	telnet	Telnet
25	TCP	smtp	Simple Mail Transfer Protocol
37	TCP/UDP	time	Time Server
43	TCP	whois	Who Is
53	TCP/UDP	domain	Domain Name Server
70	TCP	gopher	Gopher
79	TCP	finger	Finger
80	TCP	http	World Wide Web HTTP
512	TCP	exec	BSD rexecd
513	TCP	login	BSD rlogin
513	UDP	who	BSD rwhod
514	TCP	shell	BSD rshd
514	UDP	syslog	BSD syslogd
515	TCP	printer	BSD lpd
531	TCP	conference	Chat
6667	TCP	irc	Internet Relay Chat

C.9 HTTP requests

HTTP is the protocol that underlies the WWW; the current version of HTTP is 1.0, however a new version has already been proposed. An HTTP request is the message that a Web browser sends to a Web server when it is requesting a document.

A.9.1 A simple get request

A simple get request follows the old HTTP 0.9 specification which, while still in use, is becoming obsolete. Note that the requst is followed by two CRLFs.

```
GET /document.html[CRLF][CRLF]
```

A.9.2 A full get request

A full get request follows the HTTP 1.0 specification, and includes the HTTP version number in the request.

```
GET /document.html HTTP/1.0[CRLF][CRLF]
```

A.9.3 A full get request with headers

HTTP/1.0 supports optional headers in a request. The following request tells the server the type of browser being used and requests that the document only be returned if it has been modified more recently than the specified date. This particular header allows the browser to use a cached version of the document of the original has not changed.

```
GET /document.html HTTP/1.0[CRLF]
User-Agent: Blah/2.13 libwww/2.17b3[CRLF]
If-Modified-Since: Sat, 29 Oct 1994 19:43:31 GMT[CRLF][CRLF]
```

A.9.4 A post request

A post request allows the client to include a significant amount of data in a request. This is used, for example, to submit information to a CGI script or to upload a file to a Web server.

```
POST /cgi-bin/code.cgi HTTP/1.0[CRLF]
Content-Type: <mime-type>[CRLF]
Content-Length: <length>[CRLF][CRLF]
<body>
```

A.9.5 A head request

A head request requests just the headers of a particular file; this allows the browser, for example, to determine whether a file has been modified and should therefore be downloaded again.

```
HEAD /document.html[CRLF][CRLF]
```

C.10 HTTP responses

The response of a Web server varies with the type of request and whether or not the request could be serviced.

A.10.1 A simple response

A simple response of this form is only returned in response to a simple (HTTP 0.9) request, and consists of simply the requested document.

```
<body>
```

A.10.2 A full response

A full response includes the HTTP version number and a status code, followed by the body of the document. The status code indicates how successfully the request was serviced.

```
HTTP/1.0 200 OK[CRLF][CRLF]
<body>
```

A.10.3 A full response with headers

A full response may also include some headers that include additional information about the requested document, such as its content type, whether it is compressed and when it was last modified.

```
HTTP/1.0 200 OK[CRLF]
Content-Type: text/html[CRLF]
Content-Encoding: x-gzip[CRLF][CRLF]
<body>
```

A.10.4 HTTP response codes

This table lists the status codes that are included with HTTP 1.0 responses. The most common status code is 200 which means that the request was serviced successfully; 301 means that the document has moved (the response will include the new location); 404 means that the document was not found.

Code	Meaning
200	OK
201	Created
202	Accepted
204	No Content
301	Moved Permanently
302	Moved Temporarily
304	Not Modified
400	Bad Request
401	Unauthorized
403	Forbidden
404	Not Found
500	Internal Server Error
501	Not Implemented
502	Bad Gateway
503	Service Unavailable

C.11 MIME types

Multipurpose Internet Message Extension (MIME) allows different types of message content to be sent across the Internet. This table lists some of the common content types that are delivered over the HTTP protocol, and includes the file extensions that are most commonly associated with such files. Full HTTP responses usually include the content type of the document in a `Content-Type` header.

MIME type	Extension
application/octet-stream	.bin .dms .lha .lzh .exe .class
application/postscript	.ai .eps .ps
application/rtf	.rtf
application/x-compress	.Z
application/x-gtar	.gtar

MIME type	Extension
application/x-gzip	.gz
application/x-httpd-cgi	.cgi
application/zip	.zip
audio/basic	.au .snd
audio/mpeg	.mpga .mp2
audio/x-aiff	.aif .aiff .aifc
audio/x-pn-realaudio	.ram
audio/x-pn-realaudio-plugin	.rpm
audio/x-realaudio	.ra
audio/x-wav	.wav
image/gif	.gif
image/ief	.ief
image/jpeg	.jpeg .jpg .jpe
image/png	.png
image/tiff	.tiff .tif
image/x-cmu-raster	.ras
image/x-portable-anymap	.pnm
image/x-portable-bitmap	.pbm
image/x-portable-graymap	.pgm
image/x-portable-pixmap	.ppm
image/x-rgb	.rgb
image/x-xbitmap	.xbm
image/x-xpixmap	.xpm
image/x-xwindowdump	.xwd
multipart/mixed	
text/html	.html .htm
text/plain	.txt
text/richtext	.rtx
text/tab-separated-values	.tsv
text/x-sgml	.sgml .sgm
video/mpeg	.mpeg .mpg .mpe
video/quicktime	.qt .mov
video/x-msvideo	.avi
video/x-sgi-movie	.movie

appendix D

Classes from this book

All of the classes and examples that we developed in this book are supplied on the accompanying CD-ROM, with the exception of the cryptographic framework. This appendix provides a quick reference to these classes and the packages into which they are divided. Most of the reusable classes are provided in the `prominence.*` packages; the examples are collected into the `part?.*` packages.

D.1 Examples from part II

part2.chapter4.SimpleIn   Using `InputStreams`.

part2.chapter4.SimpleOut   Using `OutputStreams`.

part2.chapter4.Tee   A tee-joint class.

part2.chapter5.AltAppendFileOutputStreamEg   Using `AltAppendFileOutput-Stream`.

part2.chapter5.AppendFileOutputStreamEg   Using `AppendFileOutputStream`.

part2.chapter5.Copy   A simple filecopier.

part2.chapter5.MarkResetFileInputStreamEg   Using `mark()` and `reset()`.

part2.chapter6.ASCIIStreamsEg   Using the ASCII streams.

part2.chapter6.DataFileOutputStream   An enhanced stream.

part2.chapter6.FilterTest   Using filter streams.

part2.chapter7.MyBufferedInputStreamEg   Using `MyBufferedInputStream`.

part2.chapter7.TeeOutputStreamEg   Using `TeeOutputStream`.

part2.chapter8.ByteArrayInputTest   Using `ByteArrayInputStream`.

part2.chapter8.ByteArrayOutputTest   Using `ByteArrayOutputStream`.

part2.chapter8.PipeTest   Using piped streams.

part2.chapter9.GrabPage   Sending an HTTP get request.

part2.chapter9.InetEg   Using `InetAddress`.

part2.chapter9.PostTest   Using `PostOutputStream`.

part2.chapter10.MTEchoServer   A multithreaded echo server.

part2.chapter10.NBServer   A nonblocking relay server.

part2.chapter10.STServer   A singlethreaded echo server.

part2.chapter11.SureDelivery   A UDP client that resends lost requests.

part2.chapter11.UDPEchoServer   A UDP echo server.

part2.chapter12.PageViewer   Using the URL framework.

part2.chapter12.URLConnectionEg   Using `URLConnection`.

part2.chapter12.URLEg   Using `URL`.

part2.chapter13.Consumer   A producer/consumer using `wait()` and `notify()`.

part2.chapter13.ThreadDemo   Implementing `Runnable`.

part2.chapter13.SubThread   Subclassing `Thread`.

part2.chapter14.AuthException   A custom exception class.

D.2 Examples from part III

part3.chapter15.ChatClient   A standalone chat client.

part3.chapter15.ChatHandler   A connection handler thread.

part3.chapter15.ChatServer   A multithreaded chat server.

part3.chapter16.MessageEg   Using the message streams.

part3.chapter16.TransactionClient   A transaction client.

part3.chapter16.TransactionServer   A transaction server.

part3.chapter17.QueueEg   Using `Queue`.

part3.chapter18.Chatboard   A text-based chat component.

part3.chapter18.CollabTool   A standalone collaborative tool.

part3.chapter18.Whiteboard   A whiteboard component.

part3.chapter21.ChatboardClient   A `GenericClient` text-based chat component.

part3.chapter21.GenericChat   A `GenericClient` collaborative tool.

part3.chapter21.WhiteboardClient   A `GenericClient` whiteboard component.

D.3 Examples from part IV

part4.chapter27.DateClient   An `ObjectInputStream` date client.

part4.chapter27.DateServer   An `ObjectOutputStream` date server.

part4.chapter27.FavoriteColors   Using object streams for persistence.

part4.chapter28.DateClient   An RMI-based date client.

part4.chapter28.DateServer   A date server remote interface.

part4.chapter28.DateServerImpl   A date server remote object.

part4.chapter28.MyRemote   A remote interface.

part4.chapter28.MyRemoteImpl   A remote object.

part4.chapter28.jdk11.DateClient   An RMI-based date client for JDK 1.1.

part4.chapter28.jdk11.DateServer   A date server remote interface for JDK 1.1.

part4.chapter28.jdk11.DateServerImpl   A date server remote object for JDK 1.1.

part4.chapter28.jdk11.MyRemote   A remote interface for JDK 1.1.

part4.chapter28.jdk11.MyRemoteImpl   A remote object for JDK 1.1.

D.4 Chat system classes

prominence.chat.Chat   An internet chat client.

prominence.chat.ChatClient   An extended `Client` interface.

prominence.chat.ChatSystemClient   An extended `GenericClient`.

prominence.chat.ChatSystemHandler   An extended `GenericHandler`.

prominence.chat.ChatSystemServer   An extended `GenericServer`.

prominence.chat.Chatboard   An text-based chat component.

prominence.chat.Registry   A naming registry component.

prominence.chat.Whiteboard   An whiteboard component.

D.5 Encryption framework*

prominence.crypt.CBCCipher   A CBC-mode `Cipher`.

prominence.crypt.Cipher   The generic superclass for encryption algorithms.

prominence.crypt.CipherInputStream   An encrypted `InputStream`.

prominence.crypt.CipherOutputStream   An encrypted `OutputStream`.

prominence.crypt.Crypt   Some useful data manipulation methods.

prominence.crypt.DEA   The internals of DES encryption.

prominence.crypt.DES   A DES encryption implementation.

prominence.crypt.EDECipher   An EDE-mode `Cipher`.

prominence.crypt.Hash   The generic superclass for hash algorithms.

prominence.crypt.HashException   A `HashInputStream` exception.

prominence.crypt.HashInputStream   A hashed `InputStream`.

prominence.crypt.HashMAC   A `Hash`/`Cipher` message authentication code.

prominence.crypt.HashOutputStream   A hashed `OutputStream`.

prominence.crypt.Password   Password-key generation.

prominence.crypt.SHS   A SHS hash implementation.

prominence.crypt.TripleDES   Triple-DES encryption.

---

* Not included on the CD-ROM.

prominence.crypt.TripleDESCBC   Inner CBC-mode `TripleDES`.

prominence.crypt.X9_17KeyGen   X9.17 session key generation.

D.6 I/O classes

prominence.io.ASCIIInputStream   An ASCII data `InputStream`.

prominence.io.ASCIIOutputStream   An ASCII data `OutputStream`.

prominence.io.AltAppendFileOutputStream   An appending `FileOutputStream`.

prominence.io.AppendFileOutputStream   An appending `FileOutputStream`.

prominence.io.MarkResetFileInputStream   A `FileInputStream` that supports `mark()` and `reset()`.

prominence.io.MyBufferedInputStream   A buffered `InputStream`.

prominence.io.PostOutputStream   A HTTP post `OutputStream`.

prominence.io.ResetByteArrayOutputStream   An automatically resetting `ByteArrayOutputStream`.

prominence.io.TeeOutputStream   A tee-joint `OutputStream`.

D.7 Message stream classes

prominence.msg.Client   The component interface for `GenericClient`.

prominence.msg.DeliveryOutputStream   A `MessageOutput` that delivers to a `Recipient`.

prominence.msg.Demultiplexer   Routes messages from a `MultiplexInputStream`.

prominence.msg.GenericClient   A generic message-based client.

prominence.msg.GenericHandler   A generic message-based connection handler.

prominence.msg.GenericMessageCopier   A `MessageCopier` with error handling.

prominence.msg.GenericServer   A generic message-based server.

prominence.msg.MessageCopier   Copies message from a `MessageInput` to a `MessageOutput`.

prominence.msg.MessageInput   The generic superclass for message input streams.

prominence.msg.MessageInputStream   A `MessageInput` that reads from an `InputStream`.

prominence.msg.MessageOutput   The generic superclass for message output streams.

prominence.msg.MessageOutputStream   A `MessageOutput` that writes to an `OutputStream`.

prominence.msg.MultiplexInputStream   A multiplexing `MessageInput`.

prominence.msg.MultiplexOutputStream   A multiplexing `MessageOutput`.

prominence.msg.QueueInputStream   A `MessageInput` that reads from a `Queue`.

prominence.msg.QueueOutputStream   A `MessageOutput` that writes to a `Queue`.

prominence.msg.Recipient   The receiving interface for `DeliveryOutputStream`.

prominence.msg.Router   Routes messages from a `RoutingInputStream`.

prominence.msg.RoutingInputStream   A routing `MessageInput`.

prominence.msg.RoutingOutputStream   A routing `MessageOutput`.

D.8 Extended message stream classes

prominence.msgx.GenericRegistryHandler   A `GenericHandler` that supports a naming registry.

prominence.msgx.GenericRegistryServer   A `GenericServer` that supports a naming registry.

prominence.msgx.GenericSourceIDClient A `GenericClient` that supports message source identification.

prominence.msgx.GenericSourceIDHandler A `GenericHandler` that supports message source identification.

prominence.msgx.GenericSourceIDServer A `GenericServer` that supports message source identification.

prominence.msgx.SourceIDClient A `Client` interface that supports message source identification.

D.9 URL-framework classes

prominence.url.ContentHandlerFactoryImpl A `text/plain` `ContentHandlerFactory`.

prominence.url.HTTPURLConnection A HTTP `URLConnection`.

prominence.url.HTTPURLStreamHandler A HTTP `URLStreamHandler`.

prominence.url.TextPlainContentHandler A `text/plain` `ContentHandler`.

prominence.url.URLStreamHandlerFactoryImpl A HTTP `URLStreamHandlerFactory`.

D.10 Utility classes

prominence.util.Alarm A timed callback mechanism.

prominence.util.Alarmable The receiving interface for `Alarm`.

prominence.util.Queue A blocking object queue.

index

error handling 292–294, 297
Exception 209
exception 499, 500
    catching 208, 209, 212
    generating 210, 211
    handling 211–213
    passing on 211
    user 214, 215

F

File 54–57
FileDescriptor 57, 67, 70
FileInputStream 51, 63, 64, 70
FileOutputStream 51, 62, 63, 67, 68
FilterInputStream 78, 79, 86, 100
FilterOutputStream 77, 78, 84, 106
finally 146, 148, 149, 213
firewall. *See networking/firewalls*
flush() 39, 98

G

GenericClient 300–307
GenericHandler 291–296
GenericServer 289–291
getByName() 125
getInputStream() 129
getOutputStream() 130

H

Hash 332, 333
HashInputStream 345–348, 375
HashMAC 375–377
HashOutputStream 343–345, 375
HTTP 132, 134, 180
    get 174
    post 135–140
    request 503, 504
    response 504, 505

I

InetAddress 124–128
InputStream 43–48
IOException 40, 46

IP address. *See networking/IP addresses*

J

JDK 1.1 427

K

key 379

L

LineNumberInputStream 81
loopback address 146

M

mark() 45, 46, 69
markSupported() 46
marshaling 401, 402
message stream
    multiplexing 259
    routing 280
MessageInput 233, 234
MessageInputStream 237, 238, 244
MessageOutput 232, 233
MessageOutputStream 234–236
MulticastSocket 430
MultiplexInputStream 262, 263
MultiplexOutputStream 259–261
Multipurpose Internet Message Extension
    (MIME) types 505, 506
multithreading
    synchronization 191–195
    variable scope 190, 191

N

naming service 416, 419, 422, 423
network byte order 91
networking 437
    address resolution protocol (ARP) 8
    ADSL 448
    ATM 449–451
    B-ISDN 444, 445
    bridge 440
    CIDR 457, 458

Guide to the CD-ROM

The CD-ROM which accompanies this book isn't just window dressing. It contains the code examples and codebase developed in the book, along with documentation. This code is pretested, production-level networking code, which will be immediately useful to programmers developing networked applications of all types. Programmers producing realtime interactive or collaborative Internet and intranet applications of any sort will be able to directly apply this code to development projects.

In addition, programmers can write client/server and peer-to-peer applications-layer Java software directly on top of the CD-ROM codebase. This significantly eases the process of writing these applications because programmers do not need to worry about writing servers—a generic server is provided—or about writing the networking side of the clients—a generic client is provided.

Also included on the CD-ROM is a complete World Wide Web-based chat application built from the message streams library. Developers can directly extend this code to provide realtime collaborative applications.

Documentation for these classes is on the CD-ROM, and takes the form of a complete HTML API listing for each class in standard Javadoc format. This is the familiar format used in the standard core Java API documentation.